CENSUS
THE FAMILY HISTORIAN'S GUIDE, SECOND EDITION

Peter Christian and David Annal

BLOOMSBURY
LONDON · NEW DELHI · NEW YORK · SYDNEY

First published in the United Kingdom in 2008 by
The National Archives Kew, Richmond Surrey, TW9 4DU, UK
www.nationalarchives.gov.uk

The National Archives logo © Crown Copyright 2014

The National Archives logo device is a trade mark of The
National Archives and is used under licence.
© Text copyright Peter Christian and David Annal, 2014

The right of Peter Christian and David Annal to be identified
as the Authors of this work has been asserted by them in
accordance with the Copyright, Designs and Patents Act 1988.

Bloomsbury Publishing Plc
50 Bedford Square
London
WC1B 3DP
www.bloomsbury.com
London, New Delhi, New York, Sydney

A CIP record for this book is available from the British Library.

First Edition ISBN: 9-781-9056-1534-6
Second Edition ISBN: 9-781-4729-0293-1

MIX
Paper from
responsible sources
FSC® C013604

Design by Fiona Pike, Pike Design, Winchester

Typeset by Saxon Graphics Ltd, Derby
Printed and bound in the United Kingdom by
CPI Group (UK) Ltd, Croydon, CR0 4YY

Contents

What you will find in this book

On 2 January 2002, a remarkable event occurred which thrust the previously quiet and peaceful world of family history research into the glare of the national media. An ambitious plan to make the records of the 1901 census for England and Wales available online proved a victim of its own success when thousands of family historians who had been waiting ten years for its release and many others, inspired by press coverage but with perhaps no more than a passing interest in the subject, logged on to the 1901 census website – causing it to crash within hours of its launch. The 1901 census included the details of more than 30 million people, and this was the first time that an attempt had been made to provide access to such a large volume of family history data via the internet. Earlier censuses had been made available on microfilm and although each successive release had provoked excitement and interest in the family history community, no previous census release had captured the attention of the national press in quite the same way.

The experience of the 1901 census release, together with advances in online technology, led to a successful and trouble-free launch of the 1911 census. As a result of a ruling made under the Freedom of Information Act, the National Archives released the 1911 returns for England and Wales early – that is, before the customary 100 years had passed. The records were released gradually, county-by-county during 2009, and are now fully available online.

The release of the 1921 census is (at the time of writing) some eight years away, and as the terms of the 1920 Census Act mean that the records will not be released early, family historians will have to be patient for a while yet.

But why is such importance attached to census returns? Why does the release of another set of census records provoke such avid, some might even say obsessive, interest? What is it about the census that has led to questions being asked on a number of occasions in the House of Commons? This book will attempt to answer these questions, as well as explaining what the census is, how and why it was taken, and most importantly how researchers can use, understand and access the returns today – with the focus on online research.

Census returns are one of the key nineteenth-century sources for family historians, delivering a wealth of information about their ancestors including names, addresses, ages, family relationships and occupations. The documents may appear on the surface to be quite straightforward, but the process by which they were compiled means that the unwary researcher can easily fall foul of them. This book aims to help you navigate your way through the census returns and show you how to avoid the major pitfalls.

We begin with an exploration of the origins of the census in Chapter 1. The returns for the years 1841 (the first that recorded our ancestors' names) to 1901 are fully open, and we take a detailed look at these remarkable records in Chapter 2. The 1911 census is treated separately in Chapter 3. Although there are broad similarities between it and its Victorian predecessors, the layout of the schedules, the range of questions asked and, perhaps most importantly, the process that led to the creation of the records are different enough to warrant a separate chapter.

In Chapter 4 we explain why finding your ancestors in the returns isn't always as easy as it might be and we will offer some advice to help you to untangle these problems.

The book then goes on to explain how to access the census returns. Chapters 5 to 7 cover the census online, what you can access for free, and the best techniques to maximise the success of your searches. Chapters 8 to 15 take you on a guided tour of the most important census websites. Appendix A looks at the advantages and disadvantages of each of the sites and helps you to decide which best suits your needs.

For the most part, the book deals with the census returns for England and Wales, the Channel Islands and the Isle of Man, which were taken every ten years from 1841 to 1911 – essentially the records held by The National Archives of England and Wales. The Scottish census is generally treated alongside the English one because it is similar in most respects while reference is made to Ireland, highlighting the significant differences, in the relevant chapters. Chapter 14 looks at the ScotlandsPeople website while Chapter 15 explores the most important websites for accessing the surviving Irish censuses.

Chapters 16 and 17 cover topics that may seem old-fashioned, but will still be incredibly useful for some researchers. Chapter 16 is about the census products available on CD-ROM, and in Chapter 17 we will take a brief look at some of the offline search tools available to help you to access the census on microfilm. Some people prefer to access the returns this way and in certain cases it might be the best option for you.

Serious researchers will want to ensure that the results of their work are fully accessible and that the sources they use are correctly cited. Chapter 18 explains how the various National Archives' referencing systems work and provides a guide to citing census returns.

Lastly, the book assumes that most readers are interested in census returns from a family history perspective, but we need to remember some important points here. Firstly, the census was not taken with family historians in mind; the arrangement of the returns and the information they record may sometimes make us feel that this was the case but we have to put that idea out of our minds. The census returns were taken by the government of the day for a variety of social and political reasons, which we will explore below. Also, although family historians may form the main body of users today, we must not ignore the requirements of academics and local historians; the census returns can be vital to their research and this book is aimed at them too. To that end, Chapter 19 takes a look at the supplementary sources that researchers can access to help provide a more in-depth understanding of these remarkable records. Appendix B contains a list of the dates of all the UK censuses together with some useful notes regarding their status.

Online

The chapters devoted to the main census websites describe them as they were at the start of 2014. All of these data services are on the whole very mature and very stable, but they are subject to the occasional facelift so you should not be surprised if what appears on your screen is slightly different from our screenshots. Also, the large data services are regularly making improvements, whether to enhance existing features or to add new facilities. For this reason, you may also encounter less superficial differences by the time you access sites yourself. FamilySearch in particular (Chapter 6) is constantly being improved or tweaked. In the case of Ancestry (Chapter 7) and Findmypast (Chapter 9), both the search options and the image-viewing facilities had recently been updated when we tested them, and may well have been further modified in the light of user feedback by the time you read this. In June 2014, Findmypast announced that it had purchased Origins, and this may have an impact on the census offerings on both sides.

The chapters on the major data services are in many cases the most detailed discussions of census records on these sites ever published. Nonetheless, the coverage is not and could not be exhaustive. It is simply not realistic to try out every possible combination of search fields for every census year on all the sites. Ancestry, for example, has 35 different census datasets for the British Isles, while TheGenealogist has over 300. There will certainly be slight differences in search options that we have failed to spot. Occasionally — not too often, we hope — we may have overlooked some useful trick that solves what seems to be a problem on a particular site.

In the discussion of individual sites, we have given a number of examples of errors in indexing and transcription. However, with any luck, some of them at least will have been corrected by the time you read this (indeed, we submitted a number of corrections during the testing process). You may, therefore, not be able to locate the specific errors cited, but they retain their value as an example of the *types* of error found in online censuses. Likewise we have occasionally felt compelled to comment on poor site design or poor navigation, things that make life difficult for the user, but we are glad to report that some sites have already taken note of difficulties we raised queries about during writing, and all the sites *do* take feedback on usability from users seriously. While the data services have been very helpful in responding to our queries, we have not submitted the text to them for comment or correction, so we remain entirely responsible for any errors and omissions in the description. However, we would like to think that if, after weeks of testing a site, we have failed to spot something important it offers or misunderstood some aspect of how it works, then it is not *entirely* our fault!

In the first instance, the descriptions of the census data services are designed to guide the newcomer. Although the major sites have much more data than just the censuses, these are probably the most important single group of genealogical records available online for the British Isles, and the benefits and limitations of each site are often not readily apparent at first glance. You cannot see what the search results are like, for example, until you have signed up, and often limitations only become apparent when you have repeatedly failed to get something to work the way you have been expecting it to. It is simply not possible for the newcomer, whether to family history in general or to using the Web for genealogical research, to make more than a superficial comparison of what these sites have to offer, and one aim of this book is to remedy that difficulty. We hope also that it will be of help to those involved in the teaching of family history by providing an overview of all the main census sites.

On the other hand, if you have already signed up with a particular data service, we hope that the description of that particular service will help you to get more out of it by alerting you to features you may have missed and showing you which limitations you have to live with and which you can get round. But when renewal time comes round or you run out of pay-per-view credits, the descriptions of the other services should also help you re-evaluate your needs.

While we have attempted to give you all the information you need to decide which of the commercial services (if any) best meets your needs, there is one aspect of them we have not attempted to test: the response to customer support requests. The various companies have very different reputations in this regard, but since the comments found in the online discussion groups have only anecdotal value and could not easily be verified, we have felt it was inappropriate to take them into account. If you want to find out what others think of a particular data service, a question in a suitable discussion forum will undoubtedly elicit a range of responses. You can easily find past comments from users in the archives of relevant mailing lists. The archives of GENBRIT at <lists.rootsweb.com/index/other/Newsgroup_Gateways/GENBRIT. html> or <groups.google.com/group/soc.genealogy.britain/> would be a good place to start.

When evaluating sites, we have used Firefox 25.0 and Internet Explorer 8.0 running on Windows 7 PC systems, and have drawn attention to one or two browser problems encountered. However, we have not attempted to test the sites methodically for browser compatibility, check how these sites look with Macintosh or Linux browsers, or look at how well they work on smartphones and tablets.

The traditional caveat about the longevity of internet resources applies. Web addresses for the long-established commercial sites are not very likely to change – these sites are *very* stable in internet terms – but one or two of the smaller websites mentioned in the text, particularly those run by individuals or informal volunteer groups, are bound to move or even, alas, close down in the lifetime of this book.

Diagrams

In general, all the websites offering census data and images of the original records work in the same way (see Fig. 1): you complete a search form and click on the search button. This brings up a list of matching individuals, from which you select the one you want to see the full details of. From there you can choose to look at a digital image of the original census enumeration schedule. Beyond this commonality, though, there are usually many more options and they differ considerably from site to site. For this reason, we have provided flowcharts showing you how all the main screens and options inter-relate. The census images usually pop up in a separate browser window (with controls for zooming, panning and saving the image), and this is indicated by the rounded corners on the box. For pay-per-view sites, the flowchart will also indicate which steps you need to pay for and how much each costs.

Figure 0.1 Census websites' process for delivering search results.

Acknowledgements

We are indebted to those data services which provided free access to facilitate in-depth exploration and testing of their data and facilities. They also provided detailed answers to our questions. We would like to thank: Nigel Bayley (TheGenealogist), Debra Chatfield (Findmypast), Ian Galbraith (Origins), Laurence Harris (MyHeritage), Hannah Morris (Genes Reunited), and Bryony Partridge (Ancestry). Our coverage of surname matching has been helped by discussions with Steve Archer over many years. A special mention must go to Jeanne Bunting and John Hanson, the 'Census Detectives', who have done much to identify the types of error in the online censuses and to analyse the problems of finding individuals.

The publishers would like to thank Audrey Collins at The National Archives for her valuable contribution to the writing and production of this book.

ACKNOWLEDGEMENTS

Introduction

The internet has revolutionised the way we look at census returns. Online access to the census returns, together with comprehensive indexes, has without question improved our ability to find particular individuals in the records. In fact, as anyone who spent hours on end back in the 1970s and 1980s winding through microfilms, waiting for a name to jump off the page at them, would no doubt tell you, it has changed the whole process of family history research beyond recognition.

Not so long ago, anyone looking for their ancestors in the census would have had to visit an archive, a record office or a local library to view the records on microfilm. The only complete collection covering the whole of England, Wales, the Channel Islands and the Isle of Man was held by the Public Record Office (PRO). Public access to the collection was provided at a succession of locations: Portugal Street, Chancery Lane and latterly at the Family Records Centre.

Nowadays, the census is rightly viewed as an essential primary source for family historians and this is, at least in part, due to the easy access provided by the internet, but this wasn't always the case. A major book on Scottish research published in 1971 (*In Search of Scottish Ancestry* by Gerald Hamilton-Edwards) dedicated just one page to the subject of census returns. At that time, the Scottish returns were accessible to the public on payment of a 'special inclusive fee' at New Register House in Edinburgh. Microfilm copies were eventually produced, but it was always the case that a visit to Edinburgh was necessary to carry out an effective search in the Scottish census. The situation in Ireland has always been complicated by the loss and destruction of the vast majority of the pre-1901 census returns.

There were some alternatives. Most county record offices and many of the larger local libraries had microfilm copies of the censuses for their own areas of interest, but the biggest problem was not getting access to the records: the challenge facing family historians in this pre-digital age was actually finding their ancestors in the returns.

As we will see in Chapter 1, the census returns are arranged by place and not by name, so unless your ancestors were amongst the minority who spent the whole of their lives living in the same place, tracking them down in each successive census was potentially difficult. To stand a good chance of finding a particular individual or family, you really needed to know where they were living at the time. Ideally, you had to know the name of the village or, if they were living in an urban area, the name of the street and preferably the house number.

The census is of course a snapshot – taken once every ten years on a particular date. Sunday nights were chosen, as this increased the chance of finding people at their usual place of residence, but it was no guarantee. People working away from home, visiting relatives or simply travelling from one place to another will not be recorded where you would expect to find them. The number of people who fell into one or other of these categories was in fact quite small, and thus unlikely to have a noticeably negative impact on your research. What did have an impact was the fact that the vast majority of the Victorian urban population lived in rented accommodation: our city-dwelling ancestors moved from one address to another at a rate which is quite difficult for our twenty-first-century minds to come to terms with. The moonlight flit when the rent was due was no urban myth!

So even if you had a copy of a certificate recording a birth or a death in the family occurring within a few weeks of the date of the census, there was no guarantee that you would find them living at the address shown on the certificate. It was likely that the family would be somewhere in the same general area, possibly quite nearby, but in the most heavily-populated areas of the larger industrial towns and cities, tracking them down could be an exhausting process. Winding through reel after reel of microfilm, examining every name on every page, hoping against hope that you would stumble upon the family you were looking for was, for family historians of a certain vintage, a necessity and a way of life!

Online access to the entire collection of surviving census returns for the British Isles, from 1841 to 1911, fully indexed by name and other key pieces of information such as age, place of birth and residence, has changed all that. The number of websites offering access to the census returns for England and Wales is always on the increase and you no longer need to visit an archive to carry out your research. The Scottish and Irish censuses are also easily accessible online, although your choice of websites is more limited here. Now, in theory at least, tracking down anyone who was living in the country at the time of one of the censuses should be a fairly straightforward process, and it does not matter where they were living. Provided that you have enough information about your ancestor to make a positive identification, you should be able to find them – even if they were visiting relatives on the other side of the country! You simply enter their name, click on the search button and, within a matter of seconds, their details should appear on the screen in front of you.

Well that is the theory – and sometimes it works – but more often than not you will find that you come up against one of two problems: either your search turns up too many results or it offers you none at all. That is why, before you even begin a search in the census, you need to ask yourself an important question: do you have enough information about the individual or family that you're hoping to find, to carry out an effective search? In other words, if you're presented with a list of names, will you be able to pick out the person you're looking for?

Census returns are a gateway into the nineteenth century but they're not necessarily the best starting point for your research. Before you set off on your journey, you should aim to arm yourself with as much information as possible about your ancestor: their name and an approximate date of birth are essential, and some idea of their place of birth and parentage is also desirable. Without this sort of information your search is likely to be fruitless.

Although we now take 24 hours a day, seven days a week, worldwide access to these records for granted, this is a relatively recent phenomenon. Family historians and other researchers have been using the records for over a hundred years and the research techniques which have been developed over time are just as valid today as they have always been. The records have not changed, merely the means by which we access them.

Also, there's a very real danger that, by providing us with these instant results and leading us straight to the page containing our ancestors' details, the websites may actually be doing us a disservice. In any type of historical research, context is crucial. When you're viewing a census page on your computer screen, it's important to look beyond that single entry. Look at the neighbours; look at the size of the families; consider the social aspects – are there servants living in the households? What sort of trades or industries are the occupants involved in? Are they living in a rural or an urban district? The census can tell us so much more about our ancestors and the way they lived than the basic facts of age, occupation and birthplace.

Finally, the census should not be used in isolation, as it is just one of many tools available for you to use in the course of your research. The information that you get from other sources such as birth, marriage and death certificates, parish registers, wills, gravestones and contemporary newspapers will, to a large degree, shape your investigations into the census and provide you with a structured research strategy. Similarly, what you find in the census can lead you off into all kinds of new – and sometimes unexpected – directions.

1

COUNTING THE PEOPLE

To fully understand the census, it helps to know a bit about its origins. Over the years, a number of excellent books have been written outlining the background to the UK censuses, most notably *Making Sense of the Census Revisited* by Edward Higgs. Higgs' book provides a definitive guide to the legislation that led to the taking of the censuses and to the political, social and economic issues that shaped the questions asked on the schedules. Even more detail can be found on the Histpop website, including the full text of the relevant Acts of Parliament and examples of the various forms used by the General Register Office, the census enumerators and the individual householders, by visiting <www.histpop.org> (see Chapter 19).

The year 1753 was a momentous one for family historians – or rather, it nearly was. This was the year in which Thomas Potter's Bill for 'taking and registering an annual account of the total number of people, and of the total number of marriages, births, and deaths, and also of the total number of the poor receiving alms from every Parish and Extra-parochial Place in Great Britain' was presented to Parliament. The Bill had already passed through both Houses and despite some forthright objections from certain parties, the *Gentleman's Magazine* of December 1753 reported that 'it was carried for bringing in the bill and Mr Potter [and several others] were ordered to bring it in.' However, the Supplement to the *Gentleman's Magazine* for 1753 sheds light on the Bill's eventual fate:

> This bill, tho' it was opposed with great steadiness and vigour, passed the commons; but the lords, at the second reading, threw it out.

That, as far as proposals for a national census were concerned, was that – at least for another fifty years or so. It's difficult not to see this as an opportunity missed and, even if the results of the 'annual account' would probably have proved to be little more than a mass of statistical data, the systems and processes that would have been necessary to generate the required data would surely have produced an abundance of valuable genealogical material. Family historians are left to salivate at the thought of what might have been.

Nevertheless, population – and the thorny issue of whether it was growing or shrinking – became one of the hot topics of debate in the late-eighteenth century. Thomas Malthus, Britain's first professor in Political Economy, developed his controversial 'Principle of Population', which was originally published as *An Essay on the Principle of Population* in 1798. Malthus believed that increases in wages led to a growth in population – a growth which could not be matched by the required increase in levels of food production and, therefore, ultimately led to subsistence living for most labourers. His views were heavily criticised by social reformers such as William Godwin and Robert Owen, and have now been largely discredited, but at the time he gained influential support – most notably from the Prime Minister, William Pitt the Younger.

The idea of 'counting the people' was hardly a new one, and the practice was well established in other countries long before the UK embarked on its first census. In fact the UK lagged far behind many other European states. The Netherlands (1795), Denmark (1769), Spain (1768), Sweden (1749), Prussia (1719) and Iceland (1703) can all claim an earlier start date, and across the Atlantic the Americans beat us to it – with the first census of the United States taken in 1790.

Another name worthy of mention alongside Thomas Malthus as a prime mover in the campaign for a national census in the UK is that of John Rickman. Rickman was a staunch opponent of Malthus, but the two agreed on one point: the need to have an accurate count of the population of the UK and, most importantly, to know whether it was rising or falling. Rickman set out twelve reasons why taking a census would benefit the nation, ranging from military matters to concerns about food supply, but at the forefront of his philosophy was his statement that 'the intimate knowledge of any country must form the rational basis of legislation and diplomacy'. His idea was to hold a national census every ten years, and ultimately he got his way: in 1800 it was John Rickman who was responsible for drawing up the first

Census Act (also known as the Population Act), which resulted in the taking of the first national census of England, Wales and Scotland on 10 March 1801.

Unfortunately for the vast ranks of family historians around the world with British ancestry, the opening words of Rickman's 1800 Census Act – 'Whereas it is expedient to take an Account of the total Number of Persons within the kingdom of Great Britain' – make it clear that this was simply a numbers game. There was no requirement in the 1801 census, or in the legislation behind the three censuses that followed it, to record the names or any other details of individual inhabitants. The pre-1841 censuses were therefore no more than headcounts: of huge interest to local and social historians, providing exactly the sort of information that the government had hoped for, but of little or no direct use to those of us searching for our ancestors.

All the same, under the direction of Rickman, the 1801 census was a masterpiece of planning and execution and a fine example of what late-Georgian Britain could achieve when it set its collective mind to it. At a time when central government had little day-to-day impact on our ancestors' lives, Rickman employed the services of an unlikely alliance of parish officials, town clerks, overseers of the poor, clergymen, teachers and householders to carry out the various tasks required by the Act.

By the standards of modern censuses the questions asked in 1801 were very simple and undemanding, but viewed from an early nineteenth-century perspective they were ambitious enough. The census was divided into two parts, the first of which consisted of just three questions which were designed to fulfil the primary aim of the Act – namely to 'take an Account of the total Number of Persons within the kingdom of Great Britain.':

- the number of houses (inhabited and uninhabited);
- the number of persons (separate counts of males and females);
- the number of persons 'chiefly employed' in three categories;
  - agriculture
  - trade, manufactures or handicraft
  - other, i.e. everything else.

In England and Wales, this part of the census was to be administered by the local overseer of the poor, while in Scotland the role was to be fulfilled by a local schoolteacher. The legislation allowed for a 'substantial householder' to undertake the task if there was no available overseer (or schoolteacher) and the appointed person was allowed to ask for the assistance of one of a number of church officials.

The second schedule, which was to be completed by the 'Rector, Vicar, Curate, or other Officiating Minister' of each parish, would help John Rickman to build up a picture of what he described in the Act as 'the progressive Increase or Diminution [of the population]'. The task for the clergymen was to complete two tables (questions four and five respectively) showing firstly the numbers of baptisms and burials (separate totals for males and females) recorded in their registers for specific years in the eighteenth century; and secondly, the total number of marriages recorded each year from 1754 (the year in which Hardwicke's Marriage Act came into force) up until 1800.

The next two censuses (in 1811 and 1821) were conducted on almost exactly the same lines. There were some changes to the layout and some minor alterations to the way the questions were formed, but the information requested was essentially the same. The only significant advance came in 1821, when the overseers were instructed to provide a breakdown of the ages of those enumerated. While this was clearly a step (albeit a small one) towards a truly modern census, the wording of the relevant section in the 1820 Census Act demonstrates that there were still some serious concerns about the ability of the 'enumerators' to obtain the sort of accurate information which might be genuinely useful:

> If you are of Opinion that...the Ages of the several Individuals can be obtained in a Manner satisfactory to yourself, and not inconvenient to the Parties, be pleased to state (or cause to be stated) the Number of those who are under Five Years of Age, of those between 5 and 10 Years of Age...

It is clear, therefore, that the Act did not require exact ages to be given. Instead they were to be grouped in five-year bands for those up to 20 and in ten-year bands up to 100, with separate totals for males and females.

In the event, the administrators appear to have been unnecessarily pessimistic. The 'Preliminary observations' on the 1821 census indicated that eight-ninths of the population responded to the new question about their ages and reported that this proportion 'shews so much general good will in execution of the Population Act.'

The 1831 census, which turned out to be Rickman's last, was a somewhat more ambitious venture: the range of occupational categories was increased, a new question was asked about servants, and the clergymen were asked to provide data on illegitimate births occurring in their parish.

It's clear from the legislation that the overseers were expected to keep records showing how they had arrived at the totals for their parish, but there was no prescribed method for undertaking the work. The overseers' task, as stipulated in the four pre-1841 censuses, was simply to 'inform themselves of the several Particulars relating to the Matters specified...by proceeding together or separately from House to House, or otherwise, as they shall judge expedient for the better Execution of this Act'. The legislation required that the records should be 'safely kept and preserved by the churchwardens' and eventually sent to the Home Office where they would be 'digested and reduced into order'.

What is also clear is that certain efficient and dedicated overseers decided, for one reason or another, to compile lists of the names and other details of the people they were supposed simply to be counting. According to *Census schedules and listings, 1801–1831: An introduction and guide* by Richard Wall, Matthew Woollard and Beatrice Moring (University of Essex, 2012) nearly 800 such lists survive for England alone. Only a handful are known from Wales, but the picture in Scotland is more promising.

It seems likely that many more lists were at one time in existence and it is possible that more will turn up. Edward Higgs, in his essay on the 1821 census <**histpop.org/ohpr/servlet/View?path=Browse/Essays%20 %28by%20kind%29&active=yes&mno=2013**>, writes that printed forms were produced in some areas for the use of overseers wishing to draw up nominal lists. However, many of the surviving lists record only the names of the head of the household, and overall probably fewer than 100 can truly be counted as full censuses.

Nevertheless, the discovery of one of these pre-1841 lists for your ancestors' parish can be a major boost to your research. The surviving returns are spread around the country; every English county (with the exception of Rutland) has at least one. Yorkshire tops the list with 77 and London/Middlesex and Essex are close behind with 71 each. The counties of Norfolk, Suffolk, Surrey and Warwickshire are also relatively well represented while, at the other end of the scale, Durham, Herefordshire and Northumberland each have just two known surviving lists. More pre-1841 English censuses survive for 1821 (271) than for any other year. Perhaps surprisingly, six complete listings survive from Orkney – all from 1821.

The parish of Marnhull in Dorset provides a good example of a detailed list from the 1821 census. The original document is held by the Dorset Record Office (reference: MIC/R/1044) and was compiled by Thomas Hayward, the local Schoolmaster. Hayward was clearly a methodical and conscientious man; in addition to the questions required by the Census Act he recorded the name of each of the 'Homes and Residences', along with the names of the heads of the families, their individual occupations and their religious persuasion. He also requested that the resulting document should be 'Preserved by the Churchwardens and Overseers of the Poor, in succession, in order for referring to at any future period.' Of the population of 1273 people, the names of 285 individuals are recorded. A partial transcript of the document can be found online at: <**www.opcdorset.org/MarnhullFiles/ 1821Marnhull.htm**>.

An even more comprehensive list survives for the 1821 census of the parish of South Ronaldsay in Orkney. The document is a copy of the original, probably transcribed in the 1880s by local antiquarian, James Thomson, and now held by the Orkney Library & Archive. It records the residences, names and ages of every one of the 2227 inhabitants of Orkney's southernmost island parish together with some of their occupations. This remarkable document has been fully indexed and digitised and is available online at: <**www.southronaldsay.net/1821**> (see Fig. 1.1).

The surviving pre-1841 census records have generally ended up in County Record Offices amongst the miscellaneous parish material. It's important to note that they are not held by The National Archives (although there are a few transcripts available at Kew).

The records, along with a whole host of other 'census equivalents' dating as far back as the early-sixteenth century, have been extensively researched and listed both by Gibson and Medlycott in *Local Census Listings: 1522–1930* and by Colin Chapman in *Pre-1841 Censuses and*

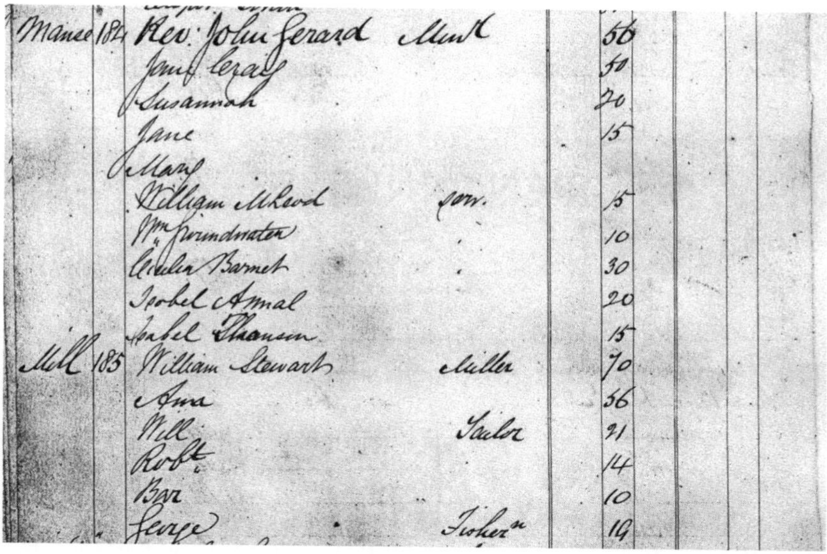

Manse	184	Rev: John Gerard	Minr	56
		Janet Craig		50
		Susannah		20
		Jane		15
		Mary		
		William McLeod	Serv.	15
		Wm Poundwater		10
		Cecilia Barnet		30
		Isobel Annal		20
		Isabel Thomson		15
Mill	185	William Stewart	Miller	70
		Ann		56
		Will	Sailor	21
		Robt		14
		Bar		10
		George	Fisher	19

Figure 1.1 Detail of a page from the 1821 census of South Ronaldsay, Orkney.

Population Listings in the British Isles. Both books are essential reading and include excellent introductions to the topic of pre-1841 censuses as well as lists of those that are known to have survived, together with their present whereabouts.

2

THE VICTORIAN CENSUSES (1841–1901)

The 1841 census

The 1841 census was the first to be taken under the auspices of the recently formed General Register Office (GRO). It was also the first census of England, Wales and Scotland to record the names of every inhabitant. Replacing the ancient counties, hundreds and parishes, the GRO's own hierarchy of Registration Districts and sub-Districts, which had already been established for the purposes of registering births, marriages and deaths, provided an ideal framework to use for the taking of the census. Each sub-District was further divided into Enumeration Districts and thousands of enumerators were appointed, each one responsible for collecting the returns for a particular district.

The original Act was passed in August 1840 but just two months before the census was due to be taken, an amendment was rushed through Parliament which changed three crucial aspects. The untimely death of John Rickman (on 11 August 1840) had left the responsibility for taking the census in the hands of the recently-appointed Registrar General Thomas Lister, and it appears that Lister was keen to introduce some of his own ideas at the earliest possible opportunity.

Unfortunately, one of the changes that Lister made was a retrograde step: the 1840 Census Act had stated that the enumerators should 'take an Account in Writing of the Name, Sex, Age, and Occupation of every living Person' in their district, the implication here being that the precise age of every individual would be noted. Under the terms of the 1841 Census (Amendment) Act, Lister simply adapted the system used in 1831: exact ages would now only be recorded for children under 15 and the five-year age bands used ten years previously would extend from 15 to 100. The wording of the 1841 Act makes interesting reading and suggests that Lister had anticipated resistance to the original question about age:

> ...the Persons charged with taking the said Accounts shall not be required to ascertain the Age of any Person above the Age of Fifteen Years more nearly than is herein provided, nor shall any Person be liable to any Penalty for refusing to tell his or her Age to any Person so charged more nearly than is herein provided;

The date of the census was brought forward from 30 June (a Wednesday) to 6 June (a Sunday) but the most important change brought about by the Census Amendment Act was one that fundamentally changed the process by which the census was to be taken. The original 1840 Act had introduced the concept of enumerators in England and Wales but Lister realised that the task of recording the names, sex, ages, and occupations of the entire population of one of the new enumeration districts was, in practical terms, an impossible one for one person to carry out, door-to-door in a single day. Instead, Lister devised a new printed schedule which was to be completed not by the enumerator but rather by the householders themselves.

The data would still have to be collated but the challenge (which Lister saw as critical) of completing the actual survey on a single day was met. Each enumerator was issued with the required number of blank householders' schedules, as well as a summary book and a memorandum book – the latter was to be used to make any notes which the enumerator felt might assist the registrar and the Census Office. Having collected the completed householders' schedules, the enumerator's next task was the considerable one of copying the details into the summary book. This system was used for each of the censuses from 1841 to 1901.

The process devised by Lister of delivering forms to the householders in the week leading up to census night and collecting them during the following week has stood the test of time and indeed was still in place for the last national census taken in 2011.

The original householders' schedules were destroyed many years ago (along with the memorandum books) but the enumerators' books were kept and it's these that we generally refer to when we talk about the census returns today. Each summary book had a number of nominal pages with space for a set number of entries. The enumerator copied the details from the householders' schedules into the summary book and then drew a line to indicate the end of the returns for one household and the start of the next. The precise manner in which this was to be done changed from year to year but in most censuses you should look out for the small, angled double lines to the left of the individuals' names.

The result of this process is that each nominal page contains the returns for several households and also that the returns for a particular household may begin at the bottom of one nominal page and continue at the top of the next.

In addition to the nominal pages, the summary books also contain a number of forms and tables which had to be completed by the enumerator, recording such information as a description of the Enumeration District, the administrative hierarchy, and abstracts and summaries of the statistical data. These pages provide essential background information about the district that our ancestors were living in. They also occasionally include additional comments by the enumerators and if you're very lucky, you may come across a hand-drawn map showing the Enumeration District boundary. Unfortunately, there is no access to these supplementary pages on most websites.

The question of how to record people who were not living in traditional family households was one that now presented a challenge to the administrators. In the pre-1841 censuses, when it was simply a matter of counting the number of inhabitants in each parish, this wasn't really an issue, but now that the householders were to complete their own schedules, a system had to be devised to deal with those whose 'residence' was, for example, a prison, a hospital or the workhouse. The answer was for the 'Master or keeper of every Gaol, Prison, or House of Correction, Workhouse, Hospital, or Lunatic Asylum, and of every public or charitable Institution' to be issued with special schedules, which closely resembled the enumerators' summary books. The main differences were that the individual pages did not include an address column and that the information was written directly into the books with no equivalent of the householders' schedules. The master or keeper of the institution was designated as enumerator and was responsible for sending the completed books to the Superintendent Registrar.

The completed summary books, together with the schedules from the various institutions were then checked by the Registrars and

Superintendent Registrars to ensure that the 'Instructions in each Case have been punctually fulfilled' before being sent to the Census Office in London. Lister insisted that the abstraction of statistics should be done centrally, in the interests of uniformity, so a central office was needed to administer this, as well as the distribution of the forms and instructions to the enumerators, and their collection. The new GRO occupied part of Somerset House, but there was no space for the additional clerks needed for the census, so Lister secured temporary accommodation for them in nearby Adelphi Terrace.

The 1841 census enumerators' summary books record the following information about each individual:

- name (forename and surname)
- age (rounded down to the nearest five for those aged over 15)
- gender
- occupation
- whether they were born in the county in which they were living at the time of the census
- whether they were born in Scotland, Ireland or 'Foreign Parts' (in Scotland the question referred to England, Ireland or 'Foreign Parts' and in Ireland, to England, Scotland or 'Foreign Parts)

The forms also provided for a count to be made of the number of houses inhabited, being built, or uninhabited.

Although this is clearly far more informative than the headcounts of the previous years, it still leaves something to be desired, and the usefulness of the 1841 census to family historians suffers in comparison with the later Victorian censuses.

There are a number of important points to consider when using the 1841 census. Although every individual is named, the enumerators were asked to enter just their first forename and the surname. This instruction was not always strictly observed but it's fair to say that finding middle names recorded in 1841 is the exception rather than the rule.

There wasn't a great deal of space allowed for names on the schedule so forenames are frequently abbreviated. The most common abbreviations to look out for are:

Jno.	=	John
Jas.	=	James
Wm.	=	William
Thos.	=	Thomas
Rbt. or Robt.	=	Robert
Chas.	=	Charles
Geo.	=	George
Eliz. or Elizth.	=	Elizabeth

This tendency of the enumerators to abbreviate forenames should not be confused with the use of 'pet' names such as 'Bessy' for Elizabeth or 'Fanny' for Frances. The abbreviation of forenames (and indeed the use of initials) also occurs in later censuses but it is a particular problem with the 1841 census and therefore worth highlighting here.

One feature of the censuses which occurs throughout the years is the use of ditto marks or the abbreviation 'Do.' to indicate that the entry is the same as the line above. Ditto marks occur particularly in the surname, occupation and birthplace columns.

To get the best out of the 1841 census it is absolutely vital that you understand the practice of rounding down the ages of those aged 15 or over. Someone whose age is given as 40 would actually be aged between 40 and 44, someone entered as 65 would be aged between 65 and 69 and so on. In Chapter 4 we'll look at some general problems surrounding ages in the census, but the situation in 1841 is made that bit more troublesome by the lack of precise ages.

An individual's gender is not explicitly stated in any of the censuses but instead is indicated by the presence of their age either in the 'Male' or 'Female' column.

Occupations can cause problems here, again because of the frequent use of abbreviations. In addition to the ubiquitous Ag Lab (short for Agricultural Labourer and used throughout all the censuses) there are a few other abbreviations commonly used in 1841:

F.S	=	Female Servant
M.S.	=	Male Servant
Ind.	=	Independent (i.e. of Independent Means)
M.	=	Maker (e.g. Shoe M. = Shoe Maker; Boot M. = Boot Maker)

F.W.K. = Frame Work Knitter (common in Nottinghamshire and surrounding counties)

Straw Pl. = Straw Plaiter (common in Hertfordshire and Bedfordshire)

The wording in the heading of the occupation column reads 'Profession, Trade, Employment or of Independent Means' – the term 'occupation' isn't actually used at all. The aim was to categorise the type of work undertaken by the chief wage earner in each household – usually the senior adult male – but the census takers also wanted to know about the numbers of servants and about people who had private incomes so we regularly see 'F.S.', 'M.S.' and 'Ind.' in this column.

Perhaps the biggest disappointment for family historians using the 1841 census for the first time is the lack of detail regarding birthplace. The 'Where Born' section is divided into two columns: one for people born in England or Wales and the other for everyone else. A 'Y' or an 'N' in the first column indicates whether or not that person was 'born in the same county' – i.e. the county in which they are currently living. An 'S', an 'I' or an 'F' in the second column indicates that a person was born in Scotland, Ireland or 'Foreign Parts'. The relevant columns in the Scottish and Irish censuses record people born in other parts of the UK as appropriate.

Another frustration here is the absence of a precise address. In rural areas it's not at all uncommon to find just the name of the village or hamlet given, and even in the more built up areas, where street names are usually shown, it's rare to find house numbers in the returns.

PLACE	HOUSES		NAMES. of each Person who abode therein the preceding Night.	AGE and SEX		PROFESSION, TRADE, EMPLOYMENT, or of INDEPENDENT MEANS.	Where Born	
	Uninhabited or Building	Inhabited		Males	Females		Whether Born in same County	Whether Born in Scotland, Ireland or Foreign Parts.
Parsonage House		1	Patrick Bronte	60		Clergyman	No	Ireland
			Elizabeth Branwell		60	Independent		Cornwall
			Emily Jane Bronte		20		Y	
			Ann Bronte		19	Governess	Y	
			Martha Brown		15	Female Servant	Y	

Figure 2.1 Detail of a page from the 1841 census showing the Bronte family. TNA reference HO107/1295/6, folio 41, page 1.

The 1841 census is best thought of as 'work in progress'. Huge steps had been taken and enormous advances had been made in the process of gathering information – the establishment of the GRO with its well-defined structure of Registration Districts and sub-Districts was perfectly suited for taking the Victorian censuses. By using the same administrative units that were being used to register births, marriages and deaths, statisticians could for the first time obtain meaningful data to help them understand and investigate population trends both nationally and from a local perspective.

However, after taking the 1841 census using the GRO's administrative hierarchy, Thomas Lister then decided to rearrange the books into the old format of hundreds, wapentakes, lathes and other ancient local divisions. It took the Census Office clerks two years to carry out this task, but it meant that the information gathered could be directly compared with that from the earlier censuses. This arrangement of the 1841 census books survives today (see Chapter 18).

The first few years of Queen Victoria's reign can be seen as a golden era for family historians. Two of the most important events on the family history calendar – the start of civil registration and the taking of the first genuinely useful national census – occurred within four years of each other. Thomas Lister's work in setting up the GRO and overseeing the 1841 census had proved a huge success but sadly Lister didn't live long enough to see the results of his efforts: he died in June 1842 at the age of just 42. However, this second untimely death in the story of the census ushered in the era of arguably the most influential and successful Registrar General, George Graham (plate 1).

The 1851 census

George Graham served as the head of the GRO for 38 years, continuing to build on and develop the work begun by Rickman and Lister. He was to be in charge of the preparations for the next four censuses and it was under his leadership that the design of the census form settled down into the classic layout that is so familiar to family historians today. Graham was assisted in this by Dr William Farr, who had joined the statistical branch of the GRO in 1839. He later became Deputy Registrar General, a post that he held until he retired in 1880, shortly after Graham's own retirement. The two men made a formidable team, each complementing the skills and qualities of the other. Farr was a doctor of medicine (although he never practised as a physician) and a founder of the Statistical Society of London, the forerunner of the Royal Statistical Society. Statisticians like Farr could see the potential of the information that could be gathered in a census, and wanted to add more questions. Graham, the administrator, had to balance this with the realities of the level of funding he could obtain from the Treasury, and the practical limitations of tabulating census data manually.

The premises at Adelphi Terrace used for the 1841 census had not proved satisfactory, and for 1851 the Census Office was established at Craig's Court, near Trafalgar Square, where it remained until the 1881 census. The premises consisted of three adjoining houses, each divided into several rooms. Clerks were employed on temporary contracts, since there was no permanent Census Office until the Census Act of 1920, and new staff had to be recruited each time. A number of experienced staff would be seconded from regular duties at Somerset House, including William Farr who was in charge of the Census Office. The great majority were employed only for the preparation of the census, and then for the time it took to process and analyse the results. A list had been kept of the temporary staff employed in 1841, and a number of them were re-engaged for the 1851 census.

As well as clerical staff, an office keeper, Edward Wells, was appointed to live on the premises, at £80 per annum, and the Treasury agreed to employ charwomen 'as necessary' at 12 shillings per week, and labourers at 23 shillings per week, to carry coals and deliver messages. The clerks were to be paid between 5 and 8 shillings, dependent on the standard of their work. In keeping with the practice of the time in the GRO itself, as much work as possible was to be conducted as 'task-work'. This is what we would now call piecework, and was a system greatly favoured by George Graham, particularly when dealing with temporary staff.

> If temporary clerks and writers and boys are on day pay, they may be placed at desks; but no amount of supervision can obtain from all of them a good day's work. They know that the more work they execute in a day, the sooner their temporary employment will cease and they will be again turned adrift; therefore it is their interest to do as little work as possible.
>
> (TNA reference RG 29/2 Treasury Letters Outward, 28 January 1870.)

Adelphi Terrace must have been very unsatisfactory indeed if Craig's Court was an improvement. The rooms were cramped and ill ventilated, and many of the staff complained of headaches from the fumes of the gas lights; they were burning for much of the working day, which could be as long as ten hours. In spite of this, every census from 1851 to 1881 was administered from there. It must have been difficult to find suitable office accommodation within a short distance of Somerset House, which was only required for a couple of years before and after each census, and at a reasonable cost.

Obtaining funds from the Treasury was a constant challenge for the Census Office, as Graham had already discovered when he suggested in 1846 that a set of maps would be very useful in planning the 1851 census. There was at that time no published set of maps showing parish boundaries, so Graham suggested that the new maps being drawn up by the Tithe Commissioners would be ideal and an extra set could be produced for relatively low cost. The Treasury were not quick to respond, and Graham's patience was evidently growing thin by 1848 when they offered him an alternative that he felt was not up to standard:

> Nicely designed as they are and well executed as I have no doubt they will be by Mr Saunders, I cannot but consider them as merely pretty toys, when compared with the practically useful and much required maps to the formation of which under the Tithe Commissioners I have so frequently, not I hope pertinaciously and obtrusively, ventured to solicit the attention of the Lords Commissioners of H M Treasury.
> (TNA reference RG 29/1 Treasury Letters Outward, 14 March 1848.)

The Treasury finally agreed to pay for a set of the Tithe Commissioners' maps in September 1850, four years after they had first been asked for. With that problem out of the way, George Graham next had to make the final decision on the questions to be included in the 1851 census schedules, in order to assess the amount of work involved and the optimum size for the Enumeration Districts. There were representations from various interested parties, including Farr and the Statistical Society, to include details about education, amount of taxes paid, the size, construction and ownership of dwellings and more. These were all rejected, so as not to overburden the enumerators and keep the costs to a realistic level when the final set of questions was eventually decided on for the layout of the schedules. Some of this information was available from other sources, and other elements, such as the number of rooms occupied by each family, were introduced in later census years.

The layout finally arrived at in 1851 hardly changed over the following five censuses from 1861 up to 1901; in fact the core questions asked about address, name, age, gender, relationship, marital status, occupation and birthplace are identical throughout this period.

When you look at the details recorded about our ancestors on these mid-to-late-Victorian censuses, it is difficult to imagine that they were not taken with family historians in mind. There they are, neatly arranged in conveniently packaged family groups showing their relationships, ages and places of birth – what more could we possibly ask for?

The full list of column headings on the 1851 census schedules is as follows:

1. No. of Householder's Schedule
2. Name of Street, Place, or Road, and Name or No. of House
3. Name and Surname of each Person who abode in the House, on the Night of the 30th March 1851
4. Relation to Head of Family
5. Condition
6. Age of Males/Age of Females
7. Rank, Profession or Occupation
8. Where Born
9. Whether Blind or Deaf-and-Dumb

From 1851, addresses start to become more detailed and precise. House numbers are increasingly given in large towns and cities but often you'll just get the name of the street or road – be careful not to interpret the schedule number as a house number! The addition of a number on the schedule given out to the householders provided the enumerators with an easy method of checking that they had collected in all the forms that they had given out.

Names are usually given in full (the enumerators were instructed to do so), and middle names are sometimes included, but more often they're shown in abbreviated form, as initials or omitted altogether. Occasionally even the first names are given as initials, and it's not uncommon to find the inhabitants of institutions entered solely by their initials. This is important to bear in mind when it comes to searching for your more elusive ancestors.

Columns four and five represent the first two of the significant improvements introduced by George Graham and William Farr. The relationship to the head of the family (usually the oldest adult male in the household) and the condition (i.e. marital condition) are crucial elements for family historians, as they enable us to reconstruct family groups. In the 1841 census this task involves a large amount of guesswork.

The ages (as they were originally supposed to have been in 1841) are now exact ages and the occupations tend to be fuller and more descriptive. It was important that the various 'ranks, professions or occupations' could later be categorized for statistical purposes and the enumerators were issued with extensive instructions on how they should complete this section to ensure a consistent approach. This was part of a three-stage process: first the householder wrote down his occupation as he would describe it, then the enumerator entered it in his summary book in a standard form, and finally the clerks at the Census Office in London assigned it to one of several hundred pre-defined categories.

The system worked well and was retained throughout this period, the only significant change being an increase in the number and variety of categories used by the census clerks. These categories were set out in a list known as the 'Instructions to the Clerks', copies of which are available at The National Archives and online on the Histpop website <**www.histpop.org**>. This extremely useful reference source, which can be used to identify obscure or obsolete occupations, will be discussed more fully in Chapter 19.

The eighth column on the 1851 census – the birthplace – represents perhaps the most significant improvement for family historians from the information given in 1841. Now, for the first time, we have the full place of birth – county and parish for those born in England and Wales and the country of birth for everyone else. The purpose behind asking for this information was to answer one of the crucial questions of the time – the rate and intensity of migration from rural to urban areas.

Again, in Scotland and Ireland the county and parish were to be given for people born in that country and just the name of the country was required for those born elsewhere in the UK.

When the results of the 1851 census were published, it was clear that there had indeed been a significant shift from the countryside to the towns; for the first time it could be demonstrated that more of the population lived in towns and cities than in rural areas. Overall the population of the UK rose steadily throughout the Victorian period from under 28 million in 1841 to more than 41 million in 1901. This of course included Ireland, which suffered a dramatic decrease in population during this period, largely due to the potato famine and the large scale emigration that occurred as a result. If the Irish figures are removed from the total, the rise is even more striking, with the population doubling over the same period from just over 18 million to almost 37 million.

The questions of religion and education were addressed in separate religious and education 'censuses' in 1851. These were not carried out under the auspices of the 1850 Census Act, and participation was not compulsory, but the response rate was high and the results were included in the Census Reports for that year. The returns for the Ecclesiastical Census of 1851 can be seen on microfilm at The National Archives (TNA), in record series HO 129. They include some returns from the Educational Census. However, it's important to note that these 'censuses', while of great interest to local and social historians, do not include the names of individuals, only statistical information.

At this time the Registrar General was responsible for the administration of the census for the whole of Great Britain, the Channel Islands and the Isle of Man. Scotland's own GRO was established in 1855, and took over the running of the Scottish census from 1861 onwards, but the returns from the earlier Scottish censuses remained in London for several decades to come. The Registrar General for England and Wales retained responsibility for censuses in the Channel Islands and the Isle of Man, and the returns for these places are still held by TNA today.

Another area which had always provided the census takers with a logistical challenge was how (or indeed whether) to count the relatively large numbers of Britons who lived in or worked on boats, either at sea or in ports. In the pre-1841 censuses, the administrators were quite explicit in their requirement that the overseers' counts were not to include 'Seamen either in His Majesty's Service, or belonging to Registered Vessels'. The Census Reports for these years did, however, include the numbers of seamen and marines in the Royal Navy as well as those employed in 'Registered Trading Vessels' – a total of more than 250,000 men in 1801. John Rickman's remarks on the summary population figures in his report on the 1811 census indicate that 'The Number of Males composing the Army, Navy etc. includes the Regular Army, The Artillery, and the British Regular Militia, all according to the latest Returns to Parliament...With the Navy are included The Royal Marines: and to these are added The Seamen employed in navigating Registered Vessels.' How the latter figures were arrived at is unclear.

The situation with people who lived and worked on Britain's vast network of inland waterways is also somewhat ambiguous. Edward Higgs, in his essay on 'People on Boats' (see **www.histpop.org**), states that, 'it is unclear how Rickman intended overseers to deal with people...on board ships in ports, or on barges on rivers and canals. Nor do we know how they dealt, in practice, with merchant seamen, fishermen, or bargees, who were temporarily absent.'

The 1840 Census Act and the 1841 Amendment were strangely silent on the matter. As in the earlier years, the overall figures for the Navy and for Merchant Seamen 'afloat' were published in the census report but the Acts contained no explicit instructions on how the enumerators should deal with the challenge of counting our maritime ancestors. But where Rickman and Lister had vacillated, Graham took decisive action and a key refinement in the 1851 census was the introduction of special schedules for vessels in home ports or within British territorial waters. However, the arrangements for recording the floating population were complex, and clearly not understood by many of the people involved. The schedules from merchant vessels were collected by Customs officers from vessels in port on Monday 31 March, the morning after census night, and forwarded directly to the Census Office. The totals were published in the 1851 census report and Graham stated that 'The royal navy in British Ports was returned; and arrangements were made with the Commissioners of Customs, who employed their officers to enumerate all the persons on board vessels, in each port of the United Kingdom, on the night of the Census. The population in vessels is thus included in the districts to which the ports are adjacent.' However, the schedules for merchant and Royal Navy vessels in 1851 do not appear to have survived and it's difficult to establish exactly what happened to them.

The 1861 and 1871 censuses

Having arrived at a satisfactory layout for the census in 1851, the ever practical George Graham saw no reason to depart from this tried and tested formula in subsequent census years, although there were inevitably requests from many quarters that he should do so. There was a suggestion that religious affiliation should be included in 1861, but there were many objections to this, and in practice it is unlikely that it would have been seriously considered. Another request was from the British Temperance League, as to the legality of including 'teetotaller', to which George Graham had no objection, since it would be ignored anyway! He also received requests for the inclusion of extra questions specific to particular localities, but these too were rejected on the grounds of cost. Every extra question added to the expense of taking the census, and would delay the production of the final reports, so it is quite understandable that none were added in 1861. All the same, every family historian must wish that a way had been found to include the religious question.

The format of the 1861 census meant that for the first time the results of a detailed census could be compared with its predecessor, which had not been the position with 1851 and the rather hybrid census of 1841. With one successful census under his belt, George Graham could now approach his dealings with the government with added confidence. When it came to hiring the temporary staff, he told them:

> After the experience I have had in this matter I venture to impress upon Secretary Sir George Lewis the necessity for my being armed, as I was in 1851, with considerable authority and for special powers being entrusted to me, if I am to keep in proper order 80 or 90 or perhaps even 100 of these clerks.
>
> (HO 45/7098 General correspondence and notes on the 1861 census.)

Although some of the temporary clerks had been employed in the Census Office before – it was the fourth time for William Tattershall – most were unused to the public service and came from a variety of different work backgrounds. They needed a great deal of training and supervision, and 106 of them were employed in total. Despite the difficulties, when the office was finally wound up in 1863, George Graham was pleased with his workforce, some of whom had worked for over ten hours a day. He was also pleased to report to the Treasury that the whole census had been conducted at a cost of £4 15s 8d per head of population, compared with £5 4s in 1851, just the sort of thing he knew they would like to hear.

An attempt had been made in 1851 to deal with the perennial problem of temporary mobility. If a significant number of 'settled' inhabitants were temporarily absent, or if others were temporarily present, the enumerator was supposed to record the estimated numbers in his summary book. The exercise was not a great success, but nevertheless, another attempt was made in 1861 – this time with clearer instructions to the enumerators. The returns for Gedney in Lincolnshire include, under the heading 'Persons temporarily absent', an entry reading '1 – absconded' (RG 9/2328 folio 58, page iv).

Turning to the nominal pages we come across an entry for a family consisting of a married woman (Hannah Miller) and her three children. No head of the household is entered but instead the enumerator has written the words 'Husband Absconded' (see Fig. 2.2). This only tells a small part of the fascinating story of the Miller family – in fact Hannah's husband George had emigrated to America in time to catch the tail-end of the Californian Gold Rush (RG 9/2328, folio 62, page 6).

The questions were repeated in the next two censuses and then abandoned.

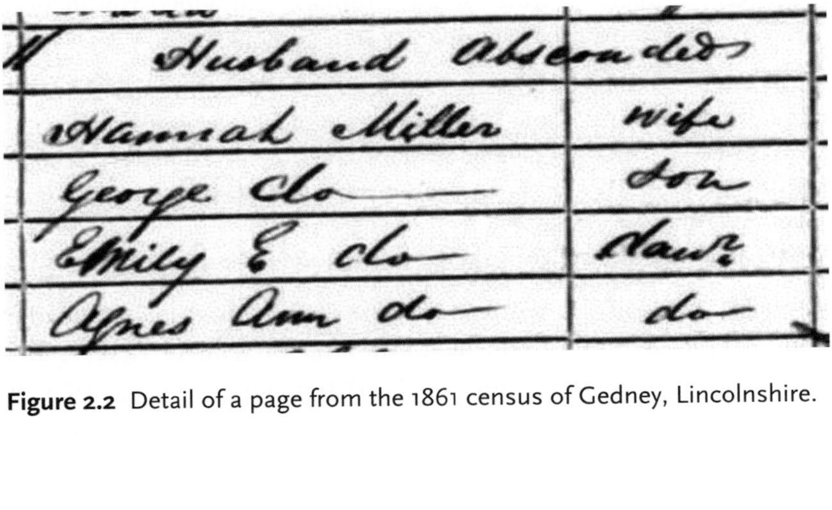

Figure 2.2 Detail of a page from the 1861 census of Gedney, Lincolnshire.

The 1861 census was the first where an explicit promise of confidentiality was made, and the GRO published a 'Memorandum on Some of the Objects and Uses of the Census of 1861', which extols the benefits of the census and reassures the populace that they have nothing to fear by way of taxation, conscription or any such evils. This 'memorandum' was effectively a press release, and parts of it were indeed reproduced in the newspapers. George Graham recognised the value of good public relations, even if he would not have recognised the term. This may have been a circular from a government department and conveyed factual information, but its literary style is unexpectedly lyrical, including a quote from Oliver Goldsmith and statements such as:

> The number of Souls, in the expressive language of the old writers, will then be known, and will remind the nation of the extent of the institutions for the advancement of religion, education and justice, required to keep pace with its numbers.
> (Memorandum on Some of the Objects and Uses of the Census of 1861 in RG 27/3 Forms and instructions issued for taking the census.)

Even when giving straightforward advice on people who subtract a few years from their age, it still tends towards the whimsical: 'Should the ages of cooks, or of others, be found by any fatality standing still, or even retrograding, it should be corrected by their masters who fill in the return.'

The returns for 1861 at last include large numbers of schedules for vessels, so for the first time family historians are able to locate their seafaring ancestors. The returns of merchant vessels were completed by the Masters or Captains and it's these forms which appear in the census. This is therefore also the first time when you might be able to identify your ancestor's handwriting on a census schedule. Previously this would only happen if your ancestor was an enumerator, or appears in one of the few household schedules to survive.

Remarkably, a collection of nearly 500 original 1841 householders' schedules has survived from the Cainham sub-district, part of the Ludlow registration district. The collection covers the returns for the parishes of Hopton Cangeford, Bitterley, Cainham, Ashford Bowdler, Ashford Carbonell and Hope Baggott and is virtually complete. Extensive research carried out by Donald Davis including a detailed comparison with the enumerators' summary books has produced some fascinating insights into 'what happened on the bottom rungs of the census implementation ladder' (*Local Historian*, Vol. 43, Number 2, May 2013).

There is another collection of household schedules for part of an Enumeration District in Newcastle upon Tyne St Andrew in 1851 (HO 107/2405, folios 276–325; plates 2 and 3) which survives with the official records. Normally the household schedules were kept until the statistical abstracting from the enumeration books was complete, so that they could be referred to in case of any queries. These ones may have been kept because part of the enumeration book was damaged or destroyed; there are other examples dotted throughout this and other census years.

Once the results were published in the form of the Census Reports, the press was always keen to publish interesting snippets, often referred to as 'Curiosities'. Following the publication in 1863 of the report on the 1861 census, *The Times* noted that the breakdown of occupations showed that there were ten solicitors enumerated as inmates of workhouses, 32 in prison for debt and 60 in lunatic asylums. It was also noted that the population of the parish of Aldrington in Sussex had doubled between 1851 and 1861 – from one inhabitant to two! The only building within its boundaries was a toll-keeper's cottage, which in 1851 was occupied by a single man, and by a married couple ten years later.

There were no significant changes in the 1871 census, and the layout is virtually identical to that of 1861, but the instructions to the householders now asked them to include in the occupation column not only their trade or calling, but also whether or not they were currently employed or unemployed. This was repeated in 1881, but then dropped again for subsequent censuses.

The 1881 and 1891 censuses

George Graham retired in 1880, by which time plans for the 1881 census were well advanced. His successor, Sir Brydges Powell Henniker, had the relatively easy task of overseeing the conduct of the census using the by now well-oiled machinery. He is not generally regarded as a great success as Registrar General, but George Graham was a hard act to follow, and Henniker encountered a set of problems that his predecessor did not have to face. Once the 1881 census was completed, early in his period of office, there were now returns from five complete census years, each bigger than the last, stored in various government buildings. These of course still included the Scottish censuses of 1841 and 1851.

Brydges Henniker was not happy with the quality of the temporary staff recruited for the 1881 census. Part of the problem was that they were recruited by the Treasury, and not directly by the GRO. Henniker tried to persuade the Treasury to hand the job over to the Civil Service Commission, but with no more success than Graham when he complained about the same thing in 1861 and 1871. Of the 98 appointments made by the Treasury, Henniker claimed that four were unfit for work of any kind and two had actually died! More than half of the remainder he considered 'indifferent', 'bad' or 'very bad'. He wrote:

> In consequence of the physical, mental and moral inadequacy of a large proportion of the clerks employed, the Census of 1881 not only cost much more money, and took a much longer time in its compilation than was necessary, but also when completed was very much less trustworthy than it should have been.
>
> (RG 29/3 Treasury Letter Book 1886–1907.)

Of course he may have been exaggerating, bearing in mind that this was his first census and he was very inexperienced. Ten years later the Treasury finally agreed to allow the expenditure for more of the census work to be done by experienced GRO staff, with only the less-skilled tasks entrusted to temporary workers. He managed to bring in the 1891 census at a lower cost than 1881.

The temporary Census Office was finally relocated from Craig's Court to a set of temporary buildings erected in Charles Street. These buildings were also used for the 1901 and 1911 censuses, but not in the same location – they were dismantled and re-erected in Millbank in 1899. Another innovation was that a telephone link was installed between the new buildings in Charles Street and Somerset House, which must have made life much easier for all concerned.

The only significant change in the 1881 and 1891 censuses related to questions regarding languages spoken (see Case study 6).

The 1901 census

Brydges Henniker was succeeded by Sir Reginald McLeod in 1900. He oversaw the 1901 census, organised from the relocated buildings in Millbank, now equipped with sprinklers in the event of fire. Women now formed a significant part of the workforce, and for the first time women clerks were employed to work on the 1901 census. A lady superintendent was seconded from the Post Office to be in charge of them. Some of these female clerks went on to become some of the first women to be employed permanently by the GRO. The War Office suggested that priority should be given to disabled ex-servicemen from the Boer War for temporary census work, although despite extensive publicity only two such men applied.

The 1901 census took the same form as that of 1891, but there had been many boundary changes during the decade, which made the administration of the census more complicated. Fortunately Ordnance Survey maps had been provided for census purposes since 1870, presumably to the great relief of George Graham in particular. A new set was provided for the planning of the 1901 census to cope with the boundary changes. The collection of maps used for census purposes dated 1870 to 1921 is held by TNA in record series RG 18 and can be viewed online at <**www.cassinimaps.co.uk/shop/tna1.asp**>.

The enumerator's lot

At the same time as the various Registrar Generals were struggling to get the resources they needed to collate, analyse and report on the results of the censuses, locally the census officials (the Registrars and Superintendent Registrars) were facing an entirely different set of problems. The most persistent difficulty was in recruiting efficient and reliable enumerators.

The lot of the nineteenth-century census enumerator was not always a happy one: some had genuine concerns about the perils of entering certain buildings. Anyone who's read the fictional works of Charles Dickens (think of Fagin's den) or the real-life accounts of poverty recorded by Henry Mayhew in his monumental study *London Labour and the London Poor* will be only too familiar with the depredation and squalor of certain types of dwelling – the rookeries, courts, cellars and 'backs', of industrial Victorian Britain. It's hardly surprising that some enumerators were less than happy at the prospect, not just of having to enter the buildings, but also of having to encourage the occupants to complete their census forms – particularly when we consider the general distrust of authority, and the appallingly low standards of literacy at the time. A letter dated 25 May 1841 from Registrar General Thomas Lister suggests that some districts were even requesting police assistance for enumerators (HO 45/146).

From time to time we come across comments and complaints written by the enumerators amongst the census records. The summary books offered the perfect forum for unhappy enumerators to voice their concerns: the enumerators could be fairly certain that their complaints would be seen by the registrars themselves. Their comments are by no means widespread, but they now form part of the official records of the census, and provide us with a fascinating insight into the life of a Victorian enumerator.

By far the most regularly heard complaint was about the rate of pay. The Home Office and the Registrar General's correspondence files, and the Treasury Letter Books, include a number of letters written by dissatisfied enumerators. In 1851, as a test case, John Cohen, an enumerator from Whitechapel in east London, sued the Home Secretary Sir George Grey for the sum of 10d which he believed was owed to him. In the event, the judge found in favour of the Home Office but there was evidence of widespread dissatisfaction with the verdict (HO 45/3579).

An article in *The Times* of 20 May 1871 reported that:

'The enumerators employed in taking the late Census, especially those in the more thickly-populated districts, are loud in their expression of dissatisfaction at the small amount of remuneration which has been fixed by the Government for their services, and within the last few days several meetings have been held ... with the view of taking measures to induce the Government to make some addition to the proposed rate of payment.' Feelings at the meetings seem to have run high: 'It was stated that the work which had been performed was not only difficult in many cases, but not altogether free from danger, an enumerator present having caught smallpox while discharging his duties.'

The problem of pay clearly wasn't going to go away – as late as 1931 a letter was written to *The Times* suggesting that 'the remuneration should be appreciably higher'.

These concerns come through loud and clear in some of the comments made by enumerators in the census returns themselves. Foremost amongst the ranks of belligerent enumerators was a man called Edward Henry Blade. In 1851 Blade was appointed to the post of enumerator for the parish of Allhallows, Barking, near the Tower of London. It was undeniably a larger than average Enumeration District – more than 2,000 people were crowded into the relatively small parish and Blade was expected to count and record them all single-handedly. He filled up his 84-page summary book and then started a second, completing 16 pages before launching into an astonishing diatribe:

> The enumeration of this district was undertaken by me in the belief that I should be fairly paid for my services. I was not aware that all the particulars were to be entered by the enumerator in a book, the work without that, being ample for the sum paid, nor had I any idea of the unreasonable amount of labour imposed. The distribution, collection etc. of the schedules together with the copying of the same, occupied between two and three hours for every 60 persons enumerated, and for this – the equivalent is – ONE SHILLING!!!
>
> (HO 107/1531, folio 193, page 18; plate 12.)

Edward Blade certainly wasn't alone in holding feelings like this. The wonderfully-named Myler Falla was employed as an enumerator for the 1871 census of Mortlake in Surrey. He used the description page of his summary book to record the following comment: 'Very badly paid. I think if Government Officials had to do it, they would be paid treble the Amount' (RG 10/870, folio 25, page i; plate 10).

In 1861 James Haliwell, the enumerator of part of Skircoat in Yorkshire, made a weary-sounding complaint on the last page of his summary book. After writing 'End of the Enumeration District' across the middle of page 27, he added the words: 'No more at this price' (RG 9/3285, folio 39, page 27).

George James Hall, the enumerator for part of the hamlet of Peckham, in 1861, had another large district to cover, containing nearly 300 households. He doesn't appear to have complained at all, but when he came to collect the schedule from number 6 Arthur Terrace it seems that he was greeted with a less than welcoming smile by the single female inhabitant, who had evidently failed to complete her form. He was able to get a name (Ann Hill) and her age (42) but no place of birth or marital status. In the occupation column he noted: 'Eccentric Lady' (RG 9/385, folio 82, page 21).

There's also no evidence that William Walker, the enumerator for part of Manchester's London Road sub-District, openly expressed any dissatisfaction about his experience, but it's clear from some of the entries in his summary book that his task was anything but straightforward. When he came to the returns for 'Pump Street Entry' he found some obstacles in his way. He listed the inhabitants of number 1 Pump Street Entry simply as a woman and her three sons; no names, no birthplaces and only approximate ages. He then went on to use the occupation column to make the following comment: 'No further information could be obtained, except that they slept in this cottage on Sunday night, April 7 1861. The cottage is "To Let" – and is left unlocked' (see Fig. 2.3).

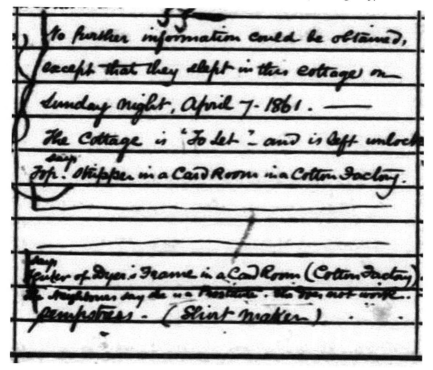

Figure 2.3 Detail of a page from the 1861 census of Manchester.

Walker was able to get full details from the inhabitants of number 2 but he wasn't too convinced by their occupations. John Mulhal, the head of the household, gave his occupation as 'Top Stripper in a Card Room in a Cotton Factory', which the enumerator prefixed with the word 'Says...'. Mary Kane, the family's 20-year-old boarder, fared even worse than her landlord. For her occupation, Walker wrote: 'Says Tenter of Dyer's Frame in a Card Room (Cotton Factory). The neighbours say she is a Prostitute. She does not work' (RG 9/2944, folio 94, page 54; see also Fig. 2.3).

The pressures placed on enumerators were real, as is clear from the tragic story of John William Hird, a grocer who had been appointed to take the returns for an enumeration district in Oldham in 1901. The *Gloucester Citizen* reported (8 April 1901) that he had 'had some difficulty in collecting his papers in the early part of last week, and on Thursday afternoon reported to the Registrar that he had not been able to complete his returns.' His body was found in a mill, four miles from Oldham and a number of census papers were found in his pockets. In the same year, Charles Tanner, a stationer from Winchester, and an appointed census enumerator, met with a similar fate. After collecting all his schedules, he went to the River Itchen where, according to a report in the *Western Daily Press* (3 April 1901), he 'took off his coat and overcoat, folded them up neatly, with his hat on top, and his bag containing his census papers by the side, and jumped into the river.'

These stories serve as a chilling reminder of the sort of stress that census enumerators could find themselves under, but thankfully it wasn't all gloom and despondency. Some enumerators even seemed to enjoy the task that they had been asked to carry out and most seem to have taken pride in what they were doing.

On 11 April 1861, *The Times* published a letter written by an enumerator who had also worked on the 1851 census. His district consisted mainly of 'tradespeople of the better class, but principally of the decent poor and the labouring class' and he remarked that his work had been made much easier by a 'great improvement in intelligence ... in the poorer neighbourhood since 1851'.

> In most families ... there was, if not a grown-up person, a boy or girl who had had sufficient schooling to enable them to fill up the schedule, and, failing this, it was taken to the baker's, or the publican's, or the

chandler's shop, or to the rent collector ... there was an eager desire manifested to get the return of each family completed before the visit of the enumerator ... But when I came to the "upper ten thousand" of my district – those persons whom I expected would have given me the least trouble – there was hardly one in three ready for me; I was to call again, and again, and again, or to wait, so that had my district been composed entirely of this class, and of the same extent, I should have required three days instead of one to complete the enumeration.'

This positive experience was echoed by an enumerator from the Portsea Island district who told a reporter from the *Portsmouth Evening News* (1 April 1901) that the forms he collected were generally completed to a high standard. 'If he [the householder] cannot fill up the paper himself because he is unable to write, he seeks the assistance of a friendly neighbour or his eldest son comes to the rescue with the "tips" that the Board School has specially given him, and hey presto, the job is done!'

An article in *The Cambrian* (the first English-language newspaper to be published in Wales) on 14 April 1871 gave another largely positive enumerator's account. Despite expressing concerns about the accuracy of information supplied by certain groups in his community ('It is the ladies – God bless them! of course – and the would be gentilities who have bothered me most') he concluded that:

The two extremes of society performed their part towards the Census Office cheerfully and satisfactorily, and the short-comings (which have, after all, been very inconsiderable) all arose among those who were uncertain as to their social position, and feared writing them-selves down in the world.'

The intrepid Portsmouth newspaper reporter, who accompanied one of the local enumerators as he went about his task of collecting the householders' schedules in 1901, noted 'the surprising amount of intel-ligent common-sense that is generally displayed.'

Despite the conflicting views expressed here, when taken as a whole, the above comments provide a remarkably clear picture of the major issues involved in the day-to-day operation of the census. As well as suggesting a number of ways in which the actions and opinions of some enumerators might have contributed to a degree of under-enu-meration, the comments provide evidence of a genuine desire to get the job done – enough evidence, we would assert, to allow us to feel confident that the census is as complete as it could possibly have been.

A new role for the census

On 7 March 1891, Mr W. H. Primrose of the Ministry of Works wrote to the Home Office asking for permission to destroy the enumeration books from the 1861 census contained in 128 boxes stored in the roof space of the Houses of Parliament: 'As it is necessary that these papers should be removed as soon as possible I am to inquire whether they may be destroyed' (HO 45/10147/b19513; plate 13).

He wrote again in June, arguing that the enumeration books were neither necessary nor useful for research purposes: 'to attempt to verify any particular fact, or to extract further information by a reference to the Enumeration Books, would be a work of labour beyond the powers of any single individual.'

It transpired that the documents he referred to included the 1851 census as well as those for 1861. There seems to have been some confusion as to which government department had the power to authorize their destruction, the Local Government Board, the GRO or the Home Office, and the delay that this caused may have been the saving of them. The matter was referred to Brydges Henniker, and, whatever his shortcomings might have been as Registrar General, it is to his great credit that he displayed such prescience in recognising the historical importance of these records and arguing so strongly that they should be kept. He wrote to the Home Office on 17 June 1891:

...in my humble opinion it would be very unwise to destroy National records, the value of which will probably be hereafter very great to those persons who wish to investigate the condition of this country in past times. It is doubtlessly true that these documents have not been hitherto consulted. Not only, however, is it within my knowledge that they would already have been examined, had not the difficulty of access to them been so great as to be practically insuperable to a private enquirer, but I would point out that the value and utility of such records depends to a great extent upon their antiquity, and that documents which are as yet only forty years old have not yet reached their stage of full utility.'

(HO 45/10147/b19513; plate 14.)

The documents were eventually moved to the Public Record Office, when it had space to accommodate them in its new building in Chancery Lane. They were not opened to researchers until some decades later, but these crucial records were at least saved for posterity. It could have turned out so differently!

Not everyone shared Mr Primrose's opinion that it would be impossible to verify any fact from the enumeration books. In 1895 a man called William Paul wrote from his home in France to request a search in the 1841 census returns for proof that his mother had been born in Britain. He was born in France of British parents and had proof of his father's birth, but needed to prove that his mother was not French, so that he would not be conscripted into the French army. This was followed over the next few years by further requests for searches in early census returns, usually for legal purposes.

The first decade of the twentieth century saw an increase in the number of requests for searches in the old census returns, particularly with the passing of the Old Age Pensions Act of 1908. For some elderly applicants who could provide neither birth, baptismal nor marriage certificates, entries in the census returns were, under the terms of the Act, accepted as proof of age. At first, the GRO was reluctant to provide this service, contending that this was not the purpose for which the census had been taken, and that there were great practical difficulties in searching these early enumeration books. Ultimately, though, special forms were provided for applications for searches. In 1909 the enumerators' books for the 1841 and 1851 Scottish censuses were transferred to Edinburgh at the request of the Scottish Registrar General. It is perhaps a measure of his exasperation with the business of allowing searches that the then Registrar General, William Cospatrick Dunbar, told his Scottish counterpart: 'I advise you not to attempt to walk on such hazardous ice as these old censuses!'

The 1901 census was not quite the last of Victorian times (Her Majesty died on 22 January 1901, just a few weeks short of Census night), but it was very much of that era. For one thing, almost everyone in it was born in or lived through Victoria's reign. It was also the last to be organised along the pattern established in 1841. The 1911 census was significantly different and was to usher in a completely new era of census taking in Britain.

Scotland

The first six censuses of Scotland, from 1801 to 1851, were administered from London. There were some slight differences in the method used to collect the information – principally the use of schoolmasters instead of Poor Law officials to take the 'accounts' and, from 1841 to distribute and collect the schedules – but for our purposes the differences are insignificant. Scotland didn't have its own Registrar General until 1855 and the 1861 census was the first to be set up under a specific census Act – the Census (Scotland) Act, 1860. Similar Acts were passed for the taking of the 1871, 1881 and 1891 censuses in Scotland but the 1901 and 1911 censuses of Scotland were taken under the terms of the Census (Great Britain) Acts of 1900 and 1910 respectively.

The passing of separate Acts made no difference to the substance of the censuses, and the questions asked and the layout of the forms in Scotland and in England and Wales remained essentially the same throughout the nineteenth century. This allowed the results to be compared both with the earlier censuses and with the returns for other parts of Great Britain.

The 1881 census saw the introduction of a question which is extremely useful for family historians. Householders were asked to write the word 'Gaelic' next to the birthplace of every individual who 'habitually' spoke Gaelic. The question seems to have been a bit of an afterthought and wasn't included on the original householders' schedules, but by 1891 it had become an intrinsic part of the census and had become more refined. This time householders were asked to give the language spoken as 'Gaelic' or 'G & E' – i.e. Gaelic and English – and the same question was repeated in 1901.

In all other respects, there was no significant difference between the Scottish census and its English and Welsh counterpart throughout the Victorian and Edwardian periods. The 1841 and 1851 census returns were eventually transferred to the General Register Office for Scotland (GROS) and along with the returns for the later years have remained there ever since.

Ireland

It is an undeniable and inescapable fact that many of the records that form the basic building blocks of our research into our English, Welsh and Scottish ancestors, simply don't exist in Ireland. A combination of the ravages of time, a catastrophic fire and some regrettable decision making by the Irish government of the time means that, for most of us, the prospects of tracing our Irish roots back beyond the nineteenth century are frankly not good.

The legislation which set up the 1801 and 1811 censuses in England, Wales and Scotland made no provision for counting the population of Ireland. Of course Ireland didn't formally become part of the United Kingdom until 1801 and, following an unsuccessful attempt to hold a census in 1813, it wasn't until 1821 that the first full Irish census was taken. However, after a slow start, things begin to look quite promising: unlike the equivalent census for the rest of the UK, the 1821 census of Ireland asked for names of individuals to be recorded along with their relationships, ages and occupations.

The 1841 census saw a further leap forward: the amount of information requested on each individual was quite phenomenal, particularly when compared with the relatively sparse forms used in England, Wales and Scotland. The householder's schedule included three tables: the first was to record the name, age, sex, relationship, marital status, year of marriage and occupation of each person living in the household at the time. An attempt was also made to gather information on literacy. The second table requested similar information on people who usually lived at that address but were temporarily absent, as well as asking for their place of residence and, finally, the third table asked for details of all those who had died in the residence of the family completing the form within the previous ten years!

The Irish census continued to expand throughout the nineteenth century with additional questions on sickness and disease, and a wide range of forms being introduced to cover those in institutions and on board ships. Questions about religion also became both a significant part of the census and a matter of some considerable dispute; the predominantly Roman Catholic population being, perhaps understandably, reluctant to provide information which they felt could potentially be used against them by the largely Protestant ruling classes.

The bad news for family historians, of course, is that virtually none of this has survived. It's worth taking a few moments here to explode a popular Irish family history myth. Anyone who knows anything about research in Ireland will have heard about the fire that destroyed 'all the primary source material' during the fighting at the Four Courts complex in Dublin in 1922. Well, first of all, not everything was destroyed; the Irish birth, marriage and death certificates had never been stored there and those records have survived, intact, from their starting date up until the present day. Also, most of the 'missing' census returns weren't lost in the conflagration either – the returns for 1861, 1871, 1881 and 1891 had already been destroyed by the government many years earlier. It's true that the pre-1861 censuses were lost, along with all the pre-1858 wills, large numbers of parish registers and a wealth of irreplaceable legal and historical documents, but fragments of these records (including some census returns) have survived and other sources that are unique to Ireland have been preserved and made accessible in an effort to redress the balance.

The good news is that the 1901 census for the whole of Ireland survives in its entirety and is held by The National Archives of Ireland in Dublin. The Public Record of Northern Ireland also has copies of the 1901 census returns for the six counties which became Northern Ireland in 1922.

The records created by the Irish Census Acts are significantly different in layout and content to the corresponding records for England, Wales and Scotland. The 1901 Irish census comprises the following documents:

- Household Return (Form A), consisting of two pages, one completed by the householder with the list of inhabitants and another completed by the enumerator with the details of the address – these are the only pages with information on individuals;
- Enumerator's Abstract (Form N) for the whole street or townland;
- House and Building Return (Form B1), with physical details of the house;
- Out-offices and Farm-steadings, (Form B2) with details of things like stables, barns, sheds.

The information contained on the additional forms (particularly Form B1) is of potential interest to family historians and certainly should not be ignored.

Case study 1 – The Evetts

Our first case study illustrates how using the census returns can be a fairly straightforward process, utilising the information you find in one census year to move back in time, identifying earlier generations as you go.

Our starting point is a woman named Dora Winifred Evett. She married William Fone in Aston, Warwickshire, in 1913, but our story starts with her appearance, two years earlier, in the 1911 census as a 24-year-old woman living at an address in School Road, Hall Green, Birmingham (RG 14/18667, schedule 207). The arrangement of the 1911 census means that we only see the entry for Dora and her family; her parents, Walter Henry Bennett Evett (a bank manager) and Sarah, and her older sister Ethel, aged 30, along with a servant and a visitor. But it's relatively easy to browse to the entries for the neighbours and it's always worth doing so. In this case, we find that the Evett's immediate neighbours were a clerk and a bank official. The houses occupied by the Evetts and their neighbours each consisted of seven rooms (not including sculleries, landings, lobbies, closets and bathrooms) and each family was employing a live-in general servant. The Evetts appear to have been relatively well to-do – they weren't rich but they probably led a fairly affluent life by the standards of the day.

The family are easily found in the 1901 census and the entry shows a remarkably similar picture, with Dora as a 14-year-old girl, living with her father, mother and sister in Whitmore Road in the Bordesley district of Aston (RG 13/2861, folio 151, page 26). Walter was already working as a bank manager and a quick glance at the census page gives us a good idea of the sort of neighbourhood in which the Evetts were living. This time their immediate neighbours were a draper and a commercial clerk and there was a gun repairer (a distinctive West Midlands trade), a plumber and a cab driver all living nearby. Apart from the draper, everyone on the page was described as a 'worker' – i.e. employed by someone else. Unlike in 1911, none of the households included a servant, but all of them were inhabited by single families. There were no boarders or lodgers and none of the families were occupying fewer than five rooms: a perfect picture of comfortable lower-middle-class life.

Dora's place of birth is given in the 1901 and 1911 censuses as Birmingham, while both of her parents were born in Shropshire. Finding the family ten years earlier in the 1891 census shouldn't prove too difficult and indeed a simple search for a Dora Evett (there's only one person of that name listed in the whole country) quickly turns up the relevant entry (RG 12/2411, folio 78, page 25).

The family was living at 54 Golden Hillock Road (very close to Whitmore Road) and it's interesting to note how little has changed over 20 years. William was already a bank manager in 1891 and, apart from a discrepancy over Sarah's age (she was 30 in 1891, 44 in 1901 and 53 in 1911) and a different place of birth for Ethel (Harborne, Staffordshire in 1891 and 1911 and Birmingham, Warwickshire in 1901), the details match precisely. There's an addition to the household in 1891 – or rather, since we're working backwards here, we should probably think of it as a disappearance since that date! In 1891 the Evett family had a servant girl called Jane Hayfield living with them. Rather than suggesting that the family were in any way better off than in 1901, this probably has more to do with Sarah's need for help in looking after her four-year-old daughter, Dora.

We now move back another ten years, when we should expect to find Walter and Sarah with Ethel as a very young child. Sure enough we come across the Evetts in the 1881 census living in Harborne at 3 Regent Villas, Regent Road, with Ethel just a year old (RG 11/2958, folio 73, page 34). Walter's occupation is given as 'Commercial Clerk (Banking)' and through the presence of Sarah's two unmarried sisters (Lucy and Martha) we get the added bonus of learning her maiden surname: Houlston. Sarah's age is given as 23, suggesting that the 1891 entry is probably the least reliable of the four that we now have.

Walter was entirely consistent in giving his birthplace in the 1881, 1891, 1901 and 1911 censuses as Shifnal in Shropshire. His given age was also consistent and points to a birth date of 1857 or 1858. These facts, combined with his distinctive name, allow us to search for him in earlier censuses with the confidence of being able to make a positive identification.

We find him in 1871 living at an address in Horse Fair, Shifnal, with his parents, James and Catherine (RG 10/2748, folio 119, page 44). James Evett is described as a 'Surgeon not practicing [sic]' and Walter is the youngest of four children living in the house. Also in the house are two domestic servants – a housemaid and a cook – suggesting that James, despite not actively pursuing his profession, was clearly doing quite well for himself.

The 1861 census goes some way towards explaining this apparent life of leisure (RG 9/1854, folio 90, page 40). The family are still (already!) living at Horse Fair in Shifnal and James's 'occupation' is given as 'Interest of Money' – he was evidently in receipt of an independent income; perhaps an annuity of some sort. There are now six children (including Walter aged three years) and the household is again supplemented by two servants: a cook and a nurse.

The research has now reached a stage where we could head off in a number of different directions. We know that James was born in Wellington, Shropshire, so we could look for him there in earlier censuses. And if we're doing our homework properly, we would discover that there is a surviving 1821 census of Wellington held by Shropshire Archives (3129/5/5 00263): James Evett is listed there as a seven-year-old boy living with his parents and two siblings. His father was also called James Evett; he also was a surgeon and left a will which was proved in 1845 – probably the source of James junior's wealth.

We could also search forward in time for James and we would discover that he lived to a ripe old age and was still around for the 1901 census. He died later the same year in Yardley, Worcestershire, aged 87. We could look for Walter's siblings and find out where they went to, to whom they were married and what children they had or we could work further back in time using the evidence from the earlier censuses to delve into the eighteenth century and beyond.

Of course, before claiming James Evett the surgeon as our ancestor, we would want to back up the details we found in the censuses with information from birth, marriage and death certificates, wills, parish registers and other nineteenth-century sources. However, you can see from the research outlined above that it's quite possible to work back through the nineteenth-century censuses, and in a matter of just a few hours trace a family back over a hundred years starting with relatively little information.

Researching a family history is not simply a lateral process. Once you start looking at a family in the census, ever-expanding avenues of research open up before you, offering virtually unlimited possibilities.

Case study 2 – The Asks

It is almost inevitable that in the course of your research you will come across at least one family where nothing about them quite seems to add up. You get to a particular event, a birth, a marriage or a census entry, and then...nothing. The Ask family of Portsmouth – also known as the Pragnell family of Portsmouth! – provide a perfect illustration of the classic family history brick wall.

Ada Denham died in abject poverty in the summer of 1904. On 16 April 1892, as Ada Ask, she had married Charles Edward Denham in Portsmouth. Ada stated that her father was George Ask, a bricklayer, and gave her age as 19. At the time of the 1901 census, Charles and Ada were living at 153 Wingfield Street, Portsmouth, with two young sons, Charles and George (RG 13/995, folio 73, page 20). Ada's age was given as 27 and her place of birth as Portsmouth; from this information it wasn't too difficult to find her in the 1891 census.

Ada was working as a domestic servant to the Bayne family in Eaton Road, Margate, aged 17. Her surname is entered as Aske rather than Ask, but since all the other details are entirely consistent with the information from the 1901 census, we can be confident that this is the right person.

Unfortunately, this is where the trail (initially) runs cold. There's no sign of Ada in the 1881 census (when she should be aged seven) and there's no trace of a birth registration for her anywhere in the Portsmouth area – or indeed elsewhere. Perhaps more worryingly, there's no sign of George Ask (her supposed father) in any of the censuses or in the GRO's birth, marriage and death indexes.

It would be easy in a situation like this to conclude that Ada had simply been missed in the 1881 census, but that would leave a lot of other questions unanswered. Although the problem might seem unsolvable, this is exactly the sort of case where the ability to carry out searches using sophisticated online search techniques really pays dividends.

The name Ask is not particularly common – there are only seventeen 'Ask' events registered in the Portsea Island registration district during the nineteenth century. The only George Ask on the hit list is the birth of a boy called George Pragnell Ask in 1865 – clearly much too young to be Ada's father, but interesting nonetheless.

A search of the birth indexes for anyone called Ada born in Portsmouth (Portsea Island registration district) between 1873 and 1874 throws up a number of results. However, it's the entry in 1873 for a girl called Ada Pragnell that really jumps off the page and demands to be investigated further.

The 1881 census provides the first hint that this is in fact 'our' Ada. The Pragnell family (entered in the returns as Prangell) is living at 86 Lower Charlotte Street, Portsmouth, as boarders with the Pond family. Ada is there (aged nine) together with three sisters; Rosinna, Clara and Sarah. Their parents are listed as George and Pollie, although 'Pollie' turns out to be a pet name: she was usually known as Rosina (RG 11/1139, folio 44, page 4; plate 16).

Ten years earlier, the Pragnell family were living at 4 George Place, Portsmouth: George and Rosina, with four children – Catherine, George, Rosaline and Clara. The births of Rosaline and Clara, as well as those of Ada and Sarah, were registered as Pragnell; however, those of the older children are in the GRO indexes under the surname Ask. So what's going on here? It appears all very confusing but, using the censuses in tandem with records of births, marriages and deaths, it's possible to put together the following story.

In 1855, Rosina Leary married a man called William Ask. William had previously been married to Julia Cox, who died in 1854, and with Rosina he had at least two children (William born in 1856 and Catherine in 1857) before he himself died in 1857.

Two years later, Rosina had an illegitimate daughter named Alice and then, sometime in the early 1860s, she met George Pragnell. There's no evidence that George and Rosina ever got married despite the fact that the 1871 and 1881 censuses both describe Rosina as George's wife. The registration of their son as George Pragnell Ask in 1865 suggests that they were together but not legally married at that stage.

George's birth was followed by the arrival of Rosaline (in 1867), Clara (1870), Ada (1873) and Sarah (1875) – all registered as Pragnell. Ada's birth certificate describes her mother as Rosina Pragnell, late Ask, formerly Leary. George Pragnell died in 1885, and at the time of the 1891 census Rosina is in the Portsea Island Union Workhouse, listed as a widow and a pauper (RG 12/860, folio 91, page 4; plate 17). Her name is given as Rosina Ask. At some stage, the whole family seem to have reverted to the name Ask, even those who were apparently George Pragnell's biological children. When Ada gave her father's name as George Ask, this was in fact an amalgam of her mother's two partners – William Ask and George Pragnell.

Rosina certainly seems to have had a hard life. She had at least eight children by two (possibly three) men and ended up in the workhouse.

She was born on the Isle of Wight (although the 1881 census is the only one to indicate this) and the 1841 and 1851 censuses both find her living there. In 1841, aged just eight years, Rosina was in the Isle of Wight 'House of Industry' in Newport. Ten years later she was still there, now described as a prostitute (HO 107/1663, folio 394, page 8; plate 15). She eventually left the workhouse to marry into a life of poverty across the Solent in Portsmouth – for Rosina, this almost certainly represented a step up in the world.

3

THE 1911 CENSUS AND BEYOND

The 1911 census may not have been the first census of the new century, but it was certainly the first to be taken in a new age of information gathering. Every census from 1851 to 1901 had been very similar to its predecessor, with only small variations and additions. In 1911, however, a completely new approach was taken by the General Register Office (GRO) as it embarked on a much more ambitious project. For the first time, it was decided that, rather than copying the information into summary books, the householders' schedules would be retained and the Census Office clerks would abstract the data directly from them.

The need for national information

There had always been pressure from the Statistical Branch of the GRO along with a variety of pressure groups for more questions to be added to each successive census. There were even proposals for a census to be taken every five years instead of ten, but the Treasury would not sanction the expenditure. Furthermore the manual methods of processing the collected data had reached their limits by 1901. There was now even more demand for information about the state of the nation's health, and there were serious concerns at the decline in the birth rate during the last decade of the nineteenth century. Combined with the scale of emigration, there were fears that Britain would fall behind the rising economies of countries such as Germany and the US. A modern industrial nation with an empire to run needed a large and healthy workforce. There was also the matter of the armed forces: many of the men who volunteered for the army in the Boer War of 1899–1902 had been rejected as physically unfit. Surveys such as those conducted by Booth in London and Rowntree in York, combined with the GRO's own statistics, confirmed that the health and living conditions of the poorer classes in Britain were very bad indeed. Despite the many improvements in public health, housing and education during the latter half of the nineteenth century, the health of poor children was not significantly better than it had been in the 1840s, and infant mortality was still very high. There was now wider acceptance of the idea that government should intervene to improve the lives of the working classes, and as the first step to solving a problem is always to find out the nature and extent of it, so there was an increasingly urgent need for additional and more detailed information.

The climate of opinion in the country was beginning to move in favour of state intervention, a trend which would eventually lead to the modern Welfare State. Charitable organisations like the Salvation Army, for example, as well as some local school boards, began to provide meals for needy children, and in 1906 a Liberal government was elected which was committed to reform. Health checks on schoolchildren were introduced, and at the other end of the age scale Old Age Pensions were introduced in 1908. This particular measure greatly increased the number of requests for searches in the Victorian census returns – an episode which appears to have exasperated the Registrar General, William Dunbar. The work involved in searching in these old census returns was considerable, and the GRO was understandably reluctant to carry them out, claiming that this was not the purpose for which the census had been taken. However, census evidence was essential to provide proof of age for some of the pension applicants, many of whom were too old to have birth certificates. Baptismal certificates were acceptable, but many people did not know the exact place of their birth or baptism, which could be supplied from what their parents had put down in the census when they were children. In other cases there was no baptism record, and the census itself was the only documentary evidence of age. In the end the GRO had not only to conduct the searches, but also to provide application forms for the purpose.

The census was the ideal method to gather the detailed information that was now required by the government. However, William Dunbar was the first Registrar General who did not have to oversee the administration of a census, being replaced by Sir Bernard Mallet in 1909.

Boundary changes

The preparations for the 1911 census had been started in 1908, and the Census Office reopened at Millbank in 1909. One of the problems identified early on was that of the many boundary changes that had taken place since 1901. In fact there had always been boundary changes between census years, but there had never been a thorough review, only piecemeal changes. This was partly caused by the fact that the census was administered through the Registration Service of the GRO, whose own districts and sub-districts had never been subject to any comprehensive revision, but were altered at odd intervals, usually to coincide with the resignation or retirement of individual registrars. This in turn was because the registrars were not salaried, but paid according to the number of events registered and certificates issued. Therefore the reduction in size of a district would directly affect a registrar's income and it was much easier to split a district that had grown too large into more manageable units when he or she left office. This was compounded by the instructions that had previously been circulated to registrars regarding the 'Plans of Division' to divide their sub-Districts into census Enumeration Districts. Up to 1891, they had always advised registrars to 'retain as far as possible the same Enumeration Districts as used at the previous census'. This was dropped from the instructions in 1901, but, owing to the limited time available for preparation, few substantial revisions were actually made. Lack of preparation time was a recurring problem with every census, since a separate Act of Parliament had to be passed each time until the Census Act of 1920 finally established a permanent Census Office. By 1911 the situation was even worse, according to a lengthy memorandum on the improvement and revision of census methods:

At present a limited number of Enumeration Districts contain parts of two or more:
Administrative Counties
Civil Parishes
Urban Districts
Wards of Urban Districts
Rural Districts

In all such cases the Enumeration Districts should, where possible, be rearranged so that in future no Enumeration Districts should comprise parts of two or more Administrative Areas of a like kind' (RG 19/45).

Machine tabulation

The same document, dated 1908–1909, recommended that the practice of filling out enumeration books should be retained, despite its disadvantages compared with that of machine tabulation directly from the household schedules. So it was at a late stage in the planning that the decision was taken to dispense with the enumeration books after all. The new Registrar General, Sir Bernard Mallet, took a keen interest in the statistical functions of the department, and was also President of the Royal Statistical Society. He was in favour of using tabulation machines, which had already been used for processing census information in other countries. Sir Bernard and his Superintendent of Statistics, Thomas Stevenson, travelled to Washington, DC, where machines had been used in tabulating census data for some years, to see them in action. As a result of their visit they decided to use 'Hollerith' machines made by the British Tabulating Machine Company (plate 18).

Using a completely new system to process the information from the census schedules was not without its difficulties, and there were many 'teething problems', but the results were worth the extra effort and expense. The advantages were considerable. First of all, the errors and ambiguities that could result from the enumerators' copying were eliminated at a stroke. Secondly, tabulating by machine meant that more questions could be included in the schedule, and the data could also be cross-referenced and sorted in a number of ways. As a result, the household schedules for 1911 could record up to 19 separate pieces of information for each individual. Some of these were simply extra levels of detail, such as in the data on occupations; people were now asked to give the kind of trade or industry they worked in, as well as their actual occupation. Much more accurate figures could now be obtained, because a bookkeeper, for example, who worked in a cotton mill, could now be listed under both categories, depending on the particular information that was being sought. But other innovations were of much greater significance, particularly for family historians.

Administering the census

Lengthy and detailed instructions were produced for all the groups of people involved in the administration of the census. These included registrars, enumerators, masters of vessels and institutions, and the police, who between them were responsible for distributing and collecting the information from individuals; the police were involved because they had to collect details as best they could on anyone found in 'a barn, shed, kiln etc., or under a railway arch, on stairs accessible to the public, or wandering without a shelter' (Police Return. TNA reference RG 27/8). This category would include any suffragettes who appeared to be carrying out their threatened boycott of the census.

The instructions to the householders were of course printed on the schedules themselves, but the GRO did not rely on these alone to convey information about the census to the population at large. Perhaps in view of the increasing complexity of the questions, they made extensive use of other means of publicity. Circulars were sent to editors of provincial newspapers enclosing copies of the detailed memoranda sent to enumerators appealing for 'accurate completion of the occupation column on census schedules' relating to the predominant industries in their areas. These memoranda and other material were also sent to school teachers for them to use in the classroom, explaining to the children how the census was to be carried out and why it was important that it should be taken accurately. The explanatory notes suggested 'that the instructions given therein should, as far as possible, be expounded with special reference to the prevailing trades or industries of the district'.

In addition to the usual schedules printed in Welsh, in 1911 the GRO for the first time produced special householders' schedules translated into German and Yiddish. Registrars 'in certain quarters of the East End of London, and in some towns where there are considerable numbers of Jewish aliens', were encouraged to select enumerators with some knowledge of Yiddish and copies of the translated schedules were forwarded to the registrars in the relevant districts. The schedules were to be presented to any householder who had a difficulty with the English language, along with a copy of the schedule in English. A letter from the Census Office dated March 1911 emphasised that 'it must be clearly understood that the English schedule must be filled up and not the translated copies'. The enumerators were also expected to offer assurance that the census was 'not for the purpose of taxation, not for enforcing military service, and not on account of religion'.

Despite all the detailed instructions, preliminary examination of the collected returns revealed many mistakes and omissions. Some house-holders appear to have been confused by several of the new questions – in particular the question relating to dead children – and the answers they gave were either ambiguous or wholly unreliable. On 30 June 1911 Bernard Mallet wrote to the Treasury: 'I have therefore reluctantly come to the conclusion that it will be necessary to examine the whole of the returns, and correct them where necessary.' He went on to ask for funds to employ ten extra female checkers, since in his judgement the work would be better performed by them than by male clerks. Moreover, he added, they could eventually be discharged on a week's notice.

As in previous census years institutions such as workhouses and industrial schools were enumerated separately using special institu-tional schedules. The questions asked on these schedules were in essence the same as those on the standard householders' schedules. The significant difference from the process with householders is that people's details were entered into enumeration books by the relevant official (as in previous years) and although there are associated enu-merators' summary books (ESBs), these only record the basic statisti-cal details.

The enumeration of people on board vessels both in the Merchant Navy and the Royal Navy was carried out in the same way as in previous census years.

Once collected, the schedules were sent to the Census Office in Millbank where an army of coders, clerks and punchers played their part in processing and tabulating the data. Although the stage of copying into enumeration books had been eliminated, a whole new operation had to be included, that of coding information into numbers in preparation for punching onto cards (plate 19). This was a skilled job, carried out by experienced clerks, who wrote the numbers that appear on the schedules in different coloured inks. By contrast, the punch card operators were recruited from girls leaving elementary schools in the area around Millbank at Easter 1911. The instructions to the coding clerks occupied several pages, while those for the 'girl punchers' comprised a single sheet. This single page, however, included the important instruction that the same code should be used for suffragettes and vagrants.

'Fertility in marriage'?

Despite the increase in the number of questions asked in 1911, much of the basic information remained the same as it had been throughout the Victorian period. The greatest innovation, however, was the addition of questions on fertility in marriage. Married women were asked to state how long they had been married, the number of children born of the current marriage, the number of those children who were still alive and the number who had died.

These questions had been a feature of the American census since 1890, and may have been directly inspired by Mallet and Stephenson's visit to Washington. This was not merely a new area of enquiry, but would be the first time that the census both recorded a moment in time, and asked people about their behaviour in the past. The answers to the 'fertility' questions can help us to trace marriage records more easily, assuming of course that the information given was accurate in the first place. It should also be easy to work out whether a man's wife was also the mother of any or all of his children, which would not be obvious from the rest of the information in the census schedule.

This is well illustrated by an entry in the 1911 census showing David Bridges and his wife Laura living at number 2 Church Road, Gillingham, Kent. David was aged 60 and employed as a dockyard labourer, while Laura was 54. The entry indicates that she had been married to David for only six years and that there were no children from the marriage. But David had two young grandchildren in the household and if the schedule hadn't included the information indicating a relatively recent marriage, it would be all too easy to assume that the couple had been married much longer and that Laura was also grandmother to the two young grandchildren. A search of the 1901 census finds David as a lodger without any other family members present, but describes him as a married man, which does nothing to contradict this assumption. Of course, the information in the census may not always be accurate, but the detail in 1911 about the marriage and children suggests that further investigation is necessary (RG 14/3937, schedule 213).

Another entry in the 1911 census reinforces how useful the information about marriages is to family historians. The Coomber family of Chiddingstone, Kent, is headed by Eliza, a widow, aged 101. Her son Ira is 62, but has only been married to his wife Caroline for four years seven months – the census only asks for whole years but the Coombers obligingly give more detail, and a search in the GRO's marriage indexes shows that this is indeed accurate, at least with regard to the date, but the correct spelling of the family name appears to be Camber, not Coomber. Ira Camber appears in the 1901 census with his widowed mother and his first wife, Eliza, but since the enumerator has (very clearly) copied his forename as 'Tar' he could prove difficult to find by means of a name search, so once again the 1911 census alerts the researcher to a late second marriage that might otherwise be missed (RG 14/4034, schedule 118) (see Fig. 3.1).

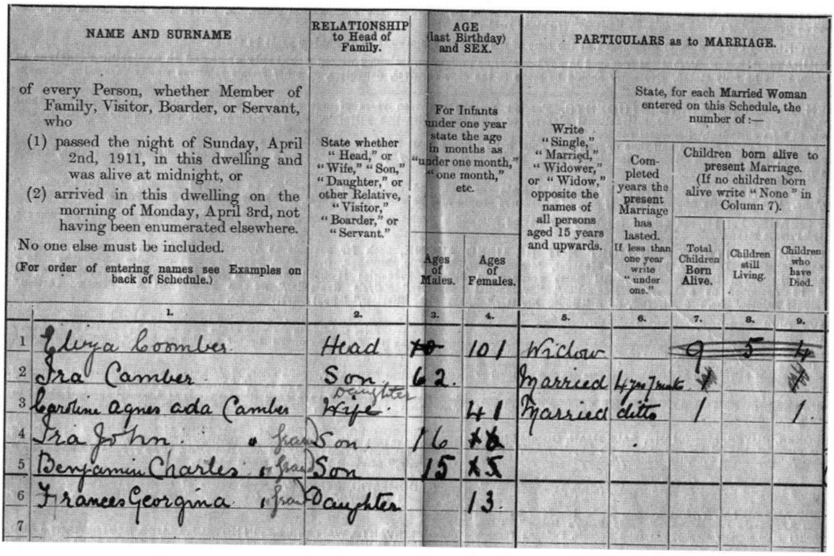

	NAME AND SURNAME	RELATIONSHIP to Head of Family.	AGE (last Birthday) and SEX.		PARTICULARS as to MARRIAGE.				
	of every Person, whether Member of Family, Visitor, Boarder, or Servant, who (1) passed the night of Sunday, April 2nd, 1911, in this dwelling and was alive at midnight, or (2) arrived in this dwelling on the morning of Monday, April 3rd, not having been enumerated elsewhere. No one else must be included. (For order of entering names see Examples on back of Schedule.)	State whether "Head," or "Wife," "Son," "Daughter," or other Relative, "Visitor," "Boarder," or "Servant."	For Infants under one year state the age in months as "under one month," "one month," etc. Ages of Males.	Ages of Females.	Write "Single," "Married," "Widower," or "Widow," opposite the names of all persons aged 15 years and upwards.	State, for each Married Woman entered on this Schedule, the number of :— Completed years the present Marriage has lasted. If less than one year write "under one."	Children born alive to present Marriage. (If no children born alive write "None" in Column 7). Total Children Born Alive.	Children still Living.	Children who have Died.
	1.	2.	3.	4.	5.	6.	7.	8.	9.
1	Eliza Coomber	Head	~~70~~	101	Widow		~~9~~	~~5~~	~~4~~
2	Ira Camber	Son	62		Married	4 yrs 7 mths	~~1~~		~~1~~
3	Caroline Agnes Ada Camber	Wife (Daughter)		41	Married	ditto	1		1
4	Ira John	Gran Son	16	~~16~~					
5	Benjamin Charles	Gran Son	15	~~15~~					
6	Frances Georgina	Gran Daughter		13					
7									

Figure 3.1 Detail from the 1911 census of Chiddingstone, Kent.

Occupational data

Another innovation in the 1911 census was the request for additional information about each individual's occupation. If all we had been given was the 'Trade or Industry' in which our ancestors were employed, this would have been useful enough, but it appears that a significant number of householders misinterpreted this question as a request for the name of their employers.

So William Bailey of number 24 Duncombe Street, Moston near Manchester, not only gives his occupation in great detail (Water Softening Plant Attendant) but also tells us that he worked for the Lancashire & Yorkshire Railway Company (RG 14/24246, schedule 142; plate 20).

Arthur Owen of number 79 Inniskillin Road, Plaistow, and his boarder William Duffin both gave their occupations as 'General Labourer' but they then went on to very helpfully inform us that they actually worked for the Gas, Light & Coke Company (RG 14/9445, schedule 301).

Arthur's near neighbour, Harry Holmes of number 100 Olive Road, Plaistow, was similarly obliging in stating that he carried out his trade of a stonemason with the Port of London Authority (RG 14/9448, schedule 105).

The records

For family historians the biggest change between this and previous censuses is that what we're looking at in the 1911 census are the actual forms that our ancestors completed, in their own handwriting and with their own errors and, occasionally, their own, unasked-for additional comments. For the first time the census has become a primary, and not a secondary, source for the researcher.

The decision to do away with the enumerator's summary books left the census administrators with the question of how to record all the supplementary details (the descriptions of the administrative districts and the statistical information) and the answer was that each enumerator should be issued with a scaled-down version of the old summary book. Confusingly, these are also known as enumerator's summary books although, unlike their nineteenth-century counterparts, they contain relatively little information about individuals.

They do, however, contain a huge amount of useful information. At the front there is a description of the Enumeration District, listing local sub-divisions, the boundary of the Enumeration District and a list of the streets covered by it. This is followed by a set of instructions to the enumerator and a number of examples of how to complete the book.

The main section of the ESBs contains the summary pages, comprising a list of the properties included in the Enumeration District. All properties are listed whether or not a census schedule was completed. Schedule numbers are given, as well as the address of each household, the type of property (i.e. domestic, shop, office, etc.), the surname of the head of the household, the title of the head (Mr, Mrs, Miss, Dr, etc.) and a summary of the number of males and females in each household.

At the back of the ESBs are the enumerator's abstract pages, which were used to add up the totals from the summary pages in order to produce the final figures for the district. The last page contains the Statutory Declaration which was signed and dated by the enumerator and the registrar.

The householders' schedules were bound into volumes, arranged by Enumeration Districts, each bound volume of schedules corresponding to an ESB as outlined above. The instructions on how to complete the form were quite clear, but it's obvious that they weren't always strictly adhered to and the quality of the information supplied varies greatly from one schedule to the next – as does the neatness and legibility of the handwriting.

As we saw in the previous chapter, householders had been completing their own census schedules since 1841 and it's certain that the forms from the earlier censuses would have contained additional unsolicited comments as well as a whole range of errors and inaccuracies. But whereas in previous census years many of these errors (and almost all of the extraneous comments) would have been 'edited out' by the diligent army of enumerators and registrars, in 1911 they have largely survived – warts and all! Some attempt seems to have been made (whether by the enumerator, the registrar or the clerks at the Census Office is not clear) to score through the incorrect entries but mostly the original data is still perfectly legible.

So when, for example, a widow erroneously enters the details of the duration of her marriage and the number of children born to it (this information was only supposed to be supplied by married women), we can still make use of this information even if it shouldn't have been given and has been partly obscured.

Jane Scully of number 10 West Bank Street, Salford, provides a good example of how this works in practice. As a widow, she shouldn't have entered the number of children she had borne – 12, with 11 of them living – but it is fortunate that she did, because only seven of them are present in the household, and they were all born in Ireland, so she has helpfully told us that she had four other children somewhere that we might otherwise not have known about (RG 14/24046, schedule 96).

Civil disobedience

Throughout the first decade of the twentieth century there was increasing political activity from trade unions and other radical groups. The Labour Party was formed in 1900 and, three years later, the Women's Social and Political Union was founded, with the aim of campaigning for women's suffrage. Although the suffragettes are remembered for their militant activities during this period, it is perhaps less well known that it wasn't until after the First World War that all adult males finally got the vote and there was continuing agitation from this direction too. It was the suffragettes, however, who had the idea of boycotting the 1911 census as part of their campaign. The boycott was perhaps not as successful as they might have hoped, but it certainly earned them a great deal of publicity. The idea may have come from Emmeline Pankhurst, who was employed as a registrar of births and deaths from 1898 to 1907, and had therefore been actively involved in the administration of the 1901 census.

A great deal of research has been carried out into the Suffragette boycott of the 1911 census, particularly by Jill Liddington and Elizabeth Crawford. Liddington's recent book on the subject (*Vanishing for the Vote*) tells the story in some detail and highlights some of the ways in which women (and a significant number of men) attempted to disrupt the census. Probably the most bizarre of these was Emily Davison's decision to spend the night of the census hiding in a cupboard in the Houses of Parliament.

Mrs Pankhurst herself attempted to evade enumeration but was 'captured' along with fellow-suffragette Ada Wright as a visitor at the Inns of Court Hotel in Holborn (RG 14/1181, schedule 149). Other than their names, no additional information is entered about either of them and indeed Emmeline is incorrectly listed as Mrs G Pankhurst – but it is clearly her. A handwritten note describes the two as 'Suffragists' and tantalisingly adds 'see letters attached'. The Superintendent Registrar, Sydney Ashley, then added his own comment:

> I am of the opinion that at least one of the above, viz. Mrs Pankhurst was counted at the Aldwych Skating Rink. I find however that this lady returned to the Hotel at 5 o'clock AM on the morning of the 3rd April 1911. Under these circumstances I have allowed her name to stand and be counted herein.

An article on Elizabeth Crawford's website (Woman and her Sphere **<womanandhersphere.com/>**) sheds more light on the incident:

> So it was that, after a late-evening rally in Trafalgar Square, the suffra-gettes promenaded down the Strand to the Aldwych where it was esti-mated by the Census Office that 500 women and 70 men gathered at the Skating Rink. Although the numbers were recorded, the identity of most of that 570 is lost – only those whose names are mentioned in the *Votes for Women* report (7 April 1911) can be placed there with certainty. These included Mrs Pankhurst...no trace of a census paper for Christabel Pankhurst has been found – but she was there in the Skating Rink, bringing the entertainments to a rousing conclusion at 3.30 am.

Another one of the 570 people known to have been present at the Aldwych Skating Rink on census night was women's rights activist Emmeline Pethick Lawrence and when the enumerator for number 4 Clements Inn, London returned to collect Emmeline's schedule (RG 14/1194, schedule 218) he found that she had failed to give any personal details but instead had written:

> Until the Government recognizes my position as a citizen of this country by according to me and other duly qualified women the right to take part in the election of representatives in Parliament I have a conscientious objection to assisting the Government by providing them with information and I accordingly refuse to fill in the particu-lars requested.

Not every attempt to avoid the census was successful. In April 1911 Eleanora Maund, the wife of Edward Arthur Maund, an African explorer and friend of Cecil Rhodes, was living with her husband, three children and two servants in West Kensington, west London. The census schedule was completed by Edward but, at some time before it was collected, Eleanora crossed out her name and other details and wrote 'Wife Away' at the bottom of the form (RG 14/227, schedule 4; see also Fig. 3.2).

Unfortunately for Eleanora, that was not the end of the story. Edward appears to have discovered her attempt to avoid enumeration and took a remarkable step. After reinstating Eleanora's details Edward embarked on an extraordinary tirade:

> My wife unfortunately being a Suffragette put her pen through her name, but it must stand as correct. It being an equivocation to say she is away she being always resident here & has only attempted by a silly subterfuge to defeat the objects of the census. To which as "Head" of the family I object.
>
> E. A. Maund

The case of Victor Prout demonstrates the depth of feeling that the subject inspired in certain quarters and the lengths that ordinary people were prepared to go to, to support the cause of women's enfranchisement. Prout was an engraver and illustrator, the son of a pioneering photographer, and as founding member and Honorary Secretary of the Men's Federation for Women's Suffrage, was actively involved in the campaign.

When Percy Cooper, one of the enumerators covering the district of Palmers Green, north London, called to collect the schedule that he had left the previous week at number 6 Stonard Road, he was confronted with an unexpected problem. Instead of completing the schedule with

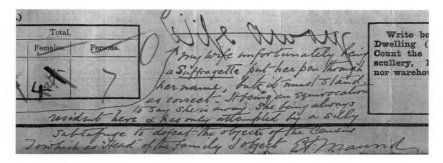

Figure 3.2 Detail from the 1911 census schedule for the Maund family of West Kensington.

the required details, Cooper discovered that the householder had written the following across the form (RG 14/7386, schedule 13a):

> I wish to protest against the terrible treatment women have been recently subjected to as the result of the Liberal Government's method of repressing the agitation in favour of Women's Enfranchisement and I refuse to fill this census form because women are claiming that until they are given the rights of Citizenship they shall not be counted and I leave out the men as an act of sympathy with that claim.
>
> All the withheld information will be freely given as soon as a Women's Enfranchisement Bill becomes law.

The householder in question was Victor Prout and he was quite adamant that he had no intention of completing the form. Cooper's next step was to write to the registrar, John Harman Judd, explaining what had happened and we can only assume that Judd then wrote to Prout asking if he would reconsider his stance as the next document that we have is Prout's reply to Judd in which he thanks the Registrar for his 'courteous and kindly note' and then goes on to say:

> My protest is of course not directed to you but the Government and my reason is as stated on the form. Please do not feel anxious that any action which it may be your duty to take on account of my having refused to fill up the Schedule will cause any unpleasantness... Believe me when I say that any action you may feel it your duty to take I shall welcome most gladly...

It is clear that Prout was expecting and indeed hoping to be prosecuted under Section 12 (2) of the 1910 Census Act which states that:

If any occupier for whom a schedule is left under this Act

(a) wilfully refuses, or without lawful excuse neglects, to fill up or cause to be filled up the schedule to the best of his knowledge and belief, or to sign and deliver it as by this Act required; or

(b) wilfully makes, signs, or delivers, or causes to be made signed, or delivered, any false return of any matter specified in the schedule; or

(c) refuses to answer, or wilfully gives a false answer to, any question necessary for obtaining the information required to be obtained under this Act; he shall for each offence be liable on conviction under the Summary Jurisdiction Acts to a fine not exceeding five pounds.

A £5 fine for a man of Prout's status would have been relatively negligible but the publicity surrounding the resulting court case would have been like manna from heaven for the suffragette cause.

The final piece of surviving correspondence on the case (a letter from Archer Bellingham, the Secretary of the Census Office, to the Registrar, Mr Judd) clearly demonstrates that there was no desire on behalf of the government to prosecute suffragettes or their supporters for refusing to complete their forms. The letter thanks him for his trouble in the matter and instructs him to 'fill up a schedule with the best possible information available, concerning Mr Prout and the other occupants on the night.'

The result of all this is that there are two schedules in the records; firstly, the original, 'spoilt' by the householder and, secondly, the registrar's effort. As the local registrar of births and deaths, he was able to get accurate information about the children in the family but some of the details about the older members of the household are pure guesswork.

Ultimately, the attempts by the women's suffrage movement to disrupt the census were thwarted by the government's determination not to allow attention to be drawn to them.

Dead people in the census?

As we have seen, the 1911 census required all married women to state how many years they had been married and then to indicate the number of 'Children born alive to the present marriage', how many of those children were still alive, and how many had died. This group of questions seems to have caused an inordinate amount of confusion amongst householders. For a start, they were frequently answered by married men, widows and even widowers when the instructions quite clearly stated that the information was only required for married women.

This inefficiency on our ancestors' part is good news for family historians because while the information they supplied in error may have been crossed out by the enumerators, it was normally done in a way that left the details quite legible – the intention was not that it shouldn't be read but that the data shouldn't be extracted. But the confusion extended beyond this basic misunderstanding about who should and who shouldn't answer the questions. The very mention of dead children appears to have led some householders to believe that the names and other details of their deceased children were supposed to be included on the census! Several instances of this have been found and it's clear from the reaction of the Census Office at the time that they were aware of the potential problem.

A memorandum issued to Registrars shortly after the census was taken includes the following statement:

> There is reason to believe that the entering of the number of children in columns 7–9 has caused some confusion to the Occupier: and that in some cases, he may have erroneously included among the Occupants of the dwelling on census night, children who were absent and even children who had died.

A further document (RG 27/8, page 131) entitled 'Instructions To Clerks Employed On Revision Of Schedules, Coding And Institutions' includes the following direction under *Section II – Examination of Schedules part (2) Columns 6, 7, 8 and 9*:

> Examine the entries relating to the number of children born alive, the number living, and the number dead. If the number of children described, either as son or daughter in Column 2 and returned as being within the age covered by the period in Column 6, exceeds the number entered in Column 8 by that given in Column 9, examine the schedule for evidence indicating which children are deceased. If any direct evidence be found of an erroneous entry (RG 14/20868, schedule 138), the entry must be deleted, the totals at the foot of the schedule corrected, and a record kept. If there are more than two cases per thousand persons where such evidence is absent, the schedules for the enumeration district must be handed to the superintendent for further inquiry.

However, despite the best efforts of the Census Office, it's clear that many of these errors were not picked up, as a result of which a number of deceased children have ended up being recorded in the census. It's certainly true that the number of children recorded was higher than predictions had suggested. One of the first exercises carried out by the Census Office was a count of the children aged under ten. This quick count can be seen on the schedules in the form of the numbers written in red ink at the foot of the page, immediately to the right of the box containing the totals of males, females and persons.

Using figures based on the registration of births and deaths, with allowances made for immigration and emigration, statisticians have calculated that the 1911 census recorded 1.6 per cent more children than expected. This has been explained by the re-formatting of the questions in 1911 leading to better enumeration of children – while others have suggested that it's the result of under-registration of births in the preceding decade. There is, however, a possibility that neither of these explanations is true and that in fact it's the inclusion of a significant number of dead children which skewed the figures.

It's difficult to see how the GRO clerks could possibly have identified the schedule completed by Robert Ashfield of Balaclava Road, Derby as one that contained an erroneous entry. Robert dutifully recorded details of himself, his wife and his eight children aged between 13 years and one month. What he failed to indicate was that the youngest child had actually died (aged one month) a year before the census was taken. There's a further mystery here however: the details relating to the marriage were originally written next to the name of the head of the household, rather than on the line below. The figures he gave indicated that eight children had been born to the marriage, of whom seven were living and one had died. These figures have been crossed through and copied onto the correct line (i.e. his wife's) but at some later stage they have been changed to read: nine born, eight living and one died. Has the registrar noticed a discrepancy but reached the wrong conclusion and added a (non-existent) living child to the family?

A similar case can be found on the schedule for the Annal family of number 48 Kempthorne Street, Gravesend (RG 14/3823, schedule 264; see also Fig. 3.3). The head of the house, Alexander Annal, was a dock labourer and according to the census schedule, was living with his wife, Louisa and their six children on the night of the census. However, a glance at the data in columns 7 to 9 reveals that only five of Louisa's children were living and that one of the six had died. Closer examination of the form throws up some further discrepancies. Whereas the 13-, 12- and seven-year-old children are clearly described as being at school, there is a dash under the 'occupation' of the 10-year-old, Alexander. And although the word 'single' has been entered as Alexander's marital condition, this has been crossed out. Like so many of the problems that we encounter

NAME AND SURNAME	RELATIONSHIP to Head of Family.	AGE (last Birthday) and SEX.		PARTICULARS as to MARRIAGE.						PROFESSION of Persons aged
of every Person, whether Member of Family, Visitor, Boarder, or Servant, who (1) passed the night of Sunday, April 2nd, 1911, in this dwelling and was alive at midnight, or (2) arrived in this dwelling on the morning of Monday, April 3rd, not having been enumerated elsewhere. No one else must be included. (For order of entering names see Examples on back of Schedule.)	State whether "Head," or "Wife," "Son," "Daughter," or other Relative, "Visitor," "Boarder," or "Servant."	For Infants under one year state the age in months as "under one month," "one month," etc.		Write "Single," "Married," "Widower," or "Widow," opposite the names of all persons aged 15 years and upwards.	State, for each Married Woman entered on this Schedule, the number of :—					Personal Occupation. The reply should show the precise branch of Profession, Trade, Manufacture, &c. If engaged in any Trade or Manufacture, the particular kind of work done, and the Article made or Material worked or dealt in should be clearly indicated. (See Instructions 1 to 8 and Examples on back of Schedule.)
		Ages of Males.	Ages of Females.		Completed years the present Marriage has lasted. If less than one year write "under one."	Children born alive to present Marriage. (If no children born alive write "None" in Column 7).				
						Total Children Born Alive.	Children still Living.	Children who have Died.		
Alexander.	2.	3.	4.	5.	6.	7.	8.	9.		10.
1 *A.F.B. Annal*	*Head*	*39*		*Married*						*Dock Labourer* 080
2 *Louisa Annal*	*Wife*		*45*	*Married*	*15*	*6*	*5*	*1*		
3 *Clara Annal*	*Daughter*		*13*	*Single*	—	—	—	—		*School* 390
4 *James Annal*	*Son*	*12*		*Single*	—	—	—	—		*School*
5 *Alexander Annal*	*Son*	*10*		*Single*	—	—	—	—		
6 *Beatrice Annal*	*Daughter*		*7*	*Single*	—	—	—	—		*School*
7 *Arthur Annal*	*Son*	*4*		*Single*	—	—	—	—		
8 *Nellie Annal*	*Daughter*		*3*	*Single*						

Figure 3.3 Detail from the 1911 census of Gravesend.

trying to get to grips with the information supplied by our ancestors, it's impossible to say precisely what was going on here, but Alexander and Louisa were apparently unsure what to do and it must have been a painful experience for them to have to work out that their second son, who had in fact died in 1903 aged just two, would have been 10 if had he lived.

All we can say for sure is that the inclusion of these two dead children, Edward Ashfield and Alexander Annal in the 1911 census are not isolated incidents and that we need to look even more closely than usual at these records – and not take anything we see at face value.

Welsh language in the 1911 census

The household schedules for the 1911 census were also printed in Welsh, and Welsh speakers were able to complete them in their native language. As a result, the UK census includes, for the first time, a significant amount of information written in a language other than English. According to the 1911 census report, around 8.5 per cent of the population of Wales were monoglot Welsh speakers, and 35 per cent were bilingual in English and Welsh. It's probable that the vast majority of heads of household who were monoglot Welsh speakers would have completed their household schedule in that language – how many bilingual speakers did so is unknown.

The fields on the census form which are affected by being completed in Welsh are mainly those for relationship and occupation, which will naturally use Welsh vocabulary. The birthplace field will also tend to have the Welsh forms of place names — these are sometimes identical to the English forms but often not.

The Association of Family History Societies of Wales has a comprehensive set of pages providing help with the Welsh vocabulary found in the household schedules for the 1911 census. The main page can be found at <**www.fhswales.org.uk/censuses/Schedules.htm**> and there are links to pages on:

- Welsh forenames, with variants;
- Welsh patronymic surnames;
- English translations of the Welsh terms found in the columns for:
  - marital status
  - relationship
  - occupation
  - infirmity;
- Welsh-language place-names found in the birthplace column, covering:
  - the counties of Wales
  - individual places in the counties of Cardiganshire, Glamorganshire, Monmouthshire and Pembrokeshire
  - major towns, cities, and islands elsewhere in the UK
  - foreign countries;
- Welsh place-name elements found in addresses (e.g. 'road', 'inn', 'farm');
- Help with looking up Welsh words in a dictionary.

This last point is important because, as is the case with Irish, the first consonant in a Welsh word can change according to the last sound in the previous word ('mutation'). Since Welsh dictionaries do not list words under all possible initial consonants, you need to be able to work out which is the dictionary form before looking them up.

A substantial selection of this material is reproduced on the help pages relating to Welsh-language returns on Findmypast and 1911census (both covered in Chapter 8). The relevant help topics will be found by following the 'help & advice' link on the navigation bar near the top of the page on each of those sites. These help pages are accessible without registration or login so can be used to help with 1911 census records in Welsh on other sites where that census is available, such as Ancestry and TheGenealogist.

There are many other online resources which can be of help in reading Welsh census entries, though of course these will not be designed specifically for the genealogist. Welsh terms for occupations can be looked up in the online Welsh–English/English–Welsh dictionary created by the Department of Welsh, University of Wales, Lampeter, at <**www.geiriadur.net**>.

For place-names not listed on the Association of Family History Societies of Wales site, you can consult the National Gazetteer of Wales at <**homepage.ntlworld.com/geogdata/ngw/places.htm**>. Where a place in Wales has an entry in the English Wikipedia at <**en.wikipedia.org**>, the Welsh form of the name will usually be given in the first line of the article. Indeed, from any topographical article in the English Wikipedia, if there is an equivalent Welsh article there will be a link to it marked 'Cymraeg' under 'Languages' in the left-hand panel and this will give you the Welsh name. The Welsh-language Wikipedia has a list of Welsh town names at <**cy.wikipedia.org/wiki/Rhestr_trefi_Cymru**> with around 150 entries.

The British Army

Just three and a half years after the 1911 census was taken, war broke out in Europe. This was the 'war to end all wars' and despite the confident assertion that it would be 'over by Christmas', as we know, it actually raged on for another four years, by which time nearly a million Britons had lost their lives. While previous censuses had done no more than provide a headcount of the officers and men of the British Army, the 1911 census saw a hugely significant development. For the first time, a full enumeration of the British Army serving overseas, in such places as India, South Africa, the West Indies and Ireland, was carried out. In theory all of these men should be listed in the 1911 census, providing us with a poignant glimpse of Britain's lost generation.

For the first time, therefore, we have access to all the usual census details for this important section of British society: their details are recorded in 23 volumes of schedules, as are the details of the wives and families who had accompanied the men on the often perilous journeys to the far flung corners of the earth. The names, ages, marital conditions, occupations and birth places of almost 135,000 officers, men (and their families) serving overseas at the time of the 1911 census are recorded in the returns for 288 military establishments. The schedules also record the soldier's rank and the name of the unit with which they were serving.

The forms themselves are very similar in layout to the standard householders' schedules although there are far fewer columns (eight in total). There is also an additional column headed: 'If absent on Census Night, write "Absent" and for those in the United Kingdom specify whether in England, Wales, Scotland or Ireland.' The lack of a column indicating gender makes it quite clear that all serving 'officers and men' in the British army were indeed male – the assumption is also that they had no physical or mental infirmities.

There is one aspect of the arrangement of these returns which may cause some confusion. By the time of the 1911 census, it was common practice for wives and children to accompany the men when they were on overseas duty. But when the authorities came to listing the occupants of the various overseas military establishments, they divided them into two separate sections: one covering the officers and men, and another for their families.

The forms for the wives and children are significantly different in terms of content. There are seven columns recording each individual's name, relationship to the head of the family, age (divided into separate columns for males and females), birthplace, nationality (if born in a foreign country) and infirmity. In addition, for each married woman, we get the 'particulars as to marriage' recorded in the now familiar five columns recording the marital status, the number of years married, the number of children born to the present marriage, and of those, the number living and the number who have died.

The problem for family historians is that there is no explicit link between the two and while, in most cases, this will not cause too many difficulties, if the name of your military ancestor is Smith, Brown or Jones for example, it's more than likely that there will be more than one potential family group with the same surname and linking them to the correct soldier may not always be as straightforward as it might be.

There are no such problems in the case of Harry Culpin. Harry was born at Tur Langton, Leicestershire in 1877 and after joining the army as a young man, married Benedicta Jane Rhydderch at Colchester in 1897. By the time of the 1911 census Harry Culpin had risen to the rank of Battery Sergeant Major in the 96th Battery of the Royal Field Artillery. He is listed immediately after five commissioned officers on the census page (RG 14/34976). His unit was garrisoned at Tempe, near Bloemfontein in the Orange Free State, South Africa and his wife and children are easily identified in the associated returns for the married quarters. Benedicta Jane is listed along with four children, born in Woolwich, Langford, Preston and Ewshott respectively. Harry Culpin had a distinguished army career – he was mentioned in dispatches during the First World War, was commissioned from the ranks in December 1914 and eventually attained the rank of Captain.

Scotland

The 1911 census returns for Scotland differ significantly in their layout from their English and Welsh equivalents. For a start the documents used to record the details are not the householders' schedules but instead a specially adapted enumerator's summary book, which combines the functions of the ESBs and the schedules. The details are recorded in 22 columns spread across two pages of the summary book and include all the information recorded in the English and Welsh returns with the exception of the question regarding the number of children who have died. As in the three previous censuses, data was collected about people who spoke Gaelic or Gaelic and English.

Ireland

As in 1901, the 1911 census returns for Ireland include a number of additional forms which will be unfamiliar to those of us who are used to the layout of the returns in the rest of the UK (see p. 40). The main household return form (Form A) is similar in content to the householders' schedules in England and Wales but doesn't include details of the numbers of deceased children and lacks the additional information regarding occupations and nationality. The questions about religion and education (essentially, whether they could read or write) which appeared in 1901 are present again but, unfortunately, the information requested about birthplaces is once again very limited. For those born in Ireland, the 'County or City' of birth was to be recorded; for everyone else, simply the 'name of the Country'.

Lloyd George's 'Domesday' survey

The 1911 census can be used in conjunction with another major record source of around the same date, namely, the Valuation Office Survey, also known as 'Lloyd George's Domesday'. As the name suggests, this was a survey to establish the value of property throughout England and Wales for Estate Duty purposes, carried out following the 1910 Finance Act, when David Lloyd George was Chancellor of the Exchequer. Since the survey was carried out at around the same time as the census, it is possible to find out a great deal about the actual buildings that your ancestors lived in, once you've found their address in the census. Conversely, local and house historians using the Valuation Office records can use the 1911 census to find out more about people that lived in them and the communities in which they resided. The records for England and Wales are held at The National Archives (TNA), and enquiries about the records of the survey in Scotland and Ireland should be referred to The National Archives of Scotland and the Public Record Office of Northern Ireland respectively.

The twentieth century

No book on the census should resist a glimpse forward to the returns that family historians will have access to in the future. The 1920 Census Act allowed for a census to be taken every ten years without needing to pass an individual Act each time and, with the exception of 1941 when our minds were on other more pressing matters, this is exactly what has happened ever since – the most recent census having been taken in 2011.

The story of the last hundred years of the census is a long and complex one; but since the returns themselves are not yet open to public inspection, and the statistical results are therefore only of passing interest to family historians, this is not the place to tell that story. Unfortunately for future family historians, the problems which the absence of a 1941 census will no doubt cause are exacerbated by the accidental destruction of the 1931 returns for England and Wales resulting in a gap of thirty years between the 1921 and 1951 censuses. The Scottish returns for 1931 have survived unaffected while in Ireland, there was no census taken in 1921 and the returns for the 1926 census taken in Northern Ireland are believed to have been destroyed.

There is, however, some good news. The records created as a result of the National Registration Act (1939) will (eventually) go some considerable distance towards filling this gap. As the outbreak of World War Two became ever more inevitable, Parliament moved quickly to create a 'register of all persons in the United Kingdom at the appointed time' with a view to issuing identity cards and, within a month of the declaration of war, the National Registration system was up and running. But unlike the decennial censuses, the register was to be a living document. The Act required that all persons entering or born in the UK after [the appointed] time should also be recorded. The appointed date was 29 September 1939 and, using the tried and trusted 'census' process of enumerators delivering householders' forms and collecting the completed paperwork, the register was successfully created and more than 45 million identity cards were issued.

The data gathered by the National Registration system falls somewhat short of what we've come to expect from the traditional decennial census. The following information was recorded about each individual:

- names
- sex
- age
- occupation, profession, trade or employment
- residence
- condition as to marriage
- membership of Naval, Military or Air Force Reserves or Auxiliary Forces or of Civil Defence Services or Reserves

The place of birth is perhaps the most crucial item that's missing here and, as the aim was to create individual identity cards, there is no information regarding relationships. However, despite the fact that the Act stated that the age was to be entered in the registers, it seems that what was actually recorded was the precise date of birth – something which will be of significant interest to family historians.

There is already some degree of public access to the 1939 National Registration records. As a result of a Freedom of Information ruling made in 2009, the Health and Social Care Information Service (the present custodian of the records) will provide data from the register 'only where the individual is recorded as deceased (or where clear evidence of death can be provided by the applicant)'. A three-part application form must be completed and signed, and sent to the following address along with a fee (currently £42) made payable to the Health and Social Care Information Centre (do not send cash):

The Health and Social Care Information Centre
The 1939 Register Team
Smedley Hydro Rm B108
Trafalgar Road
Birkdale Southport
PR8 2HH

Information can be requested on named individuals or on the residents of a specific address – in each case, if the search is successful details will be provided on up to ten residents listed at the relevant address. The search take will take up to 20 working days.

Further details, together with the necessary application form can be found at <**www.hscic.gov.uk/register-service**>.

The changing nature of the questions asked in the twentieth-century censuses reflects the particular concerns of the government of the time. Whereas the nineteenth-century censuses had focused on health, poverty and mobility, now the emphasis, beginning in 1911, shifted towards two main themes: fertility and social class. The analysis of occupations broadened and although the 1931 census (which was taken at a time of economic decline) saw a significant reduction in the number of questions asked, the trend in the post-war years was very much one of expansion, which reached a peak in 1971.

The 1981 census included just 21 questions and, remarkably, nearly half of them were identical or directly equivalent to the questions asked one hundred years earlier in 1881.

The process by which the census is taken has remained essentially the same since the first detailed enumeration was made nearly 170 years ago, and many of the same issues crop up year after year: acts of civil disobedience and attempts to disrupt the census are not recent developments. The 1991 census was certainly affected by protests about the Poll Tax, but in a similar way the 1911 census was targeted by the suffragette movement. And of course the 2001 census has its very own urban myth: encouraged by an internet campaign, the idea grew that if enough people entered their religion as 'Jedi Knight' this would somehow force the government to recognise it as an 'official' religion. As a result, some 390,000 people (roughly 0.7 per cent of the population) are recorded as following the Jedi religion – it would be interesting to know quite what the descendants of those people will make of that!

After more than 200 years of 'counting the people', the future of the census is now unclear. The next decennial census (which would be the UK's twenty second) is due to be taken in March 2021 but there is a very real chance that it may not happen. A government-launched think tank – the Beyond 2011 Programme – is looking at a range of alternatives and has identified six options which it is examining in depth. The Programme is due to report its findings sometime in 2014.

Case study 3 – The Peters

The nineteenth century was a period of huge social change and the census returns provide an excellent illustration of one aspect of this. Between 1801 and 1901 the population of Great Britain nearly quadrupled, but it's not just the overall increase that is significant here. At the start of the nineteenth century, nearly three-quarters of the population lived in rural areas. By the end of it, however, a dramatic shift had taken place: the 1901 census revealed that 74 per cent of people now lived in towns and cities.

There are a number of factors behind this change. The development of the railways, improvements in communications and some quite spectacular advances in the world of science and technology combined to transform Britain from a predominantly rural society into the most urbanized nation in the world – all in the space of just one hundred years.

The Peters family had lived in Gloucestershire for hundreds of years, making their homes in a number of small parishes in and around the Tewkesbury/Newent area. On 18 January 1801, just a few months before the first UK census was taken, a boy named Richard Peters was baptized at St Michael's church in the parish of Tirley. The population of Tirley, as recorded in the 1801 census, was just 405, increasing to 550 by the time of the 1841 census. This was very much a rural area and the census shows that a significant proportion of the inhabitants were employed either in agriculture or, thanks to Tirley's location on the River Severn, as fishermen or watermen.

Richard Peters married Elizabeth Geers in the neighbouring parish of Deerhurst in 1820, and the following year their son John was born. The 1841 census finds Richard and Elizabeth living back in Tirley with four children (HO 107/354/28, folio 10, page 13). Richard was a shoemaker by trade, but the majority of his immediate neighbours were agricultural labourers. He continued to live in Tirley until his death in 1862, but his older brother James was more adventurous.

James Peters married Martha Gannaway in Tewkesbury in 1818, but in the late 1830s he moved to London, settling in the Paddington area. His son Peter was a shoemaker, like his father and uncle before him, and although he stayed in the London area, he moved away from the city to the slightly more rural surroundings of Staines, Middlesex.

Richard's son John meanwhile had also left Tirley, and in April 1841 he married Amelia Cox in Harborne, Staffordshire. Two months later the young couple were living in Oldbury (HO 107/908/11, folio 24, page 7), which was then in Shropshire (it was transferred to Worcestershire in 1844 but continued to form part of the West Bromwich registration district which was in the administrative county of Staffordshire!). By the time of the 1851 census John and Amelia had settled in Rowley Regis, Staffordshire (HO 107/2028, folio 38, page 15). They had seemingly developed an unusual taste in boys' names: their first three children rejoiced in the names Theophilus, John Eliphaz and Zenas!

John Peters had kept up the family tradition of shoemaking, but the 1861 census shows that two of his sons were employed in the local iron works. John lived the rest of his life in Rowley Regis, dying in 1903 at the age of 81.

His sons John Eliphaz and Zenas moved to Spennymoor in County Durham. It was almost certainly the prospect of work in the rapidly expanding Tudhoe Iron Works that prompted these two young men to make the journey to the Northeast. They were not alone: the census tells us that the population of the parish of Tudhoe (which included Spennymoor) increased from just 400 in 1861 to over 5,000 twenty years later.

In the 1871 census the Peters brothers are recorded as boarders living with the Perry family – fellow exiles from Staffordshire – in the Mount Pleasant area of Tudhoe (RG 10/4964, folio 78, page 5). Sadly, John Elpihaz died in 1872, aged only 28, and soon after Zenas seems to have moved back to Staffordshire. On 5 May 1873 he married Margaret Parkin at St Giles' church in the parish of Rowley Regis. Margaret was originally from Tudhoe, and we can only speculate as to why the couple married in Staffordshire and not in Margaret's native Durham. There's also an intriguing suggestion that Margaret may previously have been married to John Eliphaz Peters, but this is one problem that the census returns can't answer. It's important to remember that a lot can happen to a family over a ten-year period. The census is simply a snapshot, recording the population on a single day.

Zenas and Margaret remained in Staffordshire for a few years (their first two children, Flora and Thomas, were born there). However, they soon moved back north and the 1881 census finds them living with Margaret's parents in Tudhoe (RG 11/4921, folio 70, page 64). Another tragedy was soon to strike the Peters family as Margaret died later that year, aged only 29. Zenas then moved back to Rowley Regis once more, where he had a further four children with his second wife, Caroline Deeley.

Our final subject here is Flora Peters – Zenas and Margaret's oldest child, who was living with her parents in Tudhoe in 1881. Ten years later she was working as a domestic servant to the Major family in Handsworth, Staffordshire (RG 12/226, folio 64, page 18). In 1894 she married Albert Holmes, a widower from Birmingham and a bookbinder by trade; by the time of the 1901 census he was employed as a foreman bookbinder. The family – Albert, Flora and their first four children, Mabel, Hilda, Irene and Cyril – were living in Walsall (RG 13/2704, folio 98, page 13), but they were soon on the move again. Their youngest daughter, Dorothy Flora Holmes, was born in Birkenhead, Cheshire, in 1907 and the 1911 census finds the family living at 11 Frodsham Street, Tranmere (RG 14/22008, schedule 189).

From Dorothy Flora Holmes and her mother Flora Peters, we have traced the family back over 100 years. Over that period we found the family living in seven different counties: Gloucestershire, Shropshire, Worcestershire, Staffordshire, Durham, Cheshire and Middlesex/London. We also saw them move from the village of Tirley in rural Gloucestershire to the 'dark satanic mills' of the West Midlands and then to the booming industrial Northeast. The story of the Peters family may be exceptional, but it serves well to illustrate the transformation that took place in nineteenth-century Britain.

Case Study 4 – The Jewish East End

Many Jewish families migrated into the East End of London during the nineteenth century and the first decade of the twentieth century. By 1911 there were so many recent Jewish immigrants from Eastern Europe that the Census Office decided to issue householders' schedules in German and Yiddish to help with the enumeration of this community (RG 27/8; plate 21). These schedules were not for the actual enumeration, which was always carried out using the English version, but to help explain to these newly-arrived immigrants what was required of them. In fact since 1891 the census authorities had been assisted by Jewish organisations with the translation and distribution of information circulars and schedules into Yiddish, Hebrew and German. Many of the recent arrivals were refugees from oppression, and it was feared that they might be reluctant to fill in the papers, particularly with details of their foreign birthplaces. However, as a result of the co-operation of the Chief Rabbi, the Board of Guardians of British Jews and others, the GRO was confident that accurate returns were obtained from the Jewish parts of the East End of London (RG 27/6 and RG 19/11).

In 1911 Abraham Lazarus Shedletsky and his family lived at 37 Lolsworth Buildings, 79 Commercial Street (RG 14/1459, schedule 30; plate 22). The ages and birthplaces of his children show that they must have arrived in England in the late 1890s. Abraham was a kosher butcher aged 42, and his wife Deborah, who was a year younger, helped him in his business. They and their 16-year-old son Lewis had been born in 'Russia (Poland)', but their other children were born in Whitechapel: David, 12; Deborah, 10; Samuel, 6; and Fanny, 5. As a married woman, Deborah was asked for the duration of her current marriage and the number of children, living and dead, of that marriage. She had been married 22 years, and in addition to the five children present in the census she had given birth to two others who had since died. The family seems to have been doing well in their adopted homeland; Abraham was in business on his own account and they could afford for their eldest son to be a student of theology and not earning a wage at the age of 16. They also had a servant, Annie Nehmann, who was born in 'Russia (Lithuania)'. The birthplace information is interesting because Russia is often used to indicate the whole Russian Empire, extending well beyond the borders of Russia itself. In this case more specific information is supplied, but it is worth remembering that a birthplace given as Russia might be Lithuania, Latvia, Poland, Ukraine or one of a number of other places.

The 1901 census shows that the Shedletsky family was at the same address in Commercial Street (RG 13/298, folio 30, page 4). Abraham was already well established in his business, since he is described as an employer, and, again, they have a servant. The names are recorded a little differently from 1911, although this is undoubtedly the same family. Abraham and his son Lewis appear in exactly the same way, but his wife Deborah appears as Dorah, his son David as Davis, and his three-month-old daughter Deborah as 'Berby'. When comparing any other two census years, we might suspect that the man had married twice, first to Dorah and then to Deborah, but the information collected in 1911 about the length of the marriage means we can be sure this is the same woman.

In 1901, the birthplaces are simply given as 'Russia', the Shedletsky family being described as Russian subjects, but in 1911 they describe themselves as naturalized British subjects. Such claims often turn out to be untrue, but in this case they have included the date of naturalization,

1903, which gives a ring of truth. Sure enough, a search in The National Archives' online catalogue reveals that Certificate of Naturalization 13938 was issued to Abraham Shedletsky on 23 November 1903 (HO 144/718/110322).

A number of other immigrants who had become British subjects added the year of naturalization to their 1911 census schedules. Another such example was Esther Cohen, a widow and provisions dealer at 25 Wentworth Street, Spitalfields (RG 14/1466, schedule 24). She was born in Russia, but all of her five children – Rachel, Augusta, Blumah, Solomon and Jessie, ranging in age from 14 down to five years old – had been born in Spitalfields. As a widow, she was not required to enter the duration of her current marriage, or the number of children she had borne. However, she misunderstood the question and gave the information anyway, and her confusion is our gain. She had married 15 years previously, and as well as the five children present in 1911 there had been another child who died. Like the Shedletsky family, the Cohens had occupied the same address since 1901, when Esther's husband Joseph was still alive. Joseph had been a little older than Esther, 30 years old to her 27, and both described themselves as Russian subjects who had been born in Russia (RG 13/299, folio 127, page 17). In 1911 Esther gave 1904 as her year of naturalization, which is the year when Joseph was naturalized.

These two families were not typical of Jewish migrant families in London; more prosperous than most, they also went to the trouble and expense of becoming naturalized. However, the extra details gathered in 1911 are particularly helpful with regard to all migrant families because foreign nationals were asked, for the first time, whether they were resident in this country or only visiting. There was a tendency to give more detail than was asked for, perhaps because the schedules were more complicated. Perhaps people took the view that when in doubt, it was better to give too much information than too little. Whatever the reason, it's certainly true that the 1911 census provides a huge boost for researchers with immigrant ancestors.

4

WHY CAN'T I FIND MY ANCESTOR?

It's very easy for an inexperienced researcher to carry out a few basic searches in the census and, on failing to find their ancestors, conclude that they aren't there – that they somehow managed to escape the clutches of that army of enumerators, registrars and Census Office clerks that we learnt about in the last two chapters. The aim of this section of the book is to convince you that, if your ancestors were living in the country at the time of the census, they were almost certainly recorded and, unless you are particularly unlucky, you should be able to find them. The odds are very firmly stacked in your favour.

In Chapter 6 we will take a look at some online search techniques which will help you to track down your more elusive ancestors but we need first to consider the undeniable fact that some individuals were genuinely missed out of the returns and we'll start by taking a brief look at some of the reasons why and how this might have happened.

Civil disobedience

Avoiding the census was never easy: even in the early years of the census, the system was fairly watertight. The registrars recruited local people to be enumerators – people with an intimate knowledge of their areas, who were expected to be familiar with the whereabouts of every house, however isolated or remote. Slipping through the net was never easy: despite an organised and well-publicised campaign to avoid the census in 1911 (see Chapter 3), the suffragettes found that the enumerators were usually one step ahead of them. If, however, someone was genuinely successful in deliberately avoiding enumeration, proving that they did so would be virtually impossible.

Refusing to give information to the census officials was an offence and the legislation was quite clear on this point. Clause XXIV of the 1851 Census Act stated that 'every Person refusing to answer or wilfully giving a false Answer to such Questions or any of them shall for every such Refusal or wilfully false Answer forfeit a Sum not exceeding Five Pounds nor less than Twenty Shillings'.

Evidence of the attention to detail employed by the census officials, together with their determination to get the job done – and done well – is easy to find. The extent to which the authorities were prepared to go to ensure that an accurate return of the population was taken is made abundantly clear by the case (reported in several newspapers in August 1841) of a school teacher in Ballachulish, Inverness-shire, who was fined £1 for giving false information to the census enumerator. She had apparently given her age as 20 but 'it was proved that she was baptised 44 years ago'.

The *Birmingham Daily Post* of 7 April 1891 reported the story of an enumerator having been 'menaced by an irate head of a family with violence':

> He was then distributing the papers, and he left the man without one. At headquarters he received instructions to try again yesterday, and to warn the man of the fine consequent on refusal. This policy of firm mildness had its due effect, and the census-paper was filled up, in the enumerator's presence, with nothing more serious than grumbling.

James Seaton, a retired baker from Grandborough in Buckinghamshire also failed in his attempt to avoid the census, and ended up serving time in prison as a result. A report on the Winslow Petty Sessions in the *Bucks Herald* of 16 April 1881 stated that Seaton:

> ... not only refused to take the schedule and fill it up, but flatly refused to give [the enumerator] any information to enable him to make his return to the registrar.

Seaton was initially fined £1 plus 18s. and 6d. costs, but when it transpired that he was unable to pay the fine, he was 'forthwith removed to the cells'. The registrar was able to get sufficient information to record James Seaton in the census. The entry appears at the end of the enumerator's summary book and also records details of the fine imposed by the court (RG 11/1477, folio 94, page 14; see also Fig. 4.1).

Figure 4.1 Detail of a page from the 1881 census of Grandborough, Buckinghamshire.

Another instance of census refusal appears in the 1841 census returns for the parish of St Swithin's in the City of London. The enumerator entered the following note on page six of his summary book regarding one of the inhabitants of St Swithin's Lane: 'John Travers will not give any information respecting the persons who abode in his house on the night of June 6th only that the number was 12 (males) 5 (females).' A later note added by the registrar on the same page states: 'Mr Travers fined Five Pounds at the Mansion House by Sir Peter Laurie. June 23, 1841. Alfred Nelson Wickes, Registrar' (HO 107/723/12, folio 6, page 6; plate 23). It appears that in this case the names of the 17 people were not recorded and we can conclude that they will therefore not be found in the census.

While it's clear that fines could be – and often were – imposed, it wasn't always felt that this was necessary. George Graham, the Registrar General at the time of the 1851 census, adopted a more relaxed approach to the problem: 'I treat these cases of obstinacy as more or less connected with insanity; and being isolated cases not very frequently met with, I do not think it necessary to prosecute the recusants.' Increasingly, the authorities were able to obtain the necessary information without resorting to fines, perhaps adopting the policy of 'firm mildness' to get results instead.

In 1861 the enumerator of Highgate in north London evidently had some problems when he came to call for the census forms at the house of a coal merchant called Thomas Lea. Thomas had provided the required information about himself, his wife, their 12 children, a visitor and three servants, but a fourth servant, Elizabeth Green, was (initially) less forthcoming. The enumerator made a note at the foot of the page stating: 'Elizabeth Green refuses to state her age or place of birth.' This was later crossed through and the words 'afterwards gave particulars' were entered together with the missing details (RG 9/792, folio 146, page 44; plate 24).

The number of people who refused to complete their schedules remained low throughout the nineteenth century and the number who did so successfully, and were therefore not recorded in the census, must have been infinitesimal. Action to obtain the necessary information was almost always taken and the evidence suggests that the chances of your ancestors having successfully and deliberately avoided the census are slim.

Under-enumeration?

Of course not all the enumerators employed to undertake the task were as efficient as we might hope. It's inevitable that the system did break down from time to time and that some properties and certain individuals living at a particular address may have been missed out altogether. As we saw in Chapter 2, there were some enumerators who were less than happy about having to enter certain buildings to deliver and collect their schedules.

One group of people who were particularly vulnerable to omission from the census were lodgers and boarders – more correctly, these are in fact two distinct groups and the instructions for enumerating them were quite clear: lodgers were supposed to be issued with their own schedules, whereas boarders should be included on the householder's schedule. However, it's not too difficult to see how some householders could mistakenly omit such people who were not strictly part of the household.

In the spring of 1851, Charles Darwin's beloved daughter Annie fell seriously ill with a stomach complaint. On 28 March, Darwin took Annie, together with her younger sister Henrietta (Ettie) and their nurse Jessie Brodie, by train from London's Euston Station to Worcester, from where they travelled on to the spa town of Great Malvern. The idea behind the trip was for Annie to spend a month in Malvern, taking the waters under the supervision of Doctor James Gully, a specialist in this developing area of medicine. After getting the girls settled in lodgings at Montreal House, on the Worcester Road, Charles returned to London, intending to stay for a few weeks with his brother, Erasmus.

The landlady of the lodging house was called Eliza Partington and we know from a letter which Ettie wrote to her mother the following week that there were 'a great many ladies' in the house at the time.

The girls arrived in Malvern on Thursday afternoon – just three days before the 1851 census was due to be taken. The schedules had almost certainly been distributed to the householders by then and it may be that the ultra-efficient landlady had immediately completed her form, listing all the people then living in her lodging house. Perhaps Annie, Ettie and nurse Brodie arrived after the form had been filled in – their names certainly do not appear in the census for Montreal House. We know, beyond reasonable doubt, that they were staying there on the night of the census, but the only people listed in the returns for the lodging house are Eliza Partington (described as a Lodging House Keeper) and her two servants, along with four female visitors (presumably the 'ladies' mentioned in Ettie's letter) and one of their servants. (HO 107/2043, folio 148, page 44)

A sad postscript is that Annie's treatment was not successful. She died on 23 April, without returning home from Malvern.

This is as close as you can get to incontrovertible evidence of under-enumeration in the census, but it's only possible to prove that the girls and their nurse were omitted thanks to the existence of contemporary sources such as the letter written by Ettie and Darwin's own diaries. Proving that your own ancestors were missed in this way might be rather more troublesome.

Our feeling is that this sort of instance was rare. Of course, the system was run by fallible human beings, but the General Register Office (GRO) was a model of Victorian efficiency managed by a succession of gifted and dedicated men. The very idea of a significant number of people being allowed to slip through the net would have felt like failure to men such as George Graham and Brydges Henniker. (It's interesting to note here that statisticians have often argued that any shortfall in the population count caused by these deficiencies in the system would almost certainly be balanced out by the number of people who were recorded twice!)

Beyond the seas?

Failure to find a family in the census can inspire researchers to come up with all kinds of elaborate 'solutions'. One that is frequently suggested is that their ancestors were temporarily absent from the country, and while some people may have had cause to travel overseas (soldiers serving in the British Army, sailors, merchants, engineers etc.), as a possible explanation for why an agricultural labourer from Wiltshire is missing from the census, it lacks a certain credibility!

There was undoubtedly a small body of 'unsuccessful emigrants' who left to start a new life beyond the seas but found that the streets of their new home were not paved with gold and later returned to the UK (and the ability, afforded by internet technology, to carry out global searches has brought many such cases to light) but by and large, the vast majority of the population would never have set foot on any foreign shore.

Occasionally you might get a clue from a later census to suggest that a family had indeed been out of the country for a while. Joseph Rhodes, an engine fitter from Alfreton in Derbyshire, married Ann Simpson in the spring of 1849. The couple went on to have a succession of children, born in the small Derbyshire town of Ripley, before moving to Greenwich where their son George was born in 1859. There is no sign whatsoever of this family in the 1861 census which, as it turns out, is hardly surprising: the 1871 census provides the answer, through the listing in the returns of a 10-year-old daughter, Emma, who had been born in Spain (RG 10/748, folio 65, page 12). Joseph had evidently taken a short-term job on the continent, meaning that the family were out of the country at the time of the 1861 census.

This book does not attempt to cover the census records created by the authorities in the United States but it's worth noting that the complete collection of federal censuses from 1790 to 1940 is openly available and fully searchable on Ancestry. It's also worth bearing in mind that the decennial US census was always taken a year earlier than the one in the UK; 1840 rather than 1841, 1850 not 1851 and so on. Finding your ancestors in the US census can of course be useful to your research, not just for the information you'll get from the very detailed schedules but also because it means you can probably stop looking for them in the equivalent UK census. Occasionally a family can be found in both: Louisa Kendall, for example, was living in Fulton County, New York at the time of the 1880 census, recently widowed, and with a young family, but the following year she was back in England with three of her children (who had all been born in America) living in Hornsey, north London (RG 11/1374, folio 39, page 6).

One of the primary aims of each census was to provide an accurate count of the total population of the country. A nation such as Great Britain with its rich military, naval and commercial heritage presented the census takers with an extra difficulty: how to record the significant population which was living (albeit temporarily) beyond its borders at the time of the census. The official report on the 1861 census remarked that:

> The people of these islands are more moveable than other nations, and large numbers of them are always abroad, sometimes on distant voyages, sometimes on the Alps, sometimes in the deserts of Africa, or in the strangest places; but generally in ships at sea, in the great commercial entrepôts, in the capitals of Europe, in our Colonies, or in the States of America.

It seems entirely logical for the vast numbers of British merchants who were resident in all these major foreign ports and cities not to be included when it came to taking the census. They may or may not have intended to return to these shores, but at any rate their numbers would almost certainly have been balanced by a similar number of foreign merchants living in places such as London, Birmingham, Manchester, Liverpool, Norwich, Bristol and Glasgow.

Neither would it have been desirable to attempt to include the thousands of Britons who had emigrated to the far flung corners of the Empire, the vast majority of whom were permanent emigrants, unlikely ever to return. Having said that, a fairly comprehensive census of the British Empire was taken as early as 1861, recording the population of each of Britain's colonies, dependencies and foreign possessions. Individual colonies had previously carried out their own censuses but now it was, in the words of the official report: 'desirable on many grounds that the population of the Queen's dominions should be enumerated simultaneously'. Unfortunately, comparatively few lists of names have survived, so while they may be invaluable for political and social historians, for us, as family historians, they tend to be of limited interest.

Canada represents a notable exception: the returns of various Canadian censuses from 1851 to 1921 have survived in full and are easily searchable online. The news for Australia, New Zealand and South Africa is not so good. With the exception of a couple of early censuses of New South Wales dating from 1828 and 1841, nothing of any value to family historians survives for Australia. The individual Australian states each took censuses throughout the nineteenth century, covering the whole of the country from 1861 onwards, but the records of these have all either been lost or deliberately destroyed. A national census of Australia has been taken every ten years since 1901 but again, the returns are systematically destroyed after the statistical information is abstracted from them.

With the exception of a few isolated returns from other parts of the former British Empire, nothing else survives. Many of the most populous former colonies, including New Zealand and South Africa, are a complete blank as far as census returns are concerned.

An appendix to the 1861 census report indicates that an attempt was made to count 'British-born subjects in foreign countries'. The returns include the remarkable fact that the population of the US included over 2 million people who were born in Great Britain. This was at a time when the total population of the UK was no more than 30 million. Further research reveals that nearly three-quarters of the British-born subjects living in the US in 1861 were natives of Ireland. Figures also show that over 40,000 British civilians were living in India – over 8,000 of them in Bengal alone.

These emigrant populations may have provided the Census Office with some useful data (although many of the figures were felt to be inaccurate) but realistically they were beyond the concerns of the Government as far as the main purposes of taking the census were concerned. An understanding of what the population of the country would look like in ten, twenty or thirty years was hardly going to be affected by groups of people who were unlikely ever to set foot in the UK again. But there were two significant groups whose absence from our shores on census night was merely temporary: firstly, those at sea (whether serving with the Royal Navy or on a merchant vessel) and secondly, the thousands of officers and men of the British Army stationed in India, South Africa, Canada, the Far East, the Mediterranean and other outposts of the British Empire.

We have touched on the enumeration of people in these groups in earlier chapters. The return rate varies from census to census, as do the arrangements in place for issuing and collecting the forms. The problems inherent in the process are readily apparent: delivering the forms may be straightforward but if the ship was no longer in port on the Monday following census night, what did you do? It may, by then, be at sea, in a foreign port, or even in another British port. And what of the ship which arrived in port on the Monday, without having been previously issued a census form elsewhere? It's evident from the notes of various census committee meetings that these questions came up year after year, and it seems as if the authorities were ultimately content to do the best possible job and accept that the results would be neither comprehensive nor 100 per cent accurate.

By the time of the 1911 census, the responsibility for collecting and collating schedules for merchant vessels lay in the hands of the Customs Office. The method deployed in 1911 may have led to a degree of under-enumeration in this area as the window of opportunity for collecting forms from ships returning to British ports after census night was significantly reduced from previous census years. It's also fair to say that the instructions issued to the Customs officials were far from clear:

> 'You are not required to collect Schedules from vessels which were at sea on the night of Sunday, April 2nd, and returned to Port after Monday, April 3rd. Vessels may, however, arrive subsequently which passed the Census night at a Port in the United Kingdom, but left before the Schedules could be collected. A good look-out should be kept for such vessels up to Saturday, April 15th, and any Schedules on board should be taken up.'

It's hardly surprising in the circumstances that many vessels seem to have slipped through the net!

The Admiralty was responsible for co-ordinating the census returns for all Royal Naval vessels, whether in British or foreign ports, or at sea. The results have always been more comprehensive than those for the merchant navy although the returns for 1891 and some of those for 1901 are missing.

In the light of this unrelenting effort to record the details of our maritime forebears, it's perhaps surprising that a similar attempt was not made on behalf of the vast ranks of men serving Queen and country overseas during the latter half of the nineteenth century – the War Office was simply asked to furnish the GRO with a head count. So the decision to carry out a full enumeration of the British Army overseas in 1911 (see Chapter 3) represents a major landmark in the history of the census.

As we've seen, the success of the government's attempts to include those who were temporarily absent from these shores varied over the years and there is a real possibility that your absent ancestor was not recorded, particularly if they were in the British Army. Whether their apparent absence can be explained in this way depends very much on the circumstances of their lives and you will probably want to consult a variety of other sources such as shipping lists before considering this as an explanation.

Name unknown

The final category of ancestors who might genuinely be missing from the returns is also one of the trickiest to spot – and in certain respects the people in this group are only partially 'missing'. This is where the enumerator was unable to get the required information but still managed to provide some sort of headcount.

It's difficult to say what the story might be behind the somewhat deficient returns for number 70 Landells Road, Camberwell, in the 1891 census. Judging by the occupants in the neighbouring houses (a civil servant, a silver polisher, an insurance agent and a painter and grainer), this was a fairly respectable lower-middle-class area – the families didn't have servants but all the houses were single occupancies. These neighbouring families are all fully enumerated, but all we know about the family at number 70 is that it comprised a man (aged about 40), his 32-year-old wife and a succession of children aged twelve, ten, seven, six, four and two years. No places of birth are given but intriguingly we have an occupation for the head of the household: 'Supposed Serjt. Major in Army.' How could the enumerator have known all this while being unable to obtain the rest of the information? (RG 12/471, folio 84, page 32; plate 25.)

Another entry which leaves us with more questions than answers is to be found amongst the 1861 census returns for West Street, Stepney. The enumerator had evidently returned to number 21 to collect the lodger's returns only to find that not only had the lodger departed, but he had also taken the schedule with him. The enumerator made the following note in his summary book: 'Lodger left Saturday and took schedule with him – gone to Woolwich.' (RG 9/298, folio 60, page 5.) It would be interesting to know whether the enumerator in Woolwich managed to 'capture' the lodger.

The census aimed to provide a true and accurate count of the population, but it was always recognised that there were groups of people who lived either on the edge of, or entirely outside, 'normal' society and that these people would be very difficult, if not impossible, to fully enumerate.

The various groups of people that the census legislators described as vagrants, tramps or gypsies form the majority of the unknowns. In most cases there was a genuine effort to count the numbers of these 'itinerant travellers', but if your ancestor is described in the census as an unknown 45-year-old living in a caravan on the common this will be scant consolation to you as, without a name, you will have no way of identifying him or her.

You'll often find these people listed at the end of an enumeration book and sometimes you are fortunate enough to get their names. No fewer than 162 travelling showmen, toy dealers and stallholders living in tents and caravans were recorded in the 1861 census returns for the parish of St Paul's, Deptford.

The enumerator had found it 'impossible to deliver' any schedules to work from and, according to a note at the top of page 28 of his summary book, had copied the details from his memorandum book: 'The following persons slept at an intended casual Fair on the night of the 7th April 1861 in a field adjoining the Boundary of the St Paul Deptford, but no information could be obtained respecting the place of birth.' (RG 9/396, folios 135–138; plate 27.)

At the end of the list of names, on page 34, the enumerator expands on his previous note:

> Sir, I forward to you a List of those persons who slept at the intended Fair on the night of the 7th instant. The enclosed was as correct as could be ascertained there being a great deal of difficulty to gain any information – especially the place of Birth – I had to forego that enquiry for the more important information respecting names & ages which was given with much reluctance, not being willing to be disturbed.

The distrust of the authorities is quite obvious here and we can only admire the commitment of the enumerator in getting as much information as he did. Other enumerators weren't quite as successful.

The 1881 census for the Berkshire village of Shottesbrook includes entries for five people (in two separate groups) who were living in sheds.

The first group consisted of a man (an Edge Tool Grinder), a woman and a child. It's tempting to assume that this is a family group, but, other than the occupation and some intelligent guesswork regarding their ages, no details are recorded about them. In the second shed we find two men whose ages are given as 48 and 35. This time we get a name for the one of them – William Neal – and an occupation of sorts; the enumerator has written: 'None (too idle)'! (RG 11/1315, folio 65, page 7).

In 1871 the enumerator for Balcomb in Sussex included five 'tramps' and one named individual at the end of his summary book. William James's residence was given as 'Edmunds Barn': he was described as a 50-year-old, unmarried Ag. Lab.– birthplace unknown. Underneath the entry for William James, the enumerator had initially written 'Tramps Names N. K. Man, Woman & 3 children', but this was scored out and an attempt of sorts was made to come up with some approximate ages – these were presumably no more than guesses (RG 10/1060, folio 126, page 18).

There are hundreds, probably even thousands, of people recorded in the censuses in this way. Some of them are our ancestors and it's just possible that the family in Balcomb or the edge tool grinder living in the Berkshire shed are the very people that you're looking for. But the chances of ever being able to prove anything are remote.

People living in prisons, workhouses and asylums can also be difficult to trace and the habit developed by the Masters of these institutions of using initials when listing the inmates certainly doesn't help. The best that we can say here is that it's worth bearing this in mind when all other approaches have failed. A search for Ann Basing from North Sherborne in Hampshire in the 1881 census, for example, will not succeed as she is listed in the returns for the Hampshire County Lunatic Asylum under the initials A. B. (RG 11/1169, folio 73, page 22).

Missing censuses

The number of people who fell into any of the categories we've looked at so far is relatively small and (with the possible exception of people serving in the British Army or at sea) these 'solutions' are unlikely to explain the apparent absence of your ancestors. Of greater concern to us are the large sections of the census that are known to be missing.

Our census records have had a somewhat chequered and confusing history. The original householders' schedules were destroyed and it perhaps says something about the lack of importance attached to the records in general that the enumerators' summary books have not been well looked after for much of their existence. At various periods in the nineteenth and early twentieth centuries the whereabouts of some of the records was unclear – indeed for a while the whole of the 1851 census was thought to be lost!

Initially, of course, these were working records: clerks at the Census Office spent months going through them, checking them for accuracy and then annotating them and extracting data from them for statistical purposes. As a result, some of the books suffered a significant amount of wear and tear. In the 1861 returns there are numerous instances, particularly in the London districts, where the front and back pages of the books or other single pages have been lost. An extensive survey of these missing pages has been carried out by staff at The National Archives and the data can be found on the Discovery catalogue.

As a researcher, it can be particularly frustrating to find that the returns for the family you're looking for have only partly survived, offering only a tantalising glimpse of what might have been. For many years, the Swale family lived at number 3 Leicester Place, Saffron Hill, in Holborn, London. They were listed at that address in 1851 and were evidently still there at the time of the 1861 census. However, we only have the details of the head of the house. William Swale is listed at the bottom of page 80 but pages 81 and 82, which would have included the returns for the rest of the Swale family, are unfortunately missing (RG 9/187, folio 85, page 80).

But it's not just the odd page here and there that's missing. Some whole sub-districts and in one case an entire registration district have, over the years, been misplaced, destroyed or possibly even stolen! The most significant gaps in the collection are:

1841:   the whole of the parish of Paddington, a few parishes in Kent, Northamptonshire and significant parts of North Wales, particularly in Denbigh and Flint

1851:   parts of the Newmarket district and the whole of the Dunmow (Essex) district

1861: the whole of the Belgravia (Westminster) and Woolwich Arsenal sub-districts, a small number of parishes in Wales

1871: part of Leicester, a few places in Wales

1901: the whole of Deal (Kent)

1881, 1891 and 1911 have no significant gaps.

The Findmypast website has a comprehensive list of known missing pieces of the census at: <**findmypast.co.uk/help-and-advice/knowledge-base/census/known-issues**>.

No one has ever been able to explain what happened to these documents and no one knows when they disappeared. Perhaps some of them were 'borrowed' by interested parties – the fact that the returns from the early censuses were stored for a while in an attic at the Houses of Parliament (apparently in a haphazard and disorganised manner) made them particularly vulnerable to this sort of pilfering. It's possible that in the fullness of time some of them will turn up amongst collections of private papers. As recently as the 1970s, an 1841 enumerator's summary book for part of Wrexham was discovered in a second-hand bookshop, so hope is not fully extinguished. It goes without saying that the surviving records are secured for posterity and that there is no danger of any further losses occurring.

Clearly, if your ancestors were living in any of these 'missing' areas at the time of the census, you're not going to find them; but even if we add the total in this category to the unfortunate few on the missing pages and then include those not enumerated in the first place, we're still looking at a very small percentage of the total population.

It's important to understand this point: our ancestors were almost certainly 'captured' by the census enumerator. If you've failed to find them, then the reason is unlikely to be that they are not recorded: it is much more likely that one or more of the pieces of information that you're using to carry out your search is, in some crucial way, 'wrong'. We have used inverted commas here to highlight the fact that this simple word can hide a multitude of meanings.

We'll now go on to look at the many reasons why your ancestors may not appear in the census as you would expect to find them.

Is the census wrong?

It's very easy to fall into the trap of thinking that, since the census returns were created by a highly efficient nineteenth-century government department, they will necessarily be totally accurate and comprehensive. We have to remember that the primary purpose of the census was to provide the government of the day with workable and meaningful statistical data – and with this in mind it was undeniably fit for purpose. The question we have to ask is whether, as a source of family history data, it can be relied upon in the same way.

We've already looked at the various problems that the enumerator might have faced in delivering and collecting the householders' schedules. Now we need to follow him home and consider the conditions in which he carried out the task of copying the details into his summary book. The enumerators were not salaried GRO employees; they were local people who, in most cases, had another, full-time job and who, therefore, had to complete this work at home in the evenings, with no separate office, no electric lighting and, quite possibly, a large family around them, providing ample distractions. If we're looking for reasons why information recorded in the census returns might be inaccurate, here's a prime candidate. Even the most diligent and conscientious enumerator, working in conditions like this, is capable of making a mistake or two with crucial details like names, ages or places of birth.

As we've seen from some of the complaints made by the enumerators, there was little incentive for them to create a quality product. They were supposed to get the job done quickly and their payment wasn't based on any measure of quality; they were simply paid a fixed amount for each completed schedule. Edward Blade (the 1851 enumerator from Allhallows, Barking) made a crucial point when he asked the question, 'How then can a correct return of the population be expected?' Yes, the quality of their work was checked, first by the local registrar and then by the Superintendent Registrar, but with the best will in the world these can only have been superficial checks.

This is just one of the stages at which errors can be introduced into the records. From the family historian's point of view, it doesn't really matter whether the mistake was made by the householder, the enumerator or a modern transcriber. Any mistake in the records is liable to cause us problems when attempting to locate our ancestors in the returns, but it's important nonetheless to consider the various possibilities so that we can gain a better understanding of how we can overcome these problems.

Reading the writing

The enumerators' summary books are, as we have seen, the census records that we use in our research today and it's from these books that the online indexes have been created. There can be no question that these indexes have improved, beyond all recognition, our ability to find individuals in the census, but it's true to say that they have also created some new problems. Put in very simple terms, it's inevitable that a further transcription process will introduce a further set of errors.

However you look at it, there's no denying that some of the transcription on some of the census websites leaves a lot to be desired, but thanks to the power and flexibility of modern search engines this shouldn't prevent us from finding our ancestors – in Chapter 6 we'll take an in-depth look at how to search the various online indexes.

But let's not be too quick to criticise the modern census transcriptions. Anyone with experience of using the returns would no doubt confirm that the handwriting, possibly as a result of the poor working conditions and low morale amongst the enumerators mentioned above, can be extremely difficult to read. Any attempt to interpret and copy handwritten documents from an earlier era is naturally going to be fraught with difficulties. However much we may be familiar with the form of writing, it's the little nuances – the exceptions to the rule – that present us with the problems.

Ultimately, a researcher trying to interpret a particularly difficult piece of text needs to consider two points: first of all, what does it say and, secondly, what did it mean to say? This is an important distinction; the transcriber's job is only to copy what it actually says and to leave the second part of the process in the hands of the researcher. No attempt should be made at this stage to editorialise or to second-guess what the enumerator meant.

Interpreting our ancestors' handwriting was clearly just as much of a challenge for the enumerators as deciphering the enumerators' handwriting was for the twenty-first century transcribers. More than anything else, it's the personal names and the birthplaces which seem to have caused the enumerators the biggest problems.

Of course, the average nineteenth-century enumerator wouldn't have had access to a decent selection of atlases and gazetteers – the sort of research tools that modern researchers take for granted. So if they were unable to read or understand what the householder had written, the only option open to them other than going back to the householder to check (which, considering the need to get the job done quickly, was not usually a practical option) was to make an intelligent guess.

Over the years I've come across a number of instances where it seems that this is exactly what the enumerator did: the only problem is that the guess doesn't always seem to have been that intelligent! How else can you explain 'Essex, Coackerter', Henry Bullifant's place of birth as given in the 1881 census? It's clearly supposed to be Colchester (the 'shape' is practically identical) and the only logical conclusion must be that the Sheffield-based enumerator was unable to identify what Henry had written and simply transcribed what he thought it said, copying the shape of the letters. It does seem quite strange though that the enumerator had never heard of Britain's oldest recorded town (RG 11/4647, folio 113, page 27; plate 28) (see Fig. 4.2).

It's not obvious on first viewing what the 1851 Clerkenwell enumerator meant when he entered the birthplace of three members of the Bennett family as 'Bucks., Jugford'. There is in reality no such place in Buckinghamshire, or indeed elsewhere in England and Wales. Further research on the family in later censuses reveals that they were born in Twyford. Leaving aside for a moment the additional complication that Twyford is in Berkshire not Buckinghamshire, it's not hard to see how someone who didn't recognise the place name could come up with 'Jugford' as a possible interpretation, based entirely on the shape of the word (HO 107/1516, folio 5, page 2 and RG 10/1288, folio 70, page 16; plates 29 and 30).

It's surprising how often what initially appears to be a modern error turns out instead to be a faithful and accurate transcription of what's in the records. I clearly remember jumping to the wrong conclusion many years ago when I found an Annal family in the 1881 census indexed as Allan – only to check the original entry and find that the whole family were indeed listed as Allan and not Annal (RG 11/4539, folio 91, page 27). I suspect that this is another example of enumerator

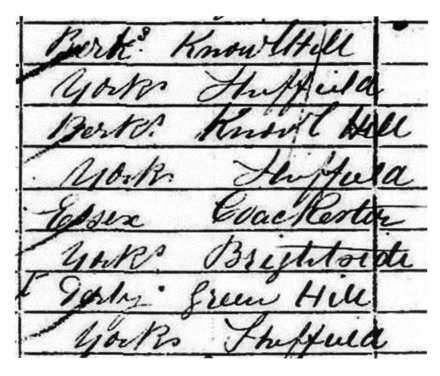

Figure 4.2 Detail of a page from the 1881 census of Sheffield showing birthplaces.

error, although it's difficult to say in cases like this whether the 'mistake' was initiated by the householder or introduced by the enumerator.

As family historians, we need to adopt an open and questioning mind when dealing with our ancestors and the information that they've left behind in the various documents that we use in our research. The challenge facing us is to work out which of the 'facts' about their lives are true and which are not.

This of course is easier said than done. The untruths we come up against comprise a wide range of eventualities: as well as the honest errors, there are the misunderstandings and misinterpretations, and lastly, and perhaps everyone's favourite, the downright lies. So how do we spot the mistakes, the lies and the half-truths?

Ignorance, errors and lies

Any data source which is based on a series of questions and answers relies in the first place on the accuracy of the initial answers. It doesn't matter how efficient the administrative process behind producing the end product is: if the original data is flawed, we're going to have problems using and understanding it. This is certainly true of the census, which relies for its accuracy and detail on people who had an astonishing number of reasons to get things wrong – namely, our ancestors.

It has been estimated that as many as one in four birth, marriage and death certificates contains an error of one kind or another, and we know from bitter experience that the information that our ancestors gave to the census enumerators is similarly riddled with inaccuracies.

Spelling must surely come right near the top of the list of issues that regularly cause errors to crop up in the census. In Chapter 7 of Charles Dickens' *Great Expectations*, the following dialogue takes place between our hero, Pip, and his brother-in-law, Joe Gargery:

'How do you spell Gargery, Joe?' I asked him, with a modest patronage.

'I don't spell it at all,' said Joe.

'But supposing you did?'

'It can't be supposed,' said Joe.

The point of this is that, not only could many of our ancestors not read and write, they also had no concept of the 'correct' spelling of their names. The significance of this to family historians is, we hope, quite clear and the lesson is an obvious one; yet it never fails to surprise us how often we hear researchers comment, for example, that the William Browne they've found can't be theirs because their name has always been spelt without an 'e'.

This fixation with 'correct' spelling is a relatively modern one. It certainly wasn't shared by our Tudor and Stuart ancestors and even into the latter half of the nineteenth century inconsistencies in spellings of place names as well as personal names were commonplace. The situation began to change with the introduction of compulsory education in England and Wales. The Education Act of 1870 began the work by allowing school boards to be set up around the country, but it was the 1876 Elementary Education Act that really opened the doors to an era of virtually universal literacy. This landmark Act compelled parents to send their children to school to receive basic education in reading, writing and arithmetic.

If the householders were unable to complete their census forms, the enumerators were supposed to help them, or even to write down the details themselves. Although all the evidence suggests it was rarely left to the enumerator, this is where regional accents, misunderstandings and misinterpretations might come into play – all of which can account for a lot of questionable information ending up in the returns.

As family historians we naturally like to think the best of our ancestors. We imagine them as fine upstanding members of their local community, as people of honesty and integrity. It can come as a bit of a shock to us therefore to discover that many of them had a rather distressing habit of lying, and when it came to filling out their census form, they had any number of reasons why they might have chosen to be economical with the truth. They could never have envisaged that we would one day be able to untangle some of the webs that they wove with their lies. Thanks to the miracles of modern computer technology, our ancestors' secrets are no longer safe.

Errors, however they originate, can of course occur right across the census form, but it's the names, ages and birthplaces which are likely to have the biggest impact on your search. Let's look at each area in turn, starting with the problems that might crop up in the 'name' field.

Names

When dealing with our ancestors' surnames, we mustn't fall into the trap of applying our modern prejudices about accuracy, detail and consistency. We need to allow for significant discrepancies in spelling occurring between one census and the next – there may be some perception of a 'usual' spelling of a name, but, as we have seen, there are many reasons why it may appear in the census in a different form.

Take the case of Henry Patterson (plate 31): he was recorded in the 1881 census, aged 40 and living in Stockton-on-Tees, County Durham, with his surname spelt exactly as we would expect (RG 11/4897, folio 28, page 51). But you might struggle to find him ten years earlier because he's entered as Henry Pattison, as indeed he is in 1861 (RG 10/4901, folio 108, page 28; RG 9/3694, folio 32, page 60). And when we go back to 1851, he's down as Henry Paddison (HO 107/2383, folio 617, page 18). So what are we looking at here? Is this a positive decision by Henry (and/or his parents) to change the name – to adopt a different spelling? Personally, I doubt it. These were labouring folk, semi-literate at best, and they were to a large degree at the mercy of the enumerator. Of course, we cannot tell from the surviving records whether the different spellings of the name were the result of the family members completing their householders' schedules themselves or the product of a succession of enumerators' attempts at interpreting the details that the Patterson family gave them, hurriedly, on the doorstep. What is clear is that examples of this kind are commonplace.

Another situation which presents plenty of opportunity for error occurs when the details on a schedule were completed by the house-holder on behalf of a lodger or servant. If that person had only recently arrived at the house in question or perhaps if he or she was someone who kept themselves to themselves and only rarely associated with the family, it's easy to see how the householder could have been unaware of some important details.

This is just one of the surname-related problems that the Critcher family of Langley Marish, in Buckinghamshire serve to illustrate. Edward was born in 1832, the son of William and Elizabeth Critcher, and the whole family are living at George Green, in Langley Marish, at the time of the 1841 census (HO 107/61/3, folio 11, page 16). Ten years later, the family are still at George Green but Edward, now aged 18, is living away from home. He's listed in the 1851 census at Hunton Bridge in the parish of Abbots Langley, Hertfordshire, where he was working as a ploughman: his surname is entered as Crutchet (HO 107/1714, folio 616, page 10).

Moving on another ten years and Edward's father William is now an inmate in the Eton Union Workhouse, but his name has been entered by the Master of the Workhouse (or perhaps by a clerk) as Crutcher. Edward meanwhile is now married and living in the Buckinghamshire parish of Chenies, 'correctly' listed as Critcher (RG 9/848, folio 10, page 14), but in the 1871 census, Edward and family are entered as Critchard (RG 10/1396, folio 6, page 5). So within a period of 20 years we have the surname spelt in four different ways: Critcher, Crutcher, Crutchet and Critchard.

But it's not just the spellings of their surnames which can make people hard to find. It may be a difficult concept for us to grasp but, of all the 'facts' that are recorded about our ancestors, it's their surnames which are the most liable to change. Take the case of Alfred Lesurf who was born in Bethnal Green in 1868, the son of James and Clara Lesurf. His father died in 1870 when Alfred was just two and the young boy can be easily found in the 1871 census with his widowed mother (RG 10/502, folio 47, page 17). In 1874 she married a man called William Bramley and in the 1881 and 1891 censuses Alfred is listed under the name Bramley instead of Lesurf (RG 11/433, folio 98, page 43; RG 12/261, folio 26, page 47). This is not a case of formal adoption but simply of a boy using, or at least being given, his step-father's surname. By the time that Alfred married in 1892, he was using his original surname, Lesurf and he continued to do so for the rest of his life.

Cases like this are not uncommon and the same thing often happens when the mother of an illegitimate child marries while her child is still young: the child just naturally takes on their step-father's surname.

Forenames tend to be less of a problem. Our ancestors worked from a relatively small palette of forenames and if we go back to the sixteenth and seventeenth centuries, we find that roughly half of the male population of England was represented by just three names; John, William and Thomas. Although there was a slightly larger pool of female names to choose from, the top five (Jane, Margaret, Ann, Elizabeth and Mary) were used by over 40 per cent of women.

So it's most likely that your ancestors' forenames will have been correctly recorded. As mentioned in Chapter 2, abbreviations were frequently used in the census, but in most cases this shouldn't present too many obstacles to your research.

The problem that we have here is more to do with the annoying habit that some people seem to have had of changing their forenames from one census to the next, often by adopting their middle name as their preferred first name.

The Swale family of Holborn (mentioned on p. 91) provide a good example of this. Ellen Jane Swale was born in 1839 and married William Hayes in October 1864. She is listed in the 1841 census as Ellen Swale but in 1851 she appears as Jane. Unfortunately, as we saw earlier, she is genuinely missing from the 1861 census but we pick her up again, by now married to William Hayes, in 1871 and 1881: in both cases her forename is once more given as Jane (RG 10/376, folio 58, page 37; RG 11/343, folio 50, page 31).

In this case, it seems likely that Ellen Jane simply chose to be known by her middle name, but sometimes our ancestors appear in the census with different forenames for no apparent reason. The case of the Foyle family of Clapham, Surrey, illustrates this quite well. Richard Foyle married Elizabeth Weatherley at Battersea in 1834 and five children were born in Clapham over the next sixteen years. It's fairly easy to find the family in the 1841 and 1851 censuses living in Clifton Street (HO 107/1053/3, folio 12, page 18; HO 107/1576, folio 143, page 20) but when we come to the 1861 census, although we can find the same family, still living in Clifton Street, the parents are entered not as Richard and Elizabeth but as William and Eliza (RG 9/368, folio 135, page 38). Where the 1861 census enumerator got these names from we'll never know. All we can say for certain is that someone, somewhere along the line, got their wires crossed and the wrong names ended up in the census.

Ages

Ages on census returns are notoriously inaccurate and it's actually not at all uncommon to find someone's age increasing by slightly more or, perhaps more often, slightly less than ten years between censuses. A Registrar General's report from 1896 stated that 'the one column in the householders' schedule which gives the most trouble to occupiers ... and is most liable to the suspicion of inaccuracy when filled up, is the Age Column'.

Birthdays weren't celebrated in the same way that they are today, and in the era before the state began to record every detail of our lives, these matters didn't always hold such importance.

Whether the problem with ages is more to do with ignorance or deception is neither here nor there, but it's certainly an area that presents us with more than its fair share of difficulties and we would do well to learn to take the ages we see in the census with a large pinch of salt. Take the example of my great-great-grandfather, James Annal, and his sister Betsy. James was born in 1837, a year after Betsy, but by the time of the 1871 census he had 'overtaken' her, and was shown as being two years older! It wasn't until the 1901 census that Betsy regained the missing years and admitted to her true age.

Henry Groves was born in Rickmansworth, Hertfordshire, in 1830. His age in five successive censuses is recorded as follows: 1851 – 20;

1861 – 25; 1871 – 39; 1881 – 42; 1891 – 60. Henry was listed as a lodger in 1861 and a boarder in 1871, which may have contributed to the discrepancies highlighted here but cannot explain the age given in 1881, when Henry was the head of his own household and therefore responsible for completing his own schedule.

Don't forget that in the 1841 census the ages of people aged 15 or over were supposed to be rounded down to the nearest five. Another important point to remember is that, from 1851 to 1911, the census was always taken either at the end of March or the beginning of April. It's easy to fall into the trap of assuming that someone who was aged two years at the time of the 1901 census was necessarily born in 1899. In fact (providing that the age was given accurately in the first place) they would have been born between April 1898 and April 1899 – with 1898 being the more likely year of birth (see p. 150).

Birthplaces

The age column may well be, as the Registrar General's report of 1896 stated, 'the most liable to the suspicion of inaccuracy', but it's our ancestors' inconsistency when referring to their birthplaces which causes family historians the greatest headaches.

Unfortunately, many of them simply didn't know where they were born. Orphans, adoptees or people who were brought up a long way from where they were born may have been unaware of the identity of their native parish, so it's not at all uncommon to find the words 'Not Known' (often abbreviated to 'NK') where you would expect to find a place of birth.

Of course, the vast majority of the population knew where they were born – the problem, however, is that they may have had a variety of ways of describing that place. At one extreme there are the (admittedly rare) cases where a precise address of birth is given – at the other, the all-too-common instances of 'NK'.

When William Barker completed his census schedule in 1881, he gave rather more information regarding his children's places of birth than he was required to (RG 11/140, folio 99, page 53; see also Fig. 4.3):

Lucy A Barker, 1 Robert St., Grosvenor Sqre.
William J Barker, 4 Brunswick Yd., Marylebone
Frederick J Barker, 25 Randolph Mews, Maida Vale

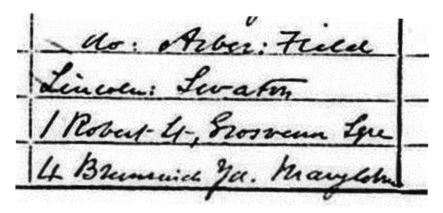

Figure 4.3 Detail of a page from the 1881 census.

A single page from the 1891 census (RG 12/39, folio 170, page 10) illustrates the huge range of possibilities that the place of birth column can throw up.

Of the 30 names on the page, only 16 gave their birthplaces in the usual 'County, Parish' format. Of the other 14, four gave the name of the county without identifying the parish, while four more were born in Scotland and one in Jersey. A further four were born overseas, two in Jamaica and two in the US (one in New York, one in New Jersey), leaving one person, Sarah Christmas, whose place of birth was given as 'London, Jermyn St.'.

It's this unpredictability which can make our searches so hard to structure. Henry Ralph Bleeze was born in London, but as a young man he moved out of the capital, first to Hitchin in Hertfordshire and then to Bedfordshire. His birthplace, as given over successive censuses, makes interesting reading:

1851 London
1861 London, Holborn
1871 Middlesex, Fetter Lane, Holborn
1881 London, Middlesex
1891 London, Fetter Lane, Holborn
1901 London, St Andrew

None of these is in any way 'wrong' – they all refer to the same place, but with varying degrees of precision.

While some were unsure of their birthplaces, others may have had cause to be less than truthful with the information they supplied. The Poor Law played a huge part in the lives of the Victorian working classes and the fear of being removed from their homes back to their parish of legal settlement (usually the parish they were born in) seems to have led many of our ancestors to claim a false birthplace in the census. The assurance of confidentiality given by the census administrators evidently wasn't enough to convince everyone.

County boundaries can also throw up a variety of issues. The Henry Grover mentioned above was born in Hertfordshire but the 1891 census records his place of birth as 'Middlesex, West Hyde'. The hamlet of West Hyde is part of the parish of Rickmansworth which is, and always has been, in Hertfordshire, but it is so close to the Middlesex border that it's easy to see how confusion could creep in.

Alfred Genner grew up around the turn of the twentieth century in the North Yorkshire village of Tollerton but, according to the 1901 census, he had been born many miles away in Ludlow, Shropshire (RG 13/4544, folio 157, page 18). However, the 1891 census gives his place of birth as Hereford (RG 12/3978, folio 36, page 11). So we have a problem here which is only partly explained by the tendency people have to be less precise when describing their birthplace the further they are away from it. A Shropshire man like Alfred's father might well give a Yorkshire census enumerator the name of the market town nearest to the village where his son was born instead of the name of the village itself. But in this case we have an extra difficulty which has as much to do with our country's often confusing geographical and administrative borders.

When we dig a bit deeper we discover that Ludlow is only a few miles from the Shropshire/Herefordshire border – indeed the Ludlow registration district includes several parishes which are actually situated in Herefordshire. It turns out that Alfred was born in one of these parishes – a small village called Ludford. An 1871 directory of Shropshire summarises the geographical difficulties rather neatly: 'Ludford is a parish joining Ludlow ... and only separated from the town by the River Teme. The village and church of Ludford is in the county of Hereford, and the townships are in Salop (i.e. Shropshire).'

So we have two different places of birth for Alfred in two censuses and neither of them is, strictly speaking, 'correct'. At least, in this case, and in the case of Henry Bleeze, it's fairly easy to explain what was going on but the next example throws up more questions than it provides answers.

Charles Lewington (plate 34) was born in 1839 in Eversley in Hampshire. He grew up in a number of different parishes on the Hampshire/Berkshire border as his agricultural labourer father moved around in search of work. In the 1851 census he was living with his family in Hartley Wintney and his place of birth was then correctly given as Hampshire, Eversley (HO 107/1680, folio 247, page 26). By the time of the 1871 census, Charles was married and living in the parish of Wrockwardine in Shropshire (RG 10/2808, folio 138, page 16). The other details in the census (his name, age and occupation) tie in precisely with what we know about him – all of which makes it very difficult to explain why his birthplace was entered as 'Warwickshire'.

But it gets even stranger: ten years later, by which time the Lewington family had moved to Liverpool, Charles gives his place of birth as 'Shropshire, Walton' (RG 11/3714, folio 50, page 40). In 1891 he reverts to the correct 'Hampshire, Eversley' while the 1901 census records his birthplace simply as 'London' (RG 12/3001, folio 101, page 22; RG 13/3450, folio 64, page 14). But he still has one more trick up his sleeve: in the 1911 census, in what must surely be his own handwriting, he gives his place of birth as 'Eversley, Essex'! (RG 14/22353, schedule 217).

This remarkable variety of birthplaces is by no means commonplace – you'd be unlucky to come across something as extreme as this in your research, but it serves to drive home a crucial point. Namely, that there is really no telling what you might find in the census returns, and that you sometimes just have to make the most of what you do find and try to work your way around the obstacles that are placed in your way. You need to find your ancestors in each of the censuses so that you can start to see the patterns in the data and, hopefully, identify the 'rogue' entries.

The examples outlined above are merely representative of the errors and inconsistencies that you might encounter: it would be impossible to cover every eventuality. Once you accept the fact that the census returns are not the model of accuracy that we'd like them to be, and train yourself to look at every piece of information they throw up with a critical eye, you'll find that the problems you had in tracking down those elusive ancestors start to fade away.

Case study 5 – The Darwins

Traditionally, family historians carry out their research backwards. We start from the present and work into the past: from the known to the unknown. However, census returns can also be used by biographers and historians to tell their stories in a chronological timeframe, working forward in time.

The family of Charles Darwin (plate 32), the scientist and evolutionary biologist, provides a good example of how this can be put into practice to tell the story of your own ancestors.

Charles Robert Darwin was born in the parish of St Chad's, Shrewsbury, in 1809. He attended the local grammar school before studying medicine at Edinburgh University and graduating from Christ's College, Cambridge, in 1831. In the same year Darwin accepted an invitation to join the HMSBeagle on its expedition to chart the coast of South America. The voyage lasted nearly five years and the events experienced by the young naturalist in the course of the expedition were to fundamentally change the way we look at the world around us. A few years after his return to England, Darwin married his cousin Emma Wedgwood and the young couple moved into a house in London.

But all of this took place before our story begins on Sunday 6 June 1841, the night of the 1841 census. Charles and Emma's second child, Annie, had been born three months earlier and in May the whole family had travelled to the Wedgwood family home at Maer in Staffordshire for Annie's christening. So at the time of the 1841 census, rather than being listed at home in Upper Gower Street in London, the Darwins were living with the in-laws at Maer Houses (HO 107/989/3, folio 3, page 1).

The Darwin/Wedgwood family tree is remarkably involved – complicated as it is by a succession of first and second cousin marriages. Staying at Maer House that night were five Wedgwood cousins, the four members of the Darwin family (Charles, Emma and the children William and Annie) and a whole host of servants including Darwin's butler, Joseph Parslow, and a young female servant named Elizabeth Harding. The head of the house (although not actually described as such in the 1841 census) was Josiah Wedgwood, Emma's father and the son of the famous potter.

The following year the Darwins moved to Down House in Kent, which was to be the family home for the rest of their lives. The story of Annie and Henrietta Darwin's absence from the 1851 census is told in Chapter 4. The rest of the family were properly recorded but are split between three different locations.

After settling Annie and Etty into their lodgings in Great Malvern, Charles returned to London and is listed in the census (as C.R. Darwin) at the house of his brother, Erasmus, in Park Street, Mayfair (HO 107/1476, folio 240, page 12; plate 33). Emma, meanwhile, was at Down House together with the four youngest children, George, Elizabeth, Francis and Leonard, and a number of servants, including Parslow the butler, Elizabeth Harding (now described as a 'House Maid') and a young kitchen maid named Margaret Evans (HO 107/1606, folio 247, page 5). Finally, the Darwin's oldest child, William, was at a boarding school in Mitcham, Surrey, preparing for his Public School entrance examinations (HO 107/1602, folio 115, page 11).

The situation in 1861 was much less complex. Charles, Emma and their seven surviving children were all living at Down House together with the usual bevy of servants (RG 9/462, folio 74, page 10). Joseph Parslow and Margaret Evans are both listed, the latter having risen in station to become the family's cook. Also among the servants is Parslow's daughter Ann.

In 1871, Charles was once more staying with his brother in London, but this time he was accompanied by Emma and four of the children: Henrietta, Elizabeth, Francis and Horace (RG 10/157, folio 81, page 16). Ann Parslow had travelled with the Darwins as Emma's lady's maid, while Ann's father, with the assistance of Margaret Evans (now the housekeeper) and four other servants, was left in charge of Down House (RG 10/875, folio 34, page 2).

The three remaining boys were by now making their own way in the world, each following their chosen profession. William was already in business as a banker in Southampton (RG 10/1201, folio 65, page 11), while George (a law student) was living in lodgings in London (RG 10/100, folio 57, page 4). Leonard had joined the army and was at the School of Military Engineering in Gillingham, where he is listed as a Lieutenant in the Royal Engineers (RG 10/913, folio 25, page 6).

The 1881 census finds the Darwins once more back at the family home, where no fewer than 21 people are listed. The household comprised Charles and Emma, five of their children, a daughter-in-law, a grandson, a cousin, a niece (actually Emma's niece) and her husband (described as a visitor), eight servants and, finally, another visitor, described as a 'Ladies Maid' (RG 11/855, folio 83, page 1). The youngest daughter Elizabeth, who never married and was a permanent inhabitant of Down House, is listed immediately after her parents, followed by the oldest son William and his American wife Sara. Next comes George, now a fully qualified barrister, and the recently widowed Francis with his young son Bernard (who was later to become the golf correspondent for The Times newspaper). Rose Frank was the daughter of Emma's brother Francis Wedgwood and just happened to be visiting the Darwins at the time of the 1881 census with her husband Herman.

The next inhabitant in the household was Charles Wood Fox, a cousin on the Darwin side. He was followed by the servants, including, once more, Margaret Evans, now aged 49 and with at least thirty years' service with the family. Joseph Parslow, Darwin's butler, friend and confidant, retired in 1875 but stayed close to the family and, in 1881, is living in the village of Downe (RG 11/855, folio 85, page 6). Harriet Wells is listed as a visitor, but her occupation is given as 'Ladies Maid' – she was in fact in the employ of William and Sara Darwin. The final name listed in the household is, somewhat surprisingly, that of Leonard Darwin, Charles and Emma's fourth son. It's impossible to say for certain why he was listed here at the foot of the schedule and not with the other family members – it may be that he had turned up at Down House unexpectedly, sometime after the form had been completed, and his details were simply added at the bottom of the householder's schedule.

Horace Darwin, the youngest surviving son, was visiting his uncle Erasmus together with his wife Emma (RG 11/140, folio 47, page 1). Henrietta was also in London, living nearby in Marylebone with her husband, Richard Litchfield (RG 11/146, folio 24, page 41).

Charles died the following year at Down House, aged 73, but the Darwin connection with the old family home continued for sometime afterwards. Charles and Emma's second son, George, moved in with his young family and is listed at Down in the 1891 census (RG 12/631, folio 38, page 18).

The remaining members of the Darwin family dispersed to various parts of the country. The stories of their families can be told using the later Victorian and Edwardian censuses.

Case study 6 – The Welsh question

Between 1841 and 1881 the layout of the schedules issued to householders in Wales was identical to that of the forms used in England. However, from 1851 a version of the schedule printed in Welsh was available for enumerators to give to those who were unable to understand English. From 1871 the enumerators were asked to indicate which schedules had been completed in Welsh by writing a 'W' underneath the schedule number in the summary book. They were also asked to enter the total number of forms completed in Welsh on page 4 of the book.

The questions asked on the census returns had always been about social demography and medical health, so the addition of a question on the Scottish census in 1881 about the use of the Gaelic language, and an equivalent question about the Welsh language in 1891, can be seen as significant departures. Both questions were introduced as the result of lobbying by special interest groups, within and outside Parliament.

The 'Welsh' question was only asked in Wales and Monmouthshire, but was supposed to be answered by all inhabitants of those areas. The wording of the question ('If only English, write "English"; if only Welsh, write "Welsh"; if English and Welsh, write "Both"') left plenty of room for misunderstanding, and the accuracy and reliability of many of the answers should be questioned. Take, for example, the Davies family from the village of Castell in Llanbedr-y-Cennin, Caernarvonshire: according to their entry in the 1891 census, the head of the household, Evan Davies, spoke Welsh while his Liverpool-born wife Jane spoke English (RG 12/4671, folio 52, page 3; plate 35). It may well be that Evan 'habitually' spoke Welsh while Jane was more fluent in English, but the correct entry for Evan (if not for Jane) must surely have been 'Both' – which indeed was the case for all of their children. In the 1901 census, the same information is given: 'Welsh' for Evan and 'English' for Jane, but this time their daughter Eveline is also shown as speaking Welsh only (RG 13/5287, folio 22, page 2).

It is clear that many householders did not understand how to answer the new question and the authorities were well aware of the problems facing them in interpreting and using the data that was gathered. The official 1891 census report stated that 'abundant evidence was received by us that it was either misunderstood or set at naught by a large number of those Welshmen who could speak both languages, and that the word "Welsh" was very often returned, when the proper entry would have been "Both"; on the ground, it may be presumed that Welsh was the language spoken habitually or preferentially'. The report went on to suggest that the figures may even have been deliberately falsified by some householders in order to 'add to the number of monoglot Welshmen'. Brydges Henniker, the Registrar General, was later forced to issue an apology, retracting this allegation (Census of England and Wales, 1891, General Report, vol. IV, 1891, p. 81).

There was also, perhaps understandably, a concern about the number of Welsh children who were entered as speaking Welsh only, when English was compulsorily taught at schools.

The language question was repeated (with some refinement) in the 1901 and 1911 censuses – the 1901 Census Act clarified the point that the data should only be gathered for those aged three years or upwards. Despite the concerns about the 'quality' of the answers, there is no doubt that this is a useful piece of additional information for those of us with Welsh ancestry, and it's interesting to be able to compare the details for our ancestors over three successive censuses.

John Richards, a coal miner from Pembrokeshire, was living in Merthyr Tydfil in 1911 with his wife Margaret Jane (née Lewis) and their six children. The census tells us that they had been married for 15 years (confirmed by an entry in the GRO's marriage index for the September quarter of 1895) and that the marriage had produced nine children, three of whom had died. We also learn that John and the children spoke English while Margaret could speak both Welsh and English (RG 14/32439, schedule 89). This information is confirmed in the 1901 census where we also discover one of the three children who sadly didn't survive infancy: a one-month-old boy called Martin Luther Richards.

According to the 1891 census, Margaret Jane's parents were, like her, able to speak both languages and perhaps her children grew up to speak some Welsh but the trend towards the dominance of the English language seemed unstoppable at the time.

It would be difficult to argue that the inclusion of the language question in the census returns played a significant role in the battle for the survival of Welsh as a living language, but it certainly helped to draw attention to the very real fear that the Welsh language might go the same way as its Cornish cousin and disappear altogether. The contemporary statistics certainly support the idea that this was a genuine possibility: while still questioning the reliability of the data, the official 1901 census report suggested that the number of people speaking Welsh only had fallen from 30 per cent in 1891 to 15 per cent in just ten years.

Thankfully the threat has long since passed and Welsh is now once more a thriving, living language.

5

THE CENSUS ONLINE

In April 2006, within a few days of each other, ScotlandsPeople and Ancestry announced that they had placed indexes to the 1841 census (for Scotland, and for England and Wales, respectively) online. This meant that, for the first time, all the released censuses (up to 1901) for England, Wales and Scotland were available in digital form to anyone with an internet connection. In 2009, these were joined by the 1911 census for England and Wales, and in April 2011 the 1911 census for Scotland came online. Finally, in May 2012, the digitisation of the Irish censuses was completed, making all the surviving censuses for the whole of the British Isles available online, by far the largest national dataset to be available in its entirety.

Since the advent of personal computers, family historians had dreamt of having the censuses in digital form so that they could be easily searched. As early as 1982 the Berkshire Family History Society had a project for transcribing the 1851 census using the BBC Model B computer.[1]

In fact the country's first census digitisation project lies even further back. Between 1972 and 1977, there was a research project based in the Sociology Department at the University of Edinburgh, which aimed to 'explore various salient aspects of the nineteenth century social and economic structure'. This involved the creation of a two per cent sample of the 1851 census (using one enumeration book in every 50). The data was not compiled for the benefit of family historians and was not orig- inally available outside the academic community. However, in about

---

1   C Bingley, 'Data Entry for Census Transcription' in *Computers in Genealogy*, Vol. 1, No. 3 (March 1983) pp. 60–63.

1995 it was made publicly available for download on a well-known genealogy server, albeit without the permission of those involved in the project, and started to be used by genealogists.[2] It was subsequently legally licensed for publication on CD-ROM and then online, and is still available, though it has largely been made redundant by more recent indexes to the full 1851 census.

Family history societies initially created census indexes to provide look-up services for their members, but soon started to publish these indexes commercially. At first these were in print, but later, with the development of CD-ROM, in digital form. The most impressive result of this development was the volunteer transcription project which created the 1881 Census Index, a combined effort by the Genealogical Society of Utah and the Federation of Family History Societies (FFHS). This led to the first publication, on microfiche, then on CD-ROM, of a complete national dataset for a single census year.

By the second half of the 1990s, record offices and family history societies were starting to have a presence on the Web, and in 2001 official census datasets started to appear online. In April of that year The National Archives (or Public Record Office, as it then was) launched an index and images for the 1891 census of Norfolk as a pilot for the subsequent 1901 census. In August, Scots Origins, launched three years earlier as a pay-per-view service for the Scottish civil registration data, added the 1891 census for Scotland to its datasets.

The most momentous event in the development of online census services was the launch in January 2002 of the 1901 census for England and Wales, digitised in a partnership between The National Archives — then still called the Public Record Office (PRO) — and the defence contractor QinetiQ. Unfortunately, it was, initially at least, dogged by problems. From the start of the project, there had been scepticism from the genealogical community about the likely quality of the indexing, and these misgivings turned out to be well-founded — the indexes contained a host of

---

2 A formal description of the project will be found on the UK Data Archive website at <**discover.ukdataservice.ac.uk/catalogue?sn=1316**>. Rosemary Lockie's article, 'The 2% 1851 Census Sample', in *Computers in Genealogy*, Vol. 5, No. 3 (Sept 1994), pp. 109–122 is probably the earliest published description of this material from a genealogist's point of view.

obvious and entirely avoidable errors.[3] The main issue was not with the content but with the popularity of the site: the unprecedented level of demand had not been adequately planned for and the service had to be withdrawn within five days because it could not cope with the load. It was November 2002 before the service was fully up and running. The National Audit Office's report, *Unlocking the Past: The 1901 Census Online* at <www.nao.org.uk/report/unlocking-the-past-the-1901-census-online/> analysed the problems and helped ensure that the launch of the 1911 census went without a hitch.

It is now strange to remember that the PRO came in for a lot of criticism at the time for prioritising online availability, now accepted as the norm. However, the overwhelming popularity of the 1901 census proved beyond doubt the huge market for online census indexes and images, and September 2002 saw the first commercial subscription service when Ancestry launched its UK data service at <www.ancestry.co.uk> with the 1891 census for England and Wales. Since then we have seen the development of a number of commercial sites offering census indexes and images.

While launching a commercial service was not a realistic prospect for local family history societies at this period, their census indexes (without images) were made accessible online with the launch of the FFHS's FamilyHistoryOnline pay-per-view service at the start of 2003. By 2009, though, the Federation was finding that the site could not be operated competitively, no doubt because all the censuses for the whole of the UK were now available elsewhere, and closed the site. Most of the societies moved their indexes to other commercial services.

Originally, under the 100-year confidentiality convention, the 1911 census for England and Wales was not expected to come online until the start of 2012. However, in 2006, after The National Archives had initially refused a Freedom of Information request from Guy Etchells, the Information Commissioner ruled that, as long as 'key sensitive information' was concealed, there was no reason why the records could

---

3   For example, Jeanne Bunting discovered 39 people with the surname Ditto, including Ada Ditto, born in Ditto Ditto — see <listsearches.rootsweb.com/th/read/SOG-UK/2002-01/1010018139>. The list archives for the UK-1901-CENSUS mailing list at <archiver.rootsweb.ancestry.com/th/index/UK-1901-CENSUS/> provide a record of initial reactions to the 1901 census.

not be made available. The National Archives decided more or less immediately that it would digitise the whole 1911 census for release in 2009 and the contract for the project was awarded to Scotland Online. The official 1911 Census site at <**www.1911census.co.uk**> was launched with an initial batch of counties in January 2009 and the material was complete by June of that year. In the initial release, the contents of the infirmity column were blocked out, in line with the Information Commissioner's ruling, but in 2012 this became visible. Scotland's different privacy legislation meant that there was no basis for an equivalent challenge north of the border, and the Scottish 1911 census went online, as expected, 100 years after the census, in April 2011.

There have been attempts to get the government to release later censuses, but these have been firmly rebuffed in the UK as conflicting with the original census legislation. However, the Irish government has undertaken to release the 1926 census of Ireland in time for the centenary of the Easter Rising. This promise is discussed in more detail at the end of Chapter 15.

It wasn't until 2003 that any significant amount of *free* census data was available on the Web, when the 1881 Census Index (albeit for England and Wales only) was finally added to FamilySearch at <**www. familysearch.org**>, the family history site run by the Church of Jesus Christ of Latter-day Saints (the LDS Church). The same year saw the launch of county-based indexes for the 1891 census by FreeCEN, a project started in 1998 to harness the efforts of volunteer transcribers to provide free census data. Another non-commercial outlet for volunteer census indexing is provided by FHS Online, a largely free service operated by S&N Genealogy, the company behind the commercial site TheGenealogist, which hosts free indexes for individual counties and years compiled by family history societies.

There has also been a major contribution to free census indexes from an official source: in 2007 The National Archives of Ireland, with support from Library and Archives Canada, set up a free site which initially provided an index and images for the 1911 census of Dublin. Over the following five years all records from the two Irish censuses which survive in their entirety, 1901 and 1911, were added, and in 2014 the surviving fragments of the pre-1901 census.

In general there has been a clear separation between the commercial sites and the volunteer projects, but a significant development took place in July 2008. FamilySearch's pilot for its Record Search site (now FamilySearch at <**www.familysearch.org**>) started to offer free of charge the 1841 and 1861 census indexes from Origins and Findmypast with links to the images at Findmypast. Further censuses have subsequently been added to FamilySearch under the same arrangement. Conversely, commercial services have started to license the free Irish census indexes. While for most people there may well be no incentive to use these rather than the free Irish government site, this development does mean that commercial services can offer census searches covering the *whole* of the British Isles, something no national official site can do.

Table 5.1 gives a timeline of the most important developments in the online provision of census records for the UK and Ireland (based on Genuki's British Isles Genealogy on the Internet Timeline at <**homepages.gold.ac.uk/genuki/timeline/**>).

	1995	Two per cent sample of 1851 census available for download by FTP
April	2001	The National Archives' 1891 census pilot goes live
August	2001	Scots Origins launches first Scottish census data
January	2002	1901 census site launched and almost immediately suspended
September	2002	Ancestry.co.uk launched with 1891 census
November	2002	1901 census finally fully operational
January	2003	Launch of FamilyHistoryOnline, with census indexes from family history societies
February	2003	1881 census index added to FamilySearch
July	2003	Launch of FreeCEN search engine with 1891 census transcriptions
November	2003	National Audit Office report on 1901 census
December	2004	The National Archives and Ancestry.co.uk launch 1881 and 1891 census indexes under the Licensed Internet Associateship initiative
February	2005	1837online (now Findmypast) launches 1861 census index and images
March	2005	1841 census launched on British Origins
August	2005	QinetiQ sells 1901 census service to Genes Reunited

December	2005	Agreement between The National Archives of Ireland and Library and Archives Canada to digitise Irish census records for 1901 and 1911
April	2006	ScotlandsPeople release the 1841 census index and images for Scotland; Ancestry release the 1841 census index for England and Wales; all censuses for England, Wales and Scotland 1841–1901 are now available online
December	2006	In response to a Freedom of Information ruling, The National Archives announce that the 1911 census will be available online from 2009 rather than 2012
March	2007	An online petition to reduce the classified period for census data from 100 years to 70 years closes with 23,602 signatories
December	2007	Irish 1911 census for Dublin goes online at the official National Archives of Ireland site
July	2008	GROS reveals that Scottish census data will no longer be exclusive to ScotlandsPeople
July	2008	FamilySearch, Findmypast and Origins announce a joint project to make UK census indexes available on FamilySearch and at Family History Centres
January	2009	Launch of the 1911 census for England and Wales
March	2009	Closure of FamilyHistoryOnline
November	2010	Ancestry and TheGenealogist announce joint project to make the 1911 census available on their sites
March	2011	Irish government makes a commitment to release and digitise the 1926 census as part of the commemoration of the 1916 Easter Rising
April	2011	The 1911 census for Scotland released on ScotlandsPeople
May	2012	Irish digitisation of 1901 and 1911 censuses completed
April	2014	Census Search Forms and surviving pre-1901 census fragments added to official Irish census site

Table 5.1 Timeline: the census online.

What's online

The websites offering census data can be classified in two ways: Is the data free or charged? Is the coverage local or national?

Free

There are three free sites with national data:

- FamilySearch at <www.familysearch.org> has indexes for all the censuses for England and Wales, along with those for Scotland 1841–1891, with links to commercially available images on Findmypast.
- FreeCEN at <www.freecen.org.uk> has indexes to censuses for England and Wales in progress, covering 1841–1871 and 1891.
- The National Archives of Ireland have a free site at <www.census.nationalarchives.ie> with the Irish 1901 and 1911 censuses, along with surviving fragments of earlier censuses.

There are many sites maintained by individuals or volunteer groups with local data, some with scope as small as a single village. The only major site with a range of individual local datasets is FHS Online at <www.fhs-online.co.uk>, which has free census indexes sourced from individual family history societies.

The free sites are covered in Chapter 7, apart from those for Ireland, which are described in Chapter 15.

Charged

There are currently five main commercial providers of national census datasets, all of whom are involved in digitisation:

- Ancestry at <www.ancestry.co.uk> — see Chapter 8;
- Findmypast at <www.findmypast.com> — see Chapter 9 — which also runs Genes Reunited at <www.genesreunited.com> (see Chapter 12); in addition, the company is responsible for the official 1901 and 1911 census sites at <www.1901censusonline.com> and <www.1911census.co.uk> respectively;
- S&N Genealogy Supplies, who have three sites: TheGenealogist at <www.thegenealogist.co.uk>, RootsUK at <www.rootsUK.com> and UK Census Online at <www.ukcensusonline.com> — see Chapter 10;

- Origins at <**www.origins.net**> — see Chapter 11;
- ScotlandsPeople at <**www.scotlandspeople.gov.uk**> — see Chapter 14.

MyHeritage and WorldVitalRecords (see Chapter 13) have not been involved in census digitisation but have licensed indexes from Findmypast and Origins. Findmypast and Origins have cross-licensed some of their datasets, and these two sites have identical census indexes for England and Wales, 1841, 1861 and 1871.

There is currently no commercial data service with only local census data, but FHS Online, mentioned above, has a small amount of charged material for individual counties.

There is also a site, **1901census.com**, which gives the impression of holding a complete set of census indexes, but in fact it just offers click-through to Ancestry's UK site.

How it's done

The original census records are held by The National Archives (TNA), The National Records of Scotland (NRS), and The National Archives of Ireland (NAI). For all the nineteenth-century censuses, these bodies have microform copies of the enumeration books, and these photo-graphic images have formed the basis of all the recent digitisations prior to the 1911 census. This was the first where the digital images were created directly from the original paper records rather than from microfilm.

The National Archives has taken three different approaches to the digitisation of census records. The 1901 and 1911 censuses have been digitised through a partnership with commercial companies, QinetiQ and Brightsolid (formerly Scotland Online) respectively. The result in each case is a website run by the company on behalf of TNA. TNA also offers what it calls 'Licensed Internet Associateships' (LIA), where a commercial data service carries out the digitisation and places the data on its own site, but the material is 'co-branded' and the company is assisted and promoted by TNA. For example, the census page on TNA's website at <**www.nationalarchives.gov.uk/census**> has links to the census data at Ancestry (see Chapter 8), which is so far the only company to have an LIA for census records. TNA gets free access at Kew for its users. Finally TNA permits companies to purchase copies of the digital images. While there is a potential conflict between conducting an official digitisation with a single commercial partner and allowing other companies to digitise the same material, which might undermine the financial viability of the official project, TNA have given the official projects a six-month monopoly before opening the material up to competitors.

In Scotland, the situation has been rather different. The General Register Office for Scotland (GROS), now part of National Records of Scotland (NRS), had an exclusive arrangement with a commercial provider for its data, making Scottish census records available on only one site, initially Scots Origins and then ScotlandsPeople (see Chapter 14). In fact the Scottish government has kept tight control over this service, and even minor changes to the way the service operates, such as how long pay-per-view credits remain valid, have to receive government approval via a Statutory Instrument.[4]

In July 2008 it was reported in the press that GROS would be granting licences to other commercial data services to provide indexes and images for the Scottish census.[5] As the first edition of this book went to press a spokesman for the Scottish government confirmed to us that: 'GROS anticipates that two possibilities will exist: a licence to enable a company to use digital images and indexes already created by GROS; and a licence that would enable a company to make digital images and indexes of the original records (most likely from microfilm).' In fact, at that point Ancestry had already created its own indexes to the Scottish censuses, apparently without GROS approval. In 2011 Findmypast also started adding Scottish census indexes to its datasets. Even though Findmypast and ScotlandsPeople are run by the same company, Findmypast's Scottish census indexes are quite separate and, like Ancestry, Findmypast has no census images for Scotland. The Scottish

---

4 You will find a description of the process in the minutes of the ScotlandsPeople User Group at <**www.scotlandspeople.gov.uk/content/images/1st%20UG%20 Meeting%20Minutes.pdf**>.

5 'Licence sale may mean money doesn't grow on family trees', *Sunday Herald*, 6 July 2008, most easily found by searching the paper's website at <**www. sundayherald.com**>.

census indexes on FamilySearch are licensed from Findmypast and are therefore also without images.

While the 2008 news had raised hopes that this situation would improve, there has been no subsequent announcement on the matter, as far as we have been able to determine. However, in response to a query from the authors, NRS have now confirmed that a decision was made to permit the creation of new census indexes (under a free license), but not to allow the licensing of census images. The rationale for this, we were informed, lies in NRS's aim of 'increasing the financial payback to the taxpayer from past investment in digitising the images of the census'. Of course, this *might* make economic sense for the Scottish government (though it would surely depend on the level of licensing fees), but, even so, it is a disappointing result from the family historian's point of view. Regardless of one's political stance on state monopolies in the commercial exploitation of public records, the one major failing of the census records on ScotlandsPeople is the poor quality, by present-day standards, of the earlier digital images. If economics are exclusively allowed to determine the matter, there might never be any motivation to remedy this. In contrast, almost all the earliest census images made available on commercial sites have been replaced at least once with superior quality scans, to match the improvements in technology and the demands of users.

In Ireland, again, the situation has been quite different. The NAI were well behind the other national archives in the British Isles in digitising census, or indeed any other genealogical records. A few small extracts appeared on commercial data services, but otherwise the commercial providers have played no significant role in getting these records online. On the contrary, the single major project has remained entirely under the control of the official repository, the NAI, and the partnership has been with another national archive, Library and Archives Canada, whose interest lay in serving the needs of Canadian family historians with Irish roots. The result is that the NAI has its own census data service as part of its own website, offering indexes and images for the whole of Ireland free of charge (see Chapter 15). Since all the available material is now freely accessible, there is no motive for alternative digitisations, though there have been some independent volunteer-based indexing projects.

Access

While there are still many census records available on microfilm or CD (see Chapters 16 and 17), the most recently released censuses, 1901 and 1911 for the UK, are mainly or entirely online resources (the 1901 census had limited release on microfiche). The majority of family historians will have access to the internet at home, but if you haven't got your own computer or internet connection, there is still no reason why you shouldn't have access to these online resources: you should be able to access the free sites from any public access computer with an internet connection. It's true that some of the commercial services may not be fully usable from a public terminal. The reason for this is that some of them require a specific browser plug-in which you are not likely to find installed on such computers, and whoever is providing the computer will certainly not let you install a new plug-in. However, there are quite a number of places where the publicly accessible computers have been specifically set up for free access to genealogical data.

Several of the data services offer an institutional subscription, which allows public libraries, among others, to provide access free of charge to the individual user from computers on library premises. If you do not have your own internet connection, or if you simply want cheaper, though no doubt less convenient access, it is worth asking at your public library. The information is likely to be given on the library's web page, which will be part of your local authority website. The most widely available service is Ancestry's Library Edition, which includes all of Ancestry's UK census indexes and images. But Findmypast, Origins and TheGenealogist also offer institutional subscriptions which you may find accessible in your public library. You will not need to pay for access to these sites, but the library will charge for any print-outs and may also charge for your time at a computer.

The computer facilities in the first-floor reading room at The National Archives in Kew offers free access to the 1901 and 1911 census data, to Findmypast census data, and to Ancestry's census data for 1841–1891. Neither search results nor images can be saved to a memory stick from these computers, but Ancestry has a facility for emailing a link to any census image (see p. 185).

Family History Centres are the local branches of the LDS Church's Family History Library in Salt Lake City. At the time of writing, The National Archives reading room at Kew is also temporarily home to the London FamilySearch Centre (<**www.londonfhc.org**>), which, since the closure of the long-established facilities in Exhibition Road, has not yet found a permanent home elsewhere. This provides computers with free access to FamilySearch's census indexes for England, Wales and Scotland, and to Findmypast's census images. There is also free access to Ancestry Library Edition. There are facilities to save to a memory stick.

Similar facilities are available in other Family History Centres in the UK and the Republic of Ireland. Details of those which are open to the public are given at <**www.londonfhc.org/content/other-uk-centres**>. (Note that the Outer London Centres in Orpington and Romford are listed on this page under their historic counties of Kent and Essex, respectively.) When planning a visit, it is probably best to contact the individual centre to find out precisely what computer facilities are available to the public.

The computers at the ScotlandsPeople Centre in Edinburgh (<**www. scotlandspeoplehub.gov.uk**>) provide free access to all the records on ScotlandsPeople, though there is a daily search room charge. There are also local ScotlandsPeople Centres in Kilmarnock, Hawick, and the Mitchell Library in Glasgow. Records can be saved to a memory stick.

Finally, in addition to the computer facilities provided for its members, the Society of Genealogists has an open access computer area available to non-members, with free access to Ancestry, Findmypast and Origins. Details will be found at <**www.sog.org.uk/ the-library/open-access-area**>.

Why pay?

When the 1901 census for England and Wales was first released, there was a great deal of concern about the fact that the index was only going to be available online, and at a cost. The general tenor was, 'These are public records — why should we pay to have access to them?' Although a much larger percentage of the population have their own internet access and there is now much more general acceptance of online information delivery and online payment, one still hears grumbles in this vein.

Disregarding the fact that family historians have always had to pay for access to birth, marriage and death certificates, there are two answers.

First, you don't have to pay to access them. The National Archives provides free access at Kew to online indexes for every census year; and, as just mentioned, many public libraries have access to one or more genealogical data services, normally free of charge. Alternatively, the microfilms for the nineteenth-century censuses are widely accessible — the LDS Church's Family History Centres have complete sets for the British Isles and these can be viewed free of charge. Central libraries, local studies centres and county record offices often have the microfilms for their own catchment area. (Census microfilms are discussed in detail in Chapter 17.)

But of course, you have to pay for your travel to Kew or a Family History Centre, and you have to take the extra time out of your schedule to do so. In fact, it makes little sense to complain about paying for online access but be happy to pay the same amount for public transport or for petrol and parking. At least with online access, the money goes to organisations making genealogical data available, with licence fees to the archives holding the original records.

Creating an online census is a massive and expensive undertaking. The 1881 Census Index took 9,000 volunteers (admittedly not working full-time) six and a half years to create, and that was without scanning the images and linking each image to all the matching index entries. FreeCEN has been running since 1998 and has almost 25 million records, but that's equivalent to just one nineteenth-century census (the population of England and Wales in 1871 was 25,974,439). In half that time, commercial data services have managed to digitise *all* the available censuses for England, Wales and Scotland, with over 230 million records for named individuals. It is only the commercial exploitation of census records that has allowed the whole body of them to be put online within a ten-year period.

For many people in fact, regardless of the expense, the availability of genealogical data on the Web from home at any time of day or night, regardless of distance from a national repository, is the only thing that makes progress with their family tree possible at all.

Technical requirements

While the volunteer-based indexes do not require any particular software or computer set-up, all the commercial census sites have some technical requirements, and it is as well to be aware of these before you start to use them for serious genealogical research.

First, like other types of commercial websites, they require cookies to be enabled. A cookie is a small text file that is stored on your computer to keep information about your connection to a site. Some people prefer, as a security measure, to set their browser to block cookies. But there is no good reason to block cookies from reputable genealogy sites and blocking them will make it impossible to use the commercial census data services. If you are worried about cookies in general, you can always switch cookies on while you use such a site and then turn them off again afterwards, and your browser will offer various ways to restrict the functionality of cookies. Cookie settings are mostly found under the heading 'Privacy' in your browser's Options menu.

Web browsers come with built-in facilities to view certain types of digital image, but have very limited facilities for anything other than basic viewing, saving or printing. For this reason, the data services generally do not provide unadorned images in these standard formats; they either use special formats or offer enhanced image viewing facilities via a dedicated image viewer. Both of these options mean that you will in some cases have to install some sort of browser plug-in before you can view the images. Brief information is given in the relevant chapters, but all the sites that use plug-ins have detailed help on viewing their census images.

One of the most common plug-ins, and one required for many other websites, is the Adobe Acrobat reader for displaying documents in PDF format. If you have not already got the Adobe Reader installed on your computer, you will need to download it from <**www.adobe.com/ products/acrobat/readstep2.html**> and install it. It will normally install automatically in your browser, so that, without any intervention on your part, your browser will use the reader to display any PDF file you encounter.

Indexing issues

The problems inherent in the census records themselves have already been highlighted in Chapter 4, but if you are consulting digitised census records there are additional issues to consider. How these affect the actual practice of searching for the census records of individual ancestors will be discussed in the following chapter, but the main issues are reviewed here to draw attention to some important limitations in online census material.

One preliminary matter, which is often overlooked, is the distinction between a transcription and an index. A transcription is an exact representation of the text of the original document; an index is a finding aid. The job of a transcription is to be accurate; the job of an index is to be helpful, to point you to the correct place in a transcription, or to the right image. If an index has to 'correct' a transcription in order to do its job, that is perfectly acceptable. Any correction of a transcription, however, is not really a 'correction' at all but rather a distortion which makes it less of a transcription.

You can see the difference between a transcription and an index if you imagine that we are looking for Charles Smith, born in Surrey. His census entry might well be 'Chas Smith, birthplace Surry'. If we have to search for Chas and Surry to find him, then we are searching a transcription, if we can find him by looking for Charles Smith, Surrey, we are searching an index. In principle, there is no reason why one could not have just an index. On the other hand, a transcription on its own, without a separate index, will bring significant difficulties.

The reason for labouring this point is that the commercial data sites, in particular, aren't always clear on the distinction. Indeed, to be pedantic, no site gives a 100 per cent accurate transcription of any census entry, and for one simple reason: in the original records, the gender of an individual is not represented by a word or mark, but is indicated by the column in which the age is placed. For very sound reasons, no commercial site attempts to reproduce this way of indicating gender. Another thing they, properly, don't do —most of the time, anyway —is transcribe literally the *dittos* used for repeated surnames and birthplaces.

All transcriptions of historical records are prone to error, and expecting a census index of 30 million or so records to be anything approaching error-free is completely unrealistic. With datasets of this size, even a very low error rate still means lots of individual errors: a one per cent error rate is well beyond anything currently achieved by the online indexes — it would mean that in every three or four pages from an enumeration book, at most a *single* entry contains an error. But even this unattainable target would leave 300,000 people potentially unfindable in 30 million records. Although it is certainly possible for the currently available transcriptions to be better than they are, it is obvious that having transcriptions done by better qualified people and instituting higher levels of quality control would add to the cost of digitization. Would you pay twice as much to consult data that was two or three per cent more accurate? Probably not. If you would, then you can effectively do so by using more than one census index. Of course, *some* identical errors may be found in two different census indexes, but they will tend to be the ones where the original document is problematic anyway.

Indecipherable text

Often, an 'error' is not really the fault of the transcriber — there are plenty of pages in the enumeration books where, with the best will in the world, a letter or a word is impossible to decipher with any certainty. The 1841 census in particular has many pages which, even with the best modern photographic or digital enhancement, are difficult to read and impossible to transcribe definitively.

The question is how to deal with these problematic entries. The 'proper' course is that taken in the professional editing of historical documents: to indicate the position of the indecipherable letters, with suggested readings, which are, after all, interpretations rather than transcriptions, consigned to notes. With a clear distinction between transcription and index, an index can then contain entries for several possible readings of an indecipherable name.

The problem is that the online censuses all offer a poor substitute: the 'best guess'. Given that this is the best guess of someone with almost certainly no professional palaeographic skills and probably little familiarity with the surnames and place names common in a particular area of the country, there is no reason to put any faith in such guesses.

(The exception would be the 1881 Census Index, where the records were transcribed by volunteers from local family history societies. To be fair, however, we are not aware of any study that actually demonstrates the superiority of this index in the indexing of, for example, birth places.) Of course, given the potential costs in both time and money of better solutions, the 'best guess' approach is understandable, perhaps even inevitable. Of the major data services, only Findmypast seems to mark indecipherable letters as such, using a question mark.

However, one or two hard-to-decipher letters may not make someone unfindable. All the commercial services have, at least for forenames and surnames, name-matching facilities that allow a certain amount of leeway and therefore can identify near-misses as well as exact matches. These facilities are discussed in general in the following chapter and as part of the coverage of the individual data services' search facilities in later chapters.

Lack of validation

One of the key techniques for ensuring the accuracy of items of data in a database is 'validation'. This means making sure that a piece of information in an index is, if not demonstrably correct, at least plausible. With types of information that can be looked up, this is easily done: there are only so many counties in the British Isles at any one time, and we know what they are. It is therefore trivial to check that text entered in a 'County' field is the correctly spelled name of a valid county. Of course, the original document may indeed include an invalid county or a misspelling of the name, which in a transcription one would want to preserve. But identifying the oddity would be a signal to check whether the error was in the original or arose in the transcription process.

It's more problematic with the town and village names given in the birthplace field, but again we have gazetteers against which these can be checked, with unrecognized entries at least flagged, if not manually corrected. For example, in several of the indexes we have noticed people born in *Parkmouth, Hampshire*. It doesn't take long to establish that there is no such place, and so far we have not come across a single one which is not, as you might expect, a misreading of Portsmouth (though *Parkmouth, Devon* is a not infrequent mistake for Plymouth). Some of these are indeed hard to read and one can appreciate the reason for the initial error. But the fact that there was a potential error here could easily have been spotted by validation against a gazetteer.

When the 1901 census for England and Wales was digitised, there was no adequate validation implemented for the age column. The result was a census index which initially had dozens of people who appeared to be over 120 years old, in some cases even over 200 years old. It is slightly puzzling that the data entry staff didn't notice this themselves without any prompting, but even so it should not take users to point out this sort of error, which it is trivial to find (if not correct) by an automated process.

Of course, misspellings of names can be very problematic to spot — there's no definitive list against which any spelling can be checked. But is it too much to expect digitisers to check that all their *Willaim*s really are *Willaim* in the original records, or all their many *Geroge*s aren't in reality *George*s?

Sometimes it's not that a single field is self-evidently wrong, but that a particular combination is implausible, suggesting that one field is wrong, and that both need checking. For example, all the census indexes seem to have a lot of girls called John. This would be a fascinating insight into nineteenth-century naming patterns, if it weren't manifest nonsense. Of course we can't be sure there were *no* girls called John in nineteenth-century Britain — there are certainly one or two with *St John* as a middle name — but clearly most such instances will be transcription errors, and the potential inconsistency should prompt manual checking. And of course, it almost always turns out that the gender has been incorrectly entered or the name has been mistranscribed (it's usually *Jane*); often it seems the transcriber has confused data from two different lines on the enumeration form, or misunderstood a correction made by the enumerator. In fact, it would be a trivial matter to scan a database, even a very large one, for inappropriate genders with the ten most common male and female forenames. Even if one does not then manually check every apparent oddity, such entries could be flagged as potentially inconsistent.

While it is not possible to spot wrong ages in general, unless they are implausibly high, the content of other fields may signal the presence of error. For example, Ancestry's census index for 1901 claims to find 3,096 individuals aged ten or under who are heads of household. However, before you shed a tear for poor little Louisa M. Jeffreys, aged two, sole member of her own household in Islington, you need to realise that she is in fact a *seventy*-two-year-old widow living on her own means (RG 13/198, folio 40, page 17).

Accuracy

While it is important to appreciate that both the problems with the source records and the constraints on the transcription process limit the accuracy of the online indexes, the practical questions are: what are the main sorts of error? What degree of accuracy will we find, both in general and in particular census indexes? The answers to these questions can indicate why searches will sometimes fail and suggest ways of getting round the indexing problems which give rise to them.

Unfortunately, neither question is easy to answer. The main issue is that it is impossible, in the absence of a major research grant and several years' work, to capture a significantly large and representative sample from all the census indexes for all the census years to draw any reliable conclusions about the levels of accuracy. This means, inevitably, that all views on inaccuracies are based on anecdotal evidence (usually of particularly crass or amusing mistakes), analysis of tiny and therefore necessarily unrepresentative samples, or very simple diagnostic tests.

The matter is complicated by differences between the various sites' search facilities, which mean that comparative searches can be carried out only for a small selection of the many error types. For example, most of the sites do not allow a search on forename only, which makes it impossible to gather any statistics for their most common forename mis-spellings. Also, many of the mistakes, even though they might be more prevalent in one index or another, are not in any way systematic; they're just a failure to recognise a particular surname or a place name. A problem with tests for surname errors is that a single misreading of the surname of the head of household will propagate to all the other family members (who will have *ditto* instead of the surname), making the number of wrong index entries much greater than the number of mistakes actually made by the transcriber.

At best, it is possible to carry out some specific test searches to identify how often some typical easily-made transcription errors occur and to look in detail at some *very* small samples which can then be treated as benchmarks — they show that the worst indexing must be at least as bad as that found in the sample, even if that is not typical.

Pioneers in this were Jeanne Bunting and John Hanson, who, when the original 1901 census was launched, analysed a complete enumeration book (for Rotherhithe in London) checking for indexing errors. They sent a list of over 900 errors for correction to the PRO. When Ancestry subsequently launched a 1901 census index, this too was checked against the originals. Here is what Jeanne had to say about the comparison:

> The Enumeration District consisted of 33 consecutive pages with 969 people. Just taking surname, first name and place of birth..., we sent in [to the PRO] a total of 378 errors (there were about another 150 occupation errors) made up from 63 first names, 192 surnames and 123 places of birth.[6]

Ancestry, on the other hand, had only 152 errors in total made up from 24 first names, 73 surnames and 55 places of birth.

Although this survey has the limitation of being for a single district (and therefore reflects the work of a single transcriber in each case reading the handwriting of a single enumerator), it does at least suggest what level of error we might expect. The fact that even the better of these two sites had 7.5 per cent of surnames mis-spelled and only 12 per cent of pages error-free is quite alarming. Certainly, while errors on the part of transcribers are inevitable, it is a pity that quality control has not always been as rigorous as it could be.

In an attempt to replicate Jeanne and John's analysis for the wider range of indexes now available, we conducted a similar survey for the first edition of this book in 2008. We carried out a detailed examination of the errors found in the indexes for two complete enumeration districts:

- the 1861 census for Pevensey, Sussex (385 individuals), from a relatively clearly written enumeration book (RG9/566, folios 73–80);

---

6 The original message can be consulted at <**archiver.rootsweb.ancestry.com/th/ read/genbrit/2004-04/1082370575**>. It is the start of a lengthy discussion thread, and a number of other types of error which were found in the comparison are mentioned in later messages.

- the 1891 census for part of Islington, London (496 individuals), the original less clearly written and with some idiosyncrasies to trap the unwary transcriber (RG12/166, folios 35–43).

Our survey looked at the indexes of three commercial sites and the results are shown in the set of tables linked from <**www.spub.co.uk/ census/tables**>. These should not be interpreted as an assessment of the relative merits of the data services examined — each enumeration district represents the work of only a single transcriber and there is no way of knowing how typical his or her level of accuracy is. And the data is certainly not current, since many of the errors in our tables have since been corrected. Nonetheless, the results indicate some general issues with the online indexes.

First, it shows clearly that there are quite a number of irreducible problem entries which are quite beyond anyone's ability to transcribe with any guarantee of accuracy. But even so, the level of error in these samples, no matter how unrepresentative, does suggest some problems in the training of transcribers and shortcomings in quality control. It demonstrates how widely transcription accuracy can vary between different services, different censuses and different enumeration books. It is obvious, too, that the failings of a single transcriber can make a whole host of individuals difficult to find.

For example, it is clear that some transcribers have not understood how to transcribe *ditto* in the surname position: some transcribers take *ditto* to mean not the immediately preceding surname, but the head of the household's surname. The result is that a number of housekeepers, widowed sisters, female lodgers and the like have children who are indexed not as theirs but as the progeny of the householder.

It also highlights the importance of local knowledge. One of the Pevensey transcriptions suggests the presence in the town of people who had moved from two towns further along the Sussex coast, Worthing and Hove. At first sight, this is not implausible, though perhaps it is slightly odd to see people moving from growing towns to a much smaller settlement. But if you know the area and look again at the original page images, you will quickly conclude that these people come not from places 30 or 40 miles away, but from the neighbouring parishes of Wartling and Hooe. One cannot, of course, expect detailed local knowledge in a commercial transcription project, but surely transcribers could have a map or a list of neighbouring localities. In one case, the transcriber could not even spell the name of the enumeration district correctly when it turned up in the birthplace column!

Although the results for the Pevensey and Islington enumeration books are in some cases better than the 7.5 per cent accuracy for surnames found for 1901, in others they are very much worse, with error rates up to 40 per cent.

A second source of information on accuracy is constituted by the corrections submitted by users. Of course, this information is not widely published, but there are two publicly available sources which can be used to assess, if not error-rates, then typical classes of error.

The original 1901 census site published details of all corrections made up to the point where the site was taken over by Genes Reunited in 2005. (At the time of writing, this material is still available on the 1901 census site but we understand that it is due to be removed. We have, therefore, with the permission of the owner, placed a consolidated list of corrections on the website for this book at <**www.spub. co.uk/census**>.)

Some of these corrections simply represent the teething problems of the 1901 census project, but others show the typical transcription errors found in other census indexes. It can be a useful exercise to look through the list for your own surnames of interest to see what might happen to them in transcription.

It's no great surprise that some of the forename errors show entirely predictable confusions between similar names: *Mary* and *May*; *Albert* and *Alfred*; *Alice, Clive* and *Oliver* for *Olive*. Two dozen *Elijahs* appeared originally as *Elizah, Eliza* or even *Elizabeth*. But who would have guessed that *Nathaniel* would be a problem, turning up as *Catharine, Katherine, Lawrence, Martha* and the desperately implausible *Wathaniel*?

In the whole batch of user-submitted corrections (35,396 records), there were over 500 corrections of *Lodnon* in the birthplace field to *London*, and over 600 corrections of the forename *Geroge* to *George* (about 20 per cent of the forename corrections). This suggests that perhaps many errors are the result simply of typing mistakes and inadequate proof-reading rather than problems with the handwriting in the originals.

The data also allows us to draw some conclusions about the misreading of capital letters. For example, there are 397 individuals with surnames beginning with *L* which has been mis-transcribed with a different initial letter. It is striking that in half of these errors (198) the wrong letter is *S*, followed by *T* with 37 examples. Conversely, the most common misreading of an initial *S* on a surname was *L* (123/600 occurrences), followed by H (99).

The other source is Ancestry. Unlike other data services, Ancestry does not replace wrongly indexed entries with corrections, but instead *adds* any user-submitted corrections as alternative readings. This makes it a very useful tool for identifying errors, since it means that a search on a particular forename or surname will show all the instances where, in the view of a user, that name has been wrongly transcribed.

Here, for example, are all the names that have been corrected to *Davis* by users of Ancestry's 1841 census index for England and Wales:

Avis, Bavis, Dabis, Dacres, Daerr, Dain, Dains, Dairs, Dais, Damis, Dams, Daner, Dani, Daniel, Danis, Dann, Dans, Daoce, Daon, Dares, Daris, Dart, Daser, Date, Daves, Daveson, Davey, Davi, David, Davie, Davies, Davir

This shows clearly the problem in transcribing correctly letters with similar strokes such as *i, m, n, r, u, v* and *w*. Similar confusions can be found between those letters with a rounded outline, which are often hard to distinguish in the less well-written pages: *a, c, e, o*. A particular problem is caused by *i*, where the dot can sometimes be a significant distance from the main stroke, making it difficult to decide exactly which stroke in the name is meant to be the body of the *i*. This is compounded in black-and-white scans, where it is not always easy to distinguish between manuscript dots and other marks on the page. The mis-reading of final *s* as *r* is perhaps unexpected but seems to be fairly common.

It is apparent that one of the basics of palaeographic training has not been sufficiently inculcated into some of the transcribers. While it would be optimistic to expect non-specialist transcribers to compile an alphabet for each enumerator's handwriting, they ought, surely, to be able to look for other examples of an individual problematic letter on the same page, or on another page of the same enumeration book. This is particularly the case for the initial capitals on forenames and surnames. To take another example from Ancestry's 1841 census index (Ancestry allows searching just on a forename, with all other search

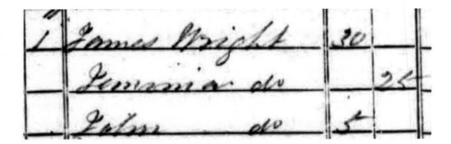

Figure 5.1 Jemima (not Lemonia) Wright in the 1841 census.

fields blank), the charmingly named Lemonia Wright, living in Lambeth (HO 107/1058/3, folio 41, page 4), is in fact *Jemima* Wright (see Fig. 5.1). Admittedly, the dot is a long way from the stem of the *i*, so the confusion at the end of the name is understandable, but how come the transcriber was unable to identify the initial *J* correctly when there are identical letters above and below, in the names of Jemima's husband and son? And this is not the only spurious *Lemonia* by any means.

If nothing else, these examples show that there are going to be some transcription errors in forenames, surnames and birthplaces which no name-matching algorithm or wildcard can compensate for.

Image quality

One of the most significant issues with the online census services is the quality of the digital images. While the most recent census digitisations, those of the 1911 censuses of England and Wales and Scotland, have produced high resolution colour images directly from the original documents, this is not the case for the earlier censuses. These were digitised not from the original documents but from the monochrome microfilm copies which had been used before the advent of the online censuses. The problem with this digitisation process is not just that the resulting images are sometimes harder to read than they might be, but that since these images were in many cases used as the basis of the indexes, any loss of clarity in the image may also give rise to an error in the index.

Starting from a monochrome source already introduces a limitation — the loss of colour means that the annotations of the clerks, originally made in a different colour ink, often obliterate information recorded by the enumerator that is easily legible on the original form. This is particularly problematic where an age has been ticked off in such a way as to become hard to read if not completely indecipherable (see Fig. 5.2, from the 1851 census for West Horsley in Surrey). Occupations, which were often subsequently annotated during analysis of the census, can be difficult to read for the same reason (see Fig. 5.3).

Figure 5.2 Check marks obscuring ages (HO 107/ 1594, folio 271, page 15).

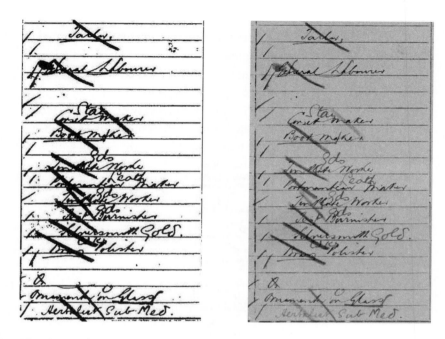

Figure 5.3 Black-and-white and greyscale images compared (RG 13/2831, folio 110, page 33).

A second limitation arises from the resolution of the images. Of course, photographic film also has a limit to its resolution, the grain size of the emulsion, but at something like 75,000 dots per inch photographic film shows over 250 times more detail than a typical digital scan of the same 35 mm frame. There are good technical reasons why digital scans are not made at the highest possible resolution: the higher the resolution of the image, the greater the file size and the longer it will take to download. This was particularly an issue in the early days of online census images, when home users had download speeds well below what is now accepted as the norm. Some of the earlier census images were scanned at around 200 dpi (dots per inch), whereas later scans tend to be at 300 dpi or higher.

Modern digital imaging technology and current broadband speeds could easily allow for much higher quality images — even the average home scanner can now scan at over 10,000 dpi. Unfortunately, the chance that the pre-1911 census records will ever be re-digitised, in colour, from the original enumeration books seems slight — it would be an expensive and time-consuming project that might struggle to recoup its costs. In any case, perhaps most genealogists would prefer the effort to be put into scanning new records rather than improving existing scans. However, in the case of the 1841 census Ancestry did in fact digitally re-photograph *some* of the hard-to-read pages in high resolution colour in order to improve the legibility of originals which were written in pencil. (Ancestry's search pages for the individual countries in the 1841 census list the piece numbers which include colour images.) And, to be fair, even with greyscale images, the ability of modern graphics software to enhance, say, the contrast in a digital scan of a microfilm frame probably means that quite a few digital census images are actually *more* easily read than the microfilms from which they were made. Again, the poor quality originals from the 1841 census have undoubtedly benefited from digitisation.

However, another factor limits the image quality: colour-depth, that is, the number of distinct shades in the image. The ideal, where we are starting from monochrome film, would be a greyscale image with the largest possible number of shades of grey. In practice 256 shades of grey is the standard for monochrome digital images. Although microfilm has much finer shading and there *might* occasionally be some benefit in re-scanning the census microfilms with more shades of grey, in fact any gains would be quite marginal. In any case, there would be the additional drawback that web browsers and much computer graphics software would be unable to handle such images.

The real problem with scanning microfilm occurs where the digitisers decide to scan the shades of grey in the film as pure black and white, i.e. every mark on the page is interpreted as either black or white, with nothing in-between. Black-and-white scans, particularly at high resolution, can be very good, but they are not the best choice where the original itself is already hard to read. This is yet another factor which can make a digital scan harder to interpret, which in turn increases the potential for errors in any transcription. The combination of black-and-white scanning with low resolution can produce particularly poor images.

The reason for creating a scanned image in pure black and white, in spite of the obvious limitations, is entirely to do with the size of the resulting file. A greyscale scan's 256 shades of grey require 8 bits of information to represent all 256 shades ($256 = 2^8$) and is therefore referred to as 8-bit greyscale. Pure black and white, however, requires only one bit (a pixel is either black, or it's not), so a black-and-white image will be an eighth of the size of a greyscale image at the same resolution. Again, this was a sound reason to use black-and-white in the early days of online censuses. However, while black-and-white can be perfectly adequate for some purposes, such as digitising printed text, it is poor for manuscript historical documents, where there are strokes of very different weight and thickness, whose interpretation may also be affected by deterioration or discolouration of the paper. Figure 5.3 (from the 1901 census for Birmingham) demonstrates the potential difference in legibility between greyscale and black-and-white images. While many of the strokes in the greyscale image are less clear, the distinction between the enumerator's writing and the later marks is much easier to see, and the ink stain at the start of 'General Labourer' no longer obliterates the text.

When a document is digitised in pure black and white, every pixel is either black or white. But of course the document itself is in many shades and more than one colour, so the digitiser has to decide: how light does a mark on the paper have to be before it is regarded as white space and represented as white, how dark does a mark have to be before it is regarded as part of the text and shown as black? Unfortunately, there is simply no right answer in the case of handwritten documents on ageing paper. Also, unlike a greyscale image, which can subsequently be made darker or lighter to bring out contrast, once the shading information has been thrown away in a black-and-white image there is no way to recover it.

Victorian handwriting can already be hard enough to read without the loss of colour contrast and the loss of detail that is inevitable in black-and-white scanning. As is apparent in Figure 5.3, black-and-white may bring indexing problems, particularly where annotations or corrections obscure the underlying text. It can sometimes also be difficult to decide which marks are part of the writing and which are just irrelevant marks on the paper, which might be interpreted, for example, as the dot of an *i*.

A final issue is image compression: in order to keep the image file smaller, some digital image formats 'compress' the image, i.e. they throw away some of the information in it. The JPEG format, which is widely used for images on web pages and is used by most of the online data services, does this. The problem is that the compression always introduces *some* distortion, and the more an image is compressed the more likely it is that the distortion will be apparent. This doesn't matter much for most purposes on the web, but with handwritten documents the distortion can make the writing appear slightly fuzzy.

At low levels of compression, you can ususally see the distortion only when the image is viewed at quite high magnification, but the greater the compression the more obvious it will be. Figure 5.4 shows an extract from a low- and a high-compression JPEG image of the same page (Thomas Hardy's entry in the 1861 census), taken from two differ-ent data services. The handwriting in the high-compression image is noticeably more indistinct — it remains readable but this might not be the case on pages with poorer handwriting or overwritten corrections. The high-compression image, as a whole, is around one quarter the size of the low-compression image.

The data services have generally recognised the need to improve image quality to keep up with the times and have been replacing images with better ones. However, there are still many black-and-white census images in the online services: many of the images for 1871 on Origins and Findmypast, images for 1861–1901 on TheGenealogist, or all the Victorian images on ScotlandsPeople.

In some cases the improvement in the images has been accompa-nied by re-indexing, but this is financially viable only when an individ-ual image is being replaced, not where new images for a whole census are being uploaded. This may perhaps explain why indexing errors sometimes seem so surprising — we may now be looking at a better quality image than the transcriber was working from.

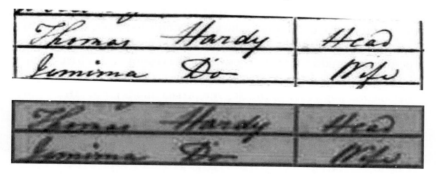

Figure 5.4 Image compression (RG9/1354, folio 89, page 2).

Terms and conditions

One question that is often raised is: what limits are there on what you can do with the data and images you download from a census site? While we are hardly qualified to offer legal advice, there are a number of issues to be aware of.

The census records are the property of the various national archives which hold them. These repositories also claim the copyright on the microfilms which are used as the basis for digital images, and digital images themselves. The individual data services purchase copies of the microfilms or the digital images and a licence to publish them. Even if there is an argument that copyright claims relating to photographs of out-of-copyright historical documents have no foundation (as is clearly the case in the USA, for example), the issue of copyright is in fact quite irrelevant: when you use a commercial data service you sign up to its terms and conditions, and these override any general copyright legislation, no matter what jurisdiction the user is in. These terms and conditions are usually quite specific about what you may and may not do with the data and images, and will set strict limits. Here, for example, are the relevant terms from Findmypast (at <**www.findmypast.com/ content/terms-and-conditions**>):

A large amount of time, money and effort has been expended to make these records and features available online. Many of these records and features have been obtained from other organizations and people. These people or organizations often own the intellectual property rights in the records (the copyright/database rights owner is displayed on most records) and website features. Accordingly, you may not use the records or features to create your own work (for example a database of records), copy or reproduce the records (either in whole or in part), or make available, share or publish them unless you have our permission (and/or that of the owner of the copyright/database rights in the work) in writing. You may however use screenshots of our website for blog postings, articles and presentations for informational and educational purposes. If you are a professional genealogist (as defined above) you may also use the records or features in preparing unpublished reports for clients. The website and services provided belong to brightsolid, and again, you must not copy or use them without our written permission. Therefore, you only have a limited license to access the website and to use the content for personal or professional family history research (including unpublished reports for clients if you are a professional genealogist).

Copyright restrictions apply to only original materials, so you can make and publish your own transcriptions from the online census images, and of course this should include information on the source. What you can't do is simply copy and paste, say, all the census entries for a particular surname from the search results on a commercial service to republish on your own website.

All the services either explicitly (as in the case of TheGenealogist — see <**www.thegenealogist.co.uk/terms.php**>) or implicitly (as in Findmypast) forbid you to use the site to offer a look-up service. You will find plenty of messages in discussion forums where someone requests a look-up in census records. If you occasionally respond to such requests, you are not likely to be in any trouble, but you would be very unwise to post a message to a mailing list announcing a look-up service.

In fact, given that all the censuses are available both by subscription and on a pay-per-view basis (not to mention the free trials), that there are free, if limited indexes on FamilySearch (see p. 158), and that the censuses are an essential genealogical source, it's difficult to find any good reason for a family historian to request a look-up at someone else's expense.

Useful census sites

Chapter 6 looks at online search techniques and Chapters 7 to 15 concentrate on the free and commercial sites offering census records, but there are many other useful sites with material relating to the censuses.

The most comprehensive general resource for online census information is Cyndi's List, which has a Census Worldwide page at <**www.cyndislist.com/census2.htm**> and a UK and Ireland census page at <**www.cyndislist.com/census-uk.htm**>. This has around 400 links, including many to individual small-scale transcriptions.

The most important single site for information about the UK censuses is Histpop ('The Online Historical Population Reports Website') at <**www.histpop.org**>, which has digitised copies of an enormous number of official documents relating to the censuses. Histpop is discussed in more detail in Chapter 19.

Genuki has a gazetteer for the places in the 1891 census at <**www. genuki.org.uk/big/census_place.html**>. This gives the county, district, sub-district and TNA piece number for any place in England, Wales and the Isle of Man.

Jeff Knaggs has two very useful pages for the 1901 census of England and Wales, with lists of institutions and naval vessels included in the census, giving the piece and folio number of the entry. If you are using a commercial site which has the facility for a reference search, then the information on these pages will save you a lot of time in locating the entries for orphanages, schools, prisons, and the like.

There are a number of discussion forums devoted to using the online censuses. RootsWeb has seven mailing lists for discussion of UK census records, though in fact most of these are for volunteer transcribers. The only general ones are UK-1901-CENSUS, UK-1911-CENSUS and the somewhat premature UK-1921-CENSUS. Links to all three will be found at <**lists.rootsweb.com/index/other/Census-UK**>. British-Genealogy has a British Census forum at <**www.british-genealogy.com/forums**>. TalkingScot at <**www.talkingscot.com**> has a forum devoted to the Scottish censuses. The online censuses are a regular topic of discussion on the main mailing list for British genealogy, GENBRIT. Details will be found at <**lists.rootsweb.com/index/intl/UK/GENBRIT.html**> with a link to the searchable archives of past messages. As this mailing list is also a newsgroup, current and past messages can be seen at Google Groups, <**groups.google.com/group/soc.genealogy.britain**>. You will often see requests for help with census records on this list.

6

ONLINE SEARCH TECHNIQUES

Although there are many differences between the various online census databases, the techniques for searching them have much in common, and there are certain general principles for successful searching that apply no matter which site you are using. The search facilities of the major census sites are described in detail in the following chapters and are summarised in Table A.4 (p. 348). The purpose of this chapter is to offer some general advice on using the most common search fields and facilities, and to highlight the benefits and shortcomings of the various options. (Some of the recommendations here apply only to the large national datasets, which tend to have the most comprehensive and sophisticated search options.)

There are three basic reasons for any problems you may have in locating people in census records:

- the records themselves are incomplete and flawed in various ways, as discussed in Chapter 4;
- you start your census search on the basis of information you already have about your ancestors, but it is quite possible for that information to be wrong or incomplete;
- the electronic indexes all contain errors or omissions resulting from the transcription process, as discussed in Chapter 5.

Together, these mean that you shouldn't be surprised if an initial search does not turn up the person you are looking for.

There is a basic dilemma when searching for ancestors in the online census indexes. The more search terms you enter, the more likely you are to enter something that does not match your ancestor's record.

Result: a failed search. On the other hand, the fewer search terms you enter, the larger the number of matching entries you will find. Result: too many entries to check.

In fact, it will often need a process of trial and error to work out which information in which fields on the search form will locate the right person. You can either start with minimal information — just a forename, surname and county perhaps — and add fields when your initial search is too broad. Alternatively, you can fill in all the fields you have information for and experiment with cutting them out to find the best combination. If a forename or surname is quite unusual, then the first strategy is recommended; for common names, the second. But which of these suits you will depend in part on what sort of site you are using. If you are using a free site or a subscription service, you can do as many searches as you like. If you are using a pay-per-view site and you are being charged for each household or census image you check, you will want to minimise the number of plausible entries in your search results.

Names

One of the hardest problems to solve in searching the census records is when there seems to be no correct entry for the surname you are looking for. Some names are inherently unstable, patronymic pairs like Richard and Richards particularly. Perhaps an enumerator, encountering an illiterate speaker with an unfamiliar accent, may not take down a name the way you'd expect. Or modern data entry staff have had trouble reading Victorian handwriting. Personal names are the most difficult textual data on the census form to validate. If a modern transcriber can't read key letters in a name, it may be impossible to make a sensible guess.

This means you need to be open-minded about surname spellings. But looking for each possible variant in turn would be a very tedious process, so the data services offer a range of options for finding variants with a *single* search.

Because of the level of variation in name spellings, you will find that many sites offer loose matching as the default type of name search and you have to select an 'exact match' option if you want to find *only* the spelling you have entered. But of course the looser the match, the more entries you will have to check.

Wildcards

One of the most useful options in any search field is the 'wildcard', a special character that can stand for any letter or letters, including no letter at all. The most common wildcard character is the asterisk (*).

At its simplest this lets you search for common surname variants that differ in their last letter: Brook, Brooke, Brooks and Brookes can be searched for simultaneously with *Brook**, though of course the results will include Brooker, Brookbank, Brookshaw, etc. Another obvious use is where there are forms of a name with a different vowel. *Blackw*ll* finds both Blackwall and Blackwell.

Wildcards are particularly useful for coping with transcription errors, since they allow you to ignore the letters which have been got wrong. The disadvantage is that you may miss odder variants or misspellings — it relies on your knowledge of, or at least ability to imagine, variants.

One limitation with wildcards as implemented in the online indexes is that they are not always permitted at the beginning of a field (Ancestry, Findmypast, ScotlandsPeople and the Irish census are the only exceptions). This is unfortunate, because it is precisely the sometimes florid Victorian initials which give rise to many transcription errors. Also you will usually have to enter at least three characters before the wildcard. So, although you can use *Alcr*ft* to find Alcraft and Alcroft, you would need separate searches to find Aldcroft and Allcroft, not to mention Oldcraft, Oldcroft and Ouldcroft.

Although wildcards are most often thought of as a tool for names, they can also be useful for place-name variants when searching for locations, particularly birthplaces.

Soundex

Soundex is a surname matching technique originally invented for the US census to try and get round the spelling variations, and some sites with census data make it available as a search option.

Soundex gives each surname an alpha-numerical code based on the first letter and the remaining consonants, with similar codes for similar sounding consonants. The code for Radcliffe, for example is R324, and a Soundex search for Radcliffe will look for all names which are coded as R324. These will include variants like Ratcliffe, Radcliff, Ratcliff, Reddcliff, as well as many others that are less likely to be misspellings or genuine variants, such as Ridgewell, Rudkin, Rattigan, and even Rothschild. So a Soundex search will always give you a lot more names, and therefore a lot more individuals, than you really want.

Soundex is designed to ignore double consonants, and ignores vowels entirely except at the beginning of a word. So Wilman and Wellman have the same code (W455). Its advantage over wildcards is that only the first letter has to be specified.

On the other hand, some very obvious surname variants have different codes and won't turn up as matches. For example, Wood has code W400, while Woods is W420. Rogers is R262, while Rodgers is R326. Again, it has the problem that it cannot cope with different initial letters.

Because of its limitations, Soundex is not now widely used on commercial sites, though you will often encounter it elsewhere. The only major census site to offer a Soundex search is ScotlandsPeople (see Chapter 14), where it is only one of several name matching options. Genes Reunited use Soundex as part of a composite search technique, which makes the limitations of Soundex much less significant.

You can find out more about Soundex and how it works at <**www.archives.gov/research/census/soundex.html**>, and there are many Soundex calculators on the Web — Cyndi's List has useful links at <**www.cyndislist.com/us/census/soundex**>.

Metaphone

Metaphone, first published in 1990, is one of a number of attempts to improve on Soundex. It uses the same approach — generating a four-character code based on the consonants in a name — but has a more sophisticated set of rules to cope with some of the complexities of English consonant spelling conventions. The revised Double Metaphone also has a method of dealing with foreign names. However, the approach suffers from the same problem as Soundex — names either match or they do not —which is poorly suited to find the closest plausible variant spellings of a name.

Metaphone is not widely used on the genealogy data services, but is available as one of the name-matching options on ScotlandsPeople (see

Chapter 14). It will also be encountered on some of the family tree hosting sites such as Geni at <**www.geni.com**> and in the advanced search of RootsWeb WorldConnect at <**wc.rootsweb.ancestry.com**>.

Ancestor Search has a brief outline of the algorithm at <**www. searchforancestors.com/utility/metaphone.php**> and a Metaphone code calculator. The Wikipedia article at <**en.wikipedia.org/wiki/ Metaphone**> has links to more technical information. The NameX Name Thesaurus discussed in the next section gives the Metaphone code and name matches for any surname.

NameX

Because of the limitations of code-matching algorithms like Soundex and Metaphone, there have been a number of attempts to find a more reliable approach. While Ancestry has an unnamed matching algorithm of its own, the system that is used by Origins, Findmypast and Genes Reunited is NameX. This is, incidentally, a proprietary system requiring a licence so the exact details of how it works have not been published and you will not encounter it on non-commercial sites.

Soundex works by giving every name a *code* and then claiming all those with the same code as matches. NameX works by taking the name you are starting with and giving every other name a *score* based on how closely it matches. This allows you, in principle, to look at only close matches or to include more distant ones (though only Origins actually offers you this choice).

Table 6.1 shows the NameX scores (out of 100) of the first 66 matches for the surname Darwin. You can see that it would be impossible to search for this group of names with wildcards or Soundex. And while some of the forms are hardly plausible variants of Darwin, there are many you would not have thought to try and which might be mistranscriptions of the name. You can try NameX out on the website of Image Partners, who developed the system, at <**www.namethesaurus.com/ Thesaurus/search.aspx**>. This will show you for comparison the much less satisfactory lists produced by Soundex and Metaphone.

Origins has background information about NameX at <**www. originsnetwork.com/namex/aboutnamex.html**>, which is also well worth reading for its explanation of the problems of identifying surname variants in historical records.

Surname	Match Score	Surname	Match Score
Darwine	99	Durwyn	85
Darwinn	99	Darwinge	84
Dearwin	99	Darwain	84
Darwina	97	Darin	83
Daarwin	97	Daryin	83
Derwin	96	Darwis	82
Dirwin	96	Daerwi	82
Dorwin	96	Dharwin	82
Durwin	96	Drwin	81
Darwins	95	Derwoin	81
Darwyn	93	Dariyn	81
Durwine	93	Darwani	81
Dorwine	93	Darwinch	81
Dirwine	93	Dartwin	80
Derwine	93	Dawin	80
Durwinne	90	Dawrin	80
Darwyne	90	Darwaine	80
Dauwin	90	Dargwin	80
Dawwin	90	Dardwin	80
Dariwin	89	Derwint	80
Daruwin	89	Derwing	80
Dorrwin	89	Derwinis	80
Derwina	89	Durwint	80
Darwinq	88	Durwind	80
Darwint	88	Dorwing	80
Darwind	88	Dorwint	80
Darwing	88	Darein	79
Darwink	88	Dairin	79
Darwinus	87	Darine	79
Derwins	87	Darwan	79
Dirwyn	85	Darrin	79
Derwyn	85	Darwid	79
Dorwyn	85	Darwen	79

Table 6.1 NameX matches for 'Darwin', from <**www.namethesaurus.com/ Thesaurus/search.aspx**>.

Forenames

Forenames also have their problems. There are three main reasons why the forename you search on may not find who you are looking for:

- the person actually uses a middle name and this is what is recorded on the form;
- the form shows a nickname rather than the formal name — for example, there are five Bill Smiths and a Billy Smith in the Origins 1871 index;
- the name has been abbreviated — William Smith could easily be recorded as 'Wm', or even plain 'W'.

Of course the data services recognise this problem and have ways of dealing with it, but they don't all deal with it in the same way so it's well worth checking any help they offer on forename searching. Most sites automatically catch a wide range of forename variants, some offering this as the default, which you can override by selecting an exact match. On Ancestry, even searching for an exact match will actually find *some* variants.

When you look at your initial search results, always look at the forename column to see what variants have been captured. Does a search for *Charles* have some entries for Chas?

You can, of course, use a wildcard — *Will** will find quite a few variants of William. But this will not identify very short forms like Wm, or nicknames like Billy which start with a different letter. It certainly won't help with pairs as different as Margaret and Peggy, or Ellen and Nell.

NameX (see above) can also be used for forenames, though only Origins offers this at present. The NameX thesaurus search page at <www.namethesaurus.com/Thesaurus/search.aspx> also has a forename search facility, which will tell you what variants are likely to be found by NameX.

ScotlandsPeople has a very useful page on Scots forename variants at <www.scotlandspeople.gov.uk/content/help/index.aspx?r=551&561>.

Age

The problems with the legibility of the ages on the census forms have already been mentioned in Chapter 5 (see Fig. 5.2). But there is a separate problem that is entirely down to the modern data services.

Ages in the censuses after 1841 are the age last birthday. Apart from the issue of people being ignorant of their correct age (see Chapter 4, p. 101), many of the census sites invite you to search not on age but on year of birth. There are good reasons for this. It is something you might already have information on, perhaps from a later census. Also it's less of a challenge than leaving you to do the mental arithmetic required to subtract the birth date from the census date to give an accurate age. However, the problem is that this switch is implemented with a fatal flaw, with the result that almost three-quarters of birth years in the census indexes are wrong!

For anyone whose birthday falls earlier in the year than the date of the census, subtracting the age from the census year will give the correct birth year. For everyone else, the calculated birth year will be one year *later* than the correct birth year. For example, a child aged one on the night of the 1901 census (31 March) will have been born on a date between 1 April 1899 and 31 March 1900. Statistically, therefore, a child who is one year old in the 1901 census is three times as likely to have been born in the latter nine months of 1899 as in the first three months of 1900, yet the year of birth calculated by the census indexes all agree such a child was born in 1900.

This means that if you use a search field which expects a birth year, you should give the right year only where an ancestor's birthday falls later in the year than census night. Otherwise, do not give the right year *and* request an exact match. Instead, give a year range or subtract one from the correct year. In recognition of this problem, some of the data services actually offer a year range as the default search option.

In general, given the likelihood of an ancestor being mistaken as to his or her age, it is always best, initially at least, not to carry out a search on a precise birth year but rather to specify a range of years to start with.

Geography

There are three groups of geographical information for each person recorded on an enumeration schedule:

- the administrative units under which a household falls, at the top of the form;
- the street address;
- the birth place, to the right.

The most reliable by far is the first of these. The enumerator will have started out with this information, derived from official documentation, not gathered it from a resident; since it will be identical for a whole group of pages, there's every reason to expect the digitisation process to capture this information accurately. Some sites offer a very precise set of fields for searching this information — see, for example, the options offered at Findmypast, shown in Figure 9.3 — but the problem with using this information to search is less the accuracy of indexing than your own geographical knowledge. You need to put exactly the right information in exactly the right fields in order for the search to work.

In general these fields can be useful for searching if it is at a high level (county, town), but unless you are a local historian or you have an authoritative source (e.g. a birth certificate of similar date), it is probably best to avoid fields like civil parish, municipal borough, ward etc. This may be unproblematic for a rural parish, which will have no sub-divisions, but for towns of any size and particularly major metropolitan areas with a complex set of administrative divisions, you are almost certainly better off using a general purpose Location field, into which you can type any place names without worrying about the exact type of place each one is.

The address information in the first column on the form is in fact not always searchable in a person search in the online census indexes, but if you have a street name which you think is reliable it can be worth trying it out in a general Location field. If your interest is local rather than genealogical, you may find the separate address search offered by some sites useful (see Table A.4, p. 348). It is also a good potential standby if name searches fail but you have some idea where your ancestor lived.

Depending on who you are searching for, the birthplace field may be essential or useless. If you are tracing backwards, this may in fact be the one piece of information you are using the census to try to discover. But it will be useful if you have already found an ancestor in an earlier or later census. It can also be useful, initially at least, to enter just the county from some later evidence of an address. This will at least narrow down the list of possible entries to check, without committing you to the assumption that an ancestor grew up in exactly the same place where he or she got married.

If, on the other hand, you are tracing your family tree forwards, looking for other descendants of an ancestor, the birthplace field may be the only one which offers definitive proof that a person living in a major city or at the other end of the country is actually the offspring of an ancestor who lived elsewhere. If you are dealing with a common name, it may be the only way of distinguishing between several families. But of course, as was pointed out in Chapter 4, this is one of the most problematic fields on the original forms and is made more so by the levels of error in the online indexes. Here, too, the distinction between a transcription and an index discussed in the previous chapter becomes important.

Let's say you are looking for family members born in Guildford, Surrey. What you can't tell without testing is whether a particular index has normalised the spellings of town and county. If it has, then a search for the standard spelling will be sufficient. If not, you may need to do more searches to cope with the most common alternative spellings: Guilford, Gilford and Gildford. The 1881 Census Index on FamilySearch, for example, finds both 'Guildford' and 'Guilford' in a search for either, but there are 55 individuals born in 'Gilford, Surrey;' and 8 born in 'Gildford, Surrey', who are not found in a search for exact matches. (If you omit 'Surrey' you will get many results for Gilford in Pembrokeshire.) True, those missing 63 are only a small fraction, but some of them will have living descendants.

County spellings are usually normalised, but you can still be caught out. Findmypast's 1891 census index rather surprisingly finds that there were only 288 people claiming to be born in Dorset, which sounds like a horrific error. But in fact the index is quite correct: the people apparently missing are in fact listed on the original forms as born in *Dorsetshire*. The 288 'Dorset' people are those who claim to have been born, rather bizarrely one might think, in 'Dorset, Dorsetshire'.

One thing to look for is a drop-down list, such as the County and City/Town fields in the search form for the 1881 Census Index. By definition, these give you only valid options and will only be offered where the index has normalised the spellings. But drop-down lists can also be your enemy. By restricting what you can select, they may sometimes be effectively useless, and indeed may have hidden traps if you are unfamiliar with the local area. If you are looking for someone living in Guildford in Origins' 1871 index, you have the option, once you have selected Surrey as the county, to search for people living in a particular Surrey parish. Your natural reaction will be to select Guildford. If you do, you will get no results, because Guildford in the mid-nineteenth century comprised *several* parishes: Bowling Green, Friary, Holy Trinity, St Mary, and St Nicholas, not to mention Stoke next to Guildford. You can only select one of these at a time from the Parish drop-down list on Origins' search form. If you don't already have a specific parish to search, perhaps from a baptism or marriage record, there is no fall-back option to select all Guildford parishes. Worse, if you're unfamiliar with the area, you won't even realise the problem and will conclude, perhaps wrongly, that your ancestor wasn't living in the town in that census year.

Gender

A gender field is probably one of the least useful fields on a search form. For a start, most Victorian forenames were gender-specific, so selecting a gender doesn't really narrow down your search at all; it's just something else which can stop you finding an ancestor by being wrongly transcribed. As pointed out in Chapter 5, there are thousands of entries in the census indexes which have a mismatch between gender and forename. If you search for 'John, male' you will miss all the entries for 'John, female'. Of course many of these will be for people who were really called Jane, but some will be for Johns given the wrong gender by the modern transcriber. If you know the forename, don't bother with gender.

The real use of the gender field is to narrow down your search results when you either don't know a forename or have failed to find a match when using the forename you believe to be correct.

Occupation

Another search field that is less useful than you might think is that for occupation, which some sites offer. Even supposing you know exactly what your ancestor did for a living in the census year, there can be many different ways to express the same occupation, from trivial spelling variants such as 'coastguard' and 'coast guard' to closely related alternatives such as 'carpenter', 'joiner' and 'woodworker'. Also, a search for 'carpenter' will probably not turn up someone whose occupation has been given more precisely as 'ship's carpenter'.

Another source of problems is the fact that on the original records the occupation entries have often been partially overwritten with annotations or strokes of the pen, which makes them particularly liable to mistranscription (see Fig. 5.3). Save the occupation field as a last resort when other approaches fail. Alternatively, with a common name, it may be worth entering an occupation in your initial search, but it should be one of the first fields you abandon if that initial search fails.

Family members

One of the most useful options which is available on several of the commercial sites is a set of fields to enter the names of other family members. Table A.4 on p. 348 shows which sites offer this facility.

Even if the names themselves are quite common, a particular combination of forenames for father, mother and a couple of children may help identify a family whose surname has been horribly mangled for whatever reason. See p. 218 and Fig. 10.5 for an example of a search form with this facility.

References

There are circumstances in which it can be useful to search by census reference (Chapter 18 discusses these references in detail). For example, none of the free census sites has digital images of the census returns, so in order to check an entry you have found in the free index, you will need to use one of the commercial data services and locate the matching image. Having precise information from a free index about the name and address of an individual will often be enough, but it is completely foolproof if you can give the precise reference and go straight to the right image.

Street indexes

Another case where you will want to use the reference search is if you have used a street index.

In the days before computerised name indexes, searching for an ancestor in a census meant identifying his or her likely location, establishing which microfilm(s) held the enumeration books for that area, and then scrolling through them. The process was made somewhat easier by the preparation of street indexes for major towns, which identify precisely which enumeration book or books hold the entries for a particular street.

Now that any individual can be sought throughout the country with a single search, these street indexes might seem to have outlived their usefulness. But in fact there are two instances where they can still be useful to those searching the censuses online, for the simple reason that not all the sites provide an address search. An address search is essential if you are looking at the history of an individual house or of a small locality. But it can also be a good way to locate someone whose name has been wrongly transcribed in the index, but for whom you have an address from a date near the census.

For England and Wales, The National Archives had an ambitious plan to digitise all the paper street indexes. This project was abandoned in 2012, but the indexes for 1841–1871 and 1891 had been completed and are available, for the present at least, in the Your Archives wiki as the 'Historical Streets Project' at <yourarchives.nationalarchives.gov.uk/index.php?title=Your_Archives:Historical_Streets_Project>. (In the longer term it will be available only in the UK Government Web Archive at <webarchive.nationalarchives.gov.uk>.) You can also get to this page from the Your Archives home page at <yourarchives.nationalarchives.gov.uk> by clicking on the 'Census Street Indexes' link in the 'Contribute' panel on the left of the page. Not every part of England and Wales is covered — street

Street name ⊠	Nearby street ⊠	Remarks ⊠	Dwellings ⊠	Reference ⊠	folio ⊠
Abbey Court	Abbey Street			RG 10/3744	15
Abbey Street				RG 10/3744	12-15, 20-21, 26
Abbey Terrace				RG 10/3744	21
Abbot Street				RG 10/3744	21-26
Abbotsford Street	Seacomb			RG 10/3754	150-155
Ackworth Place	Chapel Street			RG 10/3745	46
Adelphi Street				RG 10/3745	197-198
Albert Cottage	Albert Street			RG 10/3753	72
Albert Industrial Schools	Corporation Road			RG 10/3749	98-99
Albert Place	Tranmere			RG 10/3751	39-41
Albert Street				RG 10/3744	110
Albert Street	New Brighton			RG 10/3753	71-72

Figure 6.1 Street index for Birkenhead, 1871.

indexes were created only for towns with a population of at least 40,000. Figure 6.1 shows the start of the street index of Birkenhead for the 1871 census.

For Scotland, ScotlandsPeople has a range of street indexes for major towns, and these are described in Chapter 14 (p. 279).

There is no need for street indexes to the Irish censuses on The National Archives of Ireland site (Chapter 15): you can search on a county and street (though not town and street), and the 'Browse by place' option lets you narrow down to an individual street, with a list of the inhabitants.

Of course, for the street indexes to be usable in connection with the online index, the search facilities need to include an option to search by reference, which not all the data services provide. Table A.4 on p. 348 shows which services include this type of search. As you can see from Figure 6.1, the Historical Streets Project indexes give only the piece and folio numbers, not the individual page numbers.

General advice

In addition to specific recommendations about how you formulate your search, there are some very general things to bear in mind:

- Don't be too attached to any one piece of information. Even if you haven't got it wrong (or rather, even if your source hasn't), there can be no guarantee that the enumeration schedule has the correct information and it has been correctly transcribed in the online index.

- Be flexible and imaginative with names. The name matching systems available on the online censuses can do a lot to find variants, but none of them can cope with errors in the initial letters, and few sites allow wildcards at the beginning of a name. Unfortunately, there are also some spectacular mistranscriptions of names in the indexes, so be prepared sometimes to think about how to find someone without using the surname.

- Ultimately, be prepared to use more than one online index. You may baulk at the expense of this, but if the site you normally use can't turn up your ancestor, then an alternative may be your only chance. If you choose a pay-per-view option, you may not need to pay more than £5 or £6 to find an otherwise unfindable ancestor. Before you do this, though, check the relevant chapter in this book to make sure that your second site does not use the same index as the first, or you'll be wasting your money.

7

FREE CENSUS INDEXES ONLINE

Later chapters are devoted to the individual commercial services offering census data on either a subscription or a pay-per-view basis.
However, there are many sites offering free census indexes or transcriptions, mostly for individual towns or counties.

Because these sites are free of charge, they are accessible from any
public internet terminal. If you have not got your own internet connection at home, you can access them from the networked computers
available in many public libraries.

The Irish census data available online is almost all accessible free of
charge, but the Irish censuses require separate discussion in detail and
are covered Chapter 15.

FamilySearch

The most important collection of free online census data is that available on FamilySearch at **<familysearch.org>**. It has indexes to all the
released censuses for England and Wales as well as indexes for Scotland
1841–1891.

There are two sources for this material. The first is the 1881 Census
Index, which was created by volunteers from family history societies
and the LDS Church in a mammoth project run jointly by the Federation
of Family History Societies and the Genealogical Society of Utah. It
was initially published on microfiche, and then on CD-ROM (see p. 311).
It was put online free of charge at FamilySearch in February 2003. The
indexes for 1881 available on the commercial sites covered in the following chapters are generally copies of this index and for that reason are
usually offered free of charge.

In 2008 FamilySearch entered a partnership arrangement with Findmypast and Origins to make all the other indexes for England and Wales up to 1891 available free of charge to all users of the FamilySearch site. Although the camera icon by the England and Wales indexes (see Fig. 7.1) indicates the availability of images of the original records, for home users access to the images requires a subscription to Findmypast, and all the image links from the UK censuses take you to the Findmypast home page. However, if you are accessing FamilySearch from a FamilySearch Centre or you are a 'signed-in member of a supporting organization' (in practice, the LDS Church), you will be able to view the images without payment and without leaving the site.

Subsequently the 1901 and 1911 censuses for England and Wales have been added, as have indexes, without links to images, for the nineteenth-century censuses of Scotland. This gives FamilySearch the most

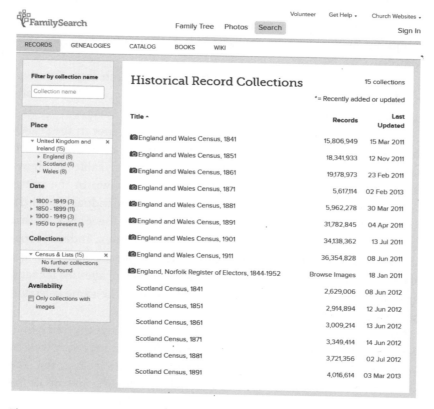

Figure 7.1 FamilySearch UK census page.

complete set of free census indexes for the British Isles, with only the 1901 and 1911 indexes for Scotland outstanding.

To search in the census indexes, select the 'Search' option from the FamilySearch home page, or go straight to **<familysearch.org/search>**. At the bottom of the page, under 'Browse by location', select 'United Kingdom and Ireland'. On the resulting 'Historical Record Collections' page, click on 'Census & Lists' in the left-hand column. From this page (see Fig. 7.1), you can select which census you want to search. If you're going to use this page often, it is worth bookmarking (the page address is **<familysearch.org/search/collection/list#page=1&region=UNITED_KINGDOM_IRELAND&recordType=Census>**).

For each census, the page gives the total number of records in the index. The figures for the 1871 and 1881 censuses for England and Wales are much lower than those for the other censuses. In these two cases this is the number of *households* in the index, not the number of *individuals*, hence the lower figure. In fact all the indexes are complete except for 1871, which at the start of 2014 was only 81 per cent complete.

The search process is very straightforward: a search form (see Fig. 7.2) leads to a list of matching individuals (see Fig. 7.3), whose details can then be viewed (see Fig. 7.4).

Unfortunately, there is remarkable lack of consistency in the search facilities for the individual censuses, both in what can be searched on and in the information displayed in search results. Table 7.1 shows which fields can be searched on (S), which are shown in the initial search results (R), and which are displayed in an individual record (I). As you can see, the index for the 1881 census is the only one that approaches the facilities available on commercial sites. Indeed, some of the omissions seem extraordinary: the complete absence of any place of residence information for 1851, and the lack of ages for 1851 and 1911. No two censuses for England and Wales offer the same selection of fields for searching and display.

The limited amount of information displayed for years other than 1871 and 1881 in England and Wales means that you may very well be unable to identify with certainty the ancestor you are looking for. The place of residence information is generally the parish, but on all the Scottish censuses it is solely the registration district and county.

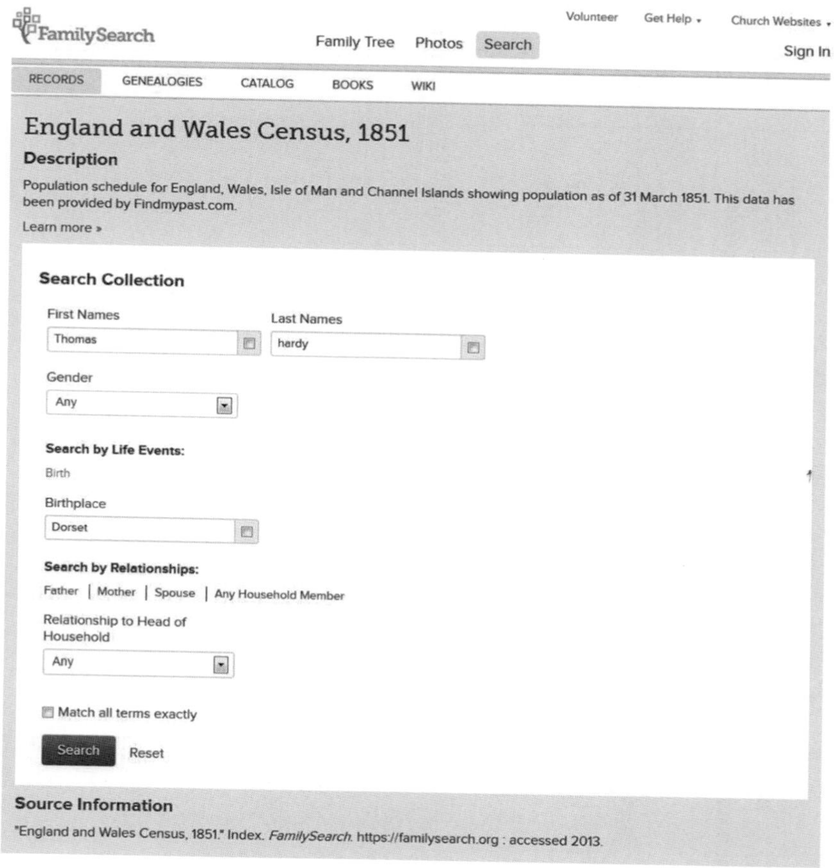

Figure 7.2 FamilySearch census search form.

A particular problem is the complete absence of National Archives references, except for England and Wales 1881, which means you cannot use the found record as an adequately documented entry in your family tree. However, at the foot of the page for an individual, there is a field 'Citing this Record' which gives a unique URL for the entry. Although web addresses are, of course, notoriously unstable, it is likely that these references, which link to Family Search's online family trees, will be more stable than most. But even so, it is far from certain that the same URL will still be valid in 10 or 20 years time, let alone 50.

By default, FamilySearch uses its own surname-matching database to offer variants for any surname or forename entered. Unlike other

| | England and Wales | | | | | | | | Scotland |
	1841	1851	1861	1871	1881	1891	1901	1911	All
	All censuses have searching and display of first name, last name and gender								
Age	I		I	I	I	I	I		I
Calculated birth year	R		R	R			R		SR
Birthplace	SRI	SRI	SRI	SRI	SRI	SR	SRI	SRI	SRI
Residence Place	SRI		SRI	SRI	SRI	I	SRI	SRI	RI
Street Address					I				
Relationship to head		SRI	SI	SRI	SRI	SI	SI		
Relation name		S		SRI	SRI	S	S		
Marital Status					I				
Occupation					SI				
Disability					I				
TNA reference					I				
Film no.					SI				SI

Key: S — search field; R — shown in search results; I — shown in individual record.

Table 7.1 FamilySearch census fields.

sites, it does *not* use an algorithm for calculating variants, but instead relies on a list that was created manually and is certainly not going to be comprehensive. It is therefore much more inconsistent than the surname-matching algorithms used by the commercial data services. However, it is likely to be quite reliable for obvious variants, though not for simple transcription errors of similar shaped letters. If you want to switch this off and search only for exact matches, you can select 'Match all terms exactly spelling' above the 'Search' button. Alternatively you can select individual fields for exact matching, using the checkbox which follows each text field (see Fig. 7.2). You can, in fact, enter just a forename or just a surname. Indeed, you can enter no name at all: if you enter just a place of residence, you'll get a list of all the inhabitants of a town or village; if you enter just a birthplace, the results will allow you to trace migration patterns.

The search results (see Fig. 7.3) list each matching individual with some basic information, but again this varies between censuses. Since the results for 1881 give the name of the parish and list other household members, you should be able spot the individual you are looking for fairly easily. But for 1851, on the other hand, only the birthplace and

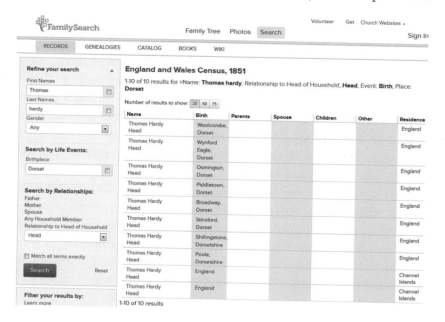

Figure 7.3 FamilySearch census search results.

relationship to head of household are shown. However, from the search results page you can refine your search by specifying additional data field in the left-hand box. In Figure 7.3, we have narrowed down the initial 26 results, by adding 'Head of Household' to the search criteria.

By default the results are displayed 20 to a screen, but buttons above the table of results allow you to switch this to 50 or 75 entries. However, you can manually edit the URL displayed in the navigation bar of your browser: the number after 'count=' is the number of records per screen and will initially say 'count=20', but you can change 20 to any other number below 500. This can be useful if you are doing a one-name study and a surname-only search turns up several hundred matches which you want to capture for adding to your database.

Figure 7.4 shows an individual record. If you are using a computer in a Family History Centre, you will be able to click through to the page image; otherwise you will be invited to sign up to Findmypast. A very useful feature is the 'Copy' button, top right. This copies the entire text of the entry, along with the citation details, to the clipboard, so that you can then paste it into your word processor or text editor — a convenient and accurate way of recording the information found.

In spite of the amount of data provided by FamilySearch, there are significant limitations which mean that it does not make other online census collections redundant.

The restricted search options can make finding an individual, unless he or she has a relatively uncommon name, rather frustrating. This is compounded by the small number of fields shown for each person, which will often make it impossible to identify a sought-after ancestor among a listing of similarly named individuals. Also, the calculated birth years are based on strict subtraction of age from census year and are therefore mostly one year out.

Most significantly, the lack of images means that you will still need to use other sites to verify the index entries before incorporating the information into your pedigree. Coupled with the absence of TNA references in most years, this means that these indexes can really only be treated as finding aids rather than as citeable sources. The exception here is the 1881 Census Index for England and Wales, which indexes all available data fields and provides a full TNA reference.

Of course, if you are accessing the site from a Family History Centre (FHC) (see p. 122), these limitations will be of no significance, since

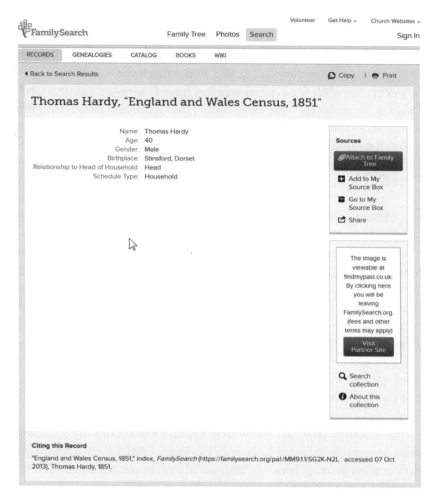

Figure 7.4 FamilySearch individual census record for 1851.

you will be able to check all details against the original images free of charge. So the real value of these census indexes, not surprisingly, is to FHC users. If you are accessing FamilySearch from anywhere else, you will need to sign up with Findmypast in order to view the images.

However, even if you are subscribed to another data service, the FamilySearch census indexes may be useful. If you have been unable to find an individual in an index provided by another commercial service, FamilySearch gives you free access to Findmypast's indexes. In spite of the limited fields provided by FamilySearch, it may well give you sufficient information to allow you to return to your usual data service and conduct a successful search. If you are on a tight budget, and are using a pay-per-view rather than subscription service, it could be worth your while to do initial searches free of charge on FamilySearch. This is particularly the case with the Scottish material, since ScotlandsPeople (see Chapter 14) charges not only for images but also for each page of search results.

FreeCEN

FreeCEN at <**www.freecen.org.uk**> is a volunteer project based on the better-known FreeBMD (<**www.freebmd.org.uk**>). It aims to provide a free online searchable database of the nineteenth-century UK census returns for England, Wales and Scotland. There is some coverage for the Channel Islands, but none for the Isle of Man or Ireland. The main focus has been on the 1891 census, and as of April 2014 the project had transcribed almost 26 million census entries, with over one quarter of these relating to 1891. Because this is only a fraction of the total 150 million records or so for the period covered, it is worth checking the coverage before you start using it. Since the 1881 census already has a free index online at FamilySearch (see above), there is almost no data for this on FreeCEN. The 1901 and 1911 censuses are not covered.

The statistics page at <**www.freecen.org.uk/statistics.html**> shows what percentage of records have been transcribed for each county in each census year. (There are individual entries on this page for the three ridings of Yorkshire, listed alphabetically by the name of the riding, not under 'Y'.) In some cases there is 100 per cent coverage, but for most there is considerably less, in some cases nothing at all. One English county, Cornwall, has 100 per cent coverage or near it for all censuses. Up to the 1871 census, the coverage for Scottish counties is very good, and you can save money on pay-per-view credits at ScotlandsPeople (see Chapter 14) by doing initial searches on FreeCEN.

The search form (see Fig. 7.5) allows you to search on any field on the enumeration schedule, including the language and disability fields.

If you wish to assist with the project, whether in transcribing or checking, there are contact details for each county sub-project at <**www. freecen.org.uk/project.htm**>.

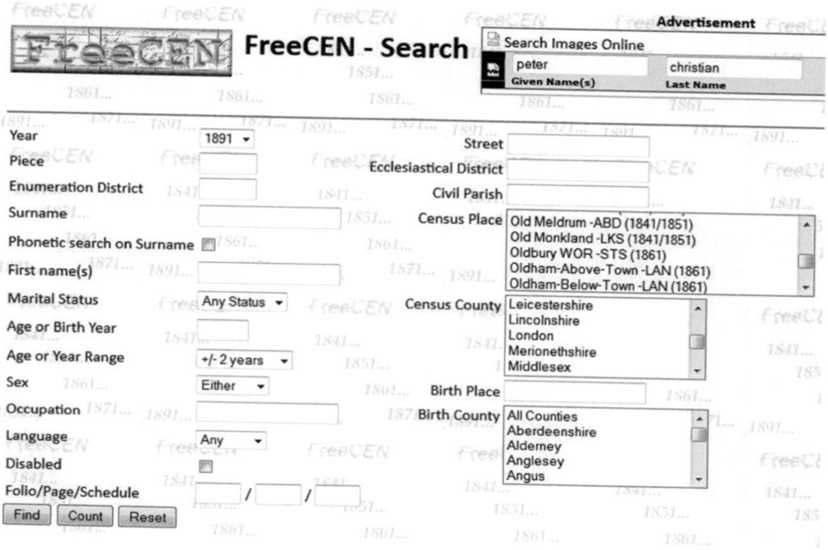

Figure 7.5 FreeCEN search form.

FHS Online

S&N Genealogy Supplies, who run TheGenealogist and RootsUK (see Chapter 10), also have a site called FHS Online at <**www.fhs-online. co.uk**>, designed to allow family history societies to publish their datasets.

It currently has around 50 county census indexes for individual years covering 33 different counties in England and Wales. Registration is required before you can search the indexes, but this does not involve payment. (The only census indexes which require payment are those for Worcestershire, which cost £14.95 for 12 months' access.)

The indexes, which can be searched on name and age, usually give TNA piece and folio number, though some give only the piece number. All the census indexes are marked as partial, so you cannot be certain to find someone, even if you are sure of their location on census night. Searching requires at least one letter of a forename. Figure 7.6 shows a typical page of search results. Clicking on 'Find this person's family' in the right-hand column brings up a list of all household members.

There is also a master search available from the home page, which searches all the databases.

Figure 7.6 FHS Online search results.

Local projects

Alongside these two volunteer projects with nationwide coverage, there are many, sometimes *very* local indexes made by local organisations or individual volunteers. Sites dedicated to particular parishes may well include census record indexes or transcriptions. Because the amounts of data are often quite small — sometimes fewer than 100 households — some of these sites offer just static pages rather than searchable indexes with search forms.

Here are just a few examples:

- The 1841 census for the Channel Islands has been transcribed by Lorna Pratt at <**members.shaw.ca/Jerseymaid/**>.
- The Sheffield Indexers have an index for the 1841 census in Sheffield at <**www.sheffieldindexers.com/1841Census_Index.html**>.

- Durham Records Online at <**www.durhamrecordsonline.com**> provides a free name index for County Durham, complete for the 1841 census and covering a large part of the county for 1851 to 1891. The site operates a pay-per-view system for access to the full individual records, though this is quite expensive at £1.50 per record.

- The Wirksworth Parish Records site includes a full transcription of the 1841–1901 censuses for 33 enumeration districts in the Wirksworth area (Derbyshire) at <**www.wirksworth.org.uk/ CENSUS.htm**>.

- The Froyle Censuses 1841-1911 site at <**www.froyle.com/census. htm**> has transcripts for all the censuses for the parish of Froyle in Hampshire.

- The Bunny Village website (Nottinghamshire) has census transcriptions for the parish for 1841–1911 at <**www.bunnyvillage.org.uk/ censusmain.htm**>.

- The website for Calverly in the West Riding of Yorkshire has searchable transcriptions for 1841–1911 at <**vitaldb.moorlandit.com**>.

Where there is an Online Parish Clerk (OPC) project for a county, you may well find a selection of census transcriptions among the project's data. The Dorset OPC site at <**www.opcdorset.org**>, for example, has census transcriptions for many individual parishes. At the time of writing there are ten county OPC projects: Cornwall, Devon, Dorset, Essex, Hampshire, Lancashire, Somerset, Sussex, Warwickshire and Wiltshire. Links to them will be found on Genuki's OPC listing at <**www.genuki.org.uk/indexes/OPC.html**>.

A special-purpose set of transcriptions is provided by the Workhouses site at <**www.workhouses.org.uk**>, with 1881 census records for many workhouses in the British Isles. There is no central listing; each is linked from the individual page for the relevant workhouse. From the home page, select 'Workhouse locations', then the Poor Law Unions for the country you want, then the county, then the individual town. At the bottom of the page you will find a link to the census data (see Fig. 7.7). In some cases there are separate lists for inmates and staff.

You can also enter a name in the search box at the top of the home page to look for individuals across the whole site. If you include both forename and surname, you will need to put them between inverted commas.

The Workhouse

The story of an institution...

Google™ Custom Search | Search

Help | News | My Books | Bookstore | Talks | Donate | Author | Contact | Copyright | Privacy

Home page
Introduction
Poor Laws
Workhouse Locations
Early Workhouses
Poor Law Union Maps
English Poor Law Unions
Summary List
Bedfordshire
Berkshire
Buckinghamshire
Cambridgeshire
Channel Islands
Cheshire
Cornwall
Cumberland
Derbyshire
Devon
Dorset
County Durham
Essex
Gloucestershire
Hampshire
Herefordshire
Hertfordshire
Huntingdonshire

1881 Census: Residents of Northampton Union Workhouse

Name	Mar	Age	Sex	Relation	Occupation	Handicap	Birthplace
Staff							
Edward ABELL	M	37	M	Husband (Head)	Master Of Workhouse (Munci)		Hatherleigh, Devon
Ann Elizth. ABELL	M	43	F	Wife	Matron Of Workhouse		Dartmouth, Devon
Annie E. ABELL		8	F	Daur			Northampton
Ernest ABELL		5	M	Son			Northampton
John REACH	M	37	M	Husband (Head)	Schoolmaster Of Workhouse		Bury St Edmunds, Suffolk
Annie REACH	M	35	F	Wife	Schoolmistress Of Workhouse		Corfe Castle, Dorset
Harry REACH		9	M	Son			Northampton
Sydney REACH		3	M	Son			Northampton
Jonah TURSELTON	M	36	M	Husband (Head)	Porter Of Workhouse (Munic)		Moulton, Northampton
Triphena TURSELTON	M	40	F	Wife	Portress Of Workhouse		Weston Favell, Northampton
May TURSELTON		10m	F	Daur			Northampton
Ellen MADGE	U	38	F	Officer	Nurse Workhouse Infirmary		Tavistock, Devon
Harriett GOSSAGE	M	44	F	Officer	Nurse Workhouse Infirmary		Churchill, Oxford
Thirza PARSONS	W	41	F	Officer (Head)	Laundress Of Workhouse		Chardgrove, Oxford
Willie PARSONS		9	M	Son			Sandhurst, Berkshire
Inmates							
Charles AASON	U	48	M	Inmate	None	Imbecile	Northampton
Ann ADAMS	W	80	F	Inmate	Charwoman		Towcester, Northampton
Hannah ADAMS	W	63	F	Inmate	Lace Maker		Gt Houghton, Northampton
John ADAMS	W	74	M	Inmate	Butcher		Northampton
Thomas ADAMS	U	60	M	Inmate	Farm Labourer		Duston, Northampton
Thomas AFLECK		11	M	Inmate	Scholar		Northampton
John ALDRIDGE		6	M	Inmate	Scholar		Northampton
Kate ALDRIDGE		11	F	Inmate	Scholar		Northampton
Mark ALDRIDGE		9	M	Inmate	Scholar		Northampton

Figure 7.7 Workhouse census transcription.

Local census indexes for Ireland are covered in Chapter 15.

Finding free census data

Many local census indexes are on small sites which may not be easy to find using a search engine unless you know what places and years they cover, though it is always worth using a search engine to look for the word 'census' along with a county and a census year.

However, more useful are the sites which provide listings of online census indexes. It is probably worth checking these first before you settle down to the rather more time-consuming business of using a search engine.

Census Online at <www.census-online.com> has links to census sites for the British Isles (separate pages for England, Wales, Scotland and Ireland), the United States and Canada. There are over 650 links for the British Isles, with a page for each county. Many pages offer a link to a subscription database, but this is only a link to Ancestry's UK Census Collection (see Chapter 8). This site is a good place to find links to transcriptions of those pre-1841 censuses that list individuals (see pp. 9–11).

Census Finder has a very comprehensive collection of links to both commercial and free census indexes at <**www.censusfinder.com**>.

Cyndi's List has a substantial set of pages devoted to online census material for the UK and Ireland at <**www.cyndislist.com/uk/census**>. There are also links to the related pages for the censuses of the United States and Canada, and there is a Census Worldwide page at <**www. cyndislist.com/census2.htm**>.

Finally, Genuki's county pages are good places to look for census indexes relating to individual counties and parishes. See <**www.genuki. org.uk**>.

8

ANCESTRY

Ancestry is a long-established US genealogical data service, launched in 1995. It unveiled a site dedicated to UK records at <**www.ancestry. co.uk**> in September 2002, with the 1891 census as the first set of records. It now provides indexes to all the released censuses for the British Isles, with the exception of the 1911 census for Scotland. Ancestry also provides images of the original records for the censuses of England and Wales, but for Scotland only the indexes are available, as the Scottish authorities have decided not to grant the right to digitise the images to companies competing with ScotlandsPeople (see p. 119).

The 1881 data for England and Wales is taken from the 1881 Census Index created by the volunteer project discussed in Chapter 7 and also available on FamilySearch at <**www.familysearch.org**>.

In 2013, Ancestry added The National Archives of Ireland (NAI) census indexes from the official Irish census site at <**census.nationalarchives. ie**> (see Chapter 15). Ancestry does not provide the images for Ireland but each record links to the free image on the NAI site. The Irish indexes are free to use and do not require a subscription.

Charges

Ancestry is essentially a subscription site. There are three subscriptions relevant to UK family historians. The UK Premium subscription includes access to all record collections relating to the UK and Ireland and costs £12.95 a month or £107.40 for a year. The UK Essentials subscription is intended for newcomers and includes only the civil registration and census records. It costs £10.95 a month or £83.40 for a year. A Worldwide subscription costs £18.95 per month or £155.40 for a year, giving access to all of Ancestry's data collections.

If you live in the US, Canada or Australia, Ancestry has sites at <**www. ancestry.com**>, <**www.ancestry.ca**> and <**www.ancestry.com.au**> with subscriptions for access to local records as well as the World subscription. For a World Deluxe membership it does not matter which national site you use to subscribe (and your username and password work on all Ancestry sites), but of course you can subscribe to the UK site only from <**www.ancestry.co.uk**>. All subscriptions on the Australian site offer UK census records as a matter of course, so for anyone interested in tracing both British Isles and Australian branches of their family it would make sense to sign up on the Australian site rather than take out a World subscription on the UK site. There is no equivalent on the US and Canadian sites, so if you have British Isles and North American ancestry, you would need to go for the World Deluxe membership.

In the case of World Deluxe subscription, it can be worth checking the prices and current exchange rates before subscribing: at the time of writing, the World Deluxe subscription was at least 10 per cent cheaper from the UK site than from the others.

There is a further money-saving option which may be worth considering, particularly if you are just starting out: the Platinum Edition of Ancestry's genealogy software Family Tree Maker (currently around £40) includes six months' UK Premium access to Ancestry UK, making it only slightly more expensive than two months' worth of subscription. The Deluxe edition of Family Tree Maker is around £10 cheaper and comes with three months' UK Essentials subscription. On occasion, both prices are substantially discounted in Ancestry's online shop (click on the 'Shop' button on the navigation bar at the top of any Ancestry page).

Although Ancestry is known as a subscription site, when it added the 1901 census it introduced a pay-per-view option, which gives you ten record views within a 14-day period for £6.95. 'Records' here means 'images of records', not just the transcriptions, which are not charged. However, while this is not necessarily bad value, it hardly compares with the unlimited access provide by the 14-day free trial, discussed below, and the monthly £9.95 subscription. Details of the pay-per-view scheme are at <**ancestryuk.custhelp.com/app/answers/detail/a_ id/2318**>. When the pay-per-view scheme was initially launched, Ancestry provided a voucher scheme for those not wanting to use a credit/debit card online, but this option is no longer available.

Some features of Ancestry do not require any form of subscription or other payment, but you are still required to register and will then be given a Registered Guest account. In the case of the census records, this means you can search all 1881 indexes for England and Wales and both the Irish censuses. These particular indexes are, of course, free elsewhere, so their inclusion is only really a way of making global searches more comprehensive and not on their own a reason to sign up with Ancestry.

The site provides a 14-day free trial. To register for this you have to give credit/debit card details and if you do not cancel the trial before it expires, the cost of a full annual subscription is charged to your card. The key thing if you do not want your trial to turn into a subscription is to ensure that you do not leave cancellation until the last minute. In particular, if your trial runs out on a Sunday, make sure you do not leave any cancellation till the Sunday itself, as it will not be processed until the following day. Ancestry provides detailed information on cancellation — click on the 'Get Help' link at the top right of any page and search for the article 'How to cancel a subscription'.

As discussed on p. 121 (Chapter 5), access to Ancestry is widely available free of charge in public libraries, as well as in The National Archives' reading room at Kew and at the Society of Genealogists, so there is plenty of opportunity to try the site out without signing up for the trial. This also means you can use Ancestry's census indexes even if you have not got your own internet connection. There are several features of Ancestry not available to those accessing the site via an institutional subscription rather than with a personal username. Depending on the policy of the host institution, you may or may not be able to download images and save them to a USB memory stick. However, Ancestry allows you to 'share' an image, which makes it possible to see and download the image from another computer. This feature is discussed later in this chapter, on p. 185.

Searching

One issue that must be mentioned at the start of any description of Ancestry's search facilities is that at the time of writing these are in flux. In 2013, Ancestry introduced its 'New Search' and warned that its 'Old Search' would be withdrawn. When a considerable body of users complained, Ancestry added an option to start incorporating the most missed features of the Old Search into the New Search, under the name 'Category Exact Search'. Since the Old Search will presumably be retired at some point, only the two flavours of New Search are covered here. If you do want to try the Old Search itself while it is still available, the Search home page at <search.ancestry.co.uk/search> has a 'Go to Old Search' link at the top right, which takes you to the Old Search home page at <search.ancestry.co.uk/oldsearch>.

When you log in to Ancestry, the Search home page (click on 'Search' from the home page) offers a form covering all the datasets included in your subscription with various ways of selecting the dataset(s) you want to search. The quickest way to get to the census records is to select 'UK Census Collection' from the right-hand panel. From the UK census Collection page at <www.ancestry.co.uk/search/rectype/census/uk> you can either search across all UK censuses or you can select an individual year and country from the panel below the search box. This does not provide an option to search England and Wales as a unit: the two countries are listed separately, as are the Channel Islands and the Isle of Man. Alternatively, you can select a year but not a country from the panel on the right of the screen. If you do this the initial search results will simply list the number of matches in each part of the UK, and you can then select the results for the part you want.

The search form in Figure 8.1 is for the basic search in a single year. The 'Show Advanced' button at the top right switches you to the advanced search form (see Fig. 8.2). The forms for the 1841 census do not have the fields for family members.

There are two main differences between the basic and advanced search. First, as you can see from Figure 8.2, the advanced search offers additional fields for location, relation to head of household, and The National Archives reference. Second, you have much more flexibility in matching your search fields — you can either select an exact match on all fields with the checkbox at the top of the form, or you can choose individual fields for exact matching. This can make a huge difference to the number of search results. A further benefit is the option to specify the year range: in the basic search the results will automatically include birth years up to five either side of the year given; in the advanced search you can make this range narrower or wider, up to ten years either side. This field can therefore be tailored appropriately for your level of certainty about when an ancestor was born.

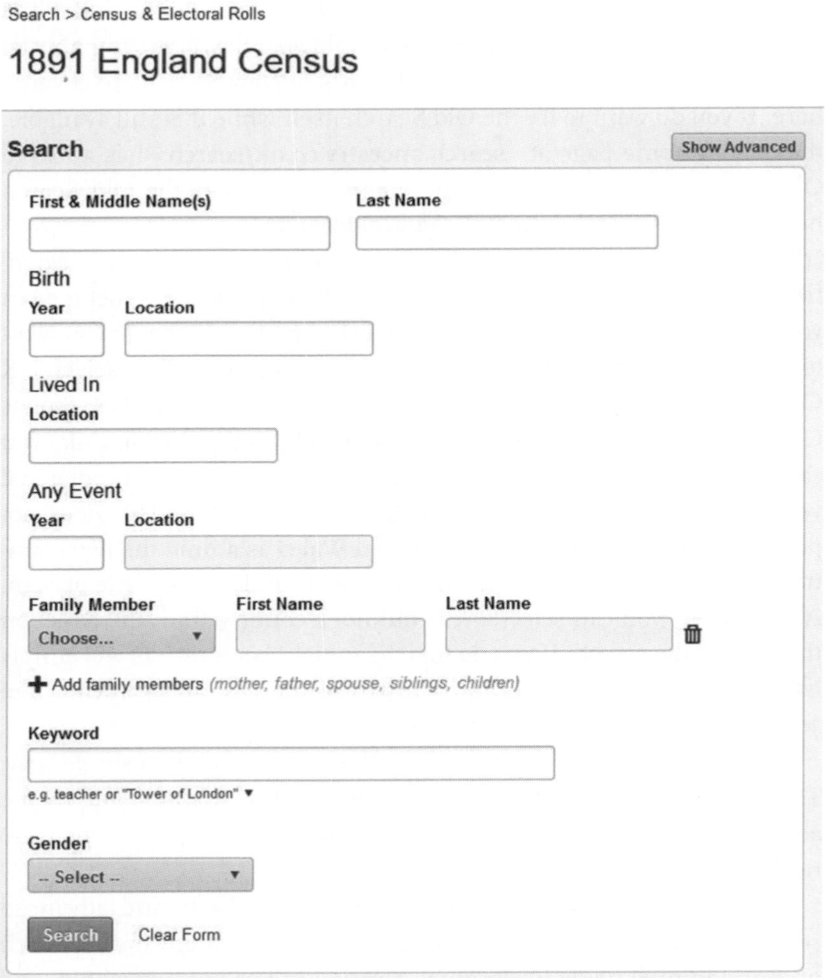

Search > Census & Electoral Rolls

1891 England Census

Search | Show Advanced

First & Middle Name(s) **Last Name**

Birth
Year Location

Lived In
Location

Any Event
Year Location

Family Member **First Name** **Last Name**
Choose... ▼

➕ Add family members *(mother, father, spouse, siblings, children)*

Keyword

e.g. teacher or "Tower of London" ▼

Gender
-- Select -- ▼

Search Clear Form

Figure 8.1 Ancestry UK Census Collection basic search form.

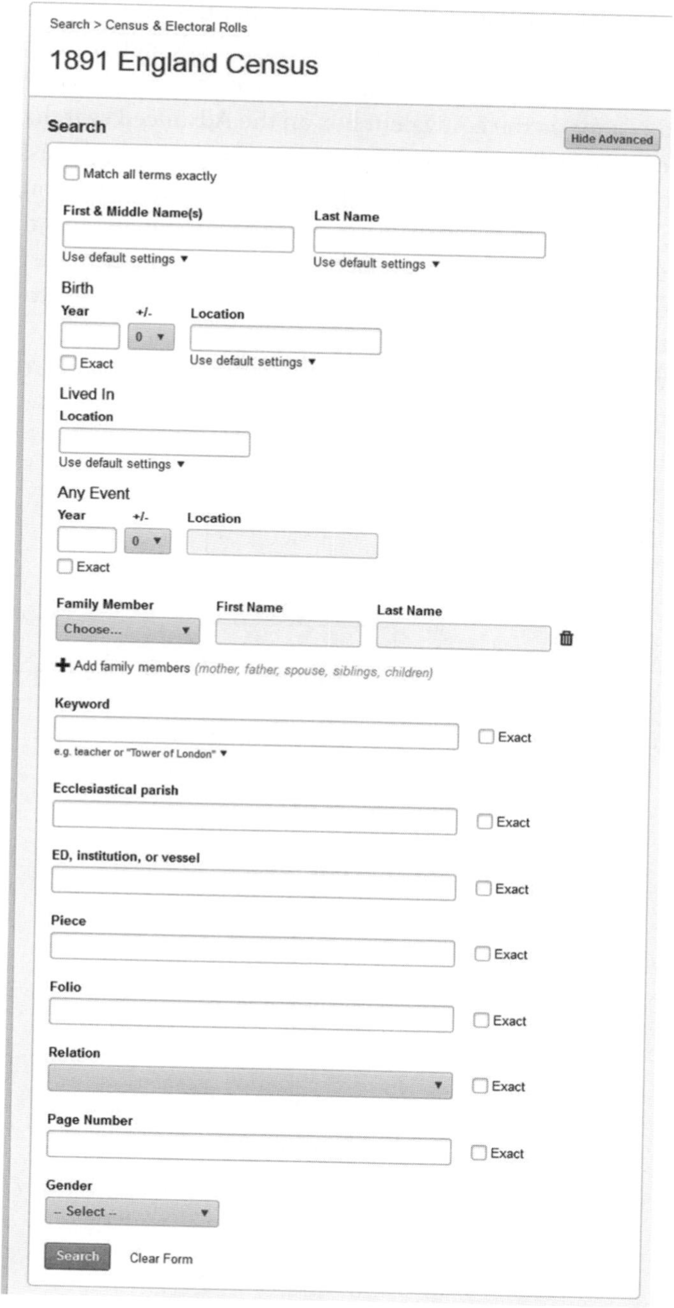

Figure 8.2 Ancestry Advanced search form for the UK Census Collection.

The 'Category Exact Search', which Ancestry has introduced to pacify disgruntled users of the Old Search, adds a single option to the Basic search: there is a check box to 'Match all terms exactly'. Since this does exactly the same as the equivalent box on the Advanced search, it is not clear that it is really very useful. In fact, it is significantly less useful than the Advanced search's exact matching options, since you cannot override it on individual fields. Also, the procedure to get this option to display on the search form is pretty tedious — you need to use the 'Site preferences' page, selected from the drop-down menu from your username at the top of the screen.

A flowchart of the search process for Ancestry's UK census records is shown in Figure 8.3.

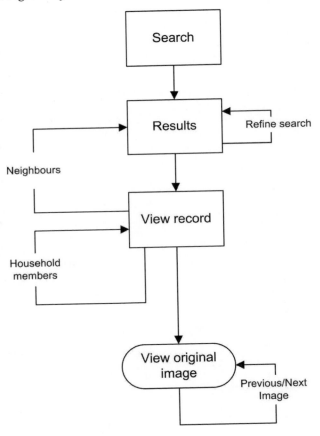

Figure 8.3 Ancestry search process.

Major George Graham (Registrar General 1842–1879) was responsible for the planning and execution of every census from 1851–1871.

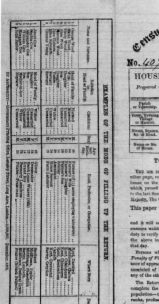

2 A rare example of a household schedule from the 1851 census for 51 Leazes Terrace, Newcastle upon Tyne, showing the instructions to the householder for filling it in. (HO 107/2405)

3 Household schedule showing attorney James Grant, 'admitted in Ireland but retired from practice', his daughter Emily, a 'retired vocalist', and their servant Susana Ball. (HO 107/2405)

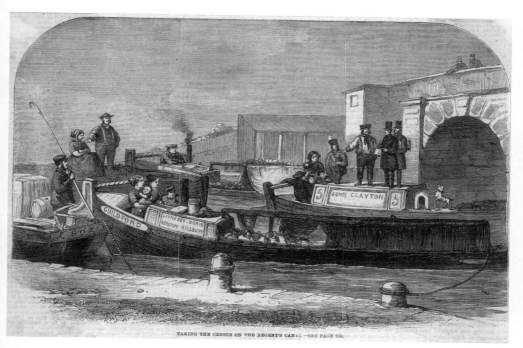

TAKING THE CENSUS ON THE REGENT'S CANAL.—SEE PAGE 250.

4 *Above:* The enumerator gathering information from the occupants of a barge on the Regents Canal in 1861.

5 *Below:* 'Memorandum respecting the Enumeration of Persons in Boats, Barges &c.' from the Census Office 1861. (RG 27/3)

MEMORANDUM respecting the Enumeration of Persons in Boats, Barges, &c.

These "Forms for Vessels" are sent for the use of the Person or Persons who may be entrusted with the enumeration of persons sleeping on the night of Sunday, April 7th, on board Boats, Barges, or other Craft, in waters within the limits of the Sub-District, but *beyond the jurisdiction of the Officers of Customs.*

Under ordinary circumstances, it will not be necessary for the Persons charged with this duty to go on board the Vessels for the purpose of leaving Forms *before the morning of Monday, April 8th.* As early as possible on that morning, every Vessel should be visited, and the Master or person in charge should be requested to fill up one of the Forms. Should he be unable to write, the Form must be filled up for him from the information which he may furnish. The position of the Vessel, or the place at which she was lying, at midnight on April 7th, should always be written in, with the other required particulars, on the back of the Form.

All the Forms, properly filled up, should be delivered to the Registrar *before the 16th day of April,* in order that, having examined them, he may enter the total number of males and females in the "Registrar's Summary."

In localities where only a small number of Barges, &c., *with persons sleeping on board,* are likely to be on the night of April 7th, it will *not* be necessary to engage the special services of a person to visit them on the day of the Census, provided the Enumerators in whose Districts the Wharves or Landing-Places are situated will be able to enumerate them in a complete and effectual manner, without inconvenience. But where the Enumerators would be unduly delayed in their progress by the necessity for going on board any considerable number of Vessels, or where the enumeration of the persons therein might be incomplete if entrusted to them, other arrangements must be made, in conformity with the Instructions already given. (See "*Further Instructions to the Registrar,*" dated 18th Jan., 1861.)

In case the total expense incurred in getting the "Forms for Vessels" duly filled up does not exceed *Five Shillings,* the amount should be defrayed by the Registrar at the time the Returns are delivered to him, and charged in his own Claim for Allowances (Accounts Form marked B), after the charges (if any) for Postage and Carriage of Parcels. But if the expense exceeds that sum, a Claim must be made out by each of the persons employed on the printed Form (marked E) provided for the purpose, and sent forward by the Registrar to the Superintendent Registrar, to be dealt with in the same manner as the Enumerators' Claims for Allowances.

Census Office, London,

4th March, 1861.

George Graham

Registrar General.

CENSUS OF ENGLAND AND WALES, 1861.

Superintendent Registrar's District of *Kensington* No. 1/3
Registrar's Sub-District of *Kensington Town*

LIST of Persons duly qualified, according to the Instructions prepared under the direction of the Secretary of State, to act as ENUMERATORS within the above-named Sub-District, and proposed for appointment in that capacity.

NAME	Age	OCCUPATION	PLACE OF ABODE	No. of the Enumeration District proposed to be assigned to him
Edward Edwin Burnes	36 Years	Grocer	Prospect Place Old Brompton	1
Charles William Cunford	51 Years	Gas Rate Collector	Victoria Terrace Notting Hill	2
Charles Graham	60 Years	Teacher	22 Kensington Park Terrace North Notting Hill	3
George Inglish	59 Years	Carpenter Waterworks &c	6 Albert Terrace Notting Hill	4
Philip Thomas Hyde	39 Years	Fishmonger	8 Bedford Terrace Kensington	5
James Hellings	58 Years	Land Agent	South Bank Villa Notting Hill	6
Joseph Mayes	30 Years	Assistant Surveyor of Taxes	43 Rudroth Kensington	7
Samuel Smith	32 Years	House Decorator	22 Upper Uxbridge Notting Hill	
George King		Commercial Traveller	15 Brunswick Brompton	
Alfred Ellis	48 Years	Collector of Christmas Rates	16 William Place Kensington	
John Charles Lindsey	35 Years	Collector of Taxes	Johns Terrace Notting Hill	
George Page	25 Years	House Proprietor	15 King St Kensington	
Thomas Taylor	35 Years	Gardener	13 Peel Street Kensington	

CENSUS OF ENGLAND AND WALES, 1861.

Superintendent Registrar's District of *Kensington* No. 1/3
Registrar's Sub-District of *Kensington Town*

LIST of Persons duly qualified, according to the Instructions prepared under the direction of the Secretary of State, to act as ENUMERATORS within the above-named Sub-District, and proposed for appointment in that capacity.

NAME	Age	OCCUPATION	PLACE OF ABODE	No. of the Enumeration District proposed to be assigned to him
George Dixe	55 Years	Office Clerk	Holland Street Kensington	21
William Henry Challis	45 Years	No occupation (House Proprietor)	Durham Place Notting Hill	22
William Cowderoy	45 Years	Jeweller	2 High Street Kensington	23
Samuel Charles Kingston	38 Years	Collector of Taxes	16 Gloucester Terrace Kensington	24
Edward Inglish	21 Years	Hinds	Murray House Holland Kensington	25
Thomas Hardy	48 Years	General Agent	15 King Street Kensington	26
Joseph Palmer	29 Years	Fruiterer	Notting Hill	27
Abel Bugler	34 Years	Merchant's Clerk	16 Devonshire Terrace Notting Hill	28
Walter Samuel Meyer	33 Years	Collector of Rates	9 Ladbroke Road Notting Hill	29
John Swindley	27 Years	Office Clerk	2 Allaton Terrace Kensington	30
Charles Green	45 Years	Grocer	13 Church Street Kensington	31
Henry Blackhall	48 Years	Master of Kensington Workhouse	Kensington Workhouse	32
Edward Brottenshire	44 Years	Master of St Margaret's Workhouse	St Margaret's Workhouse Kensington	33

6 and 7 *Above:* List of enumerators for Kensington, showing ages, addresses and occupations. These and a few other pages from 1861 are the only examples of such lists that have survived from any census year. (RG 9/4543)

8 *Right:* The enumerator's lot was not always a happy one!

THE ENUMERATOR ENDURES SOME CHAFF.

CENSUS OF ENGLAND AND WALES, 1871.

Superintendent Registrar's District ___

Registrar's Sub-District ___

Enumeration District, No. *10 B.*

Name of Enumerator, Mr. *Charles Coleman*

DESCRIPTION OF ENUMERATION DISTRICT.

[This description is to be written in by the Enumerator from the Copy supplied to him by the Registrar. Any explanatory notes or observations calculated to make the description clearer or more complete, may be added by the Enumerator.]

Col. 1.		Col. 2.
Owthorne Parish Part of	All that part of Parish called South Frodingham and Rimswell	lived in this district nearly all my lifetime so that I knew every foot of it, and nearly every soul. C.C.

This district chiefly consists of Ag. Lab. and Farmers, a people that understand hard work more than filling up a census schedule this accounts for me being detained so long in collecting them, were very truthful in giving me any information I required which I found to be of great service although I have

Very badly paid, I think if Government Officials had to do it, they would be paid treble the amount   (*Myler Falla*)

Above left: Some enumerators were unusually conscientious, such as Charles Coleman in the East Riding of Yorkshire in 1871. (RG 10/4799)

Above right: Myler Falla was unhappy with his rate of pay as an enumerator for Mortlake, Surrey in 1871. (RG 10/870)

Right: Not all householders treated the census schedule with respect.

Below: Edward Henry Blade demonstrated his displeasure at the small sum paid for a lot of work in a very crowded part of the East End of London in 1851. (HO 107/1531)

THE MAN WHO LIGHTS HIS PIPE WITH THE SCHEDULE.

18

Parish or Township of	Ecclesiastical District of	City or Borough of	Town of	Village of
Hallows Barking		London		

Name of Street, Place, or Road, and Name or No. of House	Name and Surname of each Person who abode in the house, on the Night of the 30th March, 1851	Relation to Head of Family	Condition	Age of Males	Age of Females	Rank, Profession, or Occupation	Where Born	Whether Blind, or Deaf-and-Dumb

The enumeration of this district was undertaken by me in the belief that I should be fairly paid for my services. I was not aware that all the particulars were to be entered by the enumerator in a book, the work without that being ample for the sum paid nor had I any idea of the unreasonable amount of labour imposed. The distribution collection &c of the schedules together with the copying of the same occupied from two to three hours for every 60 persons enumerated, and for this the equivalent is — ONE SHILLING !!! That man possessing the intelligence & business habits necessary for the undertaking would not be found to accept it if aware of the labour involved. How then can a correct return of the population be expected? He who proposed the scale of remuneration, should in justice be con...

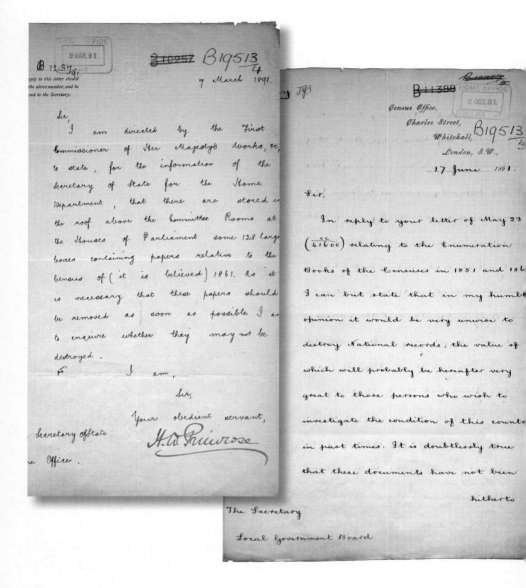

13 *Left:* In 1891 Mr Primrose was very keen to dispose of the Enumeration Books for 1851 and 1861. (HO 45/10147)

14 *Right:* Fortunately for posterity, Registrar General Brydges Henniker took the opposite view. (HO 45/10147)

Jane Whitmarsh	Do	U.		21	Servant	Hampshire, Newport I.W.	
Rosena Leary	Do	U.		18	Prostitute	Hampshire, Do Do	
Ellen Denton	Do	U.		27	Servant	Hampshire, Do Do	
Maria Hawkins	Do	U.		24	Prostitute	Hampshire, Freshwater I.W.	
Ann Cotton	Do	U.		17	Prostitute	Hampshire, Newport I.W.	
Ann White	Do	U.		20	Prostitute	Hampshire, Carisbrooke I.W.	
Charlotte Ward	Do	U.		23	Servant	Hampshire, Portsea	
	Total of Persons...		2	18			

15 18-year-old Rosina Leary in the Isle of Wight 'House of Industry' in 1851, described as a prostitute. She bore at least eight children by William Ask and George Pragnell. (HO 107/1663)

Page 4] The undermentioned Houses are situate within the Boundaries of the

No. of Schedule	ROAD, STREET, &c., and No. or NAME of HOUSE	HOUSES Inhabited	NAME and Surname of each Person	RELATION to Head of Family	CONDITION as to Marriage	AGE last Birthday Males / Females	Rank, Profession, or OCCUPATION	WHERE BORN
18	90 Lower Charlotte St	1	Arthur Villey	Head	Mar	52	Laborer R.M. Dock	Nottingham Arnsbury
			Mariam do	wife	do	49		Norfolk Norwich
19	88	do	1	John Graves	Boarder	Unm	32	Army Pensioner	Berkshire Blackburn
	88	do	1	John Worley	Head	Mar	44	Bootmaker	Hants Portsea
			Jemima do	wife	do	44		do do
			John do	Son	Unm	20	Assistant Haberdasher &	do do
			Jane do	Dgr	do	18	Dressmaker Confectioner	do do
			Alfred Worley	Son	do	15	Baker	do do
			Thomas do	do		10	Scholar	do do
			Samuel do	do		8	do	do do
			James do	do		6	do	do do
			Mary Ann do	Dgr		3	do	do do
20	86	do	1	Leonard Pond	Head	Mar	57	Stoker at Gasworks	Dorset
			Frances do	Son	Unm	18	Brushmaker	do
			Joseph do	do	do	16	do	Hants Portsmouth
			George Prangell	Boarder	Mar	40	Laborer H.M. Dock	do do
			Polly do	do	do	38		do Isle of Wight
			Rosena do	do	do	14	Scholar	do Portsmouth
			Clara do	do	do	11	do	do do
			Ada do	do		9	do	do do
			Sarah do	do		7	do	do do
21	84	do	1	Thomas Wright	Head	Mar	65	Sawyer	

16 The Pragnell family (entered as 'Prangell') boarding with the Pond family in Portsmouth in 1881. The whole family later reverted back to the name Ask. (RG 11/1139)

Page 4

RETURN of all the PERSONS who SLEPT or ABODE in this INSTITUTION on the NIGHT of SUNDAY, APRIL 5th, 1891.

	NAME and SURNAME	RELATION to Head of Family, or Position in the Institution	CONDITION as to Marriage	AGE last Birthday Males / Females	PROFESSION or OCCUPATION	Employer	Employed	Neither Employer nor Employed	WHERE BORN	If (1) Deaf-and-Dumb (2) Blind (3) Lunatic, Imbecile or Idiot
1	Austin Nancy	Pauper	Widow		None				Hampshire Fareham	
2	Ansell James	do	Single		Basketmaker				Hampshire Portsmouth	Childhood
3	Anderson Job	do	Widower		Poultry Dealer					Imbecile
4	Ask Rosina	do	Widow		Laundress				Hampshire Portsmouth	
5	Alexander Benjamin	do	Widower		General Laborer				Suffolk Bungay	
6	Akins Charles	do	Widower		General Laborer				Essex Girkwood	
7	Atkins Albert	do	Single						Marston	

17 The widowed Rosina Ask, laundress, in the Union Workhouse, Portsea Island, in 1891. (RG 12/860)

18 *Left:* A Hollerith punch-card machine as supplied to the GRO by the British Tabulating Machine Company.

19 *Centre:* An example of one of the punch-cards used to tabulate the results of the 1911 census. (T 1/11243)

20 *Below:* The 1911 census asked for information about occupations. William Bailey supplied much more detail than was actually required. (RG 14/24246/142)

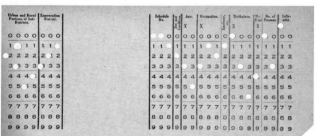

1 Household schedules and instructions for the 1911 Census translated into German and Yiddish. (RG 27/8)

2 Abraham Shedletsky, Kosher butcher, and his family in Whitechapel in 1911. The children's ages and birthplaces suggest the Shedletskys came to England in the late 1890s. (RG 14/1459/30)

CENSUS OF ENGLAND AND WALES, 1911.

NAME AND SURNAME	RELATIONSHIP to Head of Family	AGE	PARTICULARS as to MARRIAGE			PROFESSION or OCCUPATION				BIRTHPLACE	NATIONALITY	INFIRMITY
Abraham Lazarus-Shedletsky	Head	42	Married	22		Retail Butcher	Kosher			Russian Poland	Russian	
Deborah Shedletsky	Wife	41	Married	22		Assisting in the business				Russian Poland	Russian	
Lewis Lazarus-Shedletsky	Son	16	Single			Theological Student				Russian Poland	Russian	
David Lazarus-Shedletsky	Son	12				School				London Whitechapel		
Deborah Lazarus-Shedletsky	Daughter	10				School				London Whitechapel		
Samuel Lazarus-Shedletsky	Son	6				School				London Whitechapel		
Fanny Lazarus-Shedletsky	Daughter	5				School				London Whitechapel		
Annie Nehmann	Servant	21	Single			General Servant				Russia	Russian	

City or ~~Borough~~ of _London_

Parish or ~~Township~~ of _St Swithin_

PLACE	HOUSES Uninhabited or Building	HOUSES Inhabited	NAMES of each Person who abode therein the preceding Night.	AGE and SEX Males	AGE and SEX Females	PROFESSION, TRADE, EMPLOYMENT, or of INDEPENDENT MEANS.	Where Born Whether Born in same County	Where Born Whether Born in Scotland, Ireland, or Foreign Parts.
St			H George Richardson	3			Y	
Swithins		1	H James Hind	47		Book Binder	Y	
Lane			Eliza Dove		31	F. S.	Y	
			H Mary Carse		13	F. S.	Y	
D		1	Priscilla Keate		55	Char Woman	Y	
			Louisa D		12	F. S.		
D		1	Priscilla Keate		17	F. S.		
			Mr					
			John Travers					
			will not					
			give any					
			information					
			respecting					
			the persons					
			who abode					
			in his house on					
			the night of					
			June 6th					
			only that the					
			Number was	12	5			
			N Travers fine five Pounds					
			at the Mansion House by Sir					
			Peter Laurie			Alfred Aslen Miller		
			June 23 1841			Registrar.		
D		1	Jane Gronow		55	IM		S
TOTAL in Page 6	4 ✓		✓	14	11 ✓		✓	

23 John Travers in the City of London who was fined £5 for refusing to supply information about his household in 1841. (HO 107/723/12)

24 Elizabeth Green, house servant, recorded in 1861. She initially refused to give her age and birthplace, but later supplied the information. (RG 9/792)

25 An unnamed 'Supposed Serjit Major in Army' and his family, from the 1891 census whose details the enumerator could only guess. (RG 12/471)

EARLY MORNING,—THE ENUMERATOR TAKING THE CENSUS IN ST. JAMES'S PARK.

26 An enumerator gathering information from vagrants who had spent census night in the open air.

27 Enumerator's note regarding stallholders who spent the night of 7 April 1861 in a field in Deptford following a fair. Information was given with 'much reluctance'. (RG 9/396)

Top: Henry Bullifant's birthplace, Colchester, is rendered as 'Coackerter' by a Sheffield enumerator in 1881. (RG 11/4647)

Centre: Sarah Bennett's birthplace in 1851 appears to be the non-existent 'Bucks, Jugford'. (HO 107/1516)

Bottom: The same family was correctly located in 'Berks, Twyford' in 1871. (RG 10/1288)

31 Henry Patterson's surname appeared with three different spellings in four census years: Paddison in 1851 (HO 107/2383), Pattison in 1861 (RG 9/3694) and 1871 (RG 10/4901) and finally as Patterson in 1881 (RG 11/4897).

32 Charles Darwin, naturalist and author (1809-1882).

33 *Below:* Charles Darwin in 1851, visiting his brother Erasmus. His daughters Annie and Etty, then in Great Malvern, were missed from the census. (HO 107/1476)

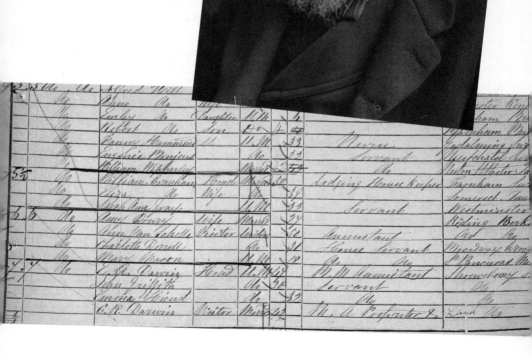

"WHAT'S THIS?"

34 *Top and centre:* Charles Lewington was born in Eversley, in Hampshire, but his birthplace was given as Warwickshire in 1871 (RG 10/2808), Walton, Shropshire, in 1881 (RG 11/3714), Shropshire in 1891 (RG 12/3001) and London in 1901 (RG 13/3450).

35 *Bottom:* The Welsh question: according to this entry in the 1891 Census for Llanbeddir-y-Cellin, Caernarvonshire, Evan Davies spoke only Welsh and his wife Jane spoke only English. (RG 12/4671)

36 *Left:* The census schedule was viewed with suspicion by many householders.

The site does not use any of the standard name-matching systems (see Chapter 6, pp. 142–148), but has its own method of identifying variants. This is nowhere fully documented but there is some limited information on the help pages:

> A Ranked Search automatically returns alternate spellings and abbreviations for name(s) of your ancestor. For example, a search for Bill Smith might return William Smith, Wm Smith, Bill Smyth or B. Smith.

You will also notice in any ranked search results (i.e. results with exact matching) that they include individuals where a middle initial might indicate the forename you have specified — so any John W. Smith will turn up in a search for *William Smith*. Ancestry allows wildcards, with the asterisk (*) standing for between zero and five characters and the question mark (?) for a single character. Unusually, wildcards are permitted at the beginning of a field.

Even the basic search form offers some quite sophisticated options, with the ability to add any number of additional search fields for family members and a Keyword field, which lets you add text for other fields not listed on the form (though some of these duplicate possible uses of the Location field):

- Ecclesiastical parish;
- Enumeration district (ED) institution or vessel;
- Relation to head;
- Age;
- Registration district;
- Sub-registration district;
- Household schedule number.

On the whole, the advanced form seems preferable, as it makes switching between exact and ranked results easy. As mentioned above, it also gives you the essential option of a birth year range, rather than a single birth year. Given the problems of birth year calculations mentioned in Chapter 6 (p. 150), being able to specify only a single year while carrying out an exact search will often lead to failed searches. There is no search which can be carried out on the basic form which cannot be carried out just as well on the advanced form.

Clicking on the 'Search' button brings up the search results. What you get here will depend on which form and matching options you have chosen.

Search results

If you have used the basic search with category exact mode or the advanced search with 'Match all terms exactly' selected, then you will get only those results which exactly match the field you have entered. In particular, any forename abbreviations and surname variants will be ignored. An exact search in the 1891 census of England for Thomas Hardy, born 1841, spouse Emma Hardy, brings up exactly one result, which, thankfully, is the correct one.

If you do a default basic search, or leave the 'Match all terms exactly' unchecked when doing a basic category exact search or an advanced search, then the first results will be the same as for an exact search but these will then be followed by other results where only some of the fields match. Without exact matching, a search for Thomas Hardy, born 1841, spouse Emma Hardy, brings up 1,819 results (see Fig. 8.4).

One of the problems with Ancestry's results listing, if you do not select exact matches, is that the results are ranked in a manner which is not made explicit and cannot be modified. As you can see from Figure 8.4, the exact match is listed first along with other matches which have the same spouse forename or its initial. Below the banner are those where there is no match on the spouse name, but a match on the year of birth. These are followed by further entries which gradually display more divergent birth years, up to five years either side of 1841; then come Hardys not called Thomas but born in 1841 and married to an Emma, followed by those with divergent birth years. At the bottom of the list are a bunch of people called Hardy, but not Thomas, born within five years of 1841, some of whom are not even married, never mind having the right spouse forename. Without extensive testing, it is impossible to say exactly how each additional search field would affect these rankings, but this example indicates that the ordering is not random and you can be reasonably sure that the most likely matches are in the first few pages of the listing.

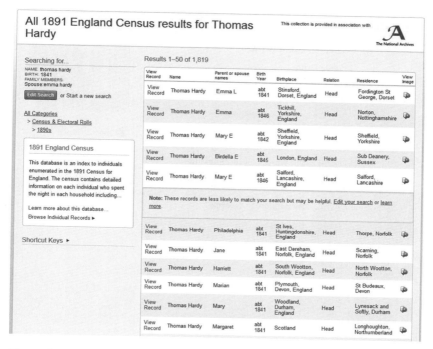

Figure 8.4 Ancestry search results.

If you have not found the ancestor you were looking for, you can use the 'Edit search' button to bring up the search form to refine your search terms, or change from an exact to a ranked search. Otherwise you can either go to the transcription of an individual census (the 'View Record' link) or go straight to the census image ('View Image'). In fact, you can get a preview of the individual record screen by moving your mouse over the 'View Record' link.

Figure 8.5 shows the transcription of Thomas Hardy's individual record in the 1891 census. From this page, you have several options:

- The 'View image' and 'View original image' links take you to the image viewer (see below).
- You can click on the name of any other household member to see the full record for that person.
- Under 'Neighbors', the 'View others on page' link brings up a results-style listing with the names of all the other people entered on the same page of the enumeration book.

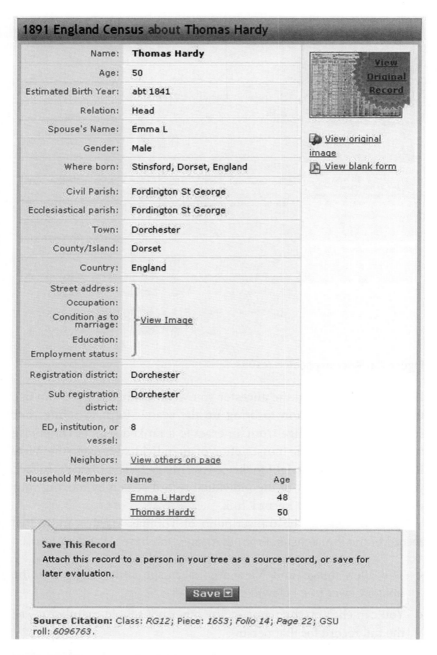

Figure 8.5 Ancestry individual record.

- The 'View blank form' simply brings up an image of a blank enumeration page as a PDF file.

- The 'Save' button offers various saving and sharing options which are discussed below.

Address search

Ancestry does not offer a separate census address search, and there is no simple way to find who is living at a particular address. But there are two facilities for finding particular places. On the main search form, you can in fact leave the name fields blank and enter a place in the Location field. Once you have typed an initial word, the form should offer you a list of options, from which you should select the one you want. You can use the 'Add Another Location' field to enter additional place elements. The Keyword field will also accept registration district and parish names. However, while this is good for finding places, it seems only occasionally possible to find a street this way — we tried entering street names in the Keyword field and had few successes (to be fair, the form does not mention street name as a candidate for this field).

An alternative is the browse option which is available for all the indexes except those for Scotland. This is quite time-consuming if you are just looking for a specific address, but will certainly be of interest to anyone using the census for local history. It can also be a last resort if you are pretty sure where an ancestor lived but have completely failed to find him or her in the search.

At the bottom of the page with the search form is a list of counties. This links to a list of each county's civil parishes, and then a list of enumeration districts (EDs) within the parish. For urban areas, there is a level of sub-registration districts before you get to the individual EDs. The districts are just listed by number so you need to read the accompanying description to see precisely what area a district covers. Unfortunately, urban areas tend to have large numbers of enumeration districts, and finding the right one for a particular street can be a long process. Clicking on the link to the ED opens up the image viewer with the first page of entries. You can then use the 'Next' button to browse through the pages.

Another use of the browse facility, which is not obvious at first glance, is to look for Royal Navy vessels. For the 1861–1881 and 1901 census indexes for England, 'Royal Navy' is listed alphabetically among the counties and the link takes you to a list of vessels, each of which in turn links to the image of the description page and to the first page of crew members.

The unofficial Ancestry Insider blog at <**ancestryinsider.blogspot. co.uk/search/label/search**> is a good place to look for independent comment on developments in Ancestry's search facilities — relevant articles can most easily be found by going straight to <**ancestryinsider. blogspot.co.uk/search/label/search**>.

Images

As with the search facilities, the image viewing options are in flux at the time of writing. In 2013 Ancestry introduced an 'interactive viewer' to replace its 'old viewer', and it has been gradually extending this viewer to more data collections. Only the interactive viewer is described here, though you may find the old viewer still accessible. At the time of writing, the US census records on Ancestry have more interactive features than the UK census records — including automatic highlighting of households — and presumably these will be added to the UK records in due course.

Ancestry's census images are greyscale and seem mostly to have been scanned at around 200 dpi. They are in JPEG format. The viewer is shown in Figure 8.6, with the zoom level set to 200 per cent. In addition to the zoom and pan controls which overlie the image itself, the Tools menu gives access to further options. Among these are the facilities to open up the index for the entries on the page (this is shown in the screenshot) and to open up a pop-up window giving the full citation details for the page, with the option of copying the citation to the clipboard. The 'Save' button offers the same facilities for saving the image within Ancestry as the Page Tools on the individual transcription page discussed above, as well as the opportunity to save the image to your computer. Very helpfully, it automatically offers a useful filename which includes the year, the country and the name of the individual (in Fig. 8.6 this would be **1891EnglandCensusForThomasHardy.jpg**). The image is saved in JPEG format. A facility for posting the image to Facebook, Google+ or email is provided by the icons in the top right.

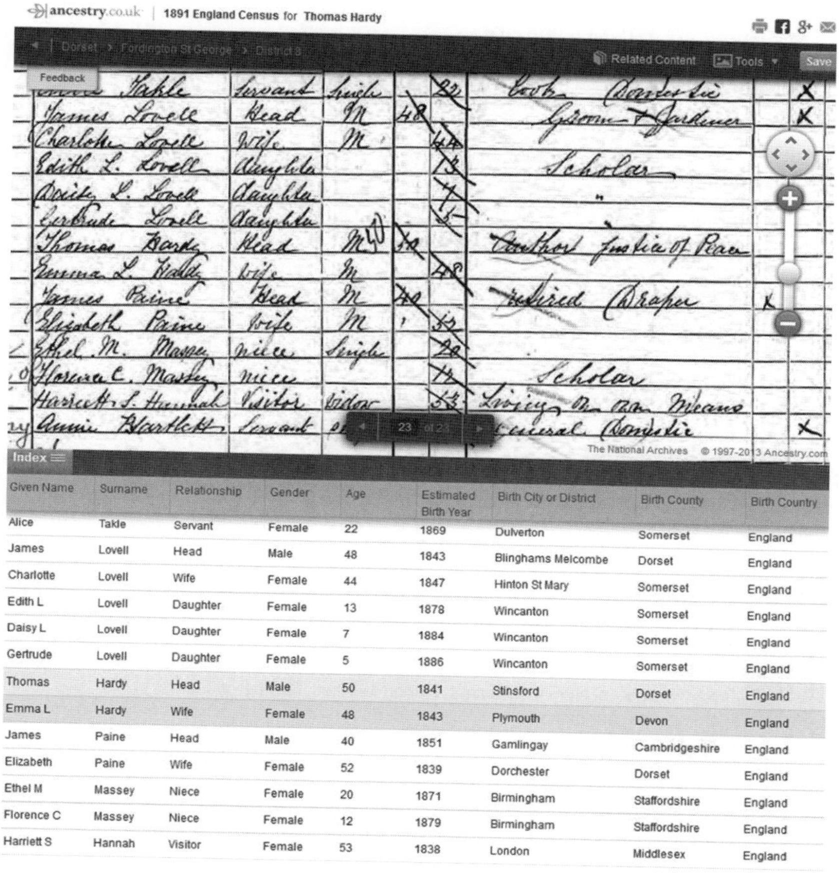

Given Name	Surname	Relationship	Gender	Age	Estimated Birth Year	Birth City or District	Birth County	Birth Country
Alice	Takle	Servant	Female	22	1869	Dulverton	Somerset	England
James	Lovell	Head	Male	48	1843	Blinghams Melcombe	Dorset	England
Charlotte	Lovell	Wife	Female	44	1847	Hinton St Mary	Somerset	England
Edith L	Lovell	Daughter	Female	13	1878	Wincanton	Somerset	England
Daisy L	Lovell	Daughter	Female	7	1884	Wincanton	Somerset	England
Gertrude	Lovell	Daughter	Female	5	1886	Wincanton	Somerset	England
Thomas	Hardy	Head	Male	50	1841	Stinsford	Dorset	England
Emma L	Hardy	Wife	Female	48	1843	Plymouth	Devon	England
James	Paine	Head	Male	40	1851	Gamlingay	Cambridgeshire	England
Elizabeth	Paine	Wife	Female	52	1839	Dorchester	Dorset	England
Ethel M	Massey	Niece	Female	20	1871	Birmingham	Staffordshire	England
Florence C	Massey	Niece	Female	12	1879	Birmingham	Staffordshire	England
Harriett S	Hannah	Visitor	Female	53	1838	London	Middlesex	England

Figure 8.6 Ancestry image viewer.

Saving information

At the top left of Figure 8.7 is a box with 'Page Tools'. If you are an Ancestry subscriber, you can use the first two options to save the individual census record to your Ancestry account. The 'Share this record' options will post the census image to your Facebook or Google+ account (see Fig. 8.8), or you can send an email to any number of recipients which includes a link to the shared image on Ancestry. This last possibility, incidentally, gets round the problem of using Ancestry in a library that will not let you save images — you can just send an email to yourself from within Ancestry. The 'Add Alternate Information' link is discussed below.

Figure 8.7 Ancestry Page Tools.

Figure 8.8 Census image posted to Facebook.

Help and feedback

Help for Ancestry will be found using the 'Get Help' link at the top right of most pages. This leads to a set of pages with a comprehensive body of answers to the most common questions. You can either browse through the list or use the search facility to find a relevant topic. The

'Help & Advice' link on the main menu bar gives access to more general help about how to conduct family history research and is not geared towards answering specific questions about searching and image viewing. The 'Help and tips' option in the image viewer (on the Tools menu) gives help only with the images and the viewer itself.

The 'Add Alternate Information' link on the individual transcription page provides a facility for submitting index corrections. If the comments on genealogy message boards are anything to go by, Ancestry has a poor reputation when it comes to correcting manifest errors, but this option makes it possible for anyone to submit not strictly a correction — it will not be used to change the existing index — but an alternative interpretation of the original record. For example, among the Hardy results is one for 'Seneca Hardy' (see Fig. 8.9). But someone has looked at the original image, realised that Seneca is a misreading of Louisa and submitted a correction. This entry now comes up in searches for both *Seneca Hardy* and *Louisa Hardy*, and a note is attached to the records along with the identity of the submitter and a reason for the correction. (As an aside, there are twelve people with the forename Seneca in Ancestry's 1891 census index: five are males genuinely called Seneca, one is an Ernest, four are Louises or Louisas, one is a Teresa, and one woman has a name which is hard to interpret but is clearly not Seneca.) If you have the index open in the image viewer (as in Fig. 8.6) you can also submit alternative information by double-clicking on the field that needs correction. These facilities are described at <**ancestryuk.custhelp.com/app/answers/detail/a_id/668/kw/corrections**> in the help pages.

The image viewer also has a facility for reporting image problems. There is a link at the top right of the image viewer, 'Having problems with this image?', which brings up a pop-up window for reporting image problems.

Figure 8.9 Census search result showing alternative transcription of the original record.

Other resources

A useful feature of Ancestry is the ability to keep family trees on the site. You can make this tree public so that anyone can see it, or you can just restrict it to individuals you have invited. The relevance of this to the site's census records is that you can link census records to individuals in your tree.

To create a tree on Ancestry, you need to go to the My Ancestry area and either create a family tree by entering individuals or upload a GEDCOM file. Once your tree is in place, then when you view the census record for an individual (see Fig. 8.5), you can click on the 'Save record to someone in my tree' link to copy data across — it will add a new 'Residence' field, giving the census year and the place. If you have no birth details for the person, you can choose to copy an approximate birth year and place of birth from the census record (see Fig. 8.10). When you then view the individual in your tree, a link to 'Historical Records' will bring up the census record.

Sometimes you will come across a census record you may feel is relevant to your tree but you are not certain enough to link it to a particular individual. Alternatively, you may choose not to have a tree on Ancestry but nonetheless want to keep a record of what you have viewed. In both cases, Ancestry's 'shoebox' feature is useful. This can

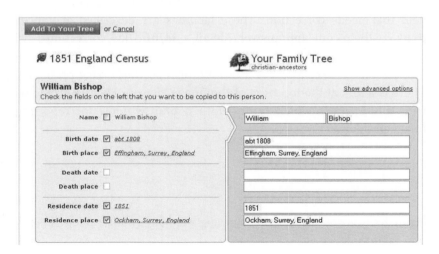

Figure 8.10 Ancestry adding census records to a family tree.

be accessed from the Page Tools box (see Fig. 8.7): clicking on the 'Save record to my shoebox' link will save the record. You can also save to the shoebox from the image viewer. When you view the My Ancestry page, it lists all the individual entries saved to the shoebox with a link to the original record.

9

FINDMYPAST AND 1911CENSUS

Findmypast at <www.findmypast.co.uk> started life in April 2003 under the name 1837online, providing images of the civil registration indexes for England and Wales, the first site to do so. It launched its first census data in early 2005, and in 2006 the site changed to its present name. In 2008, the company was purchased by Scotland Online (later called Brightsolid and now DC Thompson Family History), who run ScotlandsPeople.

Findmypast currently offers indexes and images for all the censuses of England, Wales, the Isle of Man and the Channel Islands from 1841 to 1911, and indexes without images for Scotland from 1841 to 1901. The 1841 and 1871 censuses are licensed from Origins (see Chapter 11), and Findmypast's 1861 census data is licensed to Origins, so these three indexes are identical on the two sites. Even though Findmypast and ScotlandsPeople are both run by the same company, their Scottish census indexes are different.

Findmypast's census indexes themselves are available free of charge on the FamilySearch site (p. 159), though the search facilities and results are much more limited there than on the Findmypast site itself. From FamilySearch you are redirected to Findmypast for the census images, and will need to make a payment unless you are accessing FamilySearch from a Family History Centre.

In April 2007, the contract for the digitisation of the 1911 census of England and Wales was awarded to Brightsolid and in January 2009, the official pay-per-view 1911 Census site at <www.1911census.co.uk> was launched with an initial batch of counties. The material was complete by June of that year, and in October the 1911 census was added to Findmypast's own site and became available by subscription.

Findmypast also has US, Ireland, and Australia and New Zealand sites. There are links to these at the bottom of Findmypast's UK home page.

Charges

Findmypast offers both subscription and pay-per-view access to its data collections, and details can be found by clicking on the 'subscribe' link at the top right of the home page (and many other pages).

There are two subscription types, both of which include the UK census data. The Britain Full subscription (£9.95 for one month, £99.50 for a year) includes all records for the UK. Access to records for Ireland, the US, and Australia and New Zealand requires a World subscription (£12.95 for one month, £129.50 for a year). There is currently a 10 per cent loyalty discount for renewing subscribers.

These are the options for the UK site, but a World subscription on the company's three overseas sites all offer access to UK census records. The Irish site offers and the World subscription includes an index to the 1851 censuses of Dublin City. If you are thinking of a World subscription, it is worth checking the prices on all four sites in the light of the prevailing exchange rates.

In addition to the subscriptions, there are two pay-per-view options, one offering 60 credits for £6.95, valid for 90 days, the other 280 credits for £24.95, valid for a year. Census household transcriptions and census images are both charged at five units each, i.e. just under 45p. You can see the cost in credits for other records on the site by following the 'How much does it cost to view the records?' link at <**www. findmypast.co.uk/payments**>. If you purchase more credits before the expiry of the period of validity, your remaining units will be carried forward to your new expiry date. Also, if you have credits unused at the expiry date, they are added to any new credits purchased within two years. Findmypast credits can be used interchangeably on the official 1911 census site, which has exactly the same pay-per-view charges.

Findmypast has an institutional subscription called the Community Edition, which makes the site available free of charge to the end-user at archives and public libraries. Brief details are provided at <**www.find-mypast.co.uk/content/companies-and-libraries**>, and a search of your local authority website will show whether your local libraries offer this service.

The site offers a free 14-day trial — follow the 'Take a free trial' link at the bottom left of the home page. This automatically turns into a subscription after 14 days unless you cancel; cancellation instructions are given in the FAQ ('frequently asked questions') area of the site at <**www.findmypast.co.uk/frequently-asked-questions/answer/how-do-i-cancel-my-free-trial**>. The main FAQ page at <**www.findmypast. co.uk/frequently-asked-questions**> has answers to all the common queries about subscriptions and payment.

Although, in principle, a subscription affords unlimited usage, the terms and conditions allow a subscription to be suspended if usage seems unreasonably high. However, this is mainly intended to prevent people using a subscription to offer look-up services, and in practice it would be very hard for research on an individual pedigree to get anywhere near this limit. See the heading 'Fair usage' at <**www.find mypast.co.uk/content/using-the-site/terms-and-conditions**> for an explanation of what counts as unreasonable.

Searching

In the spring of 2014, Findmypast undertook a complete overhaul of its search facilities. One of the aims was to reduce the number of different search forms and to harmonise their options. However, the unprecedented barrage of criticism these changes were met with in the genealogy discussion forums indicates that many users did not consider the changes a success, partly, no doubt, from the traditional dislike of getting to grips with a new interface, but mainly because features available on the old site were no longer available or did not work properly. In response, Findmypast set up a feedback forum (<**feedback.find mypast.co.uk**>) and started to make changes to mollify users, but in June 2014, as we make the last updates to the text of this book, there were still many outstanding problems which prevent the site offering its previous level of service. In our coverage of the search facilities, we have necessarily drawn attention to several features which appear to be poorly implemented or which fail to give expected results. Of course, our comments apply *only* to the census records on the site and should not be taken to suggest that similar problems will necessarily be found in other classes of record. The messages in the feedback forum will show which problems have been recognised by Findmypast and which remedied, but it is unfortunate that a site with a good reputation for its search facilities and the quality of the indexing has been subject to such a poorly executed, or at least inadequately tested, redesign.

Findmypast groups the census records with 'land & surveys' and the common search page for these will be found at <**search.findmypast. co.uk/search-united-kingdom-records-in-census-land-and-surveys**>, which can be reached by selecting 'Census, land & surveys' from the 'Search records' menu or the 'Census records' link under 'UK family history records', both on the home page.

The flowchart for censuses searches is shown in Fig. 9.1, and the common search form for all these records is shown in Fig. 9.2. Because this form covers not only census records, the first step is to select the exact group of records you want to search. The 'Record collection' field allows you to restrict a search to census records alone, and this is useful if you want to search *all* the census years, but mostly you will want to search a particular census year or years. In principle, the 'Record set field' can be used to select a single census year, but this requires you to scroll down through a list of 20 or so record sets. In fact it is much easier just to enter the census year in the leftmost field in the row labelled 'When'. However, selecting from 'Record sets' does give you the possibility of including *any* combination of different census years in your search.

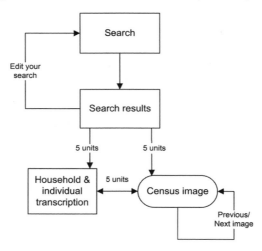

Figure 9.1 Findmypast search flowchart (unit costs apply only to pay-per-view access). Images are not available for the Scottish censuses.

Census, land & surveys

The census, taken every 10 years since 1841, provides a perfect snapshot of a day in the life of your ancestors. They show who lived where, with whom and what they did for a living.
Learn more   Search tips   Useful links

Who	First Name [ ] ☑ Name variants ⓘ Last Name [ ] ☐ Name variants ⓘ

	Year	Give or take	Year Of Birth	Give or take	Year Of Death	Give or take
When	YYYY	-/+ 2yrs ▾	YYYY	-/+ 2yrs ▾	YYYY	-/+ 2yrs ▾

Where	Britain ▾ [ ]

Other Household Member	Member First Name [ ] Member Last Name [ ]

Address	House Number [ ] Start typing a House Name Browse House Name Start typing a Street Browse Street

Record collection	Start typing a Record collection Browse Record collection

Record set	Start typing a Record set Browse Record set

🔍 Search Census, land & surveys

Figure 9.2 Findmypast general Census, land & surveys search form

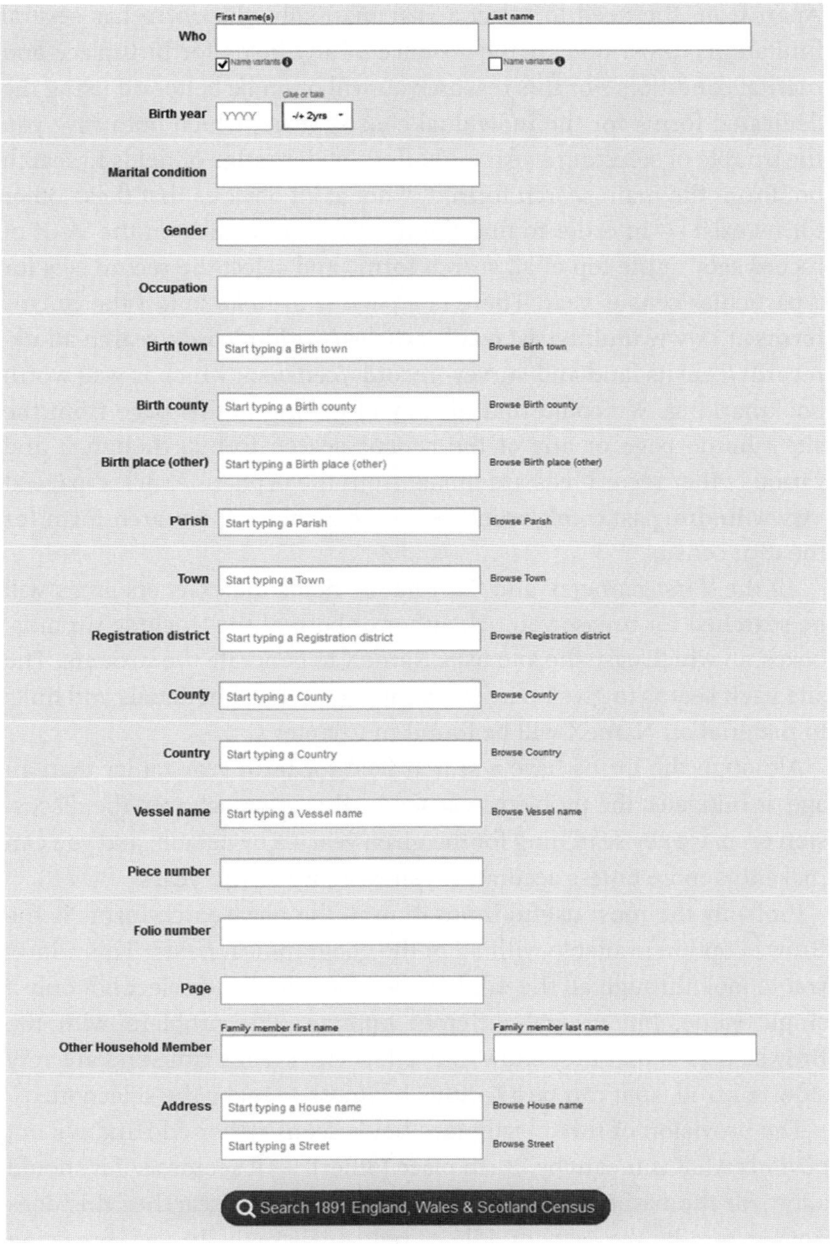

Figure 9.3 Findmypast 1891 Census search form

Apart from the need to select a year manually, this form has several limitations, most notably the absence of any fields for birthplace and marital condition. For this reason, you will often be better off using the dedicated forms for the individual census years, which both save you the trouble of selecting a year and offer a wider range of fields to search on. From the main search form it is not at all obvious that these other forms exist — in order to find them, you need to click on the 'A–Z of record sets' at the top of all search forms and select the record sets for a particular census year. There is a page with links to *just* the census forms at <**www.findmypast.co.uk/articles/world-records/search-all-uk-records/census-land-and-survey--records/census**>, which is well worth bookmarking. We could find no way of getting to this page from the site's home page or any of the census search forms, though it and various other record lists are linked from the orphan 'Articles' page at <**www.findmypast.co.uk/articles**>. Fig. 9.3 shows the search form for the 1891 census.

In the 'First name(s)' and 'Last name' fields the exact spellings will be searched for unless you tick either or both of the 'Include variants' boxes, in which case the site uses NameX to generate the variants. The site itself seems to give no information about this, but details and links to material on NameX will be found in Chapter 5.

Although the forms have a search field for birth year rather than an age, it mitigates the problems caused by this approach (see the discussion on p. 150) by searching for the given year +2 by default, and you can make this more or less accurate if you wish, up to +40 years.

Probably the most useful innovation in the new search forms is the Browse option available with all of the geographical fields. This allows you to look through all the valid entries for a field and select not only a single value, but several different options. The problem with the Browse lists is that they show only a few entries at a time and are very slow to scroll, so it can be a tedious business to make the selection.

The provision of three birthplace fields seem rather odd and it's not obvious what is meant by 'Birth place (other)' — it seems as if it should allow for the name of a country, but from our test searches this does not seem to be the case, or at least not consistently. In fact, browsing through the entries leaves the impression that it acts as a repository for exotic foreign place names and all sorts of mis-spellings and mis-transcriptions which cannot be clearly identified as towns or counties. For example, just browsing for Scottish entries in this field in the 1891 index we found Agr Scotland, Agyleshire Scotland, Alerdeen Scotland. The problem is that where a birthplace is indexed in this field, the individuals concerned will *not* be found if you enter *Scotland* into the 'Birth county' field instead. Given that the original forms have only a single field for 'Where born', the splitting of this into three fields must inevitably have been carried out automatically, though perhaps with some manual intervention. It will no doubt be quite accurate where the original entries are readily interpretable as a town and county, but where they are not, the data may end up in the 'other' field. This makes it impossible to be sure that a search has found all the relevant individuals.

It is not helped by the fact that the individual census indexes behave differently. The index to 1851 gives 19,526 people with Ireland as 'Birth county'. In the 1891 index it's just 10. The rest can be found, by entering *Ireland* in the third birthplace field, but to enter just 'Ireland' you have to scroll through probably at least a 100 entries for individual places in Ireland.

It's difficult to see the need for *three* birthplace fields. It's not just inconvenient, it means that it is impossible to know whether a search using these fields has in fact found all the matching entries. Nonetheless, there *are* two positives here: the town field seems to work much more satisfactorily, and the availability of the browse option for counties means that you can manually look through the list of entries for misspellings. For example, it is genuinely useful to discover that the index for 1851 has birth county entries not only for the expected Bedford and Bedfordshire, but also for Bedforsh, Beforshre, Bedforsh and Bedfprd. However, this does alert us to another issue with the three birthplace fields: if the original document just says 'Bedford', is this indexed as the name of the town or the county?

The place of residence fields are slightly different from one census to the next — they always include a County field along with a selection from Village, Parish, Town, City or Borough, Registration District, and Country. Since these are all based on the census administration, they are not subject to the sort of mis-spelling and transcription errors found elsewhere on the forms. As we suggest in Chapter 6, the problem is knowing whether at the date of a particular census a place name is identified as a village, parish, town or borough.

The 'County' field includes not only geographical counties, but also entries for various categories of military and naval personnel, such as 'Royal Navy at Sea', 'British Ships in Port' and 'Overseas Military'. The exact options differ from census to census and the 1891 index does not offer these at all. The Channel Islands and the Isle of Man are also treated as counties. There is some overlap with the 'Country' field, which also includes the offshore islands and, for some years, 'Ships and Overseas Establishments'.

Findmypast no longer provides separate address and vessel search forms, but includes fields for these on the main form. In both cases, searches on the fields are absolutely literal: you will not find 'H M S Albert' if you just search for *Albert* or indeed *HMS Albert*. However, you can use the Browse option to ensure you get the right spelling of the ship name, or use wildcards. The individual transcription page for vessels does not include any equivalent to the listing of 'household members' of land-based households (see Fig. 9.5), but, rather oddly, the first and last names of all the other crew members are all listed in the 'Family member name' fields.

We had real difficulties getting any sensible results searching on street name. In many cases, entering just a surname in the 'Last name' field and a street name produced exactly the same number of results as a search on the surname alone. At the very least, the address fields seem to produce unreliable results. However, the address search in the 1911 census is an exception, though it requires care to get the desired results. For 1911, if you are searching on just a street name, without a house number, it is best to start with a wildcard — if there are no house numbers, as is often the case in rural settlements, this will not matter, but without the wildcard or an exact house number before the street name, you will always draw a blank in towns. It is also advisable to put a wildcard after the street name, too, since the full address may also include the place and you can never be sure whether 'Road' and 'Street' will have been abbreviated. Of course, a common street name will turn up residents of many different places, but place fields can used to narrow this down. Alternatively, just sorting the search results on Registration District will group all the entries for a particular place together.

Finally, the form offers fields for searching on The National Archives reference. As for most census years there are the requisite fields for

'Piece number', 'Folio' and 'Page'. For 1911, the form provides for a piece number but not for the schedule number which is needed to identify uniquely the page for an individual household. For Scotland, the search form and the transcription have fields for the name of Registration District and the number of the Enumeration District. This is not enough information to identify a particular census page, but information on how to use these to locate the full reference and the matching image on ScotlandsPeople is given on pp. 280–4.

The forms for all years except 1911 cover Scotland as well as England and Wales. In some ways this is an advantage, because you can search the whole of Great Britain in a single search. On the other hand, the merging of two datasets with slight differences in field is a potential trap. For example, if you are searching for someone born in Scotland and you enter *Scotland* in the 'birth county', you won't find them if they still live in Scotland — this is rather obviously not stated explicitly in Scottish census returns — but only if they've moved elsewhere and cited Scotland as their birth country.

Figure 9.4 shows the results of a person search for Thomas Hardy in the 1891 census (specifying Dorset as his birth county). The results can be sorted on several columns, with some variation between censuses: first and last names, birth year, Registration District and parish in this case. Unfortunately, the display leaves something to be desired, with overlap between the columns unless you reduce the size of the display font in your browser. Ticks against the camera and page icons indicate that the image and transcription have already been viewed and tells PayAsYouGo customers that they will not be charged for viewing these again.

If you know a person's age and place of residence, the results listing may already provide enough information to identify the correct record so you can go straight to viewing the image — click on the camera icon at the right. But it makes sense to follow the link to the transcription— the page icon— which gives you all the information on the original census form and includes The National Archives reference. It has the advantage of listing all household members, even those entered on a previous or following page in the enumeration book. If you get too many results to spot the sought-for ancestor, or too few and your ancestor seems not to be listed, the 'Edit your search' button will take you back to the search form to tweak your search criteria.

Results for 1891 England, Wales & Scotland Census

Your search criteria

Thomas
First name(s)

Hardy
Last name

Dorset
County

✏ Edit your search

New search

17 results

Order by | Birth year ascending ▾

First name(s)	Last name	Birth year	Birth county	Registration district	Parish	County
THOMAS	HARDY	1812	DORSETSHIRE	DORCHESTER	STINSFORD	Dorset
THOMAS	HARDY	1823	DORSETSHIRE	DORCHESTER	PUDDLEHINTON	Dorset
NATHANIEL T	HARDY	1824	DORSETSHIRE	BEAMINSTER	BROADWINSOR	Dorset
THOMAS	HARDY	1829	DORSETSHIRE	WEYMOUTH	WYKE REGIS	Dorset
THOS R	HARDY	1829	DORSETSHIRE	POOLE	LONGFLEET	Dorset
THOMAS	HARDY	1834	DORSETSHIRE	WAREHAM	SWANAGE	Dorset
THOMAS	HARDY	1841	DORSETSHIRE	DORCHESTER	FORDINGTON	Dorset
THOMAS	HARDY	1842	DORSETSHIRE	POOLE	LONGFLEET	Dorset
TOM	HARDY	1856	DORSETSHIRE	DORCHESTER	PUDDLETRENTHIDE	Dorset
TOM	HARDY	1864	DORSETSHIRE	DORCHESTER	MAIDEN NEWTON	Dorset
THOMAS	HARDY	1866	DORSETSHIRE	WEYMOUTH	WEYMOUTH	Dorset
THOMAS B	HARDY	1871	DORSETSHIRE	BEAMINSTER	BROADWINSOR	Dorset
THOMAS	HARDY	1873	DORSETSHIRE	WEYMOUTH	PORTLAND	Dorset

Figure 9.4 Search results.

Figure 9.5 Findmypast household and individual transcription.

Images

From the person search results and the household transcript, there is a link to the page image, which appears in a separate pop-up window.

Apart from the 1911 census, all the images are greyscale, save for some of those for the 1871 census licensed from Origins. There is some variation in resolution, but all are at least 250 dpi and many are as high as 350 dpi. The 1911 census images are in colour.

Fig. 9.6 shows the site's image viewer, with controls for zooming and panning top left. Clicking on the 'Download' button' bottom right saves the page image in JPG format and the proffered filename includes the year and the piece number. Right clicking on the image brings up a menu which offers a 'Save image as' option. However, this is not an alternative to the 'Download' button as it saves *only* the portion of the image currently visible in the browser window.

A further useful facility which will be open to you if you are using Firefox is the ability to share the image by extracting image's unique URL. Although the image viewer itself provides a URL for the page currently being displayed, this cannot be usefully shared —if you try it without having logged in, it just brings up a page requesting you to register on the site. However, if you click on the 'Print' icon at the bottom of the viewer, it will bring up a print dialog box and the page image in its own browser window. Cancel the print dialog and you can now copy the URL in the browser's location bar. With other browsers you can achieve the same end, albeit more laboriously, by another method: if you right-click with the mouse over the 'Print' icon, the pop-up menu will have an option to copy the URL or page address (terminology differs between browsers). You then need to copy this into a text editor and replace the initial *javascript:GLB_PRINTIMAGE('/ record/image?* with *search.new.findmypast.co.uk/record?* and remove the final). You can use this as a way of making the image readily available to other family members who do not subscribe to Findmypast.

At the time of writing, for the 1911 census the new site provides no links to images other than those of the household schedules. However, messages in the Feedback Forum show that Findmypast are aware of this omission and are planning to remedy it.

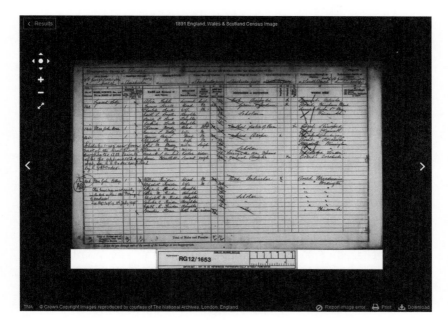

Figure 9.6 Findmypast image viewer.

Help and feedback

The site's help pages can be found by clicking on the 'Help & advice' link at the top of the home page. The FAQ covers all aspects of using the site, while there is general material on census records in the 'Expert advice' pages. Given the problems with the new site, the Feedback Forum at <**feedback.findmypast.co.uk**> is a useful place for checking which problems have been identified and which addressed.

Findmypast offers two places where you can report errors. At the bottom of the individual transcription page (Fig 9.5) you can report transcription errors in any field of the individual records. Unfortunately, to report an error common to several or all members of a household, you have to submit a separate report for each individual. From the image viewer you can report image problems, a poor quality image or the fact that the wrong image has been displayed.

1911census

The 1911 Census site (see Fig. 9.7) at <**www.1911census.co.uk**> is unusual in that it offers only the 1911 census for England and Wales.

Now that indexes and images for the 1911 census are available elsewhere, it may seem that the site is redundant. However, at the time of writing, only Findmypast, Ancestry, TheGenealogist, and Genes Reunited have 1911 indexes for England and Wales, so if you mainly use a commercial site other than these, it is probably easiest to turn to the official 1911 site. In any case, charges and credits are the same as and interchangeable with Findmypast credits, so if you have unused credits after carrying out all your 1911 census searches, you can use them for other data on Findmypast.

The site works solely on a pay-per-view basis, with 60 credits costing £6.95, valid for three months, and 280 credits costing £24.95, valid for one year. Each new census image or household transcript you view costs five credits, i.e. 58p or 45p, depending on how many credits you have purchased. For a subscription option, the site points you to Findmypast, where the cheapest option is the Britain Full subscription at £69.95 for six months.

However, if you are on a tight budget, it is worth noting that pay-per-view site Genes Reunited (see Chapter 12), which has the same index

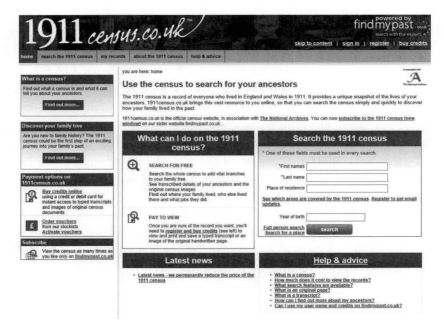

Figure 9.7 The official 1911 Census site for England and Wales.

and images for the 1911 census, is slightly cheaper at 50p per record if you are only purchasing a small number of units.

The search process is essentially the same as that on Findmypast, shown in Fig. 9.1, and is therefore described only briefly here. The basic person search form is shown in Figure 9.8. The address search is accessible on the 'Place' tab, while a census reference search is available on the advanced search form shown in Figure 9.9. The advanced search offers more sophisticated name matching, both for the person sought and for other household members, and a 'year of marriage' which works by calculating from the duration of marriage field. As with other year calculations in the census searches, this year is subject to error, which is compensated for by the automatic default range of ±3 years.

The census reference search comprises only a single field for the entire reference, rather than distinct fields for the individual components of the reference, as is more usual. As explained in Chapter 18, the references for the 1911 census are more complex than those for earlier censuses, but the site's search is very flexible: you must enter RG14 and the piece number, but then you can leave the rest of the reference out, or enter any components you know. If you are going to use this facility, you will need to look at the online help for this field (click on the question mark icon to the right of the field) for information on how to enter the various parts of the reference.

Figure 9.10 shows the results listing, from which you can either view the individual household transcript (see Figure 9.11) or image of the household schedule in the image viewer (see Figure 9.12). In each case you will have five credits deducted from your account. Since the household schedules for 1911 by definition include the entire household — in other censuses the enumeration book page may contain only part of a household — there is no real benefit in viewing the transcription unless you have difficulty reading the writing on the original form. Admittedly, the image viewer does not give the full census reference, but, as mentioned below, you can get this when you save the image to your computer.

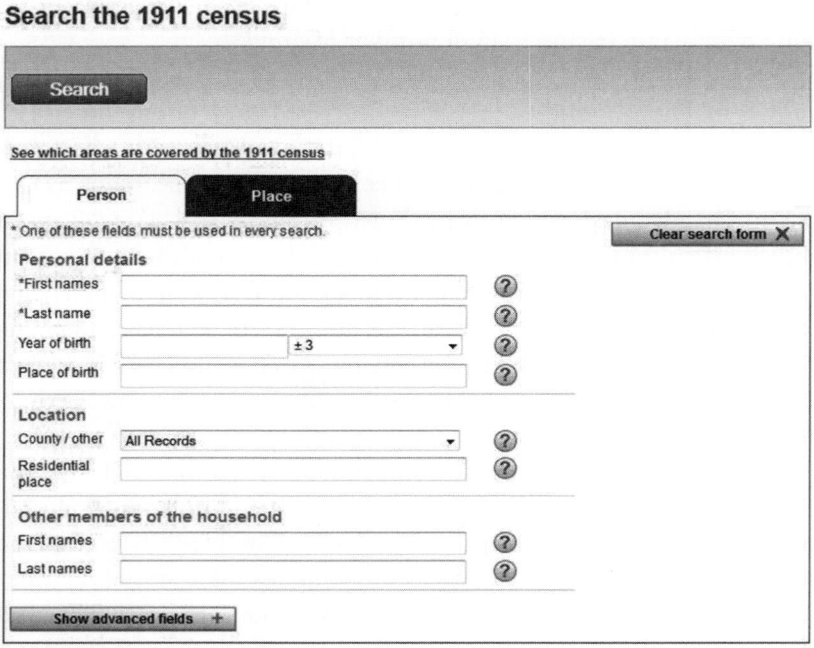

Search the 1911 census

Figure 9.8 1911census basic search form.

Unlike earlier censuses, which were digitised from existing micro-films, the digital scans of the 1911 census have been made directly from the original documents and are therefore in colour rather than grey-scale. The images are JPEG files at 300 dpi. When you save an image, it is automatically given a file name which includes the name of the individual and the full census reference.

While earlier censuses are represented solely by the enumeration schedules, for the 1911 census the documents available are the original household returns (one per household) along with the other pages described in Chapter 3 (p. 56). There is no transcription of these, but the series of buttons above the page image (see Figure 9.13) provide links to all these other documents. Once you have paid five credits to view the household return, all these other images for the same address can be viewed without further charge.

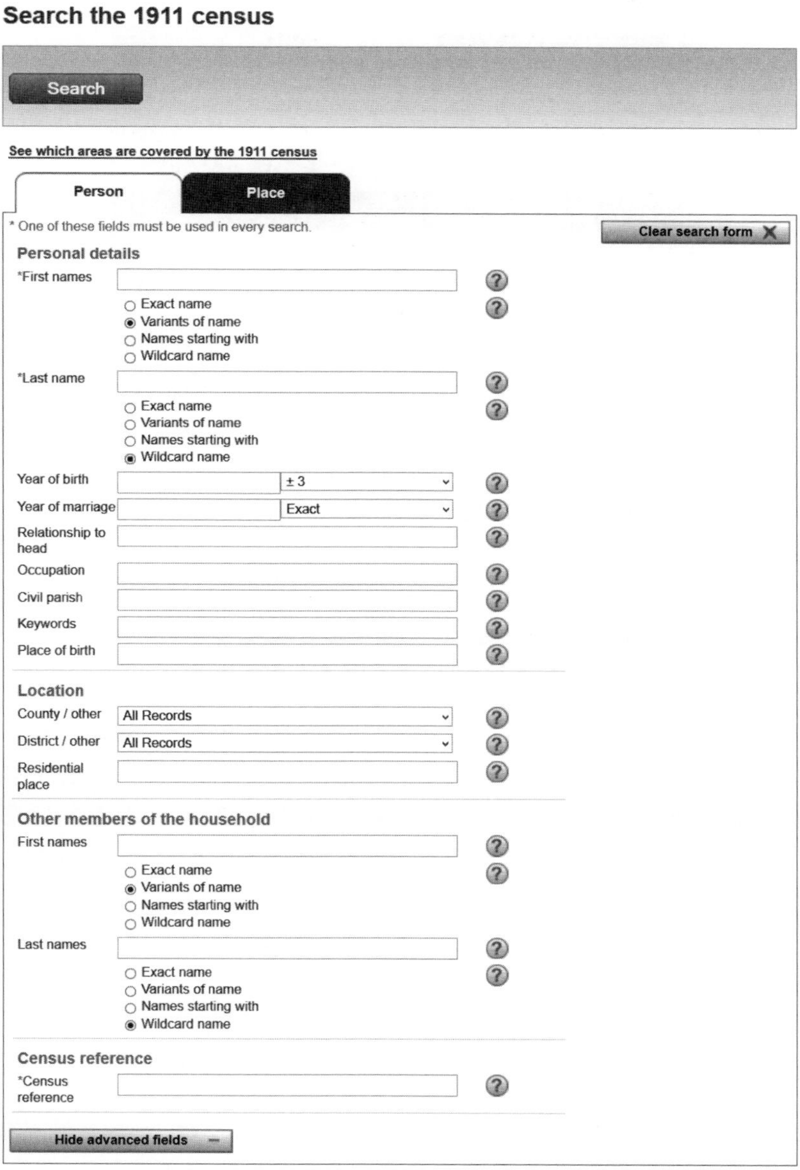

Search the 1911 census

Search

See which areas are covered by the 1911 census

| Person | Place |

* One of these fields must be used in every search.

Clear search form ✕

Personal details

*First names
- ○ Exact name
- ◉ Variants of name
- ○ Names starting with
- ○ Wildcard name

*Last name
- ○ Exact name
- ○ Variants of name
- ○ Names starting with
- ◉ Wildcard name

Year of birth   ± 3
Year of marriage   Exact
Relationship to head
Occupation
Civil parish
Keywords
Place of birth

Location

County / other   All Records
District / other All Records
Residential place

Other members of the household

First names
- ○ Exact name
- ◉ Variants of name
- ○ Names starting with
- ○ Wildcard name

Last names
- ○ Exact name
- ○ Variants of name
- ○ Names starting with
- ◉ Wildcard name

Census reference

*Census reference

Hide advanced fields —

Figure 9.9 1911census advanced search form.

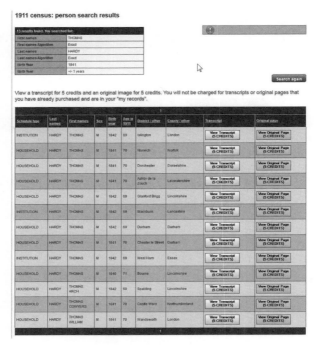

Figure 9.10 1911census search results.

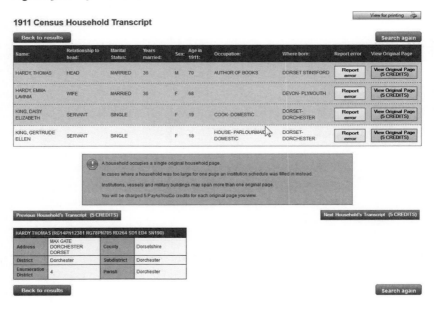

Figure 9.11 1911census household transcript.

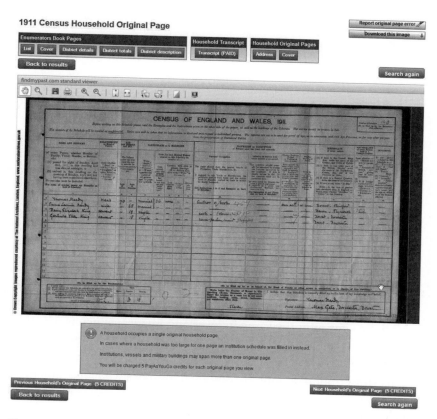

Figure 9.12 1911census image viewer.

Figure 9.13 1911census image viewer: links to other document images.

The 'help & advice' link on the navigation bar leads to articles covering general use of the site and help with searching, with material on Welsh, naval and military entries. There are also useful lists of the birthplace and occupation codes used in the 1911 census.

10

THEGENEALOGIST, ROOTSUK AND UK CENSUS ONLINE

S&N Genealogy Supplies is a long-established genealogy software retailer. It has a number of sites for genealogical data and a very comprehensive portfolio of censuses on CD-ROM (see Chapter 16). The company runs three main sites with UK census records: TheGenealogist at <**www.thegenealogist.com**> and <**www.thegenealogist.co.uk**>, RootsUK at <**www.rootsuk.com**>, and UK Census Online at <**www. ukcensusonline.com**>.

All three sites offer the same indexes and images, which is why they are treated together in this chapter, but they differ in their charging mechanisms and search facilities. TheGenealogist is the main service and its subscription options are designed for those who are going to do a significant amount of searching. It offers an extensive range of data collections, which is constantly being added to, and has sophisticated facilities for searching and viewing records.

The other two sites concentrate on the core records needed by the beginner, civil registration and the censuses, with RootsUK offering a pay-per-view service and UK Census Online a subscription service. But they might also be useful to others, such as a seasoned family historian who is just trying to fill a few gaps and may only need to make a small number of searches. They also make a good second choice if you are subscribed to another major service such as Ancestry or Findmypast, but have been unable to find an ancestor in one of their census indexes and you want to try an alternative index at reasonable cost.

All three sites have the censuses for England and Wales 1841–1911. Though the sites all refer to UK census records, only TheGenealogist has any data for Scotland. TheGenealogist also has two new pre-1841 censuses for Marylebone in London: 1821 and 1831.

S&N have a number of other census-related sites, including <www.londoncensus.co.uk>, <www.yorkshirecensus.co.uk>, <www.lancashirecensus.co.uk>, and a whole series for individual census years at <www.uk1841census.com>, etc. These simply link to the company's main census sites and to information about their census indexes on CD-ROM.

S&N also run FHS Online at <www.fhs-online.co.uk> to host census indexes and other data from family history societies. Since almost all the census data on this site is accessible free of charge, it is discussed in Chapter 7 with the other sites offering free data.

Charges

TheGenealogist

TheGenealogist's charging model is quite complex, but there are three basic types of access:

- The 'Personal Premium' subscriptions. These differ in the overall range of datasets available, but all of them give access to census indexes for England and Wales 1841–1901. The Starter and Gold subscriptions cost £54.95 and £78.95 respectively, with three-month and six-month prices also available. The Diamond subscription at £119.45 annually provides access to all the records on the site and includes the 1911 census index and some pre-1841 censuses. Prices and coverage are given at <www.thegenealogist.co.uk/compare.php>.

- The 'Personal Plus' subscription. In reality this is a halfway house between subscription and pay-per-view: you have access to all the site's datasets, but there is a limit (albeit a very high one) on how many searches you can carry out and how many images you can view. The annual subscription gives you 800 credits for £55.95, and there are two quarterly options: 75 credits for £24.95 or 175 credits for £14.95. Full details can be found at <www.thegenealogist.co.uk/nameindex/selectai.php>.

- The 'Pay As You Go' option. This gives access to a single county for a single census year, and you can sign up for either 'census records' or 'census indexes'. The indexes are name indexes only, without images, at a cost of £9.95 for 100 credits valid for 90 days and £19.95 for 200 credits valid for one year. The records contain full details with credits for 150 searches and 50 image views, costing £19.95. Details are given on the pages linked from **<www.thegenealogist. co.uk/nameindex/payg_products.php>**.

The choice is therefore between credit-free access, credit-based access to all databases, and credit-based access to a single database. If you go for a credit-based option, any credits you don't use up are carried forward to the next charging period. Also, if you use up your allowance, additional credits can be purchased. The information on how many credits things cost is not easy to find on the site, but there is a table at **<www.thegenealogist.co.uk/help/credits.htm>**.

The 'Pay As You Go' option seems quite expensive – you will need to sign up for several different census years to trace your ancestors, even if they all stayed in the same county. To get a complete run of years for a single county via this option will cost you twice the price of the All-inclusive subscription. For a local historian, this might make some sense, but for that purpose you would be better off purchasing the same material on CD-ROM, where you will have all the images and can carry out as many searches as you want. S&N's CD-ROM materials are covered in Chapter 16. Also, of course, the subscriptions give you access to all the other datasets available on the site.

The best-value option is clearly, as you would expect, the All-inclusive subscription. However, the annual Personal Plus subscription is probably sufficient for many people: the 800 credits are enough to do 100 advanced searches, and view 100 transcriptions and 100 images. By contrast, the two quarterly subscriptions are more expensive and offer fewer units. On the other hand, if you've already done a lot of work on your nineteenth-century ancestors and just need to consult the online censuses to fill in gaps and check what you've already found by other means, the single-quarter £24.95 option will be the cheapest way to access the site, though in fact RootsUK's pay-per-view charges (described below) will probably work out cheaper. In fact, RootsUK's provision of access to all census years and counties from a single pay-per-view payment makes it a much more favourable option for anyone who does not want to take out a subscription. For that reason we have omitted further coverage of TheGenealogist's 'Pay As You Go' option in this chapter.

The best way to evaluate TheGenealogist is to take advantage of the free trial, details of which will be found at <**www.thegenealogist.co.uk/freesub**>. This does not require you to give any credit card details, so it does not automatically turn into a fully-fledged subscription. The trial gives you 30 days access to all databases, with 10 credits, enough to do a couple of searches and view two images. At the end of the trial, there is a special deal on a subsequent Personal Premium subscription.

Subscriptions can be purchased online by credit or debit card (though only a credit card is acceptable for the £14.95 quarterly Personal Plus subscription). If you prefer to pay by cheque, or do not want to give your card details online, you can print off the subscription form at <**www.thegenealogist.co.uk/tg_subscription_form.pdf**> and submit it by post.

Once you have subscribed, your subscription will be automatically renewed and charged to your card, unless you cancel two weeks in advance of the renewal date.

RootsUK

Unlike TheGenealogist, RootsUK is a purely pay-per-view site and its charging structure is very simple. Credits cost £5 for 100 (i.e. 5p each) or £14.95 for 400 (about 3.75p each). Full details of how many credits everything on the site costs are given at <**www.rootsuk.com/help/credits.php**>, but for the census records there are three charged items and they are each charged at 5 credits (i.e. 25p):

- viewing the full details for an entry;
- viewing the original image;
- the advanced search and reveal details options.

Since you cannot view an image without going via the view details screen, the minimum cost for an image is effectively 10 units, which also gives you a transcription for the individual. Full details will be found at <**www.rootsuk.com/help/credits.php**>.

UK Census Online

UK Census Online is a subscription site with only census and civil registration records. Subscriptions are available for a month, quarter, six months or a year, and two of the three subscription options offer census records: census-only or all records. Prices start at £14.95 for a monthly census subscription, up to £69.95 for a year's subscription to all the records. Full details can be found at <**www.ukcensusonline. com/transaction/products.php**>.

As with TheGenealogist, all subscriptions are automatically renewed unless cancelled, and the cancellation must be made at least two weeks before the renewal date.

Searching: TheGenealogist

When you log in to TheGenealogist, you are offered two ways to search: you can select an individual database from the list appropriate to your subscription, or you can use the Master Search form at the top of the page. Generally, there are good reasons to choose the latter. In the individual database search you must choose both a year and a county and you can only search for an individual. The Master Search has person, address and family searches, and you can search all census years and all counties as well as selecting an individual county and year. Indeed, you can search *all* the records on the site with a single search form.

If you are using the 'Pay As You Go' service, you will only have access to the individual databases you have signed up for.

From the initial search form shown in Figure 10.1, you need to select 'Census' from the 'All Records' drop-down list, which will bring up the search form shown in Figure 10.2.

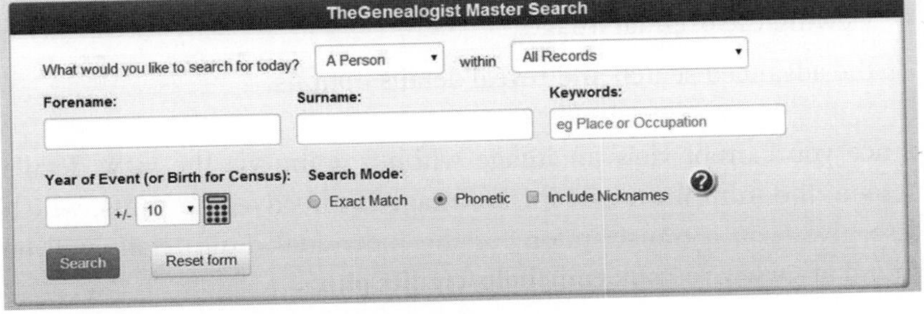

TheGenealogist Master Search

What would you like to search for today? A Person ▼ within All Records ▼

Forename: | Surname: | Keywords:
eg Place or Occupation

Year of Event (or Birth for Census): | Search Mode:
+/- 10 ▼ | ○ Exact Match ● Phonetic ☐ Include Nicknames

Search | Reset form

Figure 10.1 TheGenealogist search form.

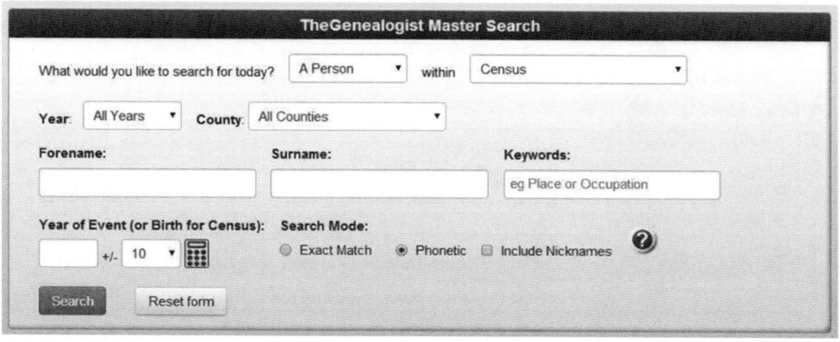

Figure 10.2 TheGenealogist census person search form.

Although the person search form has dedicated fields only for year, county, name and birth year, the 'Keywords' field allows you to enter any text found in another field, such as place of residence, birthplace, occupation, relation to head, or even part of the address. There is a slight problem in the general nature of this field: if you enter a place name, you will get results which include it as both a place of residence and a birthplace, and indeed a street name elsewhere. Searching on the keyword 'baker' will find not only bakers, but also the inhabitants of Baker Streets around the country. Nonetheless, since the search results are fairly detailed, you should find it straightforward to identify the entries that match what you were looking for.

Figure 10.3 shows the results of a search for Thomas Hardy in Dorset in the 1861 census, with 'son' in the 'Keyword' field, and the author is the third result. The site gives no information about the rules for sorting the results — these entries seem to be in order of decreasing age, but we have been unable to establish any further sorting criteria.

A useful feature of the results page is that the search form remains visible at the top of the page and you can easily modify your search to narrow down the results or change the year to carry out the same search for another census year.

Apart from the exact match, there is only one fuzzy surname matching option, labelled 'Phonetic'. Beyond the remark that this 'concentrates on looking for a name based on the way it sounds rather than the way it is spelt', the site offers no further information on the matching technique, so the site's claim that this is 'much more refined than variant searching on other sites' should be regarded with scepticism.

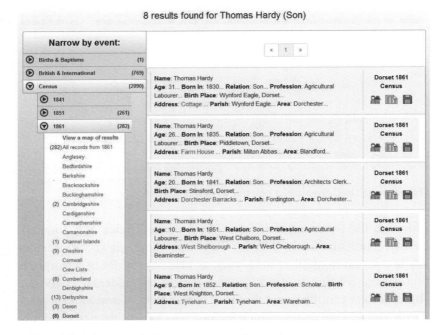

Figure 10.3 TheGenealogist person search results.

An alternative to the phonetic matching is the possibility of using a wild card with an exact match. Unusually, and very usefully, a wild card can be used even at the beginning of a name, so a search for the surname *nions will find Onions, Anions, Unions and Jenions. This offers the chance of identifying an individual even when the possible florid initial letter of their name has been mis-transcribed.

The 'Include Nicknames' option, which can be combined with both exact match and phonetic match catches names such as Eliza and Betsy in a search for Elizabeth, as well as those cases where only an initial is given instead of a forename.

The results page offers two interesting features beyond the results themselves. First, the left-hand panel shows how many results there are for the search terms not only in other census years, but also in other records on the site. Second, the 'View map of results' option brings up a map of England and Wales showing the distribution of the results by county.

From the results page, the icons to the right of each record link to 'View Household', 'View the original page' and 'Save record'. The transcript of the household (see Fig. 10.4) gives all the fields from the original form. A significant limitation is that the 'ImageReference' field gives only a partial TNA reference, including the piece number but omitting the folio and page numbers — for these you need to inspect the image itself (and, for even-numbered pages, the previous page in order to locate the folio number).

There is an additional icon in the row for each person whose age suggests they may have been born after the start of civil registration in 1837. This links to a search for the person's entry in the GRO birth indexes. In the case of Thomas Hardy, aged 20, the site finds 48 similarly named children with births registered in 1840–1842. Those born in the county of the census entry are listed first.

The Family Search allows you to search for a household with a particular set of forenames. The most obvious reason to use this rather than the normal person search is where you have failed to find a family under the surname you were expecting, whether you suspect that the family is using a different surname, or that there is an unanticipated spelling variant or transcription error. For example, in the case of a widowed ancestor who has remarried, you may not know the new surname, but you know the names of the children from her first marriage. Alternatively, with a very common surname, it will make the search results more manageable.

Figure 10.5 shows a search for any Hardy family with parents Thomas and Jemima and a son Thomas, along with the single result. Since the whole household is listed, with ages and occupations, you should be able to identify the family you are looking for quite easily, even if there

Dorset 1861 Census Transcript							
Address:	Dorchester Barracks		Parish:	Fordington	Registration District:		Dorchester
Research Log	Surname	Forename	Age	Relation	Occupation	Birth Place	ImageReference	S&N File Reference
☐	Hardy	Thomas	49	Head	Mason & Bricklayer	Stinsford, Dorset	RG9/1354/F?	CD2 R9_1354.pdf p.178
☐	Hardy	Jemima	47	Wife		Melbury, Dorset	RG9/1354/F?	CD2 R9_1354.pdf p.178
☐	Hardy	Thomas	20	Son	Architects Clerk	Stinsford, Dorset	RG9/1354/F?	CD2 R9_1354.pdf p.178
☐	Hardy	Henry	9	Son	Scholar	Stinsford, Dorset	RG9/1354/F?	CD2 R9_1354.pdf p.178
☐	Hardy	Catherine	4	Daughter		Stinsford, Dorset	RG9/1354/F?	CD2 R9_1354.pdf p.178

Figure 10.4 TheGenealogist household transcript.

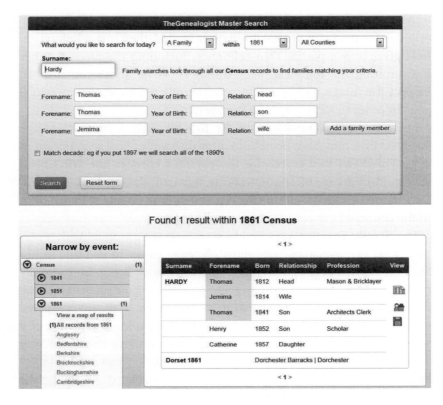

Figure 10.5 TheGenealogist census family search form with results.

were many more results, as there would be if you left the surname field blank.

The Address Search searches on a street name, and from the resulting list of matching streets (see Fig. 10.6) you go to a list of the heads of household. From there, you can view a transcript for the whole household and the page image.

The only real shortcoming of the Master Search is the very flexibility of the 'Keyword' field in the Person Search, where you can enter a search term but not specify which field it should match.

The search by a specific county and year offers an advanced search which gets around this problem. The Basic Search offers no advantage over the Master Search, but the Advanced Search (see Fig. 10.7) offers dedicated fields for district, relation to head, birth place or county, occupation, and street address. The same name-matching options are

TheGenealogist Master Search

What would you like to search for today? | An Address ▾ | within | 1861 ▾ | Dorset ▾

Street:: waterloo   Look across our census records for the addresses of your ancestors.

Search

Found 9 results

Street	Parish	Area	Piece/District
Waterloo	Stalbridge	Sturminster	Piece 1329
Waterloo Buildings	Poole St James	Poole	Piece 1340
Waterloo Cottage	Broadway	Weymouth	Piece 1348
Waterloo Cottage	Melcombe Regis	Weymouth	Piece 1349
Waterloo Cottage	Maiden Newton	Dorchester	Piece 1356
Waterloo Farm	Gillingham	Shaftesbury	Piece 1327
Waterloo Place	Melcombe Regis	Weymouth	Piece 1349
Waterloo Square	Maiden Newton	Dorchester	Piece 1356
Waterlooloo Square	Maiden Newton	Dorchester	Piece 1356

Figure 10.6 TheGenealogist census address search form and results.

Dorset Census Transcript 1861 - Credit-free Subscription | **Memory**

Forename		☐ Include nicknames	M +
Surname		☐ Use New Improved phonetics	MR
Age	(+/- 0 ▾ years)	☐ Exclude records with no age	M –
Year	1861 ▾		[Tell me more]
County	Dorset ▾		
District	Select an Option ▾		
Relation to head	Any Relation ▾		
Birth place/county			
Occupation			
Street Address			

Search   Reset

For fewer options, use a Standard Search

Images reproduced by courtesy of The National Archives, Kew, England

Figure 10.7 TheGenealogist county/year census search form.

available, but there is a restriction that you cannot search on surname alone — you must include a forename, age or district. Wildcard searches are permitted and, contrary to what it says on the search page, you do not need to enter two characters before the wildcard.

Districts are selected from a drop-down list for the specific county, which also gives the piece number. This effectively gives you a partial TNA reference search, though you cannot enter a folio or page number.

An oddity is that you enter either place name *or* a county in the birth-place field, but if you enter both, your search will fail.

While the search form is different from the Master Search, the results and the navigation from the results page are identical.

A combined flowchart for the Master Search and the single-database search is shown in Figure 10.8.

There are some differences in searches of the 1911 census. The house-hold transcript provides:

- not just the piece number, but also the full TNA reference;
- links to images of the cover and address pages;
- marriage look-up in civil registration indexes based on the name of the husband, the forename of the wife, and the duration of the marriage.

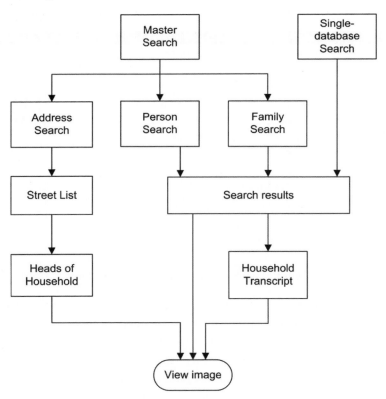

Figure 10.8 TheGenealogist search process.

In addition, there is the facility to browse the images for a particular enumeration district in the 1911 census. To access this, select '1911 images' from the drop-down list of census records on the main search page. From here you can select in turn a county, a registration district, a sub-district or parish, and finally an enumeration district. This gives a set of links to the individual schedules for that ED.

TheGenealogist does not automatically keep a record of your viewed records or images. If you are on a subscription you can view records and images as often as you want. However, in the year/county search you can record your search terms so that you can repeat a search. The right-hand panel in Figure 10.7 has three calculator-style memory buttons, and you can use these to save, retrieve or clear a search from memory. Note that this only saves a single search — saving another search overwrites the first. Apart from this, TheGenealogist does not keep track of which searches you have carried out, so if you think you will want to refer to search results again and you are on a credit-based subscription, you will need to print or save them. However, the site has two facilities for keeping a record of individuals and these are discussed below under 'Other resources'.

Searching: RootsUK

RootsUK's search screen could hardly be simpler. If you want to search all the RootsUK databases, use the search form on the home page; otherwise, clicking on the census tab will take you to the Census transcript search form shown in Figure 10.9.

You need to select a census year and enter a name — in fact you can carry out a search with a surname only, but if it produces more than 50 results for an individual county you will not be able to view them. You can also tick the forename variants box if you want to find abbreviations or nicknames. The resulting page lists how many results there are for each county, and offers two options: to view the results for any individual county for which there are matches, or to carry out an advanced search on any one county (see Fig. 10.10).

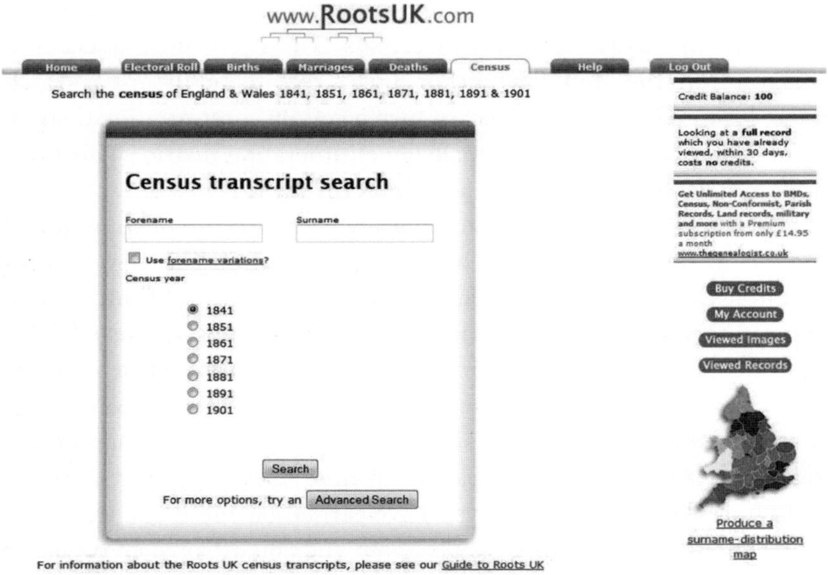

Figure 10.9 RootsUK Census transcript search.

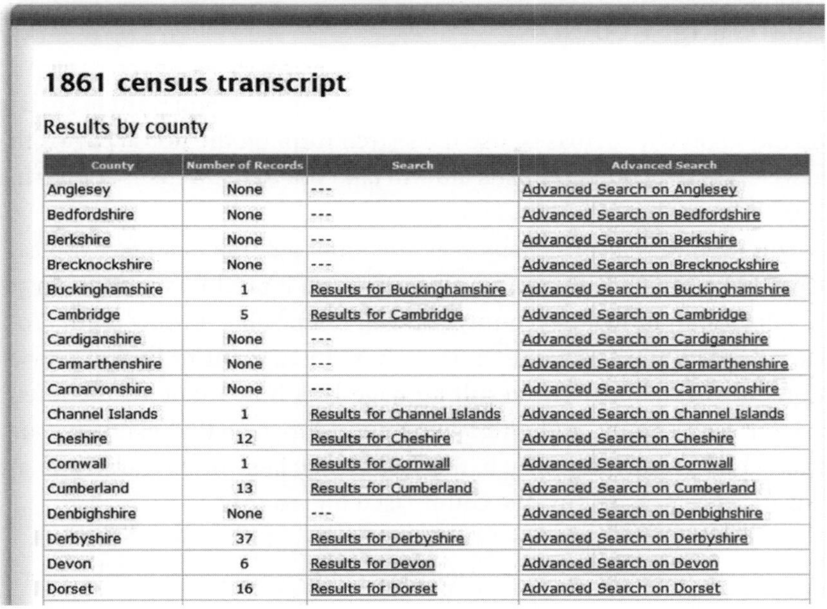
1861 census transcript

Results by county

County	Number of Records	Search	Advanced Search
Anglesey	None	---	Advanced Search on Anglesey
Bedfordshire	None	---	Advanced Search on Bedfordshire
Berkshire	None	---	Advanced Search on Berkshire
Brecknockshire	None	---	Advanced Search on Brecknockshire
Buckinghamshire	1	Results for Buckinghamshire	Advanced Search on Buckinghamshire
Cambridge	5	Results for Cambridge	Advanced Search on Cambridge
Cardiganshire	None	---	Advanced Search on Cardiganshire
Carmarthenshire	None	---	Advanced Search on Carmarthenshire
Carnarvonshire	None	---	Advanced Search on Carnarvonshire
Channel Islands	1	Results for Channel Islands	Advanced Search on Channel Islands
Cheshire	12	Results for Cheshire	Advanced Search on Cheshire
Cornwall	1	Results for Cornwall	Advanced Search on Cornwall
Cumberland	13	Results for Cumberland	Advanced Search on Cumberland
Denbighshire	None	---	Advanced Search on Denbighshire
Derbyshire	37	Results for Derbyshire	Advanced Search on Derbyshire
Devon	6	Results for Devon	Advanced Search on Devon
Dorset	16	Results for Dorset	Advanced Search on Dorset

Figure 10.10 RootsUK Results by county.

This latter option brings up the Advanced Search form (see Fig. 10.11). In addition to the fields on the initial search form, it automatically fills in the county you have selected and allows you to enter an occupation and either an estimated birth year or an age. While you can change the county selected, you cannot use this form to do a search across all counties. There is a checkbox to include forename variants, but no way to search for surname variants. Carrying out an advanced search costs five credits.

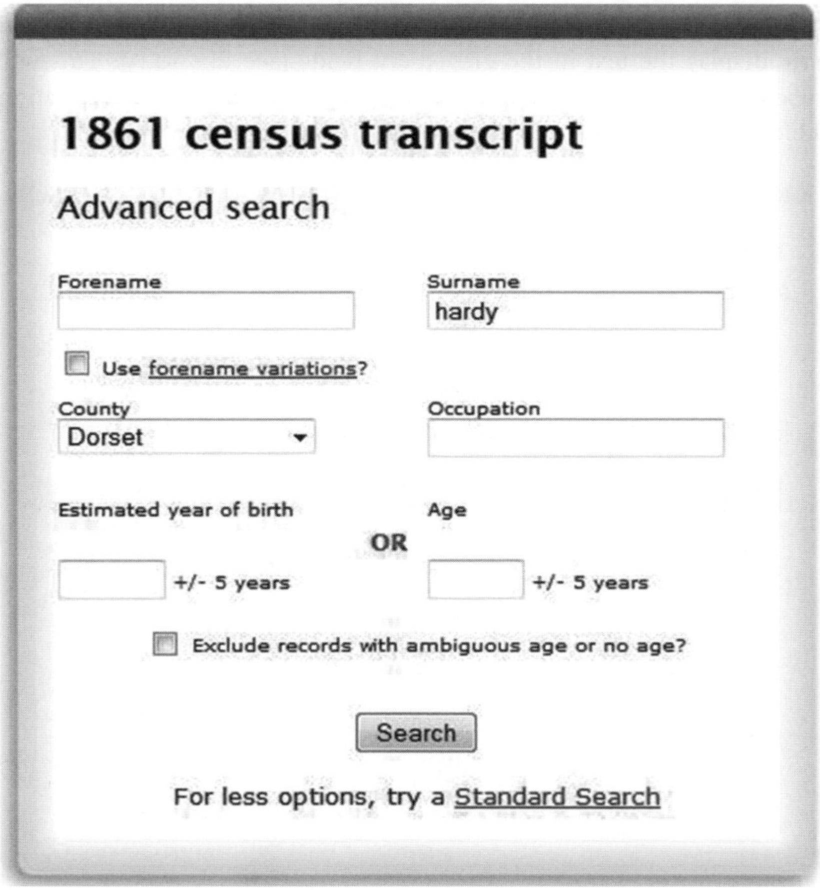

Figure 10.11 RootsUK Advanced search.

If you choose to view the matches for an individual, you get a screen showing just the items you have already searched on, with the other fields greyed out (see Fig. 10.12). Up to this point you have not been charged any credits, but if you want to go back to the county list, further screens will cost you five credits.

Although there is a link at the right to the full details for each individual, this is an item which is charged, so unless you have a very small number of entries on this page and you are sure which one you are looking for, you will want to select the option to reveal the greyed-out data by clicking on the link marked 'here' above the results table, which will display the text in the greyed-out fields (see Fig. 10.13). This will also cost you five credits, but it will give you much more information before you select the individual to see the full details of.

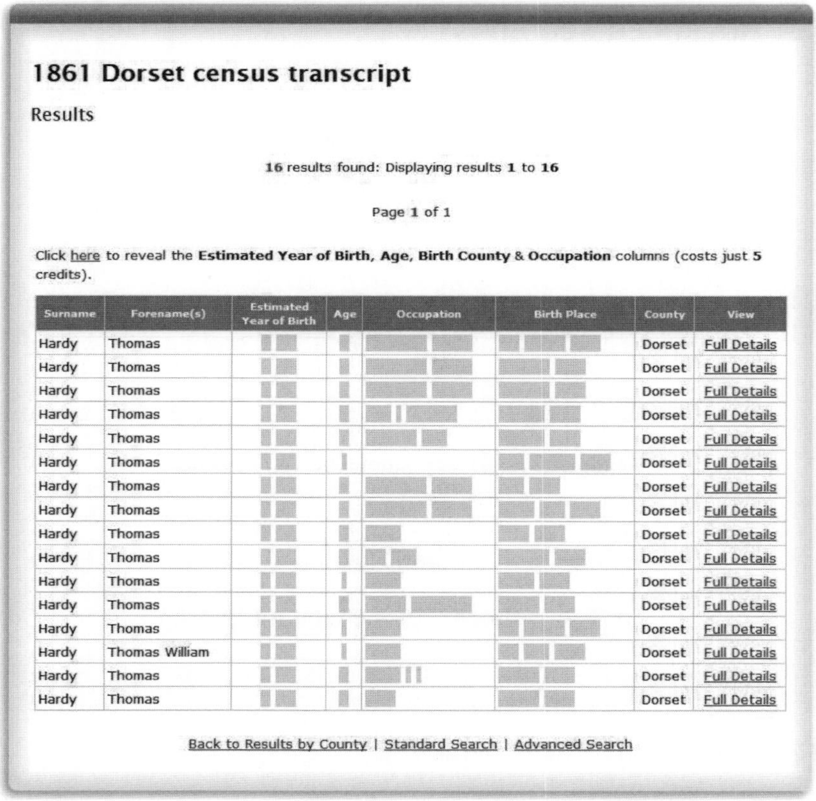

1861 Dorset census transcript

Results

16 results found: Displaying results 1 to 16

Page 1 of 1

Click here to reveal the **Estimated Year of Birth, Age, Birth County** & **Occupation** columns (costs just **5** credits).

Surname	Forename(s)	Estimated Year of Birth	Age	Occupation	Birth Place	County	View
Hardy	Thomas					Dorset	Full Details
Hardy	Thomas					Dorset	Full Details
Hardy	Thomas					Dorset	Full Details
Hardy	Thomas					Dorset	Full Details
Hardy	Thomas					Dorset	Full Details
Hardy	Thomas					Dorset	Full Details
Hardy	Thomas					Dorset	Full Details
Hardy	Thomas					Dorset	Full Details
Hardy	Thomas					Dorset	Full Details
Hardy	Thomas					Dorset	Full Details
Hardy	Thomas					Dorset	Full Details
Hardy	Thomas					Dorset	Full Details
Hardy	Thomas					Dorset	Full Details
Hardy	Thomas William					Dorset	Full Details
Hardy	Thomas					Dorset	Full Details
Hardy	Thomas					Dorset	Full Details

Back to Results by County | Standard Search | Advanced Search

Figure 10.12 RootsUK initial transcript screen.

1861 Dorset census transcript

Results

16 results found: Displaying results 1 to 16

Page 1 of 1

Surname	Forename(s)	Estimated Year of Birth	Age	Occupation	Birth Place	County	View
Hardy	Thomas	c. 1851	10	Agricultural Labourer	West Chalboro Dorset	Dorset	Full Details
Hardy	Thomas	c. 1813	48	Agricultural Labourer	Piddletown Dorset	Dorset	Full Details
Hardy	Thomas	c. 1835	26	Agricultural Labourer	Piddletown Dorset	Dorset	Full Details
Hardy	Thomas	c. 1812	49	Mason & Bricklayer	Stinsford Dorset	Dorset	Full Details
Hardy	Thomas	c. 1841	20	Architects Clerk	Stinsford Dorset	Dorset	Full Details
Hardy	Thomas	c. 1860	1		Frome Vanchurch Dorset	Dorset	Full Details
Hardy	Thomas	c. 1800	61	Agricultural Labourer	Swyre Dorset	Dorset	Full Details
Hardy	Thomas	c. 1830	31	Agricultural Labourer	Wynford Eagle Dorset	Dorset	Full Details
Hardy	Thomas	c. 1842	19	Servant	Morden Dorset	Dorset	Full Details
Hardy	Thomas	c. 1829	32	Shoe Maker	Dorchester Dorset	Dorset	Full Details
Hardy	Thomas	c. 1857	4	Scholar	Wareham Dorset	Dorset	Full Details
Hardy	Thomas	c. 1822	39	Labourer Agricultural	Broadway Dorset	Dorset	Full Details
Hardy	Thomas	c. 1852	9	Scholar	West Knighton Dorset	Dorset	Full Details
Hardy	Thomas William	c. 1856	5	Scholar	Bere Regis Dorset	Dorset	Full Details
Hardy	Thomas	c. 1829	32	Mariner M S	Weymouth Dorset	Dorset	Full Details
Hardy	Thomas	c. 1806	55	Taylor	Weymouth Dorset	Dorset	Full Details

Back to Results by County | Standard Search | Advanced Search

Figure 10.13 RootsUK transcript screen with details revealed.

When you click on the 'Full Details' link, you will get a page for the selected individual (see Fig. 10.14). Although the page is called 'Full details', it does not in fact indicate either the gender (which you probably know already!) or the marital status. Also, the TNA reference is incomplete: even though the field is labelled 'Folio reference' in some cases it does not give the folio number, but only the piece number; in cases where it does give the folio number this is often 'calculated', and may actually be incorrect; it does not give the page number.

From here, you can view an image of the original census record. The images are the same as those for TheGenealogist and the viewer for the PDF files is similar.

From the 'Full details' page, there is also a link to two 'Smart Search' options. One allows you to search the site's civil registration records for the birth of the individual, the other lists the family of the individual

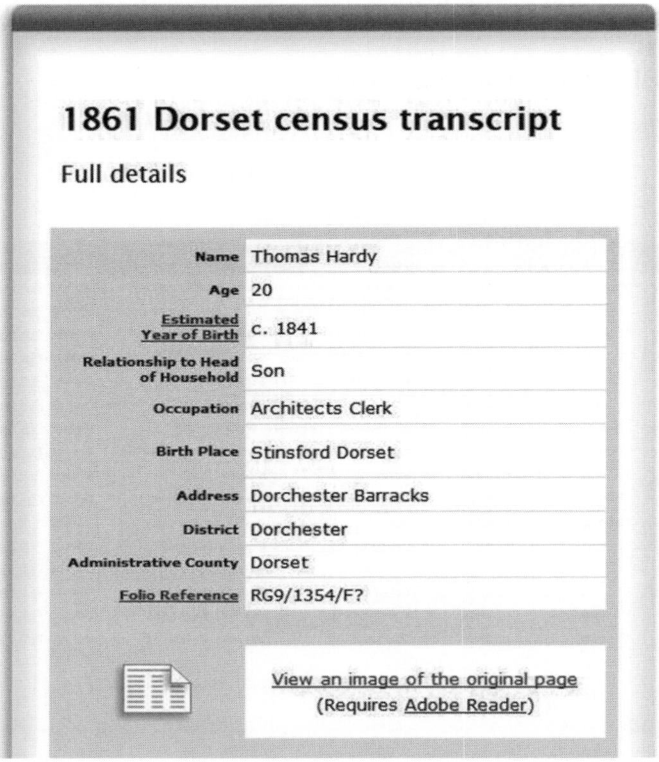

1861 Dorset census transcript

Full details

Name	Thomas Hardy
Age	20
Estimated Year of Birth	c. 1841
Relationship to Head of Household	Son
Occupation	Architects Clerk
Birth Place	Stinsford Dorset
Address	Dorchester Barracks
District	Dorchester
Administrative County	Dorset
Folio Reference	RG9/1354/F?

View an image of the original page
(Requires Adobe Reader)

Figure 10.14 RootsUK full details.

displayed. The point of this is to identify people who are in the same household but are not on the same page of the enumeration schedule — if you have searched for a child, the parents could be on a previous page; if you have searched for a head of household, the youngest children or some of the servants may be on the following page.

A flowchart for the RootsUK search process is shown in Figure 10.15.

UK Census Online

UK Census Online provides very basic search facilities and the search process is shown in Figure 10.16.

A very useful feature is the free search: without subscribing, or even registering, you can carry out an initial search on just forename and surname. The search results provide a surprising amount of detail.

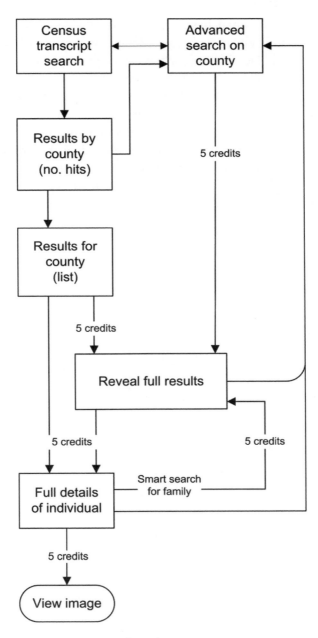

Figure 10.15 RootsUK: search flow-chart.

Alongside a count of matches in each county, the results include a list of matching individuals with age, occupation, county of residence, occupation, and place of birth. While you can't do a search on county as such, you can filter the results to view just those for a single county — Fig. 10.17 shows the results of a search for Thomas Hardy in the 1861 census, with just those for Dorset displayed.

This free search could be very useful if you mainly use another data service and have been unable to find an individual. You may have to look through a long list of individuals, but you should see enough details to identify the desired ancestor and go back to your usual site to conduct a successful search using the newly-discovered information.

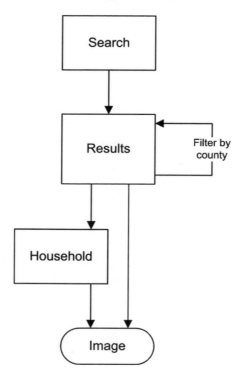

Figure 10.16 UK Census Online: search flow-chart.

Found 17 results (1 Page)

« 1 »

Forename	Surname	Age	Occupation	County	Estimated Year of Birth	Place of Birth	
Thomas	Hardy	49	Mason & Bricklayer	Dorset	1812	Stinsford, Dorset	View more details
Thomas	Hardy	48	Agricultural Labourer	Dorset	1813	Piddletown, Dorset	View more details
Thomas	Hardy	39	Labourer Agricultural	Dorset	1822	Broadway, Dorset	View more details
Thomas	Hardy	32	Shoe Maker	Dorset	1829	Dorchester, Dorset	View more details
Thomas	Hardy	32	Mariner M S	Dorset	1829	Weymouth, Dorset	View more details
Thomas	Hardy	61	Agricultural Labourer	Dorset	1800	Swyre, Dorset	View more details
Thomas	Hardy	55	Taylor	Dorset	1806	Weymouth, Dorset	View more details
Thomas	Hardy	31	Agricultural Labourer	Dorset	1830	Wynford Eagle, Dorset	View more details
Thomas	Hardy	26	Agricultural Labourer	Dorset	1835	Piddletown, Dorset	View more details
Thomas	Hardy	20	Architects Clerk	Dorset	1841	Stinsford, Dorset	View more details
Thomas	Hardy	19	Servant	Dorset	1842	Morden, Dorset	View more details
Thomas	Hardy	10	Agricultural Labourer	Dorset	1851	West Chalboro, Dorset	View more details

Select a Record Set:

(2)	Bucks 1861 Census
(5)	Cambridge 1861 Census
(2)	Channel Islands 1861 Census
(18)	Cheshire 1861 Census
(2)	Cornwall 1861 Census
(3)	Crew Lists 1861 Census
(13)	Cumberland 1861 Census
(37)	Derbyshire 1861 Census
(7)	Devon 1861 Census
(17)	Dorset 1861 Census
(90)	Durham 1861 Census
(13)	Essex 1861 Census
(1)	Glamorgan 1861 Census
(3)	Gloucestershire 1861 Census
(10)	Hampshire 1861 Census
(4)	Hertfordshire 1861 Census
(2)	Kent 1861 Census
(58)	Lancashire 1861 Census
(32)	Leicestershire 1861 Census
(43)	Lincolnshire 1861 Census
(48)	London 1861 Census
(4)	Middlesex 1861 Census
(1)	Monmouthshire 1861 Census
(8)	Norfolk 1861 Census
(3)	Northamptonshire 1861 Census
(27)	Northumberland 1861 Census
(49)	Nottinghamshire 1861 Census
(1)	Shropshire 1861 Census
(6)	Somerset 1861 Census
(16)	Staffordshire 1861 Census
(5)	Suffolk 1861 Census
(7)	Surrey 1861 Census
(13)	Warwickshire 1861 Census
(1)	Worcestershire 1861 Census
(89)	Yorkshire 1861 Census

Figure 10.17 UK Census Online free search results.

The site has only one type of search, which is indeed very basic: census year, name, birth year and keywords (see Fig. 10.18). The surname-matching options are the same as TheGenealogist's: wildcards even at the beginning of a name, and 'Smart Variants', which is simply another name for TheGenealogist's phonetic matching. There is, however, no option for including nicknames, though we found that the search results in fact include individuals with just a matching initial.

Search UKCensusOnline

Forename:

Surname:

Keywords:

Data Set:
1861 Census

Search Mode:
○ Simple ● Smart Variants* [?]

Year:

Range (+/-):
0 ▾

Search

We recommended using keywords to find your ancestor e.g. George Turner Lambeth Labourer

Please use only one forename. You can also use wildcards (*) to find your ancestors (e.g. Nor* will find Nora, Norton; Sm* will find Smith, Smitt, etc)

Figure 10.18 UK Census Online search form.

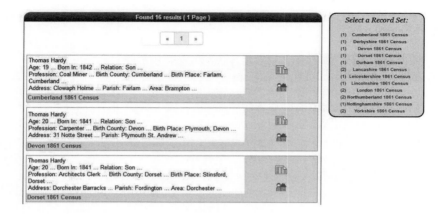

Figure 10.19 UK Census Online search results.

Dorset 1861 Census Transcript

Address: Dorchester Barracks **Parish:** Fordington **Registration District:** Fordington, Dorset

Surname	Forename	Age	Relation	Occupation	Birth Place	Image Reference	
Hardy	Thomas	49	Head	Mason & Bricklayer	Stinsford, Dorset	RG9/1354/F?	
Hardy	Jemima	47	Wife		Melbury, Dorset	RG9/1354/F?	
Hardy	Thomas	20	Son	Architects Clerk	Stinsford, Dorset	RG9/1354/F?	
Hardy	Henry	9	Son	Scholar	Stinsford, Dorset	RG9/1354/F?	
Hardy	Catherine	4	Daughter		Stinsford, Dorset	RG9/1354/F?	

Figure 10.20 UK Census Online household transcript.

The search results for subscribers are more detailed than the free search results and include details of the place of residence and address (see Fig. 10.19). From here you can view the complete household or the census image.

Images

The census images on all three sites are provided in Adobe Acrobat (PDF) format (see p. 124). Each image opens in an Acrobat window. The standard Acrobat toolbar provides options for printing, saving and zooming, while the toolbar at the top of the browser window allows you to go to the previous or following census page.

The images have been scanned at different colour depths: greyscale for the 1841 and 1851 censuses; black and white for the other Victorian censuses. The 1911 census images are the same colour images found on

Findmypast and the official 1911 site (see Chapter 9). Where customers have reported a black and white image as hard to read, S&N have been replacing these with greyscale images and targeting them for retranscription.

It is difficult to establish the exact resolution of a PDF image, but the resolution of most images seems to be around 200 dpi, with some higher and some lower. The greyscale images are quite satisfactory, but at this resolution some of the poorer quality original documents are far from easy to read where they have been scanned in black and white.

On RootsUK, any image you have already paid for can be viewed again without further payment for a period of 30 days. However, it is much better to download any images you have paid for, even those that turn out not to contain the ancestor you were looking for — that way you don't have to worry about the 30-day limit. What *is* useful is that you can return to an image without charge to check the pages either side. One thing to watch out for: if you return to an image you have already paid to view and then use the previous image or next image links to view surrounding other pages that you have not previously viewed, this will cost you an additional 5 credits each time. You can also revisit the full details for any individual you have paid for in the previous 30 days.

Help and feedback

All three sites have extensive help. TheGenealogist and UK Census Online have a Help Wizard which is accessed via the 'Help' link at the top of most pages. Most of the topics covered relate to subscribing, logging in and viewing images. Both TheGenealogist and RootsUK have detailed guides to census records.

TheGenealogist and UK Census Online have identical problem reporting, with two types of report, both accessible via the 'Add correction/Query index entry' link (the question-mark icon) on the household transcript pages (see Fig. 10.4 and Fig. 10.20). You can use the main form to provide corrections to the transcription and there is a link to a separate form for reporting problems with the page image.

On RootsUK the full details page for an individual (see Fig. 10.14) has a link at the foot of the page 'Report a problem with this record', which can be used to report apparent errors or other problems with the data. There is no form for reporting errors with the image itself.

Other resources

In addition to its short-term memory feature (mentioned on p. 221), TheGenealogist provides two ways for you to save the results of your searches. The Research Log can store the full details of any individual records you are currently viewing. If you are viewing the household or family screen, you can save the entire household or family to the Research Log. You can also add comments to the individual entries. From the Research Log you can go to the household transcript or the page image.

The other way of recording your ancestors is to save them individually, or by family, to the TreeView. It is not possible here to discuss TreeView in detail, since it is a fully-fledged online pedigree database, to which you can add individuals by hand or by uploading a GEDCOM file. When you save an individual from the census to TreeView, the details of the census entry are added to what is called the 'Exhibit List' in TreeView. You can take any record in your general exhibit list and attach it to the exhibit list for a particular individual. This way, your family tree can include the census details of all your nineteenth-century ancestors.

As mentioned above, RootsUK keeps a list of viewed images and records for 30 days. UK Census Online has no facilities for saving information on your searches or results.

11

ORIGINS

Origins was the first UK genealogical data service. It was launched in April 1998 with Scottish civil registration data and images on a site called Scots Origins. Although the Scottish data subsequently moved to ScotlandsPeople (see Chapter 14), Origins by then had launched British Origins to host datasets from the Society of Genealogists. In 2005, it started to add census data for England and Wales. It also has an Irish Origins service with data for Ireland. All are accessed via the home page at <**www.origins.net**>.

The site's census data for England and Wales comprises the 1841, 1861, 1871 and 1901 censuses. Origins carried out their own indexing and digitisation for the 1841 and 1871 censuses, while the 1861 data is licensed from Findmypast (see Chapter 9). Origins has in return licensed its indexes for use by Findmypast, as well as FamilySearch (p. 159) and MyHeritage (Chapter 13). The 1891 and 1901 census indexes were added at the start of 2014, and a new index to the 1881 census (i.e. not the index created by the 1881 Census Index project described on p. 158) was added in May 2014. The company has announced that an index to the 1851 census should also be available by the time you are reading this.

Origins was the first commercial site to host Irish census data, offering the Dublin City census for 1851 and for the Rotunda Ward in Dublin for 1901. These are discussed in more detail on p. 307. Irish Origins also has separate datasets of Irish strays in the England and Wales census of 1841 and 1871. However, these are simply extracts from the census which include only those giving Ireland as a birthplace, and do not provide any data that is not already available in the indexes to those censuses.

Charges

Origins is essentially a subscription site. Two collections of wills are accessible only on a pay-per-view basis, but all the census records require a subscription. The censuses for England and Wales require a subscription to the British Origins area of the site (prices are given in Table 11.1), and a separate subscription to Irish Origins includes access to the two Irish census indexes mentioned above. The Origins Total Access subscription covers all British and Irish census indexes.

Since the annual Total Access subscription costs less than a six-month subscription to British Origins alone, that is clearly the option to go for if you are going to be a long-term user. Subscriptions are payable only online with a credit/debit card. Monthly and annual subscriptions are automatically renewed unless the user cancels more than seven days in advance of expiry. The 72-hour subscription is not automatically renewed. The site does not offer a free trial, though searches leading to the 'Records found' screen (see Fig.11.2) are available to non-subscribers.

	British Origins	*Total Access*
72 hours	£7.00	£8.00
Month	£9.50	£10.50
Year	—	£55.00

Table 11.1 Origins subscription prices (April 2014).

England & Wales Census 1871

Enter details below and click *Search*.

Last Name (Required)

NameX [Exact only ▾] [?]

First Name

NameX [All variants ▾] [?]

County [All Counties ▾]

Parish [All Parishes ▾]

Birth Place [All Counties ▾]

Age Range [ ] to [ ]

[Search]

Help

Counties See county map and counts

NameX finds records for names which may have common variations or incorrect spelling.
Use of Wildcards will disable NameX.

Figure 11.1 Origins census search form.

Searching

Origins offers a global search across all three of its censuses and an individual search for each census. Since the global search allows you to specify only a last name and first name, its main use, unless you have an ancestor with a reasonably unusual name, is to provide initial information about how many matching records there are.

The search form for an individual census is shown in Figure 11.1. The only field you have to complete is the last name. Note that unlike some of the other sites, Origins does not have a basic and an advanced search form. You don't have to specify a county, but you can select one from the drop-down list; if you do this you will then be able to select a parish from the drop-down list below that, which initially says 'All Parishes'. This lists all the parishes in the county, so you don't have to worry about getting the correct spelling of the parish. The 'Birth Place' field allows you to select from a list of English and Welsh counties and other countries (including Scotland and Ireland).

The search form for the 1901 census is slightly different: instead of a 'Parish' field, there is a 'District' field with a drop-down list of registration districts in the chosen county.

Origins offers two ways of finding surname variants. The main one is NameX, discussed on p. 147. The default name search uses the NameX 'close variants' option, but you can switch NameX off by choosing 'Exactly only' or cast the net wider by selecting 'All variants.' The

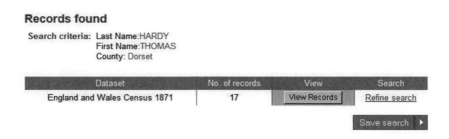

Figure 11.2 Origins 'Records found' screen.

alternative is to use a wildcard (see p. 145). If you want an exact match on the names you will need to select 'Exact only' for the two NameX fields.

When you click the 'Search' button on the search page, the initial results page, headed 'Records found,' shows you only the total number of matches (see Fig. 11.1). The aim of this is to give you some idea whether you have got a manageable number of hits or whether you want to refine your search before looking at the matching records. The page actually has a link on it saying 'Refine Search.' However, this takes you back to the original *blank* search form from which you started and there is no real reason to use this. The best way to refine your search is to modify your completed search form, which is repeated on the 'Records found' page.

Once you have refined your search as much as you think you need to, clicking on the 'View records' button takes you to the 'View records' page. This lists all the individual matching records, 20 to a page (see Fig. 11.3).

Last Name	First Name	Sex	Age	Birth County	Street	Village	Town	Parish	County		
HARDY	THOMAS	M	5	Devon	ROCOMBE VALLEY	UPLYME		UPLYME	Dorset	Image	Details
HARDY	THOMAS	M	59	Dorset	SOUTHWELL VILLAGE	SOUTHWELL		PORTLAND	Dorset	Image	Details
HARDY	THOMAS	M	41	Dorset	FARM HOUSE	WYNFORD EAGLE		WYNFORD EAGLE	Dorset	Image	Details
HARDY	THOMAS	M	5	Dorset	GROSVENOR TERRACE		SWANAGE	SWANAGE	Dorset	Image	Details
HARDY	THOMAS	M	59	Dorset	BOCKHAMPTON COTTAGE, HIGHER	STINSFORD		STINSFORD	Dorset	Image	Details
HARDY	THOMAS	M	29	Dorset	BAITER		POOLE	ST JAMES	Dorset	Image	Details
HARDY	THOMAS	M	71	Dorset	FARM HOUSE	WYNFORD EAGLE		WYNFORD EAGLE	Dorset	Image	Details
HARDY	THOMAS	M	8	Dorset	HIGH STREET		SWANAGE	SWANAGE	Dorset	Image	Details
HARDY	THOMAS	M	19	Dorset	CHALDON, EAST COTTAGES	CHALDON		CHALDON HERRING	Dorset	Image	Details
HARDY	THOMAS	M	11	Dorset	WHITEHALL ROAD			FROME VAUCHURCH	Dorset	Image	Details
HARDY	THOMAS	M	49	Dorset	CHALDON, EAST COTTAGES	CHALDON		CHALDON HERRING	Dorset	Image	Details
HARDY	THOMAS	M	46	Dorset	THE CROSS			OSMINGTON	Dorset	Image	Details
HARDY	THOMAS	M	30	Dorset	BOCKHAMPTON COTTAGE, HIGHER	STINSFORD		STINSFORD	Dorset	Image	Details
HARDY	THOMAS	M	5	Dorset	OAKLEY PLACE		WEYMOUTH	WYKE REGIS	Dorset	Image	Details
HARDY	THOMAS BURROUGH	M	0	Dorset	SANDPIT FARM HOUSE			BROADWINDSOR	Dorset	Image	Details
HARDY	THOMAS R	M	41	Dorset	OAKLEY PLACE		WEYMOUTH	WYKE REGIS	Dorset	Image	Details
HARDY	THOMAS WM	M	15	Dorset	WARGATE		WAREHAM	LADY ST MARY	Dorset	Image	Details

Figure 11.3 Origins 'View records' screen (1871 census).

For the 1871 census (shown in Fig. 11.3), this page includes the main address and personal fields, with the exception of marital status and occupation. On the 'View full record' page (Fig. 11.5) for the 1841 and 1861 censuses, there is no Relation column. Also, because the 1841 census only asked whether a person was born in the same county or not, the Birth County column will contain either the same county as the County column on the right of the screen, or the words 'OUT OF COUNTY', 'Scotland', or 'Ireland'. The listing should certainly provide enough information to identify the correct ancestor or the most likely candidates without checking every image.

The initial listing does not appear to be in any particular order, but you can sort on any of the columns by clicking on the column heading. Once you have sorted on a particular column, clicking on the heading a second time reverses the sort order. An obvious use for this is to sort by address, which will put family members together; or you can order the entries by increasing or decreasing age.

If you want to keep the details of a search so that you can run it again, Origins provides a 'Save search' facility, which is available from the 'Records found' and 'View record' screens — click on the 'Save search' button at the bottom of the screen. To view your saved searches, you click on the 'Saved Searches' link on the menu bar at the top of the screen. This brings up a list of all the searches you have saved, with details of date and time, dataset and search criteria (see Fig. 11.4). You can rerun the search from this screen and it will take you to the 'Records found' screen. Many pages have a 'view all searches' link at the bottom, but this takes you to the main list of datasets, *not* to your own saved searches. There is a bug when saving searches for the 1861 census: the 'Search criteria' field remains blank.

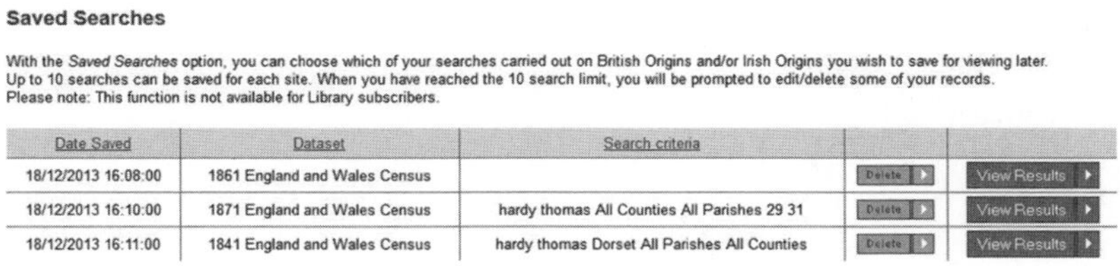

Saved Searches

With the *Saved Searches* option, you can choose which of your searches carried out on British Origins and/or Irish Origins you wish to save for viewing later. Up to 10 searches can be saved for each site. When you have reached the 10 search limit, you will be prompted to edit/delete some of your records. Please note: This function is not available for Library subscribers.

Date Saved	Dataset	Search criteria		
18/12/2013 16:08:00	1861 England and Wales Census		Delete ▶	View Results ▶
18/12/2013 16:10:00	1871 England and Wales Census	hardy thomas All Counties All Parishes 29 31	Delete ▶	View Results ▶
18/12/2013 16:11:00	1841 England and Wales Census	hardy thomas Dorset All Parishes All Counties	Delete ▶	View Results ▶

Figure 11.4 Origins 'Saved Searches' screen.

View full record - England & Wales Census 1871

Reference details

Census	1871
TNA Ref	RG10-2011
Image No	138
Folio No	68
Page No	11
Entry No	17

Location details

County	Dorset
Superintendent Registrar's District	DORCHESTER
Registrar's Sub-District	DORCHESTER
Enumeration District No	10
Civil Parish	STINSFORD
City or Municipal Borough	
Municipal Ward	
Parliamentary Borough	
Town	
Village or Hamlet	STINSFORD
Local Board	
Ecclesiastical District	
Schedule No	47
Street	BOCKHAMPTON COTTAGE, HIGHER

Record details

First name	THOMAS
Last name	HARDY
Title	
Misc	
Relation	Son
Age	30
Sex	M
Birth County	Dorset

Image

View Census Image	Image

Figure 11.5 Origins View full record.

From the 'View records' screen you have two options — to view the details or to view the images. Clicking on the 'Details' button brings up the 'View full record' page, with three tables (see Fig. 11.5). The second and third tables largely repeat the information on the results listing ('Relation' is the only significant additional field). The first table is the most useful, since it provides the full TNA reference. This page does not give you the missing columns from the enumeration book — marital status, occupation and full birthplace — and you can only get these by viewing the page image.

You can call up the image display either from the 'View records' or the 'View full record' screen and this launches the image viewer with the matching page image.

From the image viewer you can go to the next or previous page in the enumeration district, go back to the 'View records' screen, or start a new search. Figure 11.6 gives an overview of the search process at Origins.

Origins does not have an address search; the 'Search by Place' link on the navigation bar at the top of the screen takes you to entries from the 1895 *The Comprehensive Gazetteer of England and Wales*. There is no facility to search by TNA reference.

In addition to the search facility for individual census years, Origins also has a 'Search all Census Records & Substitutes' option, which covers all the census years as well as some smaller census-like data collections. This necessarily lacks search fields for places or residence and birth, but could be useful for searching on a rare name or for a one-name study.

Images

Origins is in the process of switching image formats as we write. Until the start of 2014, the census images were all in TIFF format, but with the addition of the 1901 census, the site started to use JPEG images. This format will be used in the future censuses mentioned at the start of this chapter, and Origins inform us that the older images will be converted to JPEG format in due course, though they were unable to give a firm time-scale.

The reason this matters is that, while the TIFF format is common in professional graphics work, downloaded images may not be able to

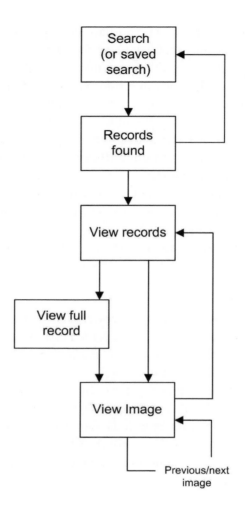

Figure 11.6 Origins search flow-chart.

display on your computer, depending on the operating system and installed software. This is not a problem with JPEG images.

Origins has its own image viewer, which can display both types of image, and has various controls such as zoom and rotate (some of the images are in portrait, rather than landscape orientation). The viewer requires a Java-based plug-in, so you will need to have Java installed on your computer. Origins has a detailed help page at <**www.origins.net/ help/helpimages-java.aspx**> devoted to using the image viewer, which explains how to install Java on your computer and how to enable it if it is already installed but not active. The first time you use the viewer, there may be a slight delay as the plug-in is downloaded.

As long as TIFF images are available on the site, Origins also has a special TIFF viewer for Windows, called AlternaTIFF, but there is no reason to use this rather than the Java viewer.

The viewer's 'Save document' icon will download the image to your computer. There is no option to select a graphics format — the file will automatically be saved in its original format. If Origins is still using the TIFF format when you read this, there is a simple way to save these images in a different and more convenient format: right-click with the mouse (or CTRL+ right-click with a Macintosh one-button mouse), this will bring up a menu, on which you can select 'Clipboard', then 'Copy image to clipboard'. This places the image in your clipboard. You can then paste the image into any application which will accept a pasted image (a word-processor or graphics editor, for example) and then save the image from that application in whichever formats it supports. In most applications the Paste option is on the Edit menu, but some graphics software has an option under the File menu to create a new image from the contents of the clipboard. Note that using the clipboard copies the entire image to the clipboard, not just whatever is visible in the viewer.

The colour-depth and resolution of the census images on Origins varies. All the page images for the 1841 and 1861 censuses and about one third of those for the 1871 census are greyscale, and generally have a resolution of 300 dpi, though some seem to be lower. The remaining 1871 images are black and white. The images for the other censuses, those added during 2014, will all be greyscale. Of this latter batch only the 1901 images were available to us at the time of writing, but they seem to be at very high resolution, perhaps double that of the earlier images.

Help and feedback

Origins has an extensive suite of help pages, accessible from the 'Help' link shown on most pages or from the 'help & resources' link on the home page. There are articles on the census and other records, as well as a general introduction on 'How to Start Tracing your Family History'.

The most important help page is probably the one on 'Viewing Images and Maps' mentioned above at <**www.origins.net/help/helpimages. aspx**> — it is probably a good idea to have a look at this before you start viewing images on the site. There is also a link to this page from the image viewer, from the 'can't view images?' link.

There is a feedback link at the bottom of many pages on the site (apart from those which form part of the record search), which leads to an e-mail form, but there is no specific facility on the record pages for reporting transcription errors or on the image pages for reporting problems with the images.

12

GENES REUNITED AND 1901CENSUSONLINE

When it was launched in January 2002, the 1901 census was the first complete census for England and Wales to go online. With some 32 million records and 1.5 million images it was by far the largest genealogical dataset for the UK on the web. It was available on a dedicated site run initially by QinetiQ and now at <**www.1901censusonline. com**>. Further details of the project are given in Chapter 5.

Genes Reunited at <**www.genesreunited.co.uk**> was launched under the name Genes Connected in 2003 as a genealogical offshoot of the immensely popular Friends Reunited. Initially it concentrated on hosting user-submitted family trees as the basis for its contact service, and did not offer any genealogical records. This changed in August 2005, when it purchased the digitised 1901 census from QinetiQ for £3.3 million, not only taking over the running of the official 1901censusonline site, but also offering the census index and images as part of a new facility on Genes Reunited.

Subsequently the two sites added the remaining censuses for England and Wales, which were licensed from TheGenealogist (see Chapter 10). However, in 2009 1901censusonline and Genes Reunited, which had meanwhile been sold to ITV, were purchased by Brightsolid and brought into the same stable as Findmypast (see Chapter 9). Findmypast's census indexes are now the source of both sites' census material, except that 1901censusonline still offers the original QinetiQ 1901 census index. The sites have more recently added the 1911 census for England and Wales, and Genes Reunited now includes indexes (without images) for the Scottish censuses up to 1901.

Charges

1901censusonline offers only a pay-per-view service but Genes Reunited has both pay-per-view and subscription options. In spite of the common ownership and the shared data, the charging regimes of the two sites differ slightly:

- 1901censusonline offers 500 credits for £5, with transcripts for an individual or a household costing 50 units and images costing 75 (i.e. 50p and 75p respectively).
- Genes Reunited gives you 50 credits for £5 or 200 credits for £17.95, with all items costing 5 units (i.e. 50p). This means that images on Genes Reunited are 25p cheaper.

On both sites, the credits have limited validity. The 1901 site's credits are valid for a mere seven days, while those purchased on Genes Reunited are valid for either 30 days or 90 days, depending on the amount purchased. The period of validity starts at the time of purchase, not the time when the credits are first used. On 1901censusonline you can only buy £5 worth of units in any one transaction, which is inconvenient if you have a lot of searches to do, while Genes Reunited has the advantage of an option for the automatic top-up of credits when they run low.

In addition to the pay-per-view system Genes Reunited also has three subscription options, for one, six or twelve months at £19.95, £49.95 and £79.95 respectively. These also give access to the site's member contact facilities, which are otherwise available, without data collections, under a Standard membership costing £19.95 a year.

Searching Genes Reunited

The search facilities on Genes Reunited are very basic, and are in some ways rather awkwardly designed. There is a home page for census records but it has a 120-character URL, and getting to it by following links is not straightforward. From the home page, click on the 'Search' link at the top of the page and then select 'Census, Land & Surveys' from the drop down menu. The search box which appears is headed

'Census' (see Fig. 12.1) and will in fact search all the census records. If, as is mostly likely, you want to search a single census, you need to select the relevant year from the 'Records to Search' panel beneath the search box, which will bring up the search box for that census (see Fig. 12.2).

As you can see from the screenshots, the basic search has limited options. Apart from the name fields, there is the possibility of adding a birth year. The 'Optional keywords' field can be used to search for a place of residence, but not a birthplace — even if you enter a birth year, a place name entered in the keywords field will not be treated as a birthplace. However, the field can also be used to specify an occupation or part of an address, such as a street name.

The 'Last Name' field accepts wildcards, and, unusually, you can use a wildcard at the beginning of a name. This allows you to find an individual where the initial letter of the surname has been mistranscribed. Fuzzy name matching can be selected by checking the 'Name variants' checkbox for First Name or Last Name. The site itself gives no information on the matching algorithms, but Genes Reunited have informed us that they use a custom system which combines listed synonyms with Soundex and NameX (see pp. 143 and 145).

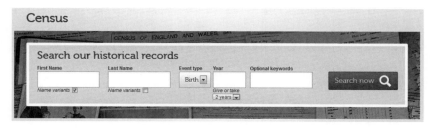

Figure 12.1 Genes Reunited general census search form.

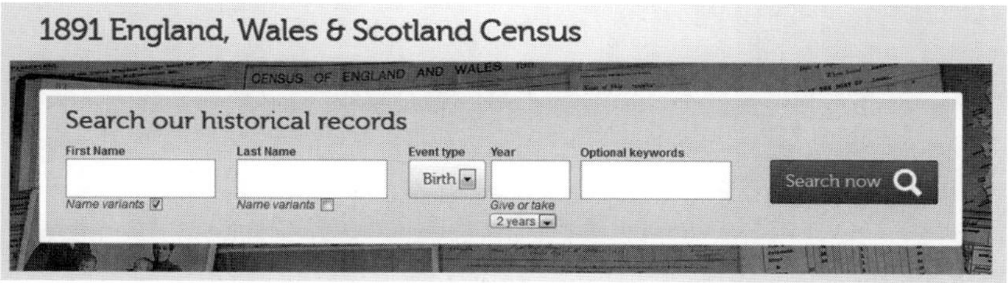

Figure 12.2 Genes Reunited search form for a specific census.

When you click on the 'Search now' button, you are presented with a page listing the first ten search results. At the top of the page it will give you the total number of search results. For each individual, the search results (see Fig. 12.3) show only registration district and county, and age and calculated birth year. Scottish census search results omit the registration district.

The limitations of the basic search are partly overcome in the advanced search. This can only be accessed after you have carried out a basic search — click on the 'Or try the advanced search' link, below the 'Search now' button (see Fig. 12.3).

The advanced search (see Fig. 12.4) adds birthplace and more specific residence place fields. There is a special 'Vessel Name' field for locating naval personnel. Having separate City, Town and Registration District fields seems rather strange. The census forms themselves distinguish parishes, cities or boroughs, towns, and hamlets, but abbreviating 'City or Borough' to 'City', in particular, seems likely to confuse even a relatively experienced user.

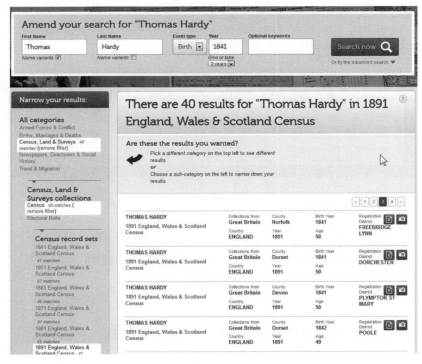

Figure 12.3 Genes Reunited search results.

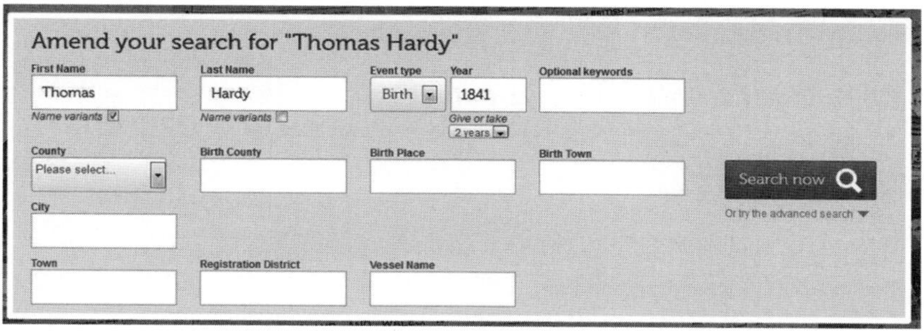

Figure 12.4 Genes Reunited advanced search.

The use of a birthplace field alongside birth county and birth town also seems rather odd and is not explained on the site. However, test searches suggest that it partly means 'country of birth' — entering 'Scotland' or 'Ireland' works — while for the Scottish census it is the only valid birthplace field. If you enter 'London' in the 'Birth Place' field, you get only results from the Scottish census indexes. Conversely, if you enter 'London' in the 'Birth Town' field, you get no Scottish results at all. Unfortunately this confusing state of affairs seems not to be explained anywhere on the site and rather undermines the merits of the advanced search.

All the searching is free of charge, so you can carry out initial searches without buying credits or using those you have bought. However, to see full details of an individual or household you must use credits to view either a transcription of the record for the individual or the image of the original records. This is done by clicking on either the document or camera icon in the row for the individual (see Fig. 12.3). You are always asked to confirm before you go to a charged page. However, if you have already used credits to view a particular record, the site remembers the fact and does not charge you again.

The Record Transcription for Thomas Hardy in the 1891 census is shown in Figure 12.5. Note that it provides, in principle, a transcription of *every* field on the original record, so you do not need to view the image to see the information, unless of course you want to check the accuracy of the transcription. However, we have noted a few examples where the full birthplace is not given in the transcription — in the case of Thomas Hardy, the original 1891 census record gives 'Dorset, Stinsford' as the place of birth but the 'transcription' says only

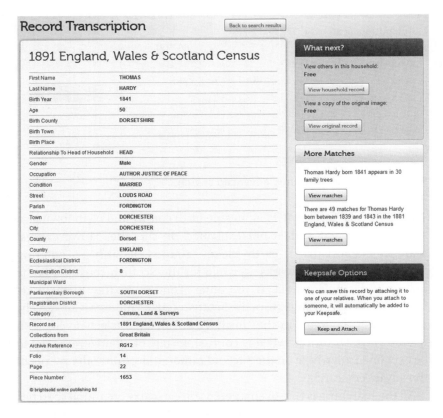

Figure 12.5 Genes Reunited Record Transcription.

'Dorsetshire'. This means, incidentally, that including 'Stinsford' in the 'Birth Town' field will find *no* matching records. This seems to be a problem with the indexing of the 1891 census on Genes Reunited, but we have not been able to establish definitively whether it is a problem that affects other census years.

From the record transcription you can select to view the page image, or you can click on the 'View household record' button to see the full record for all members of the household. As the page warns you, this costs an additional five credits, though this changes to 'Free' once you have paid to view (as you can see in Figure 12.5).

A flow-chart for the census search facilities on Genes Reunited is shown in Figure 12.6. There is no address search and no facility for census reference searches.

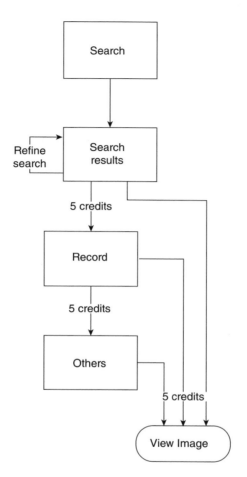

Figure 12.6 Genes Reunited search flow-chart.

All in all, the limitations and problems in the search forms make Genes Reunited's census indexes poorly suited to any but the most casual use. Certainly, most people with sufficient interest in census records to be reading this book are likely to find it frustrating. On the other hand, if you are already using other parts of the service, the census records constitute a useful additional resource. Anyone coming to the censuses as a beginner, having used the site's contact service, will find it a low-cost way to start exploring the records, but will eventually want to look elsewhere for more comprehensive search options.

1901censusonline: Person Search

While the data and images at <www.1901censusonline.com> are largely the same as those on Genes Reunited, and the overall search process is very similar (see Fig. 12.12), the search facilities are much more extensive, particularly in the case of the 1901 census index itself. However, there are differences between the individual census years, and it is not possible in the space available here to describe all the variations.

The most comprehensive options are those available for the 1901 census itself, which offers person, address, location, institution, vessel, and TNA reference searches (see Fig. 12.7). For the 1861 and 1871 censuses, person, address and vessel searches are available. For the 1841, 1851 and 1891 censuses only the person and address searches are offered. For the 1911 census, only a person search is available.

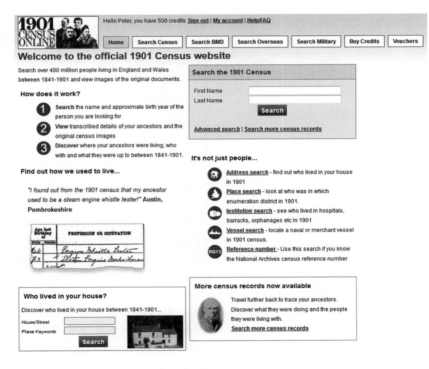

Figure 12.7 1901censusonline home page.

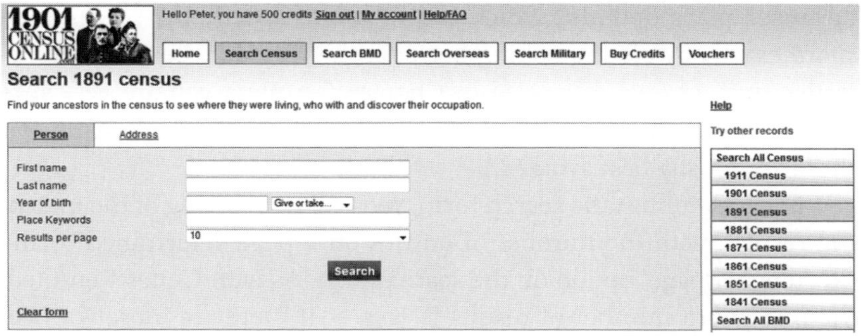

Figure 12.8 1901censusonline search form for the 1891 census.

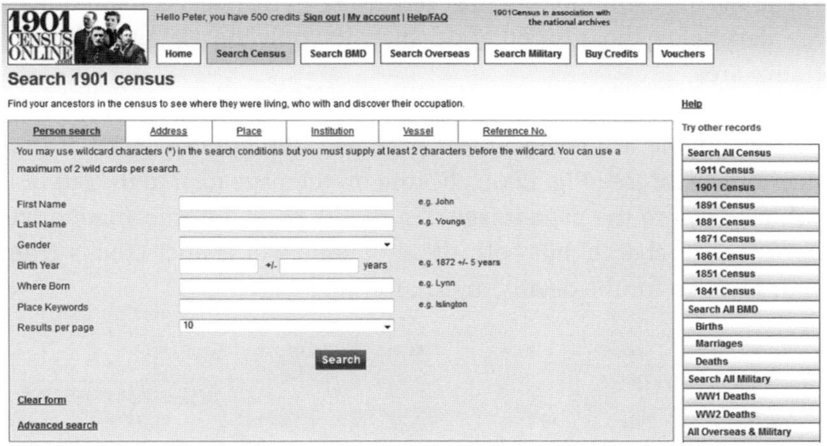

Figure 12.9 1901censusonline search form for the 1901 census.

Another important difference between the 1901 census search and the other years is that for 1901 the basic form contains more search fields and there are also two levels of advanced search. For the other years, a more limited basic search form is available. Figure 12.8 shows the person search form for the 1891 census, while Figure 12.9 shows the more comprehensive form for the 1901 census.

For the 1901 census, clicking on 'Advanced search' at the bottom of the form (this link is not available for the earlier censuses) opens up a larger form with three additional fields for Other Name(s) (i.e. middle names), Marital Condition, and Relation to Head of Family, and a checkbox to limit searches to vessels. This form in turn has a link 'See advanced place options', which allows you to specify the place much more exactly by distinguishing between the various types of administrative unit. (As we discussed in Chapter 6, unless you are very sure you know which units are relevant to the place you are looking for, these are mostly best avoided.)

When you submit the search form, you will get a listing of the matching results, with the number of entries on a page determined by the 'Results per page' option on the search form. As with Genes Reunited, the maximum number of results is 300 — if there are more you will only be shown the first 300. This is likely to make it unsuitable for a one-name study.

The results listing for the 1901 census (see Fig. 12.10) contain quite a few data fields; those for other censuses list only the age and 'administrative area'.

From the results listing, you have two main options: clicking on the person's name will take you to a page with the full census record for that individual (see Fig. 12.11); clicking on the page icon to the left of it will take you to the page image. Up to this point, all information has been free of charge, but both these options will deduct credits from your total, 50 for the details, and 75 for the image.

Person search	Address	Place	Institution	Vessel	Reference No.	

Results: 1 - 10 of 13 Matches   beta | Show results in map view

View	Name	Age	Where born	Administrative county	Civil parish	Occupation
	Thomas Hardy	17	Dorset Puddle Hinton	Berks	Stratfield Mortimer	Asst Gardener Domestic
	Thomas B Hardy	30	Dorset Broadwinsor	Dorset	Broadwindsor	Farmer
	Thomas Hardy	60	Dorset Stinsford	Dorset	Dorchester All Saints	Author
	Thomas Hardy	37	Dorset Wynford Eagle	Dorset	Maiden Newton	Groom
	Thomas H Hardy	28	Dorset ...	Dorset	Portland	Labourer In Stone Quarry
	Thomas Hardy	43	Dorset Bere Regis	Dorset	Puddletown	Agricultural Labourer
	Thomas Hardy	66	Dorset Swanage	Dorset	Swanage	Retired Master Mariner
	Thomas Masters Hardy	13	Dorset Swanage	Dorset	Swanage	Juvenile
	Thomas Hardy	66	Dorset Puddletown	Isle Of Wight	Bonchurch	Gardener Not Domestic
	Thomas Hardy	41	Dorset Frome Vauchurch	London	Battersea	Point Foreman Shuerler Railway

Figure 12.10 1901censusonline search results for the 1901 census.

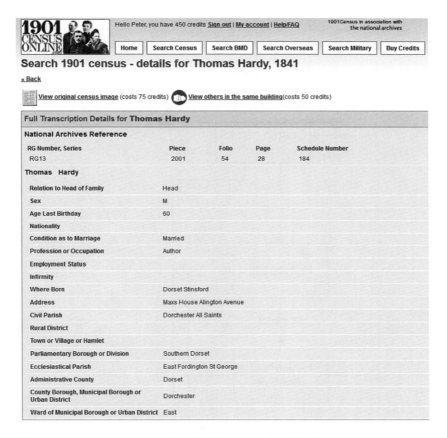

Figure 12.11 1901censusonline Full Transcription Details.

From the details page, you can also pay 50 credits to see details of the other household members, and you can also go to the image from that page.

Figure 12.12 shows the search flow-chart for a person search on the site.

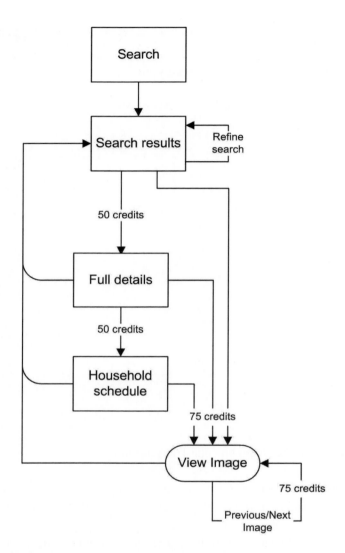

Figure 12.12 1901censusonline person search flow-chart.

1901censusonline: other searches

Unlike Genes Reunited, 1901censusonline has not only a person search, but also a range of other options for the 1841–1901 censuses.

The address search form is very simple: it has fields for just a house or street name and a place, neither of which can be left blank. In the case of the 1901 census index, there is an advanced search form which includes a range of additional place fields. The form recommends that you omit words like 'street' and 'road'. The search results list every house that matches the search criteria, with, in each case, a link to a page with details of all those at the address. Details include age, relationship, occupation and birthplace, so is almost a complete transcription. This page is free to view, which means that viewing a household via an address search is significantly cheaper than using the person search where you have to pay to view both individual and household. From this listing you then can view the page image, at a cost of 75 credits.

For 1861, 1871 and 1901 there is a vessel search. For 1901 there is also an institution search, and it is the only census year which has a TNA reference search.

The vessel and institution searches look for a vessel or institution itself by name, and do not allow for searching on the names of individuals enumerated within a vessel or institution. They work in basically the same way: you enter a name and location in the search fields and get back a list of matching vessels/institutions. Figure 12.13 shows the results of a search for 'orphanage' and 'Middlesex'.

If you click on the institution name you are taken to a list of individual names, with no other details. So far you have not been charged, but from the list of individuals it costs 50 credits to view Full Transcription Details and 75 credits to view the page containing the entry for the chosen individual. However, there is often little point in viewing the

Search 1901 census - results for orphanage

Note » On some occasions prisoners and inmates were recorded only by their initials, which makes your search a little more challenging.

Person search	Address	Place	Institution	Vessel	Reference No.

Results: 1 - 4 of 4 Matches

Name	Civil Parish	County	Image selection		View
Metropolitan & City Police Orphanage	Twickenham	Middlesex	Select an Image	▼	
Orphanage Of Mercy	Paddington	Middlesex	Select an Image	▼	
St Marys Orphanage	Heston	Middlesex	Select an Image	▼	
Victoria Orphanage	Paddington	Middlesex	Select an Image	▼	

Too many results or not found the right institution? Search again

Help

Figure 12.13 1901censusonline institution search results.

full transcription details, first because your list of individuals does not contain a list of people with identical names the way it does with a person search, and second because there's no point in paying 50 credits to see the details first when you're going to have to pay 75 to see the image anyway. Also, be prepared for a certain amount of disappointment — the details of the individuals resident in institutions sometimes comprise only name and age, or even just initials and age, with no entry in the 'where born' column.

Not all institutions will turn up in an institution search, as those with fewer than 100 inmates were not listed separately but rather included in the normal household schedules.

Figure 12.14 shows a flow-chart for institution and vessel searches.

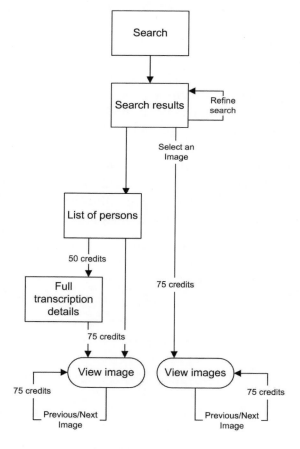

Figure 12.14 1901censusonline institution and vessel search.

Images

Genes Reunited's images are in JPEG format and open in a viewer which offers basic controls for zooming and panning (see Fig. 12.15). The 'Download' button above the image allows you to save the image, which is given by default a unique name based on the census year and the piece number. The images for the 1911 census are identical to those on Findmypast and the 1911 census sites (see Chapter 9), but *only* the household schedule image is available, not the other supporting pages.

1901censusonline treats the images of the 1901 census differently from those for other years. Images for the 1901 census are provided in PDF format and you will need to have Adobe Acrobat reader installed for them to display correctly in the browser. Moving your mouse around the browser window should cause the Acrobat icon bar to appear, and clicking on the disk icon will then enable you to save the image.

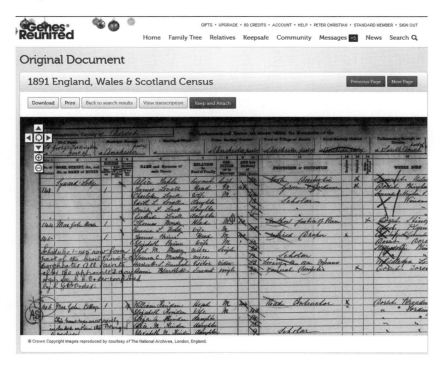

Figure 12.15 Genes Reunited image viewer (for the 1891 census).

Images for the other censuses open in a viewer in the browser window (see Fig. 12.16), with identical facilities to those of Genes Reunited. The 'Download record' button above the image allows you to save it in JPEG format. As with Genes Reunited, the site offers only a single image for the 1911 census, but in this case it is not the household schedule but just the relevant page from the enumerator's summary book, which gives only the head of household. This means, firstly, that you will have to pay to see the full household record in order to find out who else was living in the household, but also that you have no way of checking the transcription of the individual records.

Although the JPEG images for these two sites appear at first sight to be identical, in two important respects they are not. Firstly, those on 1901censusonline are at one quarter the resolution of those on Genes Reunited — two megapixels versus eight megapixels. Secondly, the 1901censusonline images are significantly more compressed (see pp. 136-137 for a discussion of image compression). Combined, these factors mean that fine detail may be less easily distinguished and hard-to-read pages may be less clear on 1901censusonline.

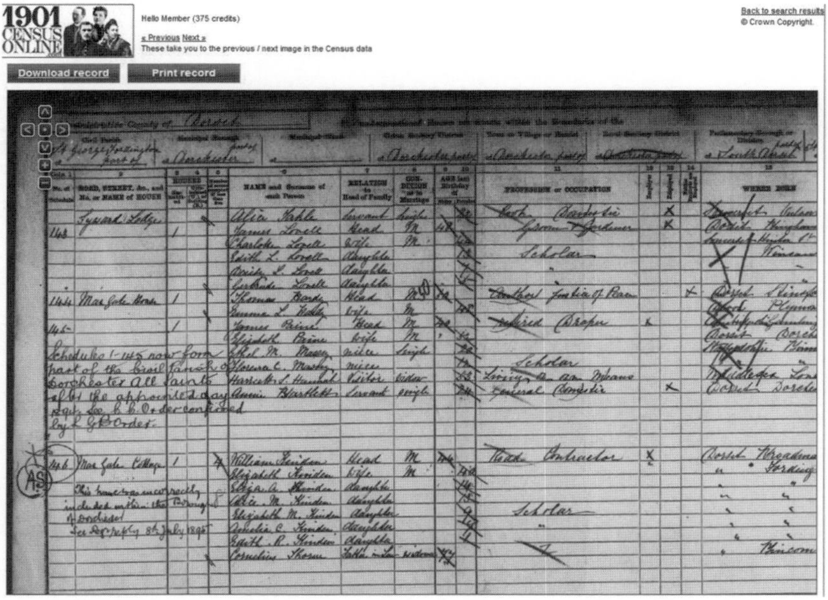

Figure 12.16 1901censusonline image viewer (for the 1891 census).

Help and feedback

Help for Genes Reunited can be found by clicking on the 'Help Centre' button near the top of the page. This provides help for all the resources on the site, and you can get census help by looking at the Records section of the FAQs, or you can type a question in the Search box. There is no dedicated mechanism for reporting errors in the indexing or problems with the images, but there is a general-purpose Contact Form at <**www.genesreunited.co.uk/help/contactus**>, which can be used for that purpose. There is a link to this form from the Feedback entry in the FAQs listing.

1901censusonline has much more extensive help for those searching census records. Since the site held the first official online census its Help Centre (accessible from the 'Help' link at the top of most pages) was designed to provide not just the data but also an introduction to census records in general, and it contains supporting material that goes well beyond the specifics of using the site. In addition, the search forms themselves have a separate Help link (just above the form) with information on how to use the various search fields. The 'Contact Us' link at the foot of every page has links to distinct forms for general feedback, payment queries, and technical help requests.

The 'Full Transcription Details' pages have links to an error reporting form, which displays the existing data and allows you to submit corrections for individual fields. You can request an email notification when the record has been updated. There is no mechanism, apart from the general Contact Us forms, for reporting image problems.

As mentioned in Chapter 5, the original 1901 Census site published details of all corrections made up to August 2005, and this information is now reproduced on the website for this book at <**www.spub.co.uk/census**>.

13

MYHERITAGE

MyHeritage at <**www.myheritage.com**> started life in 2005 as a platform for sharing pedigrees and photographs with family members and the wider world. In June 2012, the site launched its SuperSearch facility to provide indexes of genealogical records. At the time of writing the site has data for the England and Wales censuses from 1841 to 1901. The 1841 and 1871 censuses are licensed from Origins (see Chapter 11), while the remainder were originally digitised by Findmypast (see Chapter 9) and are licensed from DC Thompson Family History. Since Findmypast also licenses its 1841 and 1871 censuses from Origins, all MyHeritage's census indexes are identical to those found on Findmypast (and indeed on FamilySearch).

MyHeritage also owns WorldVitalRecords at <**www.worldvitalrecords. com**>, which it purchased in 2011. This site has the same data collections as MyHeritage, and the UK material therefore includes indexes to the censuses of England and Wales for 1841–1901, also licensed from the same sources. However, the WorldVitalRecords' census search facilities are much more limited than MyHeritage's (with no advanced option, for example), so although WorldVitalRecords' UK census indexes are certainly useful to those who are already subscribed to the site, there is no reason to recommend it to new users over MyHeritage itself.

Charges

MyHeritage offers free membership which allows you to post a family tree of up to 250 individuals on the site. Premium and PremiumPlus subscriptions provide for larger trees and additional facilities (details at <**www.myheritage.com/subscription-plans**>.) These three options do not directly give access to the UK censuses, though the site's record matching facility will alert you by email if there is a census entry which appears to match someone in your tree. Also, you can carry out what might be called 'diagnostic' searches, which will tell you how many matches there are in the individual record sets.

In order to see the detailed results of a census search and view the enumeration book images, you require a data subscription at an annual cost of £90 (£75 + VAT). This covers all of the site's datasets from all countries. Payment can also be made in Euros or US dollars (see <www.myheritage.com/FP/search-plans.php>).

Searching

At the time of writing, finding the search forms for UK census records is rather confusing. From the home page, clicking on the Research tab takes you to the SuperSearch home page at <**www.myheritage.com/research**>. There is a navigation panel on the right-hand side of this page, which offers a list of all the categories of records held. If you select 'U.K. Census' you come to a search page at <**www.myheritage.com/research/category-1200/uk-census**> which offers a joint search form for the 1841, 1871 and 1901 censuses, and links to forms for those two censuses individually. If, however, you choose 'UK Records' on the SuperSearch home page you are taken to a search page at <**myheritage.com/research/category-90000/uk-records**>, which has links to search forms for the censuses of England and Wales (some are wrongly labelled as UK censuses, but they do not in fact include Scotland) for 1851, 1861, 1881 and 1891. The rationale for having separate search pages for these two groups of censuses is that each group has its own set of search fields and options. But the site's two distinct navigation paths here make little sense, and there must be a danger that newcomers to the site will not be aware of the full range of census indexes than it in fact has.

Because of the differences, the details of the two groups of searches are treated separately here in part. However, the basic process is the same for both and the flow-chart in Figure 13.1 is valid for all census searches on the site.

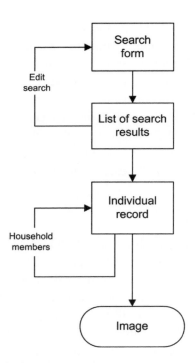

Figure 13.1 Search flow-chart for MyHeritage.

The search forms

For the 1841 and 1871 censuses, there is a basic and an advanced search. The basic search form has fields for first and middle name(s), last name, birth year and place, and place of residence, along with a general-purpose keyword field. The advanced search form is shown in Figure 13.2. This adds fields for gender, names and relationship of other household members. It also provides flexible name matching on both forenames and surnames. For forenames there is the option to match exactly, or to search for spelling variants, initials or the start of the name. The household matching only has options for immediate family: father, mother, spouse, child or sibling, though one can also enter a name without specifying a relationship.

The surname-matching is one of the most flexible of any data service: in addition to exact matches, it also offers any combination of three types of Soundex, three types of Metaphone (see pp. 143-144 for details

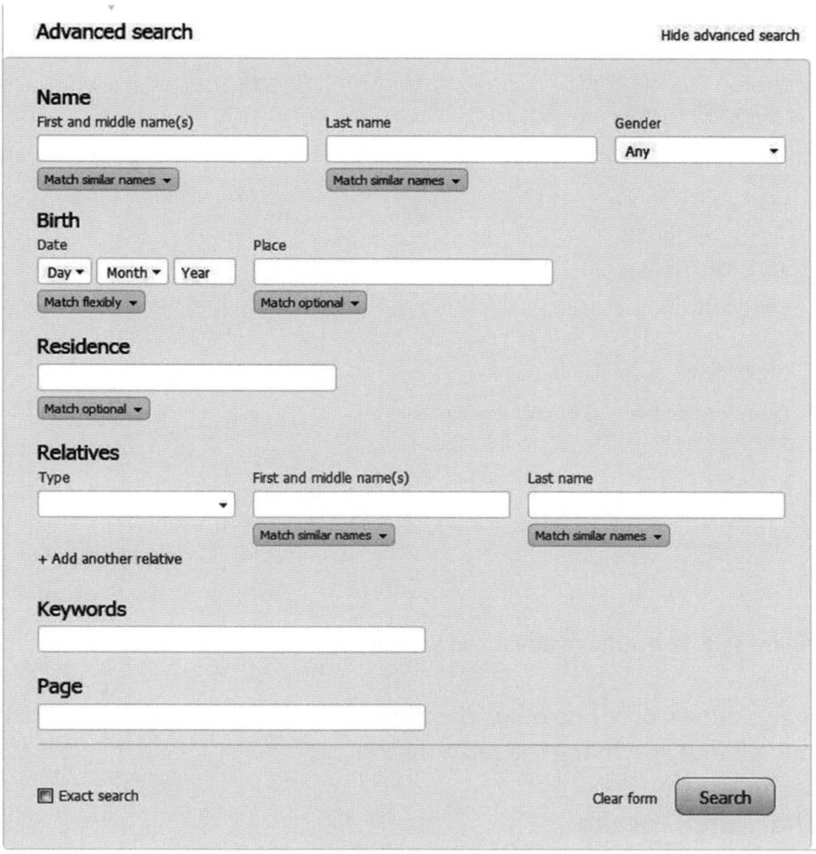

Figure 13.2 MyHeritage advanced search 1871.

of these), and MyHeritage's own Megadex system, which is explained at <**www.myheritage.com/FP/Company/megadex.php**>. However, at the time of writing, Megadex did not seem to be operating the way the help page described, though we understand this is to be remedied.

There is also a 'Page' field, but we were unable to find information on how it is used.

Figure 13.3 shows the advanced search form for the 1891 census. The only elements which are missing in the equivalent basic search form are 'Other person' fields and the ability to give a year range. The advanced search has fewer options than the advanced search form for 1871, most notably in the absence of the various name matching options.

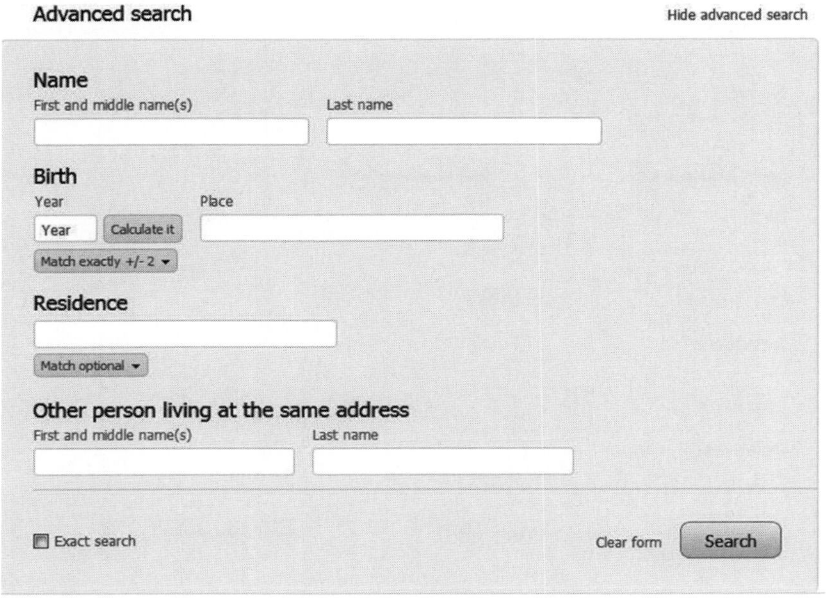

Figure 13.3 MyHeritage advanced search 1891.

It also allows only one other member of the household to be entered, and without specifying the relationship.

The search results

A typical search results page for the 1841, 1871 and 1901 censuses is shown in Figure 13.4. The occupation and marital status fields are the only ones on the original form which are not displayed here, and the results include the full house address and the names of other household members, so it should be relatively easy to identify the ancestor you are looking for. The ability to list as many as 100 results on one page also makes it easy to scan for a particular individual.

Unless you use an exact search, the results lists tend to be long, but each result is given a star rating and the results are presented in order of decreasing star rating. In Figure 13.4 you can see that the first two results have a match on name, birth date and birthplace and gets 4.5 stars, while the next result, which matches only name and birthdate, gets just 3.5. On the advanced search form, you can choose to match

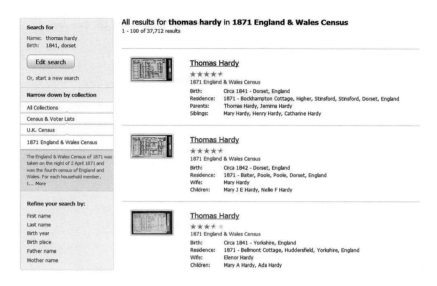

Figure 13.4 MyHeritage search results for the 1871 census.

on only the most important fields in order to control how the results are ranked after the exact matches.

For searches on the 1851, 1861, 1881, and 1891 census the results lists are less satisfactory (see Fig. 13.5). For a start, they give only birth and age, and place of residence, which may not be enough to spot the individual you are looking for without checking the details of a large number of those listed. In particular, if you have included a birth place in your search fields, there is no way to see which of the pople listed match on that field and which do not. Also, even when not using an exact search, the results seem to include only exact matches.

One slight drawback from the point of view of someone doing a one-name study is that the results list does not use a tabular format with one person per line, which means it is not a straightforward matter to import these results into a database or spreadsheet.

The link from a name in the results list takes you to the full record for that individual (see Fig. 13.6), which usefully includes all the other household members with their ages. The terminology used for The National Archives reference is idiosyncratic: instead of piece number, folio and page, these fields have been labelled 'roll', 'folio' and 'image'.

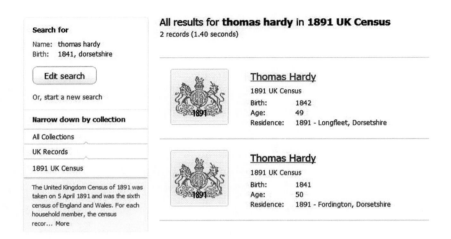

Figure 13.5 MyHeritage search results for the 1891 census.

Images

MyHeritage's images for 1841 and 1871 are the same as those available on Origins (see Chapter 11), that is, high resolution black and white. Images are in PNG format, a standard format for images on the web, though less common than JPEG. Once you have downloaded an image it will be viewable in your browser or any image viewer. The images for 1901 are greyscale images in JPEG format.

There are two ways to view the images for these censuses. Clicking on the thumbnail image at the top right of the screen brings up a full-screen image viewer in a new browser window. Alternatively, clicking on the 'View census image' button above the list of household members opens up a panel on the screen showing the census image, which can be zoomed and panned within this panel.

The full-screen image viewer (see Fig. 13.7) is very basic, with only the same zoom options as the in-page viewer. Helpfully, the full National Archives reference is provided in the banner above the page image. Clicking on the Download button displays the image on its own in a new browser window, and you have to use the browser's image-saving facility to save the image.

The images for the other censuses are all greyscale images in JPEG format. For these, the in-page viewer is opened automatically in the

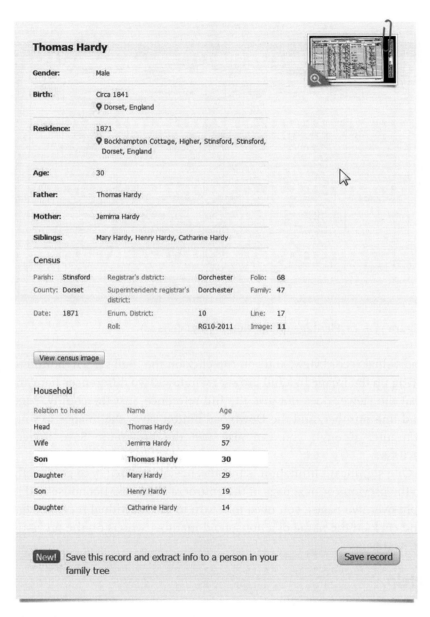

Thomas Hardy

Gender:	Male
Birth:	Circa 1841
	📍 Dorset, England
Residence:	1871
	📍 Bockhampton Cottage, Higher, Stinsford, Stinsford, Dorset, England
Age:	30
Father:	Thomas Hardy
Mother:	Jemima Hardy
Siblings:	Mary Hardy, Henry Hardy, Catharine Hardy

Census

Parish:	Stinsford	Registrar's district:	Dorchester	Folio:	68
County:	Dorset	Superintendent registrar's district:	Dorchester	Family:	47
Date:	1871	Enum. District:	10	Line:	17
		Roll:	RG10-2011	Image:	11

[View census image]

Household

Relation to head	Name	Age
Head	Thomas Hardy	59
Wife	Jemima Hardy	57
Son	**Thomas Hardy**	**30**
Daughter	Mary Hardy	29
Son	Henry Hardy	19
Daughter	Catharine Hardy	14

New! Save this record and extract info to a person in your family tree

[Save record]

Figure 13.6 MyHeritage individual record (1871 census).

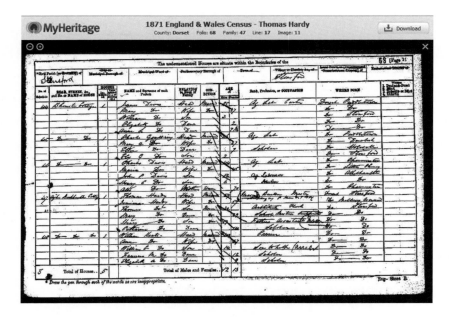

Figure 13.7 MyHeritage image viewer (1871 census).

individual record view, and you can click on the 'Full screen' button to bring up the image in a full browser window. Two differences here are that the viewer does not give the full reference, just the county, page and line number, and the Download button saves the images to your computer (though you can also use the browser's 'Save image' facility).

One significant limitation is the absence of any facility to go directly to the previous or next page of the enumeration book. If a household is split over two pages, you need to return to the individual records page and click on the name of a household member who is on the previous or next page.

Help

At the bottom of every page is a link to the Help pages at **<www.myherit age.com/help/en>**, which include an extensive collection of articles. Apart from the pages relating to subscription questions, those most relevant to the census records will be found under the 'Research' and 'SuperSearch' headings. There is also a video tutorial on using SuperSearch. The support forums at <**www.myheritage.com/support-forums**>, linked from the main help page, provide a place to post questions, which will be answered by MyHeritage staff or other users. (There are also location-based discussion forums with a home page at <**www.myheritage.com/genealogy-forums**> but these are only for genealogical discussion with other users, not for official support.)

The site has a blog at <**blog.myheritage.com**> which carries announcements and tips.

14

SCOTLANDSPEOPLE

ScotlandsPeople at <**www.scotlandspeople.gov.uk**> was launched in September 2002 as the official home of the digitised historical records of Scotland, in a partnership between the General Register Office for Scotland (GROS) and the ISP Scotland Online. Scotland had first put genealogical data online in 1998 at Scots Origins, run by Origins (see Chapter 11), and by 2002 it hosted the 1881 Census Index and an index with images for the 1891 census. Since then, ScotlandsPeople has added all the remaining Scottish censuses — the 1911 census was the most recent addition in April 2011. As well as the Scottish records from the original 1881 Census Index, the site now has its own index to the 1881 census, linked to images.

In January 2008, Scotland Online purchased Findmypast (see Chapter 9), which in July 2008 changed its name to Brightsolid and in October 2013 became DC Thompson Family History. Meanwhile GROS has merged with The National Archives of Scotland to form National Records of Scotland (NRS), which is now the custodian of Scottish census records, and has its own website at <**www.nrscotland. gov.uk**>.

For much of its existence, ScotlandsPeople was the only site with Scottish census data. However, in April 2007 Ancestry (see Chapter 8) launched a complete set of indexes to the censuses from 1841 to 1901, though without images because they had been unable to license the right to digitise them from the GROS microfilms. Findmypast now also has its own indexes to these records, again without images.

The reasons for this lack of images on other commercial sites are discussed in Chapter 5.

Charges

ScotlandsPeople is an exclusively pay-per-view site. In fact, you can do very basic searches on the site without payment, but you need to register in any case — there is a prominent 'Register' button at the top of the home page (see Fig. 14.1). Registering allows you to carry out searches, but *not* to view search results or images: when you carry out a search, the site always tells you free of charge how many search results there are and how many pages are required to display them. It also redisplays the search form so that you can refine your search to produce fewer results, requiring fewer page displays. But to view the search results you then have to purchase page credits.

An initial payment of £7 gives you 30 page credits (i.e. 23p each), and these are valid for one year from the day on which payment is made (not from the first search). If you still have credits unused at the end of that period, these will be carried forward to any subsequent purchase of credits — they remain unusable until you make a new purchase. If

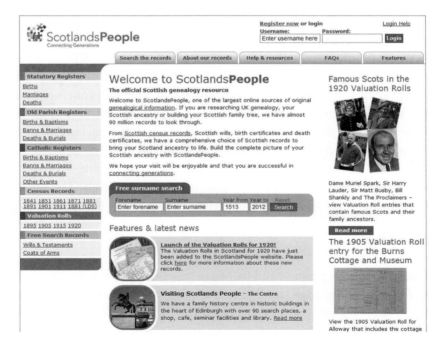

Figure 14.1 ScotlandsPeople home page.

you buy more credits before the year is up, all the unused credits have their validity extended to one year from the date of the most recent purchase.

- Searches are charged at 1 credit per page of search results (each page has a maximum of 25 results).
- Viewing an image costs 5 credits.
- For the original 1881 Census Index, where no images are available, the search results are free and viewing the full transcription costs 1 credit.

You can purchase larger numbers of credits, in multiples of 30, up to a maximum of 300. However, there is no discount on larger numbers. Also, no matter how many credits you purchase, they all have the same expiry limit. If you really need more than 30 credits, then unless you are going to use them up in a single day it is better to purchase additional credits when you run out — that way your access period will constantly be extended to one year from the last day on which you bought credits. Once you have logged in, the number of unused credits and their remaining validity are shown at the top of the screen.

You can only purchase credits online with a credit or debit card. If you do not wish to pay online, or if you are giving credits as a gift, you can print out an order form for any number of 30-credit vouchers and pay by cheque or credit card. Note that buying vouchers is slightly more expensive because you also have to pay a postage and packing charge (£1 within the UK). The vouchers are not available from retail outlets.

Credits can be used for almost all of the material on the site — census, civil registration, parish registers, and wills and testaments. The Coats of Arms have a separate payment system, which uses a shopping cart.

Searching

Once you have registered and logged in, the links to individual census years on the home page (see Fig. 14.1) will take you to the Search Census page for the chosen year (see Fig. 14.2). The initial search is free. (If you click on these links without logging in, you will just get a page of

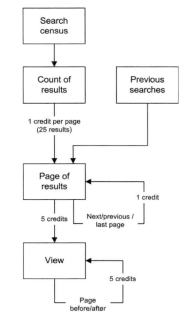

Figure 14.2 ScotlandsPeople search form.

Figure 14.3 ScotlandsPeople search flow-chart.

information about that particular census.) The 'Search the Records' tab at the top of every page will take you to the search home page from wherever you are on the site. Figure 14.3 shows the census search process on ScotlandsPeople.

Each field has a question mark button to the right, and clicking on this brings up help about using the field. None of the name fields is compulsory, which means you could, for example, search for all the males of a particular age in an individual registration district.

Name matching

ScotlandsPeople has the most flexible set of name-matching options of any genealogical data service. Alongside Soundex (p. 145) and two types of Metaphone (p. 146), it offers wildcards (p. 145), 'fuzzy matching', matching using just the beginning of words, and surname and fore-name variants. The fuzzy matching uses the Levenshtein distance formula (see <**en.wikipedia.org/wiki/Levenshtein_distance**>), which is useful where letters have been transcribed wrongly, a situation which is not dealt with well by the other methods since they tend to be based on similarity of pronunciation.

Although each of these methods has its failings, the fact that you have such a wide range to choose from gives you a much better chance of finding an individual whose name has been spelt (or even mis-spelt) in an unexpected way.

All three name fields can have wildcards. Whereas most sites only use the * character to mean any number of characters (even zero), ScotlandsPeople also uses the '?' symbol to mean exactly one character. This is most useful where there are two variants of a name with a single difference of vowel. For example, *B?rne* finds Byrne and Burne, but does not find the unwanted Blackbourne, Blanthorne or Bradbourne, which a search on *B*rne* would turn up. Unusually, the wildcards can be used at the beginning of a name. When searching for any patronymic surname in Mac or Mc, using *M*cDonald* etc. will find both forms.

Locations

There are two location fields from which you can select an option. From the County/City/Shipping field you can select a Scottish county, and the cities of Aberdeen, Dundee, Edinburgh and Glasgow. The District field initially lists all districts (i.e. Registration Districts), but if you select a county or city in the field above, the list is narrowed down to just the districts in the chosen county or city. Unless you are very sure of your geography and your ancestors' whereabouts (perhaps from the birth certificate of a child born close to the year of the census), this field is probably best avoided initially until you see how many results you have got when searching on just county or city. However, you can search an area wider than an individual district by selecting up to five districts from this list at once.

You can't in fact choose 'Shipping' itself — this is a relic of a previous incarnation of the site — but the list of counties and cities includes a 'Minor Records' option. From 1861 onwards this has as its 'districts', some or all of 'foreign register', 'marine register', 'marine return' and 'service returns', which will include individuals not physically on Scottish soil on census night.

Unfortunately, these location fields only apply to the residence address, and there is no facility to search for a birth place. However, the 1881 LDS Census Index has a different search form, which does include a field to search on birthplace.

Search results

When you click on the 'Do the search' button it brings up not a list of search results but information on how many matches there are and how many pages they will take to display (there are 25 search results to each page). The importance of this last piece of information is that *each* page of search results costs one credit to view — for each page of results, you are asked to confirm that you want to use one credit to view it. If you have more than a couple of pages, then you will probably want to refine your search rather than use up lots of credits to view all the search results, unless, of course, you are conducting a one-name study and genuinely need *all* the search results.

From here you go to the first page of search results (see Fig. 14.4). These are sorted by surname, then forename, and show only the fields available on the search form. The lack of any address information more precise than city or county and the lack of the birthplace can make it difficult to identify the right individual, particularly with a common

Your Census Search Returns

You searched for: Surname: "DOYLE"; Surname Option: Wildcard; Forename: ""; Forename Option: Prefix; Sex: "Any"; Year: 1861; City: "EDINBURGH CITY";

Help information on these records   Refine your search

Next Page (1 credit)   Last Page (1 credit)

Jump to page: 1 (Free) ▾ of 2 (45 records)

No	Year	Surname	Forename	Sex	Age	District	City/County	GROS Data	Image	Extract
1	1861	DOYLE	ADAM	M	29	ST GILES	EDINBURGH CITY/MIDLOTHIAN	685/04 002/00 002	View (5 Credits)	Order
2	1861	DOYLE	ANN	F	30	ST GILES	EDINBURGH CITY/MIDLOTHIAN	685/04 038/00 011	View (5 Credits)	Order
3	1861	DOYLE	ANN	F	10	LEITH SOUTH	EDINBURGH CITY/MIDLOTHIAN	692/02 060/00 006	View (5 Credits)	Order
4	1861	DOYLE	ANNETTE	F	4	ST ANDREW (EDINBURGH)	EDINBURGH CITY/MIDLOTHIAN	685/02 090/00 011	View (Paid)	Order
5	1861	DOYLE	ARTHUR CONAN	M	1	ST ANDREW (EDINBURGH)	EDINBURGH CITY/MIDLOTHIAN	685/02 090/00 011	View (Paid)	Order
6	1861	DOYLE	BERNARD	M	33	ST ANDREW (EDINBURGH)	EDINBURGH CITY/MIDLOTHIAN	685/02 096/00 009	View (5 Credits)	Order
7	1861	DOYLE	CATHERINE A	F	5	ST ANDREW (EDINBURGH)	EDINBURGH CITY/MIDLOTHIAN	685/02 096/00 009	View (5 Credits)	Order
8	1861	DOYLE	CHARLES ALTAMON	M	29	ST ANDREW (EDINBURGH)	EDINBURGH CITY/MIDLOTHIAN	685/02 090/00 011	View (Paid)	Order
9	1861	DOYLE	DAVID	M	18	ST GEORGE	EDINBURGH CITY/MIDLOTHIAN	685/01 052/00 009	View (5 Credits)	Order
10	1861	DOYLE	ELIZABETH	F	42	CANONGATE	EDINBURGH CITY/MIDLOTHIAN	685/03 047/00 005	View (5 Credits)	Order

Figure 14.4 ScotlandsPeople search results listing.

surname in an urban area. Absence of the relationship and marital status fields here makes it impossible to identify whether a woman is using a maiden name or a married name. The only additional information given is the census reference in the 'GROS Data' column — the use of this is discussed on p. 277, below.

At this point you can either choose to view the next page of results if there is more than one, or view the census image for an individual. (Although you can also order an 'extract', i.e. an officially certified copy of a census page, there is no reason to do this; it is really meant for ordering certificates from entries in the civil registration indexes.) If you have already viewed an image, it will say 'View (paid)' instead of 'View (5 credits)' and you will be able to view the image again without further payment.

Unlike many other sites, there is no page showing a transcription of the full record or of the full household. Viewing the image is the only way to see occupation and birthplace information. In fact, ScotlandsPeople does not recognise the unit of the household at all — there is no option to identify all members of a household except by looking at the census page; if your family is at the end of a page, you need to check visually on the image whether or not there is an 'end of household' marker after the last person or whether the household continues on the next page. If your ancestor is at the top of a census page and is not the head of the household, then you will need to view the previous page in order to be sure you have identified all the household members.

Advanced search

The Advanced Search is completely unlike the advanced search facilities on the other sites described in this book: it offers you not a range of more specialised fields but a single large text box into which you have to enter a precisely formulated query. In fact, clicking on the 'Show Advanced' button (see Fig. 14.2) also brings up a field marked 'GROS data', which, in principle, allows you to enter the document reference, but it does not seem to work for census records as the field is not long enough to contain a full census reference.

Queries are formulated by using a 'query language'. In this you create a search term which combines the name of a field in the census index with what you want that field to contain. So if you wanted to find everyone with the surname Richards, your query would be:

```
surname:Richards
```

You can combine any number of search terms using the logical connectors && (AND) and || (OR). To search for the surnames Richards and Richard, your query would be:

```
surname:Richards || surname:Richard
```

That is, find all entries where the surname is either Richards or Richard.

You might think ScotlandsPeople's excellent range of surname-matching options makes this sort of search redundant, but in fact it allows you to search for a range of name variants of your own choosing, and by-pass a name-matching algorithm which will always be much more inclusive. For example, in the index to the 1911 census for Glasgow there are 100 people with the surname Richards, and 66 with Richard. The advanced search shown above finds precisely these 166 people. On the other hand, the surname matching options produce much less satisfactory results. Putting a wildcard at the end or using the 'Surnames that begin with' option will, of course, add the 902 Richardsons to the results. Soundex and Metaphone will do likewise, since they ignore everything after the 'd', but they will also add names like Rickard and Ritchard. The surname variants option finds 1,082 matches, while a fuzzy match on Richard finds 2,756 results, which include Pritchard, Richford and McHardy!

The site offers some basic online help on the Advanced Search help page — follow the 'Advanced search guide' link from any Advanced Search page — and further pages linked from it. An essential help here is the 'Search Fields' page which tells you how to refer to the individual fields in the index. The most useful are the five fields which identify individuals:

- surname
- forename
- sex
- age
- relativeforename

together with those which identify the geographical and administrative location:

- county
- city
- rdno
- rdsuffix
- enumdist
- edsup
- pageno.

This latter group are essential for address and reference searching, discussed below, and are the only ones which are not present on the basic search form.

The search engine used for the advanced search is a widely available and well documented piece of free software called Lucene, and ScotlandsPeople has links to the official online documentation, which will be of use to those wanting help to formulate complex searches.

Street indexes

ScotlandsPeople provides only a person search. There is no facility to search for an address, even by using the advanced search. However, for each Scottish census there is a set of street index books, which can be used to identify the enumeration district in which a particular street falls.

For 1841, the street indexes cover just Edinburgh and Glasgow, but coverage gradually expands, so that by 1911 over 30 towns are included. All the street indexes are linked from the Census Street Index Books page at <www.scotlandspeople.gov.uk/Content/Help/index.aspx?2094>. (We have been unable to find any way of navigating directly to this page from anywhere else on the site, except for the 1911 Census Street Index, which is linked from the main Help menu, under 'Help With Searching'.)

The indexes are provided in PDF format and are unindexed scans of original paper documents, one volume per town. For each entry there is a volume number and suffix, which gives the registration district and registration district suffix, and an enumeration book number for the particular enumeration district.

Taking the entry in the 1861 street index for Edinburgh shown in Figure 14.5 as an example, the three pieces of information for 273–285

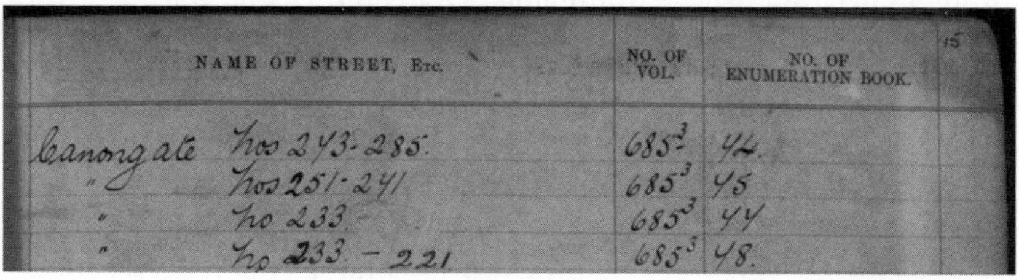

NAME OF STREET, Etc.	NO. OF VOL.	NO. OF ENUMERATION BOOK.
Canongate hos 273-285	685³	44.
" hos 251-241	685³	45
" ho 233	685³	44
" ho 233 - 221	685³	48.

Figure 14.5 Street index for Edinburgh, 1861.

Canongate at the top of the page need to be entered into the advanced search box as follows:

```
rdno:685 && rdsuffix:3 && enumdist:74
```

The search results then will list every person in the enumeration district, sorted by surname and forename, which will normally take up at least a dozen pages of search results, each of which will cost one credit to view. Unfortunately the search results do not indicate the address, so there is no way to identify the inhabitants of a particular house from the search results. Instead, you will need to browse through the census images for the whole district. The easiest way to do this is to add:

```
&& pageno:1
```

to your search terms, which will bring up the entries on the first page of the enumeration book. Once you are viewing the first page, the image viewer's 'View Page After' button can be used to go to each next page in turn.

Since each image costs five credits to view, it may cost around £20 to view an entire enumeration book, so unless your interest is in local history rather than family history and you really do want to view a whole district, you will normally want to include a surname in the 'Surname' field on the search form. Since your probable reason for using the street index is to try and find someone whose expected name does not appear in your previous search results, it can be a good idea to use a wildcard to specify as little of the surname as possible. When searching just a single enumeration book, even a very broad search for all surnames beginning with a particular letter is unlikely to give more than a manageable two pages of search results. Alternatively, if you think a surname proves unfindable, you could search on just a forename, which will surely not produce more than one page of search results.

Reference searches: using with other sites

The advanced search also allows you to conduct reference searches. The form of the reference given on ScotlandsPeople can be seen in the search results listing (see Fig. 14.4) and in the page image (see Fig. 14.8) when the 'Descriptions In Images' option is switched on (this is explained on p. 285, below). The reference for Arthur Conan Doyle's entry in the 1861 census seen in these two screenshots is 685/02 090/00 011, and this can be turned into an advanced search query by taking each number and prefixing it with the name of the field it belongs to:

```
rdno:685 && rdsuffix:2 && enumdist:90
        && edsup:0 && pageno:11
```

(In this case you could omit the 'edsup' field, since it is zero, and similarly for the 'rdsuffix' if you have a reference where the registration district number has no suffix and therefore a zero after the slash.)

If you use another data service which has indexes to Scottish censuses, you will not have been able to view the census page images because these are still exclusively available on ScotlandsPeople. But using this type of advanced search means that you can, in principle, use another site to find the person you are looking for and then locate the relevant image on ScotlandsPeople. There might seem to be little reason to do this — why not just do all the searching on ScotlandsPeople? The answer is that another site's search results may well give you much more precise information about an individual than ScotlandsPeople's (see Fig. 14.4), which give no birthplace information, for example. Where you are dealing with a common name and are not sure of the place of residence, it will be well worth doing an initial search on the other site to identify the correct individual. Then, with precise information on the age and census location, you stand a much better chance of being able to keep the number of pages of search results on ScotlandsPeople down to one. If you are already paying for a subscription to Ancestry or Findmypast, or if you can access either of the sites free of charge at a library or record office, then you can spare yourself the expense of looking through many pages of search results on ScotlandsPeople and possibly having to pay to check several different images before you find the right one.

If you are using Ancestry to search the Scottish censuses, converting Ancestry's reference information (see Fig. 14.6) into an advanced search on ScotlandsPeople is fairly straightforward. The registration

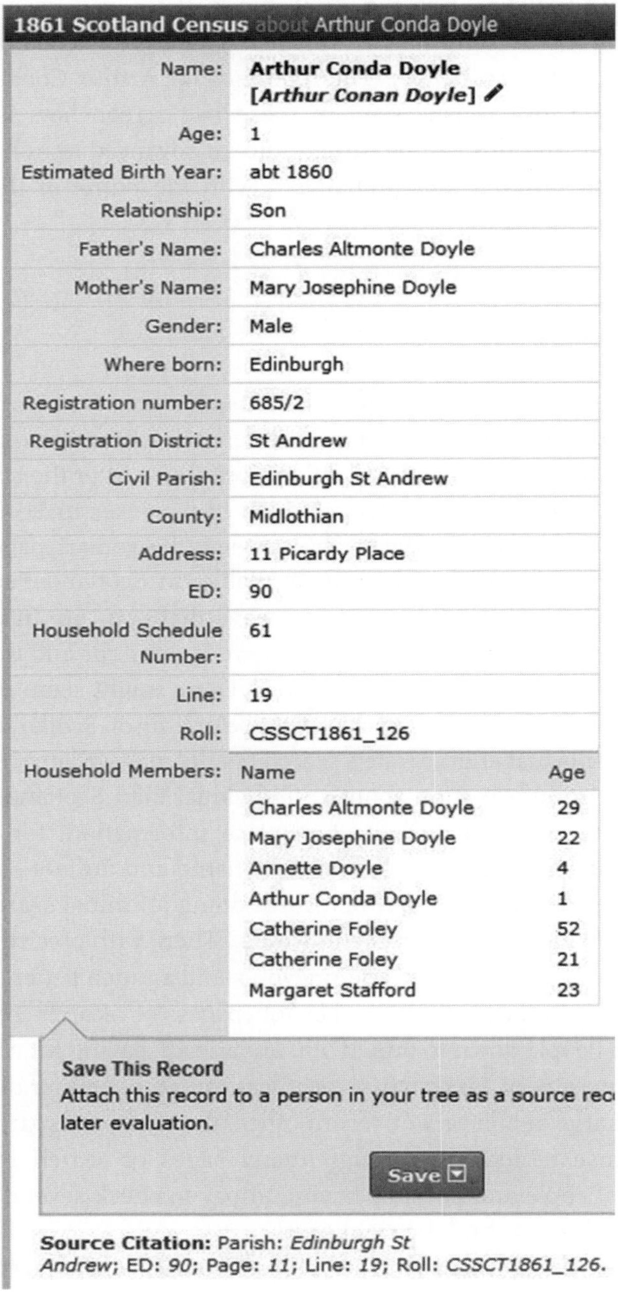

1861 Scotland Census about Arthur Conda Doyle	
Name:	**Arthur Conda Doyle** *[Arthur Conan Doyle]* ✏
Age:	1
Estimated Birth Year:	abt 1860
Relationship:	Son
Father's Name:	Charles Altmonte Doyle
Mother's Name:	Mary Josephine Doyle
Gender:	Male
Where born:	Edinburgh
Registration number:	685/2
Registration District:	St Andrew
Civil Parish:	Edinburgh St Andrew
County:	Midlothian
Address:	11 Picardy Place
ED:	90
Household Schedule Number:	61
Line:	19
Roll:	CSSCT1861_126

Household Members:	Name	Age
	Charles Altmonte Doyle	29
	Mary Josephine Doyle	22
	Annette Doyle	4
	Arthur Conda Doyle	1
	Catherine Foley	52
	Catherine Foley	21
	Margaret Stafford	23

Save This Record
Attach this record to a person in your tree as a source rec·
later evaluation.

Save ▾

Source Citation: Parish: *Edinburgh St Andrew*; ED: *90*; Page: *11*; Line: *19*; Roll: *CSSCT1861_126*.

Figure 14.6 Scottish census reference on Ancestry.

number gives the numbers for the rdno and rdsuffix fields, while the ED field gives the number for the enumdist field. In the case of Arthur Conan Doyle this gives:

```
rdno:685 && rdsuffix:2 && enumdist:90
```

Ancestry does not give the page number. This alone however, gives you 16 pages of search results, so it is worth adding:

```
&& surname:doyle
```

or entering 'Doyle' in the 'Surname' field on the main part of the search form. This cuts the results listing down to one page containing four individuals in a single household — Conan Doyle, his parents and older sister.

In the case of Findmypast, things are more difficult, since it does not cite the registration district number, but just its name, in this case St Andrew, Edinburgh (see Fig. 14.7). ScotlandsPeople has a master list of registration districts with their numbers, available in both PDF and Excel spreadsheet format, linked from **<www.gro-scotland.gov.uk/famrec/ list-of-parishes-registration-districts.html>**. This listing indicates that St Andrew, Edinburgh is registration district 685/2. There is also an unofficial listing at **<www.ktb.net/~dwills/scotref/13300-scottishreference. htm>**, which has the advantage of giving the Family History Library microfilm number, useful if you want to view images on microfilm at a Family History Centre — see Chapter 17. In this example, the 'Piece' field gives the registration district suffix, but we have found other examples where the 'Piece' shows the main registration district number. However, since you can select the district from the drop down list on the main part of the search form (see Fig. 14.2), this is not really a problem.

Unfortunately Findmypast does not give the enumeration district, but does give the page number, and the search

```
pageno:11 && surname:doyle
```

with St Andrew, Edinburgh selected as the district again gives just Conan Doyle's family.

Piece:	**2**
Folio:	**0**
Page:	**11**
Registration District:	**St Andrew**
Civil Parish:	**Edinburgh**
Municipal Borough:	
Address:	**Picardy Place, Edinburgh**
County:	**Midlothian**

Figure 14.7 Scottish census reference of Findmypast.

Of course, if you can access both Ancestry and Findmypast (which is possible at the Society of Genealogists and at The National Archives), you can get both enumeration district and page number to give the full reference:

```
rdno:685 && rdsuffix:2 && enumdist:90 && pageno:11
```

The Scottish census indexes on FamilySearch (p. 158) give only the name of the registration district, and as with Findmypast, without the enumeration district or page number, there is no point in using the advanced search.

Images

ScotlandsPeople has the most sophisticated set of image options of any of the commercial data services. On the 'My Details' page for your username you can choose between six different image viewers and six different levels of image compression.

For the compression levels, you should ensure that it is set to 'none' — in principle, higher compression means lower quality, so it is best avoided. (To be honest, we could detect no difference in the file size of downloaded images between the 'high' compression setting and 'none.') Unless you have very poor internet connection speeds, there is no reason to speed up downloads by opting for greater compression.

Another option on the 'My Details' page is to have 'Descriptions In Images'. When this option is ticked, each image will have above it the name of the individual you searched for along with the reference information, and this remains part of the image when you download it (see Fig. 14.8).

The two most basic viewing options are:

- Direct download: This will work with any browser — it does not display the image on-screen but simply downloads the image to your hard disk.

- Direct view: This is the simplest viewer, with only panning and zoom options. To download the image you need to use your browser's image saving facility (normally on the right mouse button on the PC).

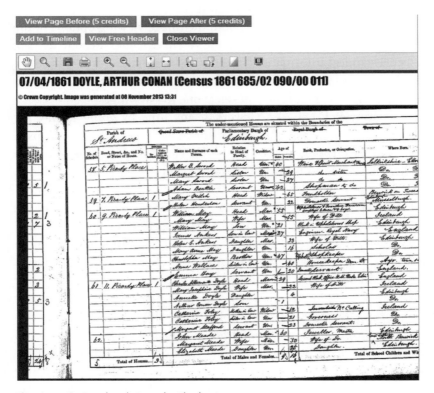

Figure 14.8 ScotlandsPeople Flash viewer.

More sophisticated viewing facilities are provided by:

- Adobe Reader: This requires the Adobe Acrobat Reader to have been installed (see Chapter 5).
- Flash: This requires the Adobe Flash plug-in, which can be downloaded from <**get.adobe.com/flashplayer/**>.
- Java Applet: The Java Applet option will work if your computer has Java installed and your browser has Java enabled. You can install it from <**java.com**>, which also has an option to test whether Java is already installed on your computer.
- ActiveX Control: this is supported only by Internet Explorer and is not available for other browsers.

A link from the account page allows you to test the various options and see whether they work with your browser.

There is further information about the image viewing options in the help section of the site: click on the 'Help & Other Resources' tab, select 'Technical Information', then 'Viewing Images'. It is well worth reading this before you start searching, to make sure you will be able to see the image the first time you select one for viewing.

You can switch between viewers at any time by going to the 'My Details' page — there is a link at the top of every ScotlandsPeople page once you have logged in (see Fig. 14.8). There is also a link to a page which allows you to test whether ActiveX and/or Java are available in your browser.

Figure 14.8 shows the Flash viewer. The buttons along the top of the viewer allow for saving, printing and zooming. The 'View Free Header' above the viewer button is useful — it brings up (free of charge) an image of the front page of the enumeration district, which provides a description of the area the district covers.

The images themselves are black and white scans in TIFF format with a resolution of about 200 dpi. This quality represented a necessary compromise when the site first launched in 2002 and download speeds were a fraction of what they are now. But it now compares poorly in terms of legibility with the 300 dpi greyscale scans available on most of the other data services. Now that the site has indexed and digitised all the censuses, it is perhaps time to look again at image quality. These issues are discussed in more detail in Chapter 5.

As mentioned in the discussion of Origins, which also uses TIFF images (see Chapter 11), TIFF images cannot be viewed in a browser, and a computer running Windows can only display a TIFF image using graphics software. However, *any* graphics software, whether a fully fledged graphics editor such as Photoshop or a simple image viewer like IrfanView or ACDSee, should be able to save a TIFF file in some other format, such as JPEG, which can then be easily viewed. The FAQs pages (see below) mention a problem with some TIFF images on Apple Macintosh systems, which will also require image conversion.

The images for the 1911 census are of much better quality — higher resolution and in colour. The image format for these is JPEG, which does not present any of the issues that may be encountered with TIFF images.

Saving information

ScotlandsPeople keeps a permanent record of all the search results and images you have viewed, and this remains accessible whether or not you have any credits remaining. Once you have logged in, all the pages on the site have 'Viewed Images' and 'Previous Searches' links along the top of the page, which bring up a list of the searches you have previously carried out and the images you have already paid to view.

On the 'Previous Searches' page (see Fig. 14.9) the 'View' link takes you to your original list of results, and indicates which records you have already viewed and which can therefore be viewed again without payment. Fields at the foot of the page allow you to filter your search by surname or location. The rows which give no name, sex or location are for advanced searches.

The previous searches can be saved to your computer in four different formats: PDF, Excel spreadsheet, CSV (comma separated values) for import into a spreadsheet or database, and plain text. This makes it easy for you to keep a complete list of all your searches on your computer without logging in to the site. This does not download the actual search results, just the details you entered in the search form. To save the search results themselves you would need to copy and paste the text from the results page.

Previous Searches ⊘

1 **2 3 4 5 6 7**

Type	From	To	Page	Name	Sex	Location	Performed	
10/01/2014								
Census	01/01/1861	31/12/1861	1				11:39:09	View
02/01/2014								
Census	01/01/1911	31/12/1911	1	ALEXANDER			10:51:50	View
11/11/2013								
Census	01/01/1861	31/12/1861	1				15:37:36	View
Census	01/01/1861	31/12/1861	1				15:25:39	View
Census	01/01/1861	31/12/1861	1				15:17:25	View
Census	01/01/1861	31/12/1861	1				15:06:14	View
07/11/2013								
Census	01/01/1861	31/12/1861	1				21:13:03	View
Census	01/01/1861	31/12/1861	1				21:10:21	View
Census	01/01/1861	31/12/1861	1	DOYLE		EDINBURGH CITY	18:34:56	View
Census	01/01/1861	31/12/1861	1	DOYLE		GLASGOW CITY	18:33:04	View
Census	01/01/1861	31/12/1861	1	DOYLE			18:32:19	View
Census	01/01/1901	31/12/1901	1	MACDONALD		GLASGOW CITY CAMBUSLANG	18:11:08	View
Census	01/01/1881	31/12/1881	1	MCCURRY			17:34:41	View

Figure 14.9 ScotlandsPeople saved searches.

The 'Viewed Images' listing works in the same way. Again, you can download a list of the viewed images in various formats. Figure 14.10 shows a listing displayed as a spreadsheet in Microsoft Excel. Usefully, it gives you the full census reference.

Viewed Images

13 January 2014   12:40

	Year	Type	Description	Purchased
	1861	Census	BRODIE, MARY (Census 1861 685/02 076/00 001)	11/11/2013
	1861	Census	DOYLE, ARTHUR CONAN (Census 1861 685/02 090/00	07/11/2013
	1901	Census	MACDONALD, AGNES (Census 1901 627/00 005/00 005)	07/11/2013
	1881	Census 1881 LDS	MC CURRY, JOSEPH (Census 1881 566432)	07/11/2013
	1881	Census	MCCURRY, JOSEPH (Census 1881 644/03 116/00 008)	07/11/2013
	1891	Census	MACARA, ALEXANDER (Census 1891 685/01 011/00	18/10/2013
	1881	Census 1881 LDS	MC CURRY, GEORGE (Census 1881 297990)	16/10/2013

Figure 14.10 Viewed Images listing in an Excel spreadsheet.

Help and feedback

There are two places to look for help on the site: the FAQs and the Help & Other Resources area. Each of these is accessible by clicking on its tab at the top of the page. The FAQs are mostly about how the site works and provide brief answers to common queries about the records and indexes. The Help & Other Resources pages are more detailed and some of their most useful content provides help with names and handwriting. This is the place to look for broader guidance rather than quick answers to basic questions.

There are no links to dedicated error reporting forms from the search results or image pages, but the 'Contact Us' link at the bottom of every page leads you eventually (after two more links) to a general form to report a problem.

The site originally had its own discussion forums, but after a number of problems these were closed down. However, the Census forum on TalkingScot at <**www.talkingscot.com/forum**> is a good place to post queries relating to ScotlandsPeople and the Scottish census records if you don't need an official answer.

15

IRELAND

The digitisation of Irish census records was slow to get started. Apart from a tiny amount of material on commercial sites, there was no attempt, official or commercial, to digitise the Irish records, until long after England, Wales and Scotland had put their entire body of public census records online. This is all the more surprising since the 1901 and 1911 censuses for Ireland have actually been open to the public since the 1960s, which means they *could* have been among the first censuses to be digitised.

In fact, it was not until the end of 2005 that The National Archives of Ireland (NAI) announced that the two Irish censuses that survive in their entirety would be digitised and made available free of charge under a cultural agreement with Library and Archives Canada, which carried out the digitisation work. The impetus for the Canadians' decision was the large number of Irish immigrants to Canada and the importance of these records for Canadian family historians. In December 2007, the first fruits of this agreement went online, the 1911 census of Dublin, at <**www.census.nationalarchives.ie**>. The remaining material for 1911 and the whole of the 1901 census followed, completed in June 2010. In May 2014 the surviving fragments of the censuses of 1821–1851 were added to the site. At the same time an important supplementary source was added to the NAI's main genealogy site at <**www.genealogy.nationalarchives.ie**>, the 'Census Search Forms', which are copies of entries in the 1841 and 1851 censuses made before the original records were lost.

Since the 2005 announcement promised free access, it is hardly surprising that the commercial data services did not make any move to digitise the Irish material, though Origins has a small amount of material from the Irish CD-ROM publisher Eneclann. However, for many years volunteers have been getting on with making up for the previous lack of an official digitisation programme, and the result is a number of small to medium census transcription projects, which also include indexes to some of the few surviving pieces of the nineteenth-century censuses.

Since the completion of the Irish indexes, Ancestry has licensed a copy of them, freely searchable, with links to the original images on the NAI site, and it may well be that other major data services will do likewise. For Ancestry users this makes it possible to include Ireland in global census searches.

The next Irish census to be digitised will be that of 1926, the first for an independent Ireland. The project is discussed at the end of this chapter.

The National Archives of Ireland census site

The NAI's dedicated census site at <**www.census.nationalarchives.ie**> includes images of the original household returns, signed by the head of the household, for *both* surviving censuses, 1901 and 1911. (For England and Wales, only the 1911 returns are available in this form — for 1901 the enumeration schedules are all that is available.)

Searching

The site offers two ways to view the indexes: search and browse. A flowchart for the search process is shown in Figure 15.1, and Figure 15.2 shows the search forms. When you first go to the Search page, only the basic options are offered, along with the start point for the 'Browse by place' facility, but clicking on a 'More search options' brings up an additional panel with advanced search options. The advanced search fields in the 'Marriage and children' box are relevant only to the 1911 census.

One of the unusual things about the search is that you can leave both of the name fields blank. This means you can easily get a list of all the inhabitants of a street (making it effectively an address search) or even all those in a certain age range (114-year-old John Connelly, living in the Irishtown workhouse, Queen's Co., is the oldest person in the 1911 census, married for 58 years).

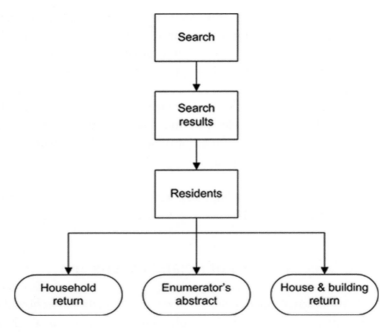

Figure 15.1 NAI census search process.

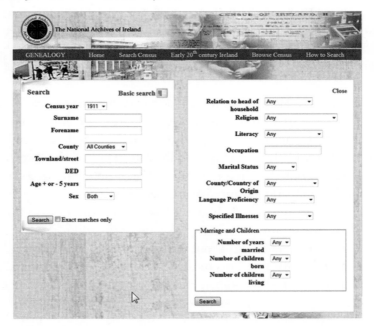

Figure 15.2 Search form for the Irish census.

The search treats any text you enter as a distinct word to be sought anywhere in the field, so a search for the forename _John_ finds _Arthur John_ and _Michael John_ too. All the text fields accept * as a wildcard, which stands for zero or more characters.

If you enter two or more words in a search field, they are treated as an OR search, i.e. the results will comprise any entry in which any one or more of the words given is found. This gives rise to an unexpected trap if you enter a street name in the Townland/street field: if you search for, say, _Iona Road_ you will find not only the 200 odd entries for Iona Road, but also all those for Iona Park and Iona Drive, which could be useful, as well as every entry that has the word _Road_ in its street name, which is rather less helpful! You can get around this by omitting the word _Road_ or by putting the whole street name in inverted commas, _'Iona Road'._

Clicking on the 'Search' button at the bottom of the form brings up the first page of search results (see Fig. 15.3). As you can see, the contents of the surname, forename, age and sex columns on the census form are given for the individual, as well as the District Electoral Division (DED) and the townland or street of the household. This list is initially sorted by surname, ten records to a page, but you can re-sort by any field, and you can choose to display 50 or 100 results per page. If you have got too many results, the search form is repeated at the bottom of the page so you can refine your search. If you select the 'Show all information' checkbox, the results are expanded to show all the remaining fields, including 'Birthplace', 'Occupation', 'Religion' and, for 1911, the fertility information. The results for the pre-1901 censuses vary slightly in presentation, giving a 'Parish' rather that a 'DED', for example. Also, where the information in one of the additional fields has been given in Irish, it will not appear in the 'all information' listing, unless a translation has been given on the original form.

You will sometimes see a name (usually male) which has no entry in the age or sex columns. This is not an error, but indicates that this is the name of the head of household entered on the _outside_ of the household schedule by the enumerator (see Fig. 15.8). It's important to note that these entries will not appear in search results if you specify a gender and age. You might not think this matters, but there is one case where it makes a real difference. As explained later in this chapter, many householders, even in essentially Anglophone parts of the

Home / 1901/1911 Census, Ireland / Search

Search results Displaying results 1 - 10 of 52

Records per page: 10 / 50 / 100   ☐ **Show all information**

Sort by: Relevance / Surname / Forename / **Townland or Street** / DED / County / Age / Sex

Surname	Forename	Townland/Street	DED	County	Age	Sex
OBrien	Edward	Abbey Street Lower	North Dock	Dublin	38	M
OBrien	Edward	Allingham St.	Merchant's Quay	Dublin	8	M
O'Brien	Edward F	Ballybrack	Killiney	Dublin	4	M
O'Brien	Edward	Ballybrack	Killiney	Dublin	58	M
O'Brien	Edward	Ballybrack	Killiney	Dublin	73	M
O Brien	Edward	Blessington Lane	Inns Quay	Dublin	39	M
OBrien	Edward	Booterstown Avenue	Blackrock No. 1	Dublin	34	M
OBrien	Edward	Bride Street	Wood Quay (part of)	Dublin	35	M
O Brien	Edward	Brunswick St. North	Arran Quay	Dublin	32	M
OBrien	Francis Edward	Buckingham Buildings (a block).	Mountjoy	Dublin	49	M

Page 1 2 3 4 5 6   Next 10

Figure 15.3 Irish census Search results.

country, entered their names in Irish, so you find James Casey recorded as Seámus Ó Cathasaigh in the household schedule (as in Fig. 15.7). However, the enumerator will have recorded the name in its English form on the outside of the schedule (see Fig. 15.8). If so, you will not find him in a search for James Casey, age 45, male, whereas if you search for just James Casey he will be included in the search results. Of course you will then need to look at the census image to check his age and make sure he is the person you are looking for.

From the Search results page, clicking on a forename or surname takes you to a listing of the household members (see Fig. 15.4). The initial listing gives only the names, age, sex, relation to head and religion, with the address at the top of the form. But here, too, selecting the 'Show all information' checkbox expands the results to show all the remaining fields. This makes it possible to copy *all* the data for a household for pasting into a text file, word processor document or spreadsheet.

Below the household listing are links to the various images which have information relating to this household. More information about viewing the images is given below.

Census Years / 1911 / Dublin / Killiney / Ballybrack / Residents of a house

Residents of a house 33 in Ballybrack (Killiney, Dublin)

☐ Show all information

Surname	Forename	Age	Sex	Relation to head	Religion
O'Brien	Edward	58	Male	Head of Family	Roman Catholic
O'Brien	Ellen Frances	30	Female	Wife	Roman Catholic
O'Brien	Thomas W	5	Male	Son	Roman Catholic
O'Brien	Edward F	4	Male	Son	Roman Catholic
O'Brien	James F	2	Male	Son	Roman Catholic
O'Brien	Susan Mary		Female	Daughter	Roman Catholic
O'Brien	Edward	73	Male	Uncle	Roman Catholic

Report any error in transcription

View census images

Household Return (Form A)
  Additional Pages: 2

Other original census images available

Enumerator's abstract (Form N)
  Additional Pages: 1, 2, 3, 4, 5, 6, 7, 8, 9
House and Building Return (Form B1)
  Additional Pages: 2, 3, 4, 5, 6, 7, 8
Out-Offices and Farm-Steadings Return (Form B2)
  Additional Pages: 2, 3, 4

You will need Adobe Acrobat Reader to view the images.

Get Acrobat 📄

How do I view the images?

⚠ Report errors in transcription

Visit Ireland

Figure 15.4 Irish census household listing.

The browse is organised geographically, by county, then DED, then street. For each street, there is a page listing the houses with the surname of the head of household and links to a list of occupants and the image of Form A. For rural areas, the listing will be based on townland rather than street.

There is no census reference search in the site, and indeed it does not cite references at all, though they are visible on the cover of the household schedule. References of the sort used in this chapter (see the footnotes on p. 297 for examples) can be used as the basis for a geographical browse to locate the correct record, and this is discussed in more detail in the coverage of Irish census references in Chapter 18, p. 326.

Surnames

One important issue with the Irish census is that surnames with the prefix 'O' (meaning literally 'grandson of', but more generally 'descendant of') are recorded in various ways. So O'Brien is sometimes O Brien, sometimes OBrien and sometimes O'Brien. This means there is no way to formulate a *single* search which will find all three forms. Just to make things even harder, there are even a few cases of O' Brien. However, doing a search on *Brien* alone will find Brien, *O Brien* and O' Brien. O*Brien finds OBrien and O'Brien. However, in the 1911 census there are around 1,800 individuals whose surname is recorded with the Gaelic form of the prefix, *Ua* and more rarely *Uí*, as well as over 5,000 (mainly) females who use the traditional feminine equivalent *Ní* (occasionally without the accent as *Ni*). This means you may need to search for *Ua Briain* or *Ní Bhriain* as well.

In other families the girls have adopted English-style gender-neutral surnames. You will also see wives in Irish-speaking families recorded sometimes as *bean Uí X* (wife of O'X), where the husband is called Ó'X. See, for example, Brigidh bean Uí Dhuinn at 5 Allingham Street, Dublin, in 1911, whose husband is Micheal Ó Dúinn.[1] There are just over 550 of these in the 1911 census. In this particular household both parents speak only English, incidentally, and the husband's occupation of 'Ex-Policeman' is given in English though he signs the Irish form of his name. On the reverse of the form his name is given as Michael Dunne.

With the patronymic prefix Mac, there are three forms: Mac, Mc and M'. A search for *M*Donald* finds MacDonald, McDonald, and M'Donald. However, a search for *M* Donald* (with a space after the wildcard) is not entirely helpful for finding the forms which have been recorded with a space after the patronymic prefix — it finds every name with Mac or Donald as a distinct element. In fact the best approach is probably just to use the forename part: a search on *Donald* finds Donald, Mc Donald, Mac Donald and M Donald. Unfortunately you cannot use a wildcard at the start of a name, so you cannot use *Donald as a way to capture all the variant forms.

One interesting difference between the two Irish censuses is that there is a significant increase in the number of households where the names, even if not the remaining columns, have been entered in Irish.

---

1 <www.census.nationalarchives.ie/pages/1911/Dublin/Merchant_s_Quay/
Allingham_St_/62230>.

This means that you cannot even assume that an individual's name will be identical in the two censuses. For example, James Lennon of Cornararagh (1901 census, Drumcarrow, Co. Monaghan) becomes Seamus Ó Lionáin in 1911.[2] John M'Glynn of Kilrean (1901 census, Cloghan, Donegal) turns up as Seaghan Mhac Fhloinn in 1911, while his wife Mary M'Glynn becomes Máire Nic Fhloinn.[3]

This can make identification problematic unless the addresses, ages and other family members are sufficiently similar. For a young man who has moved away from home and married between the two censuses, it may be impossible to find the two matching census entries. The number of individuals this affects is probably quite small, but it is something to bear in mind if you can locate an ancestor in one census but not the other.

There is a detailed guide to Irish names and how they are constructed on the Nualéargais website at <**www.nualeargais.ie/gnag/ainm.htm**>.

The Irish language

An additional complication in the Irish census is that in 1911 over half a million people (almost 18 per cent of the population) spoke Irish, though the number of monoglot Irish speakers is naturally a good deal smaller.[4] In many cases, their Form A has been completed in Irish and using the Gaelic script, which is quite different from English scripts of the same period. Table 15.1 shows the letter-forms for this script, though bear in mind that handwritten letters of individual householders will often be significantly different from the printed font.

---

2 <www.census.nationalarchives.ie/pages/1901/Monaghan/Drumcarrow/
   Cornararagh/1624192> and <www.census.nationalarchives.ie/pages/1911/
   Monaghan/Drumcarrow/Cornalaragh/797497>.
3 <www.census.nationalarchives.ie/pages/1901/Donegal/Cloghan/
   Kilrean/1197771> and <www.census.nationalarchives.ie/pages/1911/Donegal/
   Cloghan/Kilrean/507579>.
4 The Central Statistics Office Ireland provides historical data on the number of
   Irish and non-Irish speakers in the counties of the Republic (i.e. excluding the
   six Ulster counties which now make up Northern Ireland) since 1861 at
   <beyond2020.cso.ie/Census/TableViewer/tableView.aspx?ReportId=1208>
   (summary) and <www.cso.ie/en/media/csoie/census/documents/vol11_entire.
   pdf> (very detailed).

A	B	C	D	E	F	G	H	I	L	M	N	O	P	R	S	T	U
𝔞	B	C	ꝺ	e	F	ᵹ	ƕ	ı	ⱡ	𝔐	N	O	P	R	S	ⲧ	u
ᴀ	b	c	ꝺ	e	F	ᵹ	ƕ	ı	l	m	ꞃ	o	p	ꞃ	ꞃ	ⲧ	u

Table 15.1 The Gaelic script.

Irish does not use the letters J, K, Q, W, X, Y, Z. Note particularly that the Irish 'i' has no dot. This can make it difficult to distinguish between 'm' and 'in' (m, ın), though in handwriting the 'i' often has a noticeable descender. Dots above letters are used for a quite different purpose in Irish, and are found only above consonants (see below).

Some of the entries written in Irish have annotations in English in the family relationship and occupation columns, but the remaining columns may be hard to read if you are not familiar with the script, which you will need to be before you can look up the words in a dictionary. Figure 15.5 shows the entries for an Irish-speaking household in the Gaelic script.[5] Note that the relationship column includes English translations. You will also sometimes find English translations for the entries in the occupation column, as shown in Figure 15.6 for an Irish-speaking household in Limerick.[6]

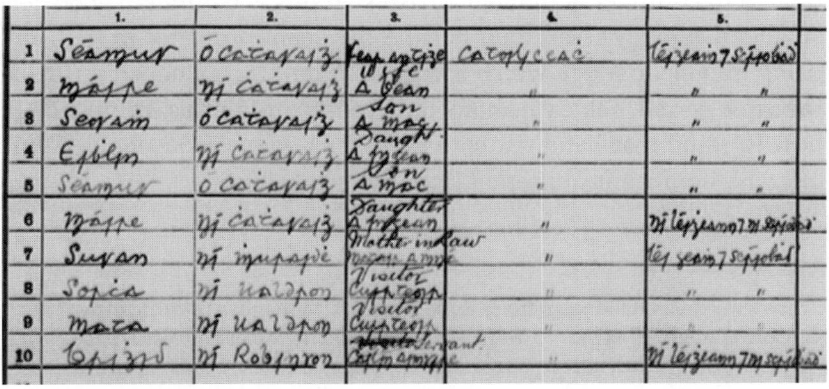

Figure 15.5 Entries for an Irish-speaking household.

5 <www.census.nationalarchives.ie/pages/1911/Dublin/Glasnevin/ Iona_Road__to_Auburn/16378>.
6 <www.census.nationalarchives.ie/pages/1911/Limerick/Limerick_No__3_ Urban/Bedford_Row/628430>.

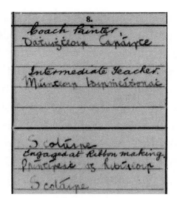

Figure 15.6 Irish occupation entries with English translation.

Census Years / 1911 / Dublin / Glasnevin / Iona Road, to Auburn / Residents of a house

Residents of a house 49 in Iona Road, to Auburn (Glasnevin, Dublin)

☐ Show all information

Surname	Forename	Age	Sex	Relation to head	Religion
Ó Cathasaigh	Séamus	45	Male	-	-
Ní Chathasaigh	Máire	37	Female	Wife	-
Ó Cathasaigh	Seosamh	13	Male	Son	-
Ní Chathasaigh	Eibhlin	11	Female	Daughter	-
Ó Cathasaigh	Séamus	8	Male	Son	-
Ní Chathasaigh	Máire	4	Female	Daughter	-
Ní Mhuraidhe	Susan	57	Female	Mother in Law	-
Ní Ualdron	Sorcha	34	Female	Visitor	-
Ní Ualdron	Mata	23	Female	Visitor	-
Ní Robinson	Brighid	24	Female	Servant	-
Casey	James	-	-	-	-

Figure 15.7 Transcription of names in Fig. 15.5.

Figure 15.7 shows the transcription of the names from the household listing. Note the entry for the head of household James Casey mentioned above.

You shouldn't assume, incidentally, that all those with Irish names are Irish speakers: if you look at the family of Tomás O hAodha at 30 Leinster Street in 1911,[7] both his wife Máire Ní Aodha and his youngest

---

7   <www.census.nationalarchives.ie/pages/1911/Dublin/Arran_Quay/ Leinster_Street_North/43742>.

son Seaghán O hAodha speak only English. Occasionally, you will find both Irish and English names within the same family: at 1 Mountpleasant Place, Dublin, in 1911 Jeremiah Hayes has a wife and five children, all called Hayes with the exception of a 22-year-old son whose name is given as Seosamh Ó hAodha, Seosamh being the Irish form of Joseph.[8] In this case, it seems likely that the use of the Irish name represents a statement of national identity by an individual family member.

You can even find forms where there is a mixture of Irish and English. For example, Kate Duffy of Cappalusk, Co. Galway, a teacher, gives all the names for her household in Irish but has completed the other fields in English.[9]

Where individuals have not got English or anglicised names, there are particular problems with searching, because the Irish vowels can also take an acute accent to indicate vowel length (the Irish term for this mark is *fada*). Our testing suggests that in the 1901 census, vowels with and without the *fada* have been indexed together, while for the 1911 they are indexed separately. However, it is impossible to be entirely sure about this and the site has no information whatsoever on this issue.

For example, the surname Súilleabháin (anglicised as Sullivan) will not be found in a search for *Suilleabhain*, you have to use the *ú* and *á* spellings. These accented characters can be entered on a PC keyboard by holding down the ALT key and typing 0225 on the numeric keypad (*not* the normal number keys on the top row of the keyboard). On the Mac, you can enter vowels with an acute accent by first holding down the Option key and the E key together, then releasing them and pressing the normal key for the vowel. The key combinations are shown in Table 15.2.

Letter	PC (Windows)	Mac
á	ALT+0225	Option+e, a
é	ALT+0233	Option+e, e
í	ALT+0237	Option+e, i
ó	ALT+0243	Option+e, o
ú	ALT+0250	Option+e, u

Table 15.2 Entering *fadas* on a keyboard.

8 <www.census.nationalarchives.ie/pages/1911/Dublin/Rathmines___Rathgar_East/Mountpleasant_Place/50561>.
9 <www.census.nationalarchives.ie/pages/1911/Galway/Cappalusk/Temple/462777>.

Alternatively, you could use a wildcard instead of the vowel in question: *S*lleabh*n* finds both the accented and unaccented spellings. This also helps to cope with the fact that mistakes in the use of the *fada* are only to be expected among a population with widely differing surname pronunciations and varying degrees of literacy. For the Irish form of Patrick, for example, you will find the normal form *Pádraig*, not to mention Pádraic, Pádraigh, Padraig, Pádráig, Padraic, Padraich, Padruig, Padráig, Padruigh, Padreag, Paádraig, Pádriac, Pádruic, and Pádruich. Matching criteria seem less strict with forenames: a search on *Pádraig* finds some Padraigs, Padráigs, and Pádráigs, but searches on each of these names gives a different number of results. Again, the wildcard comes to the rescue: *P*dr** will find all of these. If you sort the results on forename or surname, note that the letters with and without the *fada* are treated as different letters for sorting and *a* comes before *á*.

The older Irish writing system (prior to a reform started in 1948 and completed in 1957) also used a dot over certain consonants, indicating a linguistic feature called 'lenition'. In English transcriptions and in modern Irish spelling, this feature is normally indicated by an 'h' after the consonant, giving the consonant pairs 'bh', 'ch', 'dh', 'th', 'gh', 'mh', 'ph', 'sh', 'th'. Although the dot spellings are found in the actual census forms, the 'h' spellings are used in the census index, so you do not need to be able to enter the dotted consonants (just as well, as there is no way to do so!).

However, there is an additional complication: the initial consonant of a word can be affected by the final sound of the previous word (a feature also found in Welsh, see page 65) — some forms of a name have the consonant without and some with lenition. If you look at the family of Séamus Ó Cathasaigh in Figure 15.5 and Figure 15.7, you'll see that all the male family members are Ó Cathasaigh while the females are Ní Chathasaigh with a Ċ on the original form and 'Ch' in the index. The same distinction can be seen in the names of Micheal Ó Dúinn and Brigidh bean Uí Dhuinn mentioned above.

In general, Irish spellings correspond very poorly to English spelling conventions, so it is not a trivial matter for anyone but an expert to match up an Irish name with its normal anglicisation. Unless they are Irish or have lived in Ireland, English speakers have little hope of guessing the Irish spelling of a name on the basis of its form in English. Also, before the spelling reform there were many more 'silent letters'.

For example the modern name for the Irish language, 'Gaeilge,' is spelled 'ᵹᴀᵉᴆɪᴌᴈᵉ' (i.e. 'Gaedhilge') on the census forms.

Before you start using the Irish census, it is well worth consulting reputable reference works, such as the *Oxford Names Companion*, to check the surnames of any Irish ancestors to see if they are anglicisations of Irish surnames, and what Irish spellings are attested. If you are searching for Casey ancestors, for example, you are unlikely to guess that they might be concealed behind the Irish surname Ó Cathasaigh shown in the extract above. Given that the Irish language had no agreed standard form until the 1950s, you should also expect that even the best surname dictionaries will not be familiar with all the spellings used for the same name as pronounced in the many local dialects, and spelt by householders who might be more or less literate.

While this problem is mainly one for surnames, it applies equally to forenames: Séamus Ó Cathasaigh would be anglicised as James Casey, and indeed that is the householder's name given on the outside of Form A for this family (see Fig. 15.8). Forenames are less problematic simply because there are fewer of them, with the correspondences well known and easy to look up. Even so, there may be surprises: even if you know that Seán corresponds to John, you may not realise that there is an older spelling Seághan which is in fact more common on the census forms. A good online guide to the forename equivalences will be found on the Baby Names of Ireland site at <**www.babynamesofireland.com**> — follow the links to 'Girl Names' and 'Boy Names' at the top of the page.

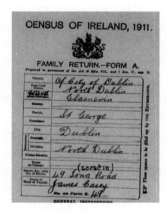

Figure 15.8 The outside of Séamus Ó Cathasaigh's Form A.

Obviously it is important to be able to understand the terms used in the 'relationship' and 'other' columns on the household schedule. Table 15.3 gives some of the most common words. You will find a list of the main vocabulary of family relationships at <**www.irishgaelictranslator. com/articles/?p=30**>, though this gives the modern reformed spelling so there will be some differences from the census records.

Back in 2008, the Irish census site was promising that, 'A list of Irish names and occupations, with translations, will appear on this site in the coming months' but at the start of 2014 this promise remained unfulfilled.

The birthplace column will usually give the name of an Irish county or city. You can find the (modern) Irish spellings for towns and cities in the Dictionary of Irish Terms at <**www.focal.ie**>. Geonames' Ireland page at <**www.geonames.de/couie.html**> gives the names of the present day county councils of the Republic of Ireland with their main

Term	Older spelling	Modern spelling
head	ceann	ceann
wife	bean	bean
son	mac	mac
daughter	inzion	iníon
mother	máċair	máthair
brother	deṗbráċair	dearthái r
sister	deiṗſiúṗ	deirfiúr
visitor	cuaiṗceoiṗ	cuairteoir
married	póſca	pósta
single	aonca	aonta
widow	baincṗeaċ	baintreach
read and write	léiżeaṁ 7 ſcṗíoḃ	léigheamh & scríobhadh
can't read and write:	ní léiżeaṁ 7 ní ſcṗíoḃ	ní léigheamh & ní scríobhadh
Irish	Zaeḋilze	gaeilge
Irish and English	Zaeḋilze 7 béaṗla	gaeilge & béarla

Table 15.3 The main Irish terms on census forms.

towns in both Roman and Gaelic letters. The equivalent material for Northern Ireland will be found at <**www.geonames.de/cougb-sub. html#gbi**>.

Images

For each household, there are several images relating to the additional census forms.

In the case of the Forms N, B1, and B2, there are links to all the pages for the street and not just the pages which related to the one household, so in a long street or a large townland you may need to look at several of these to find the right one.

The page images are greyscale and are provided in PDF format with a file size of between 500k and 600k. Because of the nature of the PDF format it is not possible to be precise about the resolution at which the images have been scanned, but they seem to have been scanned at about 200 dpi, though at very high magnification one can detect some distortion because of compression. On the whole, fine detail is easy to make out.

Help and feedback

The 'How to Search' link on the home page leads to the Help Menu with general information about the Irish censuses and basic help on using the search facilities, with details on each of the search fields.

According to the help page, the indexes will be rebuilt at two- or three-monthly intervals, and the rebuild will incorporate any verified corrections. On the household page, there is a link to an online form for correcting transcription errors. One type of error we noticed, and which will not be corrected because the error is on the original form, is where both forename and surname have been entered in the forename field. If you can't find someone by surname, it might be worth trying it out in the forename field.

Census Search Forms

While the pre-1901 census records are generally preserved only in accidental fragments, there is one significant body of copies made before the loss of the records. When the Old Age Pension was introduced in 1908, extracts were made from the 1841 and 1851 censuses as proof of age for some individuals who were born before the start of the civil registration of births in 1864 and who therefore could not produce a birth certificate. These forms survive. Where the search was successful, they list the names of all family members. But even where the search failed, they still record what the claimant believed to be their place of residence in the census year and the names of their parents, which will indicate a married woman's maiden name. Each form also gives the current address of the claimant. Figure 15.9 shows the form for a successful search, with the names of all the children in the family written in pencil in the left margin.

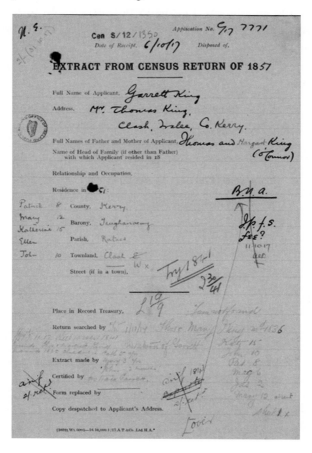

Figure 15.9 Census Search Form

Although the records for the six counties of Northern Ireland have been available in book form since 1999, in 2014 an index to all of the records, along with images of the original forms, was released on the NAI genealogy site. Since they require a quite different search form, they are not located with the other census records, but in a separate area of the NAI site at <**censussearchforms.nationalarchives.ie**>, which is linked from the main genealogy page at <**www.genealogy.nationalar-chives.ie**>.

The search form is shown in Figure 15.10. Although there are a dozen search fields, given that all the data come from potential pensioners remembering details from 60 years earlier, it is probably best to be cautious and search on as few fields as possible. Even a search on just a surname and a county will probably not produce an unmanageable list of results, and will reduce the risk of missing the entry you are looking for.

Search

Year of Census Extract	
Surname of Applicant	
Christian name of Applicant	
Applicant's present address	
Surname of Father	
Christian name of Father	
Maiden Surname of Mother	
Christian name of Mother	
Residence Location - County	All Counties
Residence Location - Barony	
Residence Location - Parish	
Residence Location - Townland	
Residence Location - City	

Search

Figure 15.10 Search form for Census Search Forms

The search results show all the fields on the search form and clicking on the surname or Christian name takes you to the 'Details' page. If the original search of the census records was successful, this will list the names of the family members. If no family members are listed, it means that the original search was unsuccessful. In both cases there is a link to an image of the original form in PDF format.

Commercial sites

Although the NAI site will obviously be the main Irish census site, some of the material is also available on commercial sites: Ancestry, Findmypast and Origins all have some overlapping record sets. In addition, Origins has an index of the 1851 census for Dublin City, created by Dr D.A. Chart before the original records were lost, and it does not duplicate the 1851 census fragments on the NAI site. It gives only the names and addresses of heads of household (around 60,000). The forenames are usually abbreviated.

The Irish Family History Foundation has a pay-per-view service at <**www.rootsireland.ie**>, launched in July 2008. This has around 3 million census records for 1901 and 1911, compiled by volunteers in the foundation's county genealogy centres, and therefore different from the official NAI indexes discussed above.

Searches are free, though you need to register first. Viewing the records costs €5 for one record, €40 for eight and €100 for twenty. These prices seem quite high, because the search results do not give any information to identify individuals other than what you have entered on the search form, so you may have to pay to view several records before finding the right person. There are no images, so you will have to re-run your search on the NAI site to check an entry. It is therefore difficult to see any usefulness in these census indexes except as a last resort if you have been unable to find a household on the NAI site or as part of a wider search in the other records on Rootsireland.

Volunteer transcriptions

During the long wait for any official plan to digitise the Irish censuses, many groups and individual volunteers set about indexing or transcribing the census for particular towns or areas.

					Head of household Surname	Head of household Given	Head of household Occupation	Other occupants
Townland	Parish	Barony	County	Description				
Corracoggil North	Tibohine	Frenchpark	Roscommon	Household	Kelly	Joseph(34)	teacher	Bridget(34)-Eugene(6)-Mary(5)-Joseph(3)-Mary Sharkey(16)niece-Ellie Sharkey(12)niece
Culleenirwan	Dysart	Athlone South	Roscommon	Household	Kelly	Joseph(48)	farmer	Bridget(36)-Mary A.(16)-Julia(2)-Norah(7mo.)
Carrick	Cam	Athlone South	Roscommon	Household	Kelly	Joseph(74)	farmer/civil service pens.	widower-Mary Kate(34) teacher/not married
Ballyardan	Ardcarn	Boyle	Roscommon	Household	Kelly	Joseph(39)	Superannuated Ins.RW Officer	Annie(46) wife-Mary(19)-Kathleen(15) scholar-Patrick(18) scholar-Kate McManus(58) unmarried/servant

Figure 15.11 Leitrim-Roscommon 1901 Census Search Output.

The largest of these seems to be the Leitrim–Roscommon material for the 1901 census at <**www.leitrim-roscommon.com/1901census**>. This includes entries for around 300,000 individuals in the counties of Roscommon, Leitrim, Mayo, Sligo, Wexford, Westmeath, and Galway. The exact scope of the data is given on the main page — data for the first four of these counties is complete — and there is a link to the search form at the foot. There are no images, but the search results give family groups with the occupation of the head (see Fig. 15.11).

The best way to find other county indexes is to consult the Ireland page on Census Finder at <**www.censusfinder.com/ireland.htm**>. Alternatively, consult the Genuki page for the relevant Irish county at <**www.genuki.org.uk/big/irl/**>.

The 1926 census

There was no census in Ireland in 1921 because of the Irish War of Independence, and the first census for the newly formed Irish Free State was taken in 1926. Under the 100-year rule stipulated in the original legislation these records were due for release in 2026. A campaign for the early release of this census to coincide with the centenary of the 1916 Easter Rising and 'to stimulate genealogy tourism' has resulted in a commitment from the Irish government to permit the early release of the 1926 census and digitise it 'subject to resources and the resolution of legal and other issues'. (Unfortunately, it has recently been established that the records for the 1926 census of Northern Ireland were probably destroyed in World War II.)

However, in spite of repeated assurances from the Minister for Arts, Heritage and the Gaeltacht, the promised legislation has been delayed by the determined refusal of Ireland's Central Statistical Office to accede to the waiving of the 100-year rule of confidentiality. In May 2013 the minister said he was nonetheless 'of the opinion that the extensive preparatory work required to facilitate the release of the data into the public domain can commence in advance of the legal restriction being addressed'. But even if this particular matter is speedily resolved, it is reasonable to wonder whether, in the current economic climate, funding will be forthcoming in time for a 2016 release.

The Council of Irish Genealogical Organisations has been at the forefront of the campaign for early access to this census and its page at <**www.cigo.ie/campaigns_1926.html**> gives background and links. A good place to look for the latest news about the 1926 census is Claire Santry's Irish Genealogy News blog — a listing of all census-related items will be found using the URL <**irish-genealogy-news.blogspot. co.uk/search?q=census**>.

16

THE CENSUS ON CD-ROM AND DVD

While the web is now the most popular way to access census data, particularly if you need to search the whole country for your ancestors, there is still much census material on CD-ROM or DVD. This material is generally in the form of indexes only, though some suppliers include images, and most CD-ROMs cover only a county, a major city, or in some cases a smaller area.

This might suggest that you should not bother with CD-ROM products. But there are a number of reasons why it might be worth your while to see what is available in that media format.

If you live close to the area where your ancestors came from, your central library, local studies library or county record office is very likely to have copies of census indexes published on CD-ROM for the local area. You will be able to consult these without signing up with a commercial data service.

For anyone consulting the census as part of a local history or one-place study, it may make sense to have the complete data for that place available without going online. It is generally quite difficult to use the online censuses for any sort of general analysis of the population of an enumeration district (e.g. what the main occupations are) — you would have to download and then merge the data for every individual household. Also, where original census images are published on CD-ROM, this can be a much more convenient alternative to downloading the images for a large area from an online service — not to mention that trying to identify all the households for a particular town or area, or even just a single street, can be extremely difficult in the online services.

Finally, there is an argument that CD-ROM census indexes will often be superior to their online equivalents. In particular, this ought to be the case with those produced by family history societies. While the data services outsource indexing to non-specialists without local knowledge, FHS census indexes have always been produced by local volunteers and have in many cases been in use by the society for many years before appearing on CD-ROM. That should mean that all obvious and many non-obvious errors will have been spotted and corrected.

There is no comprehensive master catalogue of all the publications, but some of the commercial retailers, discussed below, source their products from dozens of different suppliers and browsing their catalogues will give you a good idea of what's available.

A very comprehensive online listing, on a county-by-county basis, is provided by Daniel Morgan at <**www.mit.edu/~dfm/genealogy/census-chart. html**>. Another source is the library catalogue of the Society of Genealogists (SoG), which is linked from the SoG home page at <**www.sog.org.uk**>. This is the largest genealogy library in the UK and the catalogue lists many census indexes in a variety of media.

The largest single CD-ROM product is the 1881 Census Index, which is available online at <**www.familysearch.org**>, but it was previously published as a set of 25 CD-ROMs. The CD-ROMs are no longer available for purchase from the LDS Church, but can be found second-hand on eBay or Amazon (at the time of writing there were five sets on offer on eBay). While the CDs have been made redundant by the online availability of the data free on FamilySearch, the CD product has significantly better search facilities, which are particularly useful for the local or social historian. However, the software which provides the search facilities is now rather long in the tooth and there can be no guarantee that it will run on a computer with a recent version of Windows, so you may need to seek advice from expert users.

One thing to bear in mind is that in the last ten years the Web has taken over from CD-ROM as the publishing medium of choice for census indexes. You will therefore not find CD-ROM products for the recently released censuses, 1901 and 1911, and we are also not aware of *any* material of this sort for Scotland.

Family history societies

Many family history societies have published their census indexes on CD-ROM. Increasingly, these indexes are also available online, but many are not. Even where an FHS index is online, it may be less expensive, if you are interested in many families in a county, to buy an index on CD-ROM than to pay for lots of searches online. Of course, since they are only indexes you will still need to check the index entries against the originals. If your interest is more in local history than in genealogy, having a complete index for a town or village could be more convenient for you than carrying out place name searches in the online census collections.

For census CD-ROMs, the obvious places to look are the websites for the societies covering the area you are interested in. Few societies have their own online shop, but you can order from a society by post or from one of the commercial suppliers. You can find links to the websites of all the family history societies in the British isles on Genuki's 'Family History And Genealogy Societies' page at <**www.genuki.org.uk/ Societies**>. Many of the CD-ROM publications of societies are available from the commercial suppliers discussed below and, particularly where an area is covered by more than one society, this may be an easier way to find out what is available than visiting the individual FHS websites.

Commercial suppliers

The largest producer of census CD-ROMs is S&N Genealogy, whose online shop is at <**www.genealogysupplies.com**>. There is a link to the page for census CD-ROMs in the left-hand column.

Whereas almost all census products on CD-ROM are indexes only, S&N has concentrated on putting scanned images of the enumeration books on CD-ROM, with separate name indexes released subsequently. Prices depend on the number of CDs in a set. The smaller counties cost £19.95 for each census year, while the largest (London, Lancashire, Yorkshire) with as many as 30 CDs or one DVD cost £24.95. The images are supplied as Adobe Acrobat (PDF) files; the indexes indicate the file and page number on which the matching entry is found. The image collections come with indexes of streets and areas, so if your information on where your ancestors lived is accurate for the year in question, you may not need the name indexes. The same will apply to any with an interest in the local history of an area rather than the individuals as possible ancestors.

The indexes require the installation of a program on your computer (Windows systems), which provides a very simple search facility — you can search on name and age only. For each name that comes up in the search results, the age, location and The National Archives (TNA) piece and folio reference are given. You can also get a listing of the other family members to check that you have the right person. Figures 16.1 and 16.2 show the results of a search for Charles Dickens in the 1841 census for London, and the household listing.

With the PDF file and page reference you can now load the relevant CD (there are 41 CDs in this particular set) and navigate to the relevant page. Note that the page number you need is the page within the PDF file (which appears in a small window at the bottom of the Acrobat Reader), and not the page number printed on the enumeration book.

Another major supplier of genealogy books and CDs is GENfair at <www.genfair.co.uk>. This was previously the online shop of the Federation of Family History Societies but it is now run by S&N British Data Archive, which sells products from around 130 suppliers and which currently offers over 3,000 products under the census heading. The majority of these are from family and local history societies, but

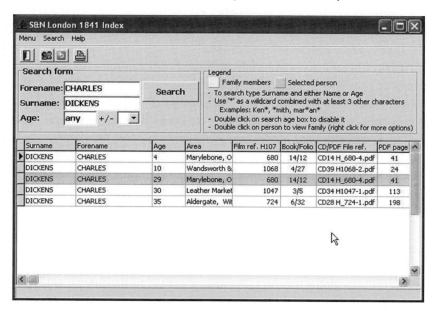

Figure 16.1 S&N London 1841 census index search results.

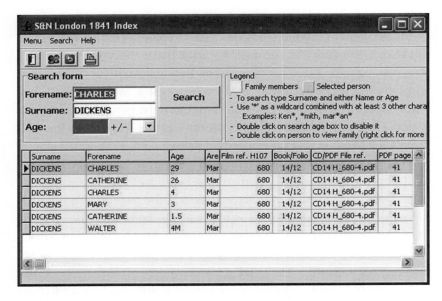

Figure 16.2 S&N London 1841 census index family listing.

products from major producers like S&N are also included. To see the census products available, either click on the 'Census' link on the home page and then search on the county, or click on a county on the map on the home page, and search on 'census'.

Parish Chest at <www.parishchest.com> sells census CDs from a range of sources (including around 75 family history societies and historical organisations, and over 120 commercial suppliers). To see the census offerings, click on the Census Records link on the home page and then select the county from the map.

One rather different type of material is available on CD for Ireland: the Irish genealogical publisher Eneclann has digitised all the official census reports for 1841–1911 and made them available on CD — each CD holds all the reports for a single county. While these are not going to be useful for tracing individual ancestors, they are invaluable for local historians and provide historical background for particular localities. The full list can be found in Eneclann's online catalogue at <www. eneclann.ie/acatalog/Census_Records_Census_Substitutes.html>.

You don't need to go online to purchase census indexes on CD — a wide range will normally be found on sale at the various family history fairs around the country and at the open days of local family history societies. You can find out details of forthcoming events from Genuki's events calendar, GENEVA, at <**geneva.weald.org.uk**> and from the Family History Fairs website at <**www.familyhistoryfairs.org**>. Parish Chest have a page listing the events they will be attending (click on the Events tab at the top of their web pages). A similar list for S&N can be found by selecting Events from the 'What's New' menu on their site.

The largest fair, the Who Do You Think You Are? Live show at Olympia is attended by all the major vendors and many FHSs and is an excellent place to see a wide range of census records on CD and DVD. See <**www.whodoyouthinkyouarelive.com**> for details of the next event.

A further source of census CDs are online auction sites such as eBay at <**www.ebay.co.uk**>. A search on 'CD' and 'census' should bring up all the relevant items. There is one caveat about bidding for genealogy CDs in an online auction: check the normal retail price of a CD before bidding. Most genealogy CDs are quite cheap, and it's easy to end up paying above the retail price on an auction site, particularly if the seller has high postage and packing charges.

Cyndi's List has a page devoted to a list of CD-ROM publishers and suppliers (listed under 'Vendors') at <**www.cyndislist.com/cd-roms. htm**>, though this is not exhaustive.

Future prospects

Although, as we have suggested, there continue to be good reasons for using census indexes on CD-ROM, it is likely that this type of product will become less common in the long term. The more family historians have internet access from home, the less need there is for local census indexes on CD-ROM. Most people will feel the need to subscribe to a data service for a wide variety of records and there is no need to spend money on duplicate data. Certainly, no one with an internet connection is going to buy several county census indexes on CD to track down a couple of families, when they can do national searches online for a fraction of the cost.

On the other hand, if many of your nineteenth-century families lived in the same area or you are conducting a one-name study for a surname with a concentrated local distribution, it may well be more economical, and indeed more convenient, to purchase a CD or DVD set than to pay for every search result and image on a pay-per-view service. If you have not got easy internet access, or anyone interested in a whole town or village from the point of view of local or social history, having the census images on CD-ROM is much more convenient. It would be a very tedious business to download from the web all the images even for a single enumeration district.

CD-ROM is not necessarily doomed as a whole for genealogy — it remains a good way of distributing other types of digital material commercially, such as scans of directories and similar books — but it is now much less important for the census than it was, and it would be surprising to see many new products in this format.

17

USING THE CENSUS ON MICROFILM

The various websites that we've looked at in Chapters 6 to 15 have one thing in common – they are essentially designed to help you find individuals in the census. As we've seen, some of them do allow you to search by place or even by address, but the emphasis is very much on the search for a person or a family.

For most family historians, this is fine – generally speaking, we can usually find our ancestors using one website or another and we have the undeniable bonus of being able to download images of the original census pages to our own PCs. The advantages of searching online are manifold and, we hope, obvious to all, but it's also true to say that there are times when what you really need to do is to go back to the originals – or at least to a microfilm or microfiche copy of the originals.

Despite the extensive drive towards digitisation of the records, The National Archives (TNA) still provide access to microfilms of the censuses in its reading rooms at Kew (the films are no longer on open access but must be ordered) and many libraries and local record offices continue to do likewise. Similarly, the microfilms of the Scottish censuses are still available at the ScotlandsPeople Centre in Edinburgh. (It's worth noting here that the 1911 census returns for England, Wales and Scotland are only available online and not on microfilm or microfiche.)

There are no signs that this is likely to change in the foreseeable future, but for researchers who have come to family history since the 'digital revolution' took place, the process behind finding the returns for a particular property using microfilm may be unfamiliar and potentially confusing.

There's also a small but significant body of researchers who either cannot or will not use a PC. Of course, we would encourage them to think again – help with using computer technology is not hard to come by: classes run by local libraries or adult education groups such as the University of the Third Age (U3A) are available all around the UK and most of us have friends or relatives who might be willing to offer some basic assistance.

Finding aids

The biggest problem facing researchers in the long years of the pre-digitisation era was how to locate the returns for a specific place or address and the solution was to produce a vast array of finding aids. Staff at the Public Record Office (PRO) were for many years at the forefront of this venture, creating lists and indexes to hamlets, townships, chapelries, villages, towns and cities the length and breadth of the country.

For the cities and the larger towns, street indexes were produced identifying the precise location of a given address in the records, and many of these have been digitised and are now available online, and discussed on p. 155.

The first problem facing anyone compiling a place-name index is what to include and what not to include. After all, when you start to think about it, what actually constitutes a 'place'? If, for example, someone asked you where you were born, you could give a variety of answers. You could give the name of the actual hospital or give the name of the town in which it was situated. You could name the district within that town or if you were born in a rural area you might say the name of the hamlet or village, or possibly even the name of the nearby market town.

A separate set of finding aids was created for each of the census years and they are still available at Kew. You start by finding the name of the place that you're looking for in the alphabetical place-name index. The place-name indexes include the names of every Civil Parish, as well as the more significant hamlets, townships and chapelries.

Next to each place name you'll find the name and number of the relevant Registration District and the number of the sub-District. Using these numbers, you can then turn to the Reference Books, which are arranged numerically by Registration District and sub-District. These books will identify the microfilm which contains the census returns for the place that you're interested in.

The lists for 1841 work slightly differently – the number next to your place name is the page number in the Reference Book, not the number of the Registration District. But once you've found your place in the Reference Book, the process is pretty much the same as with the other census years.

Genuki has a searchable gazetteer for places in the 1891 census for England, Wales and the Isle of Man at <**www.genuki.org.uk/big/census_place.html**> which gives the relevant TNA piece number along with the LDS film number. You can also use TNA's own Discovery catalogue at <**discovery.nationalarchives.gov.uk/SearchUI**> to find places in England, Wales, the Isle of Man and the Channel Islands in each of the censuses from 1841 to 1911. Simply enter the place-name in the search box together with the word 'census' and the census year that you're interested in (i.e. 'Aldenham 1851 census' – without the quotes). This will give you TNA's reference for the document or documents which include the returns for that place.

This system works well for rural areas or for small towns. If, however, the address you're looking for is in a large town or a city, you'll need a more precise reference and for each of the most heavily populated districts in England and Wales a street index has been produced, listing all the streets, roads, avenues, places and terraces in alphabetical order. Each entry in the street indexes provides you with a range of folios within a particular piece number so that you can go straight to the relevant entry without having to wind through a whole microfilm.

Finding addresses in London can be particularly difficult. Boundary changes, renaming of streets, renumbering of houses and long streets which stray into more than one Registration District can all make your search that bit more complicated. A huge amount of work has been carried out by, first, the PRO and then TNA staff to help alleviate these problems, the result of which is a number of additional finding aids designed to help you trace that elusive London address. Again, these are available at Kew.

Similarly, paper finding aids were produced in Scotland to identify the correct microfilm, including street indexes for Edinburgh, Glasgow, Dundee and Aberdeen. The situation in Scotland is less complicated than in England and Wales as each parish has a unique registration district number which is repeated across each of the censuses. So, for example, the parish of Anstruther Easter in Fife has the reference 402 whether you're looking at the 1841 census, the 1901 census, or indeed the statutory birth, marriage and death registers and the Old Parish Registers. The full list of parishes and registration districts can be found on ScotlandsPeople at: <**www.gro-scotland.gov.uk/famrec/list-of-parishes-registration-districts.html**>.

In order to carry out an effective search of the census returns on microfilm, you need to have a pretty good idea of where your ancestors were living at the time of the census. There are a number of sources that you might use to get potential addresses for your ancestors: wills, newspaper reports, obituaries, electoral registers and trade directories can all prove useful, but by far the most important source is the birth, marriage and death certificates issued by the GROs of England and Wales, and Scotland.

Armed with a contemporary birth or death certificate, finding the census returns for the address shown on the certificate is a relatively straightforward matter. As we've seen, the two sets of records use exactly the same hierarchy, north and south of the border: so if a death was registered in the Watford Registration District, the address shown on the certificate will be found amongst the census returns for the Watford District. You might need to watch out for the occasional boundary change but generally speaking this direct correlation between the two sets of records works well. Addresses on English and Welsh marriage certificates are less useful – they tend to be less precise than those given on birth and death certificates and are often inaccurate or even invented! This is not the case in Scotland.

Libraries and county record offices will all have their own ways of accessing microfilms of the census returns for their areas. Some of them may use TNA or GRO(S) references, while others will have their own systems. You may find that your local record office has copies of the relevant street indexes or, alternatively, they may have produced their own.

Another option open to you is to use the worldwide network of Church of Latter-day Saints' Family History Centres. You can order a microfilm of any census return (including Scotland and Ireland) to view at your local Centre – details can be found on the FamilySearch website at: <**familysearch.org/locations/centerlocator**>.

While staff at the PRO in London and New Register House in Edinburgh were busy working on place-name and street indexes, members of family history societies up and down the country were embarking on the monumental task of creating surname indexes to the census returns. From the 1970s onwards, a huge amount of work was done by volunteers, producing indexes to some quite significant sections of the census. 1851 was the first year to be tackled in earnest, and long before the commercial census websites got in on the act, thousands of indexes had been published covering perhaps 75 per cent of the country. And it wasn't just 1851: family history societies and a whole host of dedicated individuals moved on to other census years as well. It's certainly true that some parts of the country were better covered than others, but there was something for every county and many counties had been fully indexed for certain years.

These surname indexes are still available to researchers today – mainly as printed booklets, on microfiche, on CD-ROM or even online. TNA and the ScotlandsPeople Centre have good collections, as does the Society of Genealogists in London. Libraries and local record offices are likely to have copies of the indexes for their own areas of interest and may even have unpublished manuscript or card indexes, which are only available in their own reading rooms.

The indexes were produced by hundreds of different local and family history societies. There was no central body to establish conventions for transcribing the returns or to impose rules on how to create indexes, so the published results can vary greatly from county to county and from index to index.

Having said that, the transcription and indexing are generally of a higher standard than we've come to expect from the various census websites – they were usually created by people who had a good local knowledge of the names and places and a personal interest in the area.

One of the advantages of using census returns on microfilm is that you get a better sense of the context of the records you're looking at than you do in an online environment. Rather than dropping you in on a particular page, the microfilm forces you to wind through the returns, viewing a whole range of pages on the way. By doing this, you become familiar with both the physical structure of the records and also with the geography of the area in which your ancestors were living.

While searching online should always be your first choice, it's important not to ignore the possibilities that the microfilm alternative can offer.

18

CITING CENSUS RECORDS

Throughout this book you will see mention of census references. Each individual page of the census records has a unique archival reference which should be used when referring to a particular entry. The reference reflects the way in which the documents are organised. When we consider the arrangement and structure of the census records we are really talking about two different things: the administrative hierarchy through which the returns were compiled (Registration Districts, Administrative Counties etc.) and the physical structure of the documents themselves.

A clear understanding of these concepts is important for researchers who want to keep accurate records of their census searches and, particularly, for those who wish to cite census records in their family tree software, on a website or perhaps in a printed, published work.

England and Wales

The records for England and Wales were arranged by the General Register Office (GRO) into Registration Districts, sub-Districts (the same hierarchy used for the registration of births, deaths and marriages) and finally Enumeration Districts. There was never an exact match between this system and the ancient structure of counties, hundreds and parishes. A large parish could extend over several enumeration districts or alternatively a single enumeration district could include the returns for two or more small parishes. Also, many Registration Districts included parishes situated in more than one county, which gave rise to the rather confusing term 'Registration County' as opposed to the traditional 'Administrative County'.

Entries in the census returns for England and Wales (including those for the Channel Islands and the Isle of Man) should be referenced in line with the guide to 'Citing documents in The National Archives', available online at: <**www.nationalarchives.gov.uk/records/citing-documents.htm**>.

Essentially, all documents held by The National Archives (TNA) have a three-part reference which uniquely identifies them, comprising a department code, a series number and a piece number. The first of these relates to the government department which created, maintained or inherited the records, and in the case of the census returns this was the Home Office (HO) for 1841 and 1851 and the Registrar General (RG) for all the others. The department and series references for each of the 'open' census years are as follows:

1841	HO 107 (pieces 1–1465)
1851	HO 107 (pieces 1466–2531)
1861	RG 9
1871	RG 10
1881	RG 11
1891	RG 12
1901	RG 13
1911	RG 14 and RG 78

The census enumeration books were collected into individually numbered 'pieces', each covering a particular area, and each with a unique piece number. Before the census records were microfilmed, they were stamped with 'folio' numbers. It's important to note that each folio number relates to two pages: the numbers were stamped on the top right of every second page – this page is often referred to as 'recto' (Latin for 'right') – but the folio number also relates to the following page (the other side of the same piece of paper) which is referred to as 'verso' (i.e. 'reverse'). This is all much easier to understand when you imagine the sheets as pages in the original summary books.

Folio numbers run sequentially through an entire piece, each of which usually covers several enumeration districts. Within each enumeration district, each page has a unique page number.

As an example of how this works in practice, the full TNA archival reference for the page recording Charles Darwin's family in the 1881 census is: RG 11/855, folio 83, page 1. In this case:

- RG 11 indicates that the record is for the year 1881.

- The number 855 identifies the particular piece number within the Record Series RG 11. TNA's *Discovery* catalogue tells us that RG 11/855 covers the census returns for the parishes of Cudham and Downe.

- The folio number (83) and page number (1) uniquely identify the specific page on which the entry for the Darwin family is recorded.

We could also use the GRO's own administrative hierarchy and say that the entry is in the Bromley registration district, the Bromley sub-district and is on page 1 of enumeration district number 5.

The 1841 census

The 1841 census returns are arranged in a different way to the other censuses. The records were originally taken using the then new administrative hierarchy of registration districts, sub-districts and enumeration districts, but before the census data was abstracted by the Census Office clerks, the returns were re-arranged into the traditional English administrative units of counties, hundreds and parishes. This process was carried out in order to enable comparison with the data from the earlier, pre-1841 censuses and must have involved some considerable additional work.

The re-arrangement of the 1841 records is well illustrated with reference to the returns for the Dorset parish of Toller Porcorum. The parish, which was part of the Dorchester and Cerne registration district and the Maiden Newton sub-district, was, at the time of the 1841 census, divided into two enumeration districts, numbered 8 and 9 in the original returns. However, the two enumeration districts happened to be in two different hundreds: district 8 was part of Tollerford hundred while district 9 came under Beaminster Forum and Redhone. The two parts of Toller Porcorum are therefore separated administratively in the 1841 census and this is reflected in their archival references:

- Enumeration district 8   HO 107/286/12
- Enumeration district 9   HO 107/282/2

As an example, the full archival reference number for the entry relating to the family of William and Susanna Groves of Toller Porcorum is HO 107/286/12, folio 5, page 4. As with the other census years, the record series (HO 107) and piece number (286) are present but there is also an additional number here (12) which is known as a 'book' number. The folio numbers run sequentially through each census book.

The 1911 census

As we have seen, the 1911 census returns comprise two separate sets of documents: the householders' schedules and the enumerators' summary books (ESBs). The two sets of records have a one-to-one relationship in that each ESB has a corresponding set of schedules.

The link between the two sets of documents is through a unique three-part reference number which is made up of the following items:

- registration district number;
- registration sub-district number;
- enumeration district number.

However, these numbers do not form part of TNA's archival reference. Instead, each individual schedule can be cited using a different three part reference consisting of the series number (RG 14), the piece number, and the handwritten schedule number. For example, the 1911 census entry for the Annal family has the reference RG 14/3823, schedule 264. In the case of institutional returns, the reference will also include a page number.

The ESBs are in a separate record series (RG 78).

As mentioned in Chapter 3, a significant number of boundary changes were made prior to the taking of the 1911 census with the aim that 'no Enumeration Districts should comprise parts of two or more Administrative Areas'.

Scotland

The GRO Scotland references to census returns are very straightforward, consisting of just three parts: the registration district number (often including a suffix), the enumeration district number (occasionally including a suffix) and the page number. This referencing system applies equally across all the Scottish censuses from 1841 to 1911.

Ireland

References for the 1911 census of Ireland are quite different to those for England, Wales and Scotland. In fact on the NAI census site no document references are explicitly given: there are none in the household listings (see Fig. 15.3, p. 294) and neither the original microfilms nor the digital images made from them contain any reference information like that found on the microfilms for England and Wales.

The way in which the NAI refers to 1911 census documents is to cite the census year, county, District Electoral Division (DED) number and townland number. Lists of the latter numbers are available in printed form at the NAI itself, but they do not seem to be available online. However, they can be found on the forms themselves and can be read off the digital images. Specifically they are found on the first page of Form N, the enumerator's schedule. At the top right of the form are details of the townland, below which is an oval with a thick bar across it. The number in the left half of the oval is the DED, the number in the right half, after the word 'File', the townland number. So the reference for the household of Edward O'Brien in Ballybrack, shown in Figure 18.1, would be 1911, Dublin 93/12 (Dublin here is the county in which Ballybrack is located).

The problem with this, though, is that the census sites can only be searched on the names of DEDs, not the numbers. And while there seem to be a few indexes online which match up DED numbers and names — FamilySearch, for example, has an 'Ireland 1901 Antrim Census Townland Index' at **<familysearch.org/learn/wiki/en/ Ireland_1901_Antrim_Census_Townland_Index>** — there is no complete coverage that we are aware of.

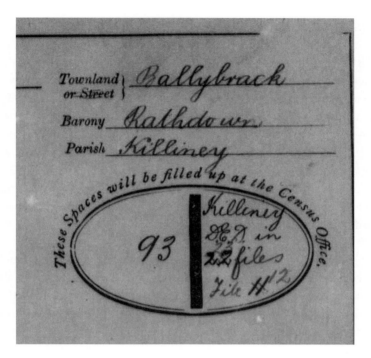

Figure 18.1 Reference from Form N in the Irish census.

An alternative is to use the web address of the household schedule – for the household of Edward O'Brien this would be <**www.census.nationalarchives. ie/reels/nai000239889**> for the image or <**www.census.nationalarchives. ie/pages/1911/Dublin/Killiney/Ballybrack/96653**> for the transcription. The problem with this is that the web address will cease to be valid when the NAI decide to redesign their system. It may still be valid in five or ten years, but it's unlikely still to be so in 50 years, while the reference taken from the document itself will always be correct. However, even if the NAI reorganises the entire website, part of the URL — 1911/Dublin/Killiney/Ballybrack — gives you year, county, DED, townland/street, which, together with a personal name, will always be enough to identify a particular census record.

At present, unfortunately, there is no way to use the county and numerical reference to check a source in the online census – the only thing you can do is conduct your own search for the person using the location information from the URL. It would be nice to see the full reference included in the household listing and searchable.

Census references and genealogy software

The information above shows you how to establish the reference for a particular entry in a census. If you are using a piece of genealogy software to record your family history research, though, it is also important to consider how and where you are going to record this information.

One of the reasons why this is not a straightforward matter is that experts have a variety of views on how it should be done, and while there are several standard approaches, there is no *one* standard. But in spite of their differences the main genealogy programs all take broadly the same approach, and all have the same three types of record for recording source information.

1. Source — often this will be a primary historical document, such as a census record or a birth certificate, but an online index is also a source, even if a secondary one. Genealogy programs often call this a 'master source' because it may be the origin of several different pieces of information about various individuals in your family tree.

2. Repository — this is where the source is to be found. It's obvious enough how this applies to unique manuscript documents, but even with a published book, it is useful to record the library in which you consulted a copy. An online data service is also a form of repository, though with a website like FreeCen, for example, which consists entirely of a single database, the distinction between a master source and a repository is perhaps less clear.

3. Source citation or source detail — once you have defined a source then every time you add to your family tree a fact which comes from that source, you create a source citation. This gives detailed information about where in the source the particular piece of information is to be found, and it needs to be sufficiently precise for someone to be able to check easily — in the case of the census, a full reference. Genealogy software always has a field to record the original text from the source, and some programs also let you include a digital image of the relevant page.

Of course, you almost certainly won't be looking at the *original* census records but at images of them on microfilm or online. For that reason, some people prefer to treat the library or data service as the source of the information rather than the relevant national archive. We prefer to regard microfilm and online images as forms of publication, and all programs should have a field for publication information. One good reason for this is that the original census records are unlikely to be moved from their present homes and their references are allocated by these archives, but a particular set of census images may at some point cease to be available at the location you used. However, this only applies to the images of the original records. Where a website (or indeed a published book) has just an index to all or part of a census, the national archive is no longer the source of the information — the book or website is the source and will need to be cited in a quite different way.

One difficulty which arises with census records which is not the case for, say, a birth certificate or a will, is that there are some questions with no obviously correct answers: is the entirety of records for a particular census a single source, or is the source an individual piece, or enumeration book? Given that all the entries in an enumeration book come from individual household schedules (which are still preserved for the 1911 census of England and Wales and both the remaining Irish censuses) shouldn't we treat each household as a single record?

Now, unless you are an archivist, you will undoubtedly not care about the philosophical aspect of these questions, but there is a practical issue to consider in citing census records as sources of information in your family tree. The three main approaches are detailed below.

A. One source per household

This has the advantage of giving every household its own unique source entry, but with the disadvantage that you have to create a new source record in your database for every new family you locate, and you will end up with a large number of sources. If you're going to fill in the 'date of source' field, then this approach commits you to typing the census date every time you add a new census entry to your list of sources! However, it has the advantage that each source is so specific that you do not need to give much further detail.

Master Source
> **Title:** England and Wales, 1881 Census, household of Thomas
> Hardy, Wandsworth, London
> **Repository:** The National Archives
> **Source reference (or 'call number'):** RG11/659, folio 56, page 43
> **Publication:** *online service or microfilm you consulted*

Source Citation
> **Where within source:** *not needed*

B. One source per piece

This has the advantage of grouping all the households from a single
area within a single source. It can be a useful approach if you have a lot
of families from the same small area.

Master Source
> **Title:** England and Wales, 1881 Census, Wandsworth, London
> **Repository:** The National Archives
> **Source reference:** RG11/659
> **Publication:** *online service or microfilm you consulted*

Source Citation
> **Where within source:** RG11/659, folio 56, page 43

C. One source per census

If you treat an entire census as a source, then you only need to create a
record for that census once. A slight disadvantage is that the place of
residence is not in the title of the source record, only in the census
address, which would be cited in the detail. Also, if you use more than
one data service, you won't be able to use the publication field to record
which service you used unless you create separate sources for each data
service. However, the source citation will have a field for notes, which
can be used for this purpose.

Master Source
> **Title:** England and Wales, 1881 Census
> **Repository:** The National Archives
> **Source reference:** RG11

Source Citation
    Where within source: RG11/659, folio 56, page 43

In each of the three cases, you would want to add to the source citation the full address and possibly the text of the record. In fact, it does not really matter much which approach you take, as long as you are consistent in how you document sources and include the full reference to the location of the particular entry. If you are just starting to use census records or a new piece of software, it is certainly best to think about this before you start entering lots of census-derived information, as it can be a time-consuming job to change the format of all your census citations at a later date.

If you are consulting an online (or published) index and entering information from it without being able to check it against the original images, then, taking Thomas Hardy in the 1881 census as an example, the source will be:

Master Source
    Title: England and Wales, 1881 Census index
    Repository: FamilySearch
    Source reference: familysearch.org/search/collection/1321821
Source Citation
    Where within source: familysearch.org/pal:/MM9.1.1/XQQ7-TKR
    Date accessed: *whenever*

The reason for including the 'date accessed' here is that online indexes change (for corrections, new data, etc.) and if the date is a significantly long time ago, anyone looking at the reference needn't think the information is wrong just because it can't now be found, though of course they would need to find a new source for it to be sure. Giving the access date is less important for references to images of original documents, but can still be a useful way of keeping track of the progress of your research. In this particular index, FamilySearch does in fact give the full TNA reference, so it would be worth noting it in the Notes field.

Incidentally, one thing missing from all these is the schedule number, which tells you exactly which entry on the page is the source, but no one seems to bother about this, except in the case of the 1911 census for England and Wales where each schedule number refers to a single document. As we have suggested above in the discussion of Irish census references, it can be a good idea to add the schedule number in the source detail for an Irish census record, as this will help to identify the correct household in a rural townland where there may well be no street addresses given.

One thing we've done in the above examples might be thought a bad idea from an information management perspective: citing the class mark or piece number twice opens up the possibility of inconsistency. But in our view, this is outweighed by the benefit of having the full reference in a single field, even if part of it is repeated elsewhere.

Because each genealogy program has its own set of options and dialog boxes for creating sources and attaching them to individual genealogical facts, it is well worth spending some time familiarising yourself with your own program's facilities in this area before you start adding multiple census sources.

19

CENSUS DOCUMENTATION

The documents which we, as family historians, think of as the census records – i.e. the enumerators' summary books and the householders' schedules from which they were compiled – are in fact merely a means to an end. The ultimate aim of each successive census was to produce a detailed report which would examine the findings of the census and, by comparison with the results of previous censuses, help to shape future government policy.

The reports included detailed statistical breakdowns of the population arranged county-by-county and parish-by-parish, and in the pre-digital age, these lists were frequently used as census-finding aids. The shelves of the former Public Record Office (PRO) reading rooms at Portugal Street, Chancery Lane and the Family Records Centre were full of these printed lists, annotated by hand with the relevant archival piece numbers.

Histpop.org

All of the surviving census reports, together with a vast array of supplementary material, are freely available online as part of a remarkable project known as The Online Historical Population Reports collection – or Histpop for short. The collection (hosted by the UK Data Archive at the University of Essex) brings together a wide range of official documentation relating to the censuses, including:

- the published census reports for England, Wales, Scotland and Ireland from 1801 to 1937;
- the full texts of the Acts of Parliament relating to each of the censuses;

- a selection of documents from The National Archives (TNA), including samples of enumerators' summary books, householders' schedules, instructions to the enumerators and Census Office clerks, maps and correspondence relating to the taking of the census.

Much of this material is of huge potential interest to family historians but it's fair to say that it has generally been underused over the years. Serious researchers would be well advised to investigate the resources available on Histpop – it will soon become apparent how the resources used to study population history can aid their own research. The instructions issued to the enumerators and clerks will explain what they were actually supposed to be doing which, along with the various Acts of Parliament and the General Register Office's (GRO) own correspondence files, can help us to interpret the answers that our ancestors gave to the questions they were asked in the census. The census reports themselves can provide invaluable background to our ancestors' lives, illustrating the changing world in which they lived.

The Histpop website <**www.histpop.org**> is relatively easy to use. From the home page, you can choose to browse the resources by category or search the website by keyword. The 'Census' category contains the main reports and is sub-divided by census year starting with 1801 (for which there are just three available documents) and moving on through the decades. Examples of enumerators' books from various census years can be found by selecting the 'TNA Enumerators' Books' section while the 'TNA Census – Other' category provides access to a variety of documents relating to the taking of the census, including samples of original householders' schedules and copies of letters from the Registrar General to registrars and enumerators clarifying their duties and responsibilities.

Histpop also features more than 100 essays written by Eddie Higgs and Matthew Woollard, two of the UK's leading experts on the subject of population history. Their general essays with titles such as 'What is a census?' and 'Introduction to administrative units of England and Wales' are clearly of interest to family historians while more specialised subjects like 'Migration', 'Armed forces' and 'Institutions' are essential reading for the serious researcher. There is also an excellent series of biographies covering the key players in the story of the UK census; Rickman, Lister, Graham, Farr et al.

Occupations

Right from the start, the question of employment was at the very heart of the census. The 1801 census asked about the numbers of people 'chiefly employed' in each of three broad categories; 'agriculture', 'trade, manufacture and handicraft', and 'other', and as the years progressed, the analysis of our ancestors' occupations in the census became more and more sophisticated.

Classification of individual occupations began to be taken seriously from 1841. One of the duties performed by the Census Office clerks was to categorise each occupation and it was therefore important that they were able to understand what was meant by the entries made by the householders on their schedules. The enumerators (and indeed the householders themselves) were given instructions on how to enter the details, but in order to enable the clerks to accurately assign each occupation to a particular category, the GRO produced a set of 'Instructions' listing every conceivable occupation and dividing them into 'Classes', 'Orders' and 'sub-Orders'. This extensive work, entitled the 'Instructions to the Clerks Employed in Classifying the Occupations and Ages of the People', was first produced for use with the 1861 census. The 'Instructions' underwent a number of revisions and improvements, with the final edition being published in 1911.

There is plenty of evidence in the census enumerators' books themselves that the clerks made good use of the 'Instructions'. The occupation columns are full of annotations made by the Census Office clerks as they went about their work assigning the occupations to the correct classification. These annotations largely consist of underlinings or other marks used to indicate that the occupation was itself a category, or abbreviations such as 'Rail.' for Railway, 'Gard.' for Gardener, 'Port.' for Porter, 'Dom' for Domestic or 'Ag.' for Agricultural Labourer, but of most interest to us are the coded numbers. These are usually in the form O20/3 and refer to the Order and sub-Order to which the occupation was to be assigned — i.e. Order 20 sub-Order 3.

The art of classifying and defining occupational terms (at least as far as official government publications were concerned) reached its pinnacle with the publication in 1927 of the extraordinarily detailed 'Dictionary of Occupational Terms'. The Dictionary comprised references to (and

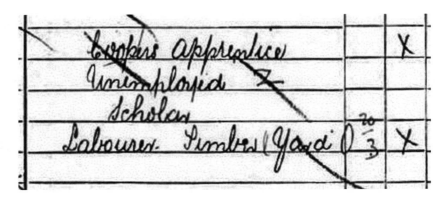

Figure 19.1 Detail of a page from the 1891 census showing the Occupational code O20/3. TNA reference RG 12/1081, folio 113, page 22.

ORDER 20.

81

309. HAY, STRAW (NOT PLAIT), CHAFF—CUTTER, DEALER.
 Fodder Dealer. Hay Compresser. Straw Joiner. Straw Mat Maker.
310. THATCHER.
 Rick Crowder. Straw Maker. Moss Thatcher.

SUB-ORDER 3.—IN WOOD AND BARK.

311. TIMBER, WOOD—MERCHANT, DEALER.

Bavin Maker.	Lancewood Spar Dealer.	Timber Measurer.
Bent Timber Manufacturer.	Mahogany Dealer.	„ Preserver.
Boxwood—Dealer, Worker.	Mahogany Cutter.	„ Squarer.
Chip Breaker, Dealer, Merchant.	Pimp (Firewood) Maker.	„ Yard Labourer.
Coppice Dealer.	Pole Dealer.	Underwood Dealer.

Figure 19.2 Extract from the 'Instructions to the Clerks' (1881) showing Order 20, sub-Order 3 which includes 'Timber Yard Labourer'. TNA reference RG 27/5, page 81.

definitions of) nearly 17,000 occupations and was arranged both alphabetically and (as it was based on the classifications used in the 1921 census) by occupational code. The work is currently out of print but a CD version was produced by the Open University in 1998 and a copy is available in TNA's library.

The National Archives

While the most important documentation held by TNA (particularly the material in RG 27) has been fully digitised and made available online on the Histpop website, the coverage of TNA's 'supplementary' holdings is by no means comprehensive. Further records can be found in a number of TNA record series, with the following being particularly worthy of further investigation:

RG 19   General Register Office (GRO): Census Returns: Correspondence and Papers

Correspondence and papers of the Registrar General and the Local Government Board on Censuses taken under the Census Acts 1900, 1910 and 1920, including information on local, special, imperial and foreign censuses. The earlier papers in this series consist mainly of correspondence between the Board and the Registrar General. Three files are of Local Government Board papers and include correspondence with the Registrar General and the London County Council. The later papers concern censuses taken under the 1920 Act, a permanent enactment requiring the Registrar General to make arrangements for taking a census in accordance with the Act, an Order in Council and the regulations made by the Minister of Health.

RG 20   GRO and Office of Population Censuses and Surveys, Establishment and Accounts Division: Correspondence and Papers

A selected sample of General Register Office correspondence with the Treasury, Ministry of Health and other Government Departments, the Industrial Court, Civil Service Clerical Association, local Registrars of Births, Deaths and Marriages and individuals. The material relates to establishment and personnel matters, arbitration and awards for search officers, cost of services rendered to other government departments, GRO estimates and certain matters concerning the indexes of birth, death and marriage registers, including the evacuation of registers and indexes from London, 1939 to 1942. Other files concern injuries received by enumerators during the 1931 census period, also a proposal to remove the General Register Office from Somerset House.

The series also includes account books, 1836 to 1854, and certain papers, 1920 to 1946, kept by R. J. R. Farrow, Deputy Registrar General (1942–1946), also staff organisation charts, mainly from 1947.

RG 26   Office of Population Censuses and Surveys and predecessors, Statistical Branch: Population and Medical Statistics: Correspondence and Papers

Correspondence of the Statistical Branch with the Ministry of Health and other government departments, the Registrars General of Scotland and Northern Ireland; universities, medical bodies, international organisations and the US Bureau of Statistics; local authorities, Registration Officers and Medical Officers of Health.

Subjects covered include national and international policy on medical, demographic and housing statistics; administrative areas and revision of maps for census and National Registration purposes; the government evacuation scheme of 1939 and the reorganisation of the Statistical Division during the national emergency; the issue of instructions to local registration authorities and methods of data tabulation. Some files include reports by experts on medical statistical matters, and others deal with the activities of League of Nations committees working in the field.

RG 27   General Register Office: Census Returns: Specimens of Forms and Documents

A manuscript statement of the practical means planned by the first Registrar General and adopted for taking the 1841 Census was prepared entitled 'History of the Census of 1841'. The volume sets out the preparatory steps, instructions and layout of the forms. Separate collections have been made for other censuses of England and Wales from 1861 to 1991. Those for the 1921 and 1931 censuses include forms and instructions used in machine and tabulation processes.*

RG 29   General Register Office: Letter Books

This series contains General Register Office letterbooks, including the Registrar General's private letter book, Treasury letters, correspondence relating to the 1891 Census and Local Government Board volumes.

RG 30   General Register Office: Census Reports and Population Abstracts

This series contains copies of the printed general reports of the censuses from 1861 to 1981 inclusive, of the enumeration abstract from the census of 1841 and of one per cent sample tables from the census of 1951. The general reports and abstracts contain various population data covering such aspects as age, sex, marital condition, birth place, occupation and area. The later volumes cover a wider range and for more detailed statistics reference should be made to the reports which deal with specific subjects. Also included is a manuscript volume of notes and workings estimating pre-census population prepared by John Rickman, the results of which were published in the report on the 1841 census.

The General Report of each census provides a full description of the particular enumeration, new developments and observations of the results. A major development was the introduction of mechanisation in the 1911 census. The General Reports of the censuses of 1901 and 1911 contain a full account of the scope of the censuses taken up to those dates and of the legislation under which they were held.

RG 41   General Register Office: Circulars

The circulars run from 1909 and mainly relate to instructions issued by the General Register Office concerning the duties imposed, largely under various acts and measures, on officers of the registration service in England and Wales, and also information to Medical Officers of Health, medical practitioners, coroners, local authorities and persons responsible for the solemnisation of marriages in certain religious denominations. The first piece contains documents relating to vital and health statistics for the period 1910-1940.

RG 60   General Register Office: Population Estimates

Volume containing a detailed analysis of population estimates for England and Wales for the years 1891 to 1929. The totals are broken down by county, towns, metropolitan boroughs and municipal counties, with intercensal increases, quarterly increases or decreases and the factors for intercensal populations. Information is also included on age (1-65, 65 and over) and male/female populations.

* Specimen forms for the 1851 census were missing at the time the documents were transferred to TNA. Copies can be found amongst a collection of Home Office documents relating to the census and boasting the rather vague catalogue description, 'Census: general' (HO 45/3579).

Other sources

Another website which brings together a range of useful information for family historians and other users of the census, including 'maps, statistical trends and historical descriptions' is A Vision of Britain Through Time <**www.visionofbritain.org.uk**>. The website can be searched by place, leading the user to information about the location such as maps, extracts from gazetteers, historical photographs and administrative descriptions as well as links to other local resources.

Access is also provided to the full text of the UK census reports from 1801 to 1971 and to a wide range of historical maps of Britain.

For those who are interested in the results of more recent censuses, the Office for National Statistics has some very useful data on their website including sample forms from each of the censuses at <**www.ons.gov.uk/ ons/search/index.html?newquery=census**>. The General Register Office for Scotland website has information about the 1991, 2001 and 2011 censuses of Scotland at <**www.gro-scotland.gov.uk/census**> while the Northern Ireland Statistics and Research Agency provides access to information about all the censuses carried out in that part of the UK since 1926 at <**www.nisra.gov.uk/Census/previous-census-statistics. html**>.

Finally, CALLS-HUB (the Census & Administrative data LongitudinaL Studies Hub) <**www.calls.ac.uk**> is an academic resource which aims to 'facilitate and encourage the use of multiple longitudinal studies for UK-wide research' by linking data from recent censuses for England, Wales, Scotland and Northern Ireland. The website provides samples of census forms from 1971 to 2011.

Appendices

APPENDIX A: COMPARISON OF DATA SERVICES

The obvious question which arises from the survey of commercial census data sites in Chapters 8 to 14 is: which one should you choose? Even if you are mainly using free sites, these are unlikely to offer census images for the foreseeable future, so they can provide no verification for the entries in their indexes.

Unfortunately, there is no simple answer to this question, and even if there was at the time of writing, there can be no guarantee it would still hold by the time you are reading this. All the commercial census sites are extending their search facilities, correcting errors found in the data, improving image quality and viewing facilities, all in an effort to keep existing customers happy and get new ones.

Also, of course, your own requirements and budget will play a role in making one service preferable to another. If you can access one service free of charge at a public library, for example, any shortcomings of that service may be relatively insignificant compared to the savings involved.

However, we here offer a set of comparison tables to provide a basis for comparison, looking at:

- coverage;
- price and payment options;
- search options;
- image quality.

Quality of indexing is another issue which ought to be included but for the reasons explained in Chapter 5 it is impossible to give a fair overall assessment of accuracy for any of the commercial sites.

Coverage

Table A.1 shows which census years and regions the commercial services offer, along with FamilySearch.

	England and Wales	Scotland	Notes
Ancestry	1841–1911	1841–1901	No images for Scotland NAI indexes for Irish censuses
Findmypast	1841–1911	1841–1901	No images for Scotland
1911census	1911		
Genes Reunited	1841–1911	1841–1901	Household schedules only for 1911; no images for Scotland
1901censusonline	1841–1911		Enumerators' schedules only for 1911
TheGenealogist	1841–1911	1851 partial	No images for Scotland
RootsUK	1841–1901		
UK census online	1841–1911		
Origins	1841, 1861–1901		1851 in preparation
ScotlandsPeople		1841–1911	1881: two different indexes
MyHeritage	1841–1901		
FamilySearch	1841–1911	1841–1891	No images

Table A.1 Coverage of commercial services.

Charges

Full details of the charges for the various sites will be found in the chapters on the commercial data services. Tables A.2 and A.3 summarise for each site the subscription and pay-per-view charges respectively. Subscriptions which do not include access to census records have been omitted.

Note that many of these subscriptions are automatically renewed unless you cancel. We have given current information in the coverage of the individual sites, but it is advisable to check before signing up.

Subscriptions

Site	Subscription	1 Month	3 Months	6 Months	Year	Notes
Ancestry	UK Essentials	£10.95			£83.40	
	UK Premium	£12.95			£107.40	
	Worldwide	£18.95			£155.40	
Findmypast	Britain Full	£9.95			£99.50	Different rates on overseas sites
	Worldwide	£12.95			£129.50	
Genes Reunited		£19.95		£49.95	£79.95	
TheGenealogist	Starter		£14.95	£28.95	£54.95	1911 census not included
	Gold		£24.95	£44.95	£78.95	
	Diamond				£119.95	1911 census included
UK Census Online	Census	£14.95	£24.95	£39.95	£54.95	
	Census+BMD	£19.95	£29.95	£49.95	£69.95	
Origins	British Origins	£9.50				
	Total Access	£10.50			£55.00	
MyHeritage					£90.00	

Table A.2 Subscription charges for the commercial data services (prices correct June 2014).

Pay-per-view

	Pay-per-view	Unit cost	Validity	Search cost	Transcript cost	Image Cost	Notes
Ancestry	£6.95 for 12 record views	58p	14 days			58p	
Findmypast & 1911census	£6.95 for 20 credits	35p	90 days	35p		35p	
	£24.95 for 280 credits	9p	1 year	9p		9p	
TheGenealogist	£14.95 for 75 credits	20p		20p		60p	Advanced searches 2 or 3 credits
RootsUK	£5 for 100 credits	5p		advanced 25p		25p	
	£14.95 for 400 credits	3.7p		advanced 19p		19p	
GenesReunited	£5 for 50 credits	10p	30 days	50p		50p	
	£17.95 for 200	9p	90 days	45p		45p	
1901censusonline	£5 for 500 credits	1p	7 days		50p	75p	
ScotlandsPeople	£7 for 30 credits (90 days)	23p	1 year	23p		£1.15	Each page of results charged

Table A.3 Pay-per-view charges for the commercial data services (prices correct June 2014).

Search options

Table A.4 summarises the search options for all the commercial sites, as well as The National Archives of Ireland. The complex variety of search options for the different censuses on FamilySearch are shown in Table 7.1, p. 162.

Where a site has an advanced search, it is the details for this that have been given, in preference to the standard search.

In principle, of course, the more search fields the better, because you then have more options for finding someone if a basic search on name, age and residence doesn't do the trick. But some of these fields are more useful than others. Lack of an occupation search field is not really a significant limitation; lack of a birth place field is a considerable drawback.

However, a 'Keywords' field ought to make it possible to search for any text in any field which does not have its own box on the form, and certainly should find occupations and birth places. If you enter more than one word in a keyword search, though, you may not get any hits if the keywords are not found in the same field, e.g. you may not be able to use the 'Keywords' field to search for both occupation and birth place at the same time. Because of the huge range of possible options and combinations provided by a 'Keywords' field, we have not been able to carry out exhaustive tests.

	Ancestry	Findmypast	Genes Reunited	1901census		TheGenealogist	RootsUK	UK Census Online	Origins	Scotlands People	MyHeritage	National Archives of Ireland
	Advanced	Advanced	Standard	1901 advanced	Other years standard	Master	Advanced	Standard	Standard	Advanced	Advanced	Standard
Name fields	2	2	2	3		2	2	2	2	2	2	2
Surname variants	Custom	NameX	Custom	Wildcards	Wildcards	Custom		Custom and Wildcards	NameX or wildcards	8 options		Wildcards
Age	Year	Year	Year	Year	Year	Year	Age or year	Year	Age range	Age range	Date	Age
Birth place	✓	3 fields	✓	✓	Place keywords				✓			County
Residence	1 field	5 fields	4 fields	10 fields	Place keywords	County	County		County and parish	County and district	1 field	3 fields
Keyword	✓	✓	✓	✓		✓		✓			✓	
Gender	✓	✓		✓		✓				✓	✓	✓
Marital status		✓										✓
Relation to head		✓				✓						✓
Occupation		✓					✓					✓
Household members	Unlimited	1				Separate family search				1 additional forename	Unlimited	
Address search	Street name in keyword field *may* work	Address fields		Separate address search	Separate address search	Separate address search						Browse
Reference	Reference fields	Separate reference search								Free-form query text		

Table A.4 Comparison of search facilities.

Image quality

The importance of image quality is discussed in Chapter 5, and Table A.5 compares key features of the image quality for the commercial census sites which have been involved in digitisation. All the other sites take their images from one of these — details will be found in the relevant chapter.

Neither colour depth nor resolution is straightforward to specify here, since both are based on downloading sample images from the sites. In the case of the images in PDF format, the exact resolution is not possible to obtain with great accuracy as there is no way to ensure that an image extracted from a PDF is the same resolution as the one that was converted to PDF. However, visual inspection suggests this is broadly correct.

In the case of JPEG images, there are visible differences in compression levels between the sites. Also, the same original image available on related sites may be offered at a different level of compression on each. Unfortunately, it has been impossible to quantify compression levels or be sure that they apply equally across a whole census.

We cannot promise that we have not overlooked some black-and-white images on a mainly greyscale site or vice versa.

Not listed are the images for the 1911 census — these are high-resolution (at least 300 dpi) colour images in JPEG format on all sites.

	Format	Colour depth	Typical resolution (estimated)
Ancestry	JPEG	Greyscale A few colour images for 1841	300 dpi
Findmypast	JPEG	Greyscale 1871 black-and-white	300 dpi
Origins	JPEG	Greyscale 1871 black-and-white	300 dpi
TheGenealogist	PDF	1841, 1851, greyscale Others black-and-white with some greyscale	200 dpi
ScotlandsPeople	TIFF	Black-and-white	200 dpi

Table A.5 Image quality comparison.

APPENDIX B: LIST OF UK CENSUS DATES

This list is partly based on a list of census dates published on **Histpop.org <www.histpop.org/ohpr/servlet/View?path=Browse/ Essays%20%28by%20kind%29&active=yes&mno=2108>.**

Year	Date	Day	Notes
England, Wales and Scotland			
1801	10 March	Monday	Details of individuals not recorded.
1811	27 May	Monday	Details of individuals not recorded.
1821	28 May	Monday	Details of individuals not recorded.
1831	30 May	Monday	Details of individuals not recorded.
1841	6 June	Sunday	
1851	30 March	Sunday	
1861	7 April	Sunday	
1871	2 April	Sunday	
1881	3 April	Sunday	
1891	5 April	Sunday	
1901	31 March	Sunday	
1911	2 April	Sunday	
1921	19 June	Sunday	Originally scheduled for Sunday 24 April.
1931	26 April	Sunday	Returns for England and Wales have not survived.
1939	29 September	Friday	National Registration.
1951	8 April	Sunday	
1961	23 April	Sunday	
1966	24 April	Sunday	
1971	25 April	Sunday	
1981	5 April	Sunday	

Year	Date	Day	Notes
1991	21 April	Sunday	
2001	29 April	Sunday	
2011	27 March	Sunday	
Ireland			
1813	1 May	Saturday	Not completed in one day. Returns have not survived.
1821	28 May	Monday	Not completed in one day. Returns have not survived.[1]
1831	----	----	Taken on various dates. Returns have not survived.
1841	6 June	Sunday	Returns have not survived.
1851	30 March	Sunday	Returns have not survived.
1861	7 April	Sunday	Returns have not survived.[2]
1871	2 April	Sunday	Returns have not survived.
1881	3 April	Sunday	Returns have not survived.
1891	5 April	Sunday	Returns have not survived.
1901	31 March	Sunday	
1911	2 April	Sunday	
1921	----	----	Cancelled – originally scheduled for Sunday 24 April.
Northern Ireland			
1926	18 April	Sunday	Returns have not survived.
1937	28 February	Sunday	
1939	29 September	Friday	National Registration.
1951	8 April	Sunday	
1961	23 April	Sunday	
1966	24 April	Sunday	
1971	25 April	Sunday	
1981	5 April	Sunday	
1991	21 April	Sunday	
2001	29 April	Sunday	
2011	27 March	Sunday	

1 The Irish census returns for the years 1821, 1831, 1841 and 1851 were destroyed by fire in 1922. The returns for a few parishes survive for each of these years and are held by The National Archives of Ireland.

2 The Irish census returns for the years 1861, 1871, 1881 and 1891 were destroyed by the government. Virtually nothing survives.

READING AND WEBSITES

SELECTED READING

Colin R. Chapman, *Pre-1841 Censuses and Population Listings in the British Isles* (2nd edn, 1991)

E. Margaret Crawford, *Counting the People. A survey of the Irish Censuses, 1813-1911* (2003)

Jeremy Gibson and Elizabeth Hampson, *Census Returns 1841-1891 in Microform: A Directory to Local Holdings in Great Britain* (6th edn, 2001)

Jeremy Gibson and Mervyn Medlycott, *Local Census Listings: 1522-1930* (3rd edn, 1997)

Jeremy Gibson and Elizabeth Hampson, *Marriage, Census and Other Indexes for Family Historians* (8th edn, 2000)

Edward Higgs, *Making Sense of the Census* – Revisited (2005)

Edward Higgs, *Life, Death and Statistics* (2004)

Jill Liddington, *Vanishing for the Vote* (2014)

Susan Lumas, *Making Use of the Census* (2004)

Muriel Nissel, *People Count: A History of the General Register Office* (1997)

USEFUL WEBSITES

Histpop – The Online Historical Population Reports Website

Everything you need to know about the background to, and history of, the UK's census returns. <**www.histpop.org.uk**>

A Vision of Britain Through Time

Detailed Historical information on places in Britain
<www.visionbritain.org.uk>

Sites with national census datasets:

Ancestry <www.ancestry.co.uk>
FamilySearch <www.familysearch.org>
Findmypast <www.findmypast.com>
TheGenealogist <www.thegenealogist.co.uk>
Genes Reunited <www.genesreunited.com>
National Archives of Ireland <www.census.nationalarchives.ie>
Origins <www.origins.net>
Roots UK <www.rootsuk.com>
ScotlandsPeople <www.scotlandspeople.com>
1901censusonline <www.1901censusonline.com>
1911 Census <www.1911census.co.uk>

There is a website for this book at <www.spub.co.uk/census/> with
updates and additional material.

Index

Census